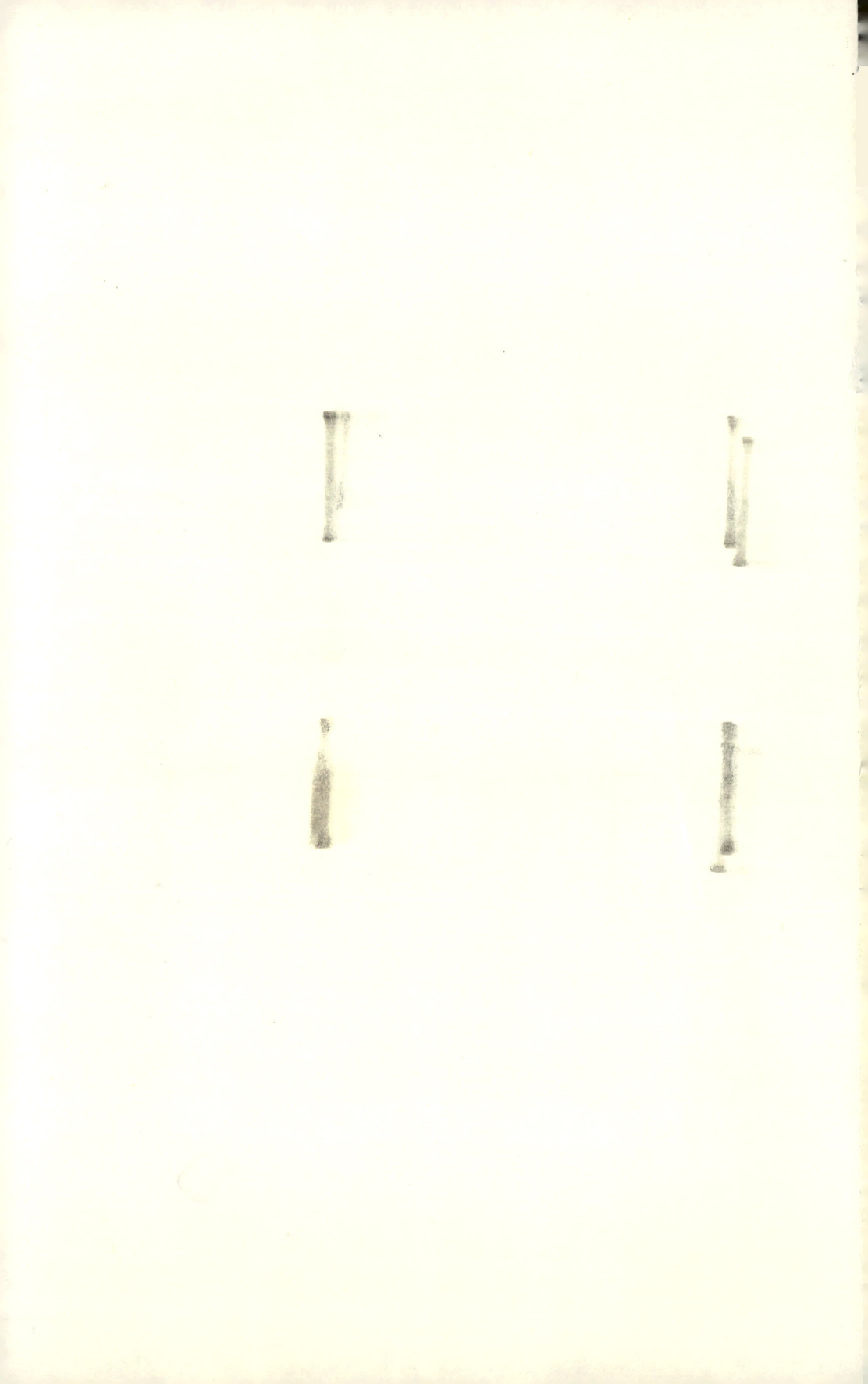

PSYCHOCRITICISM

PSYCHOCRITICISM

AN ANNOTATED BIBLIOGRAPHY

Compiled by
Joseph Natoli *and* Frederik L. Rusch

Bibliographies and Indexes in World Literature, Number 1

GREENWOOD PRESS
Westport, Connecticut • London, England

Library of Congress Cataloging in Publication Data
Main entry under title:

Psychocriticism : an annotated bibliography.

(Bibliographies and indexes in world literature,
ISSN 0742-6801 ; no. 1)
  Includes indexes.
  1. Psychology and literature—Bibliography.   I. Natoli,
Joseph P., 1943-   II. Rusch, Frederik L.
III. Series.
Z6514.P78P89   1984   [PN56.P93]   016.801′92   84-4689
ISBN 0-313-23641-0 (lib. bdg.)

Copyright © 1984 by Joseph Natoli and Frederik L. Rusch

All rights reserved. No portion of this book may be
reproduced, by any process or technique, without the
express written consent of the publisher.

Library of Congress Catalog Card Number: 84-4689
ISBN: 0-313-23641-0
ISSN: 0742-6801

First published in 1984

Greenwood Press
A division of Congressional Information Service, Inc.
88 Post Road West, Westport, Connecticut 06881

Printed in the United States of America

10 9 8 7 6 5 4 3 2 1

Contents

Preface	vii
Introductory Essay: A Survey of Psychocriticism	xi
General Studies and Essay Collections	1
Ancient and Classical Literature	46
Medieval Literature	53
Renaissance Literature	57
Seventeenth-Century Literature	78
Eighteenth-Century Literature	83
Nineteenth-Century Literature	92
Twentieth-Century Literature	150
Subject Index	243
Author Index	257

Preface

The psychology-literature relationship has been documented previously with varying purposes and scopes in mind. Norman Kiell's *Psychoanalysis, Psychology and Literature: A Bibliography* (Madison: University of Wisconsin Press, 1963) covers journals published in English-speaking countries during the period 1900 to 1961. The work has been updated by Kiell's bibliography of the same name, published by Scarecrow Press (Metuchen, N.J., 1982). In his initial bibliography, Kiell claims that "all schools of psychological and psychoanalytic thought are represented" although the impetus of the book is admittedly the "development and acceptance of Freudian theory." Kiell's bibliographies are unannotated. Also unannotated is Albert Rothenberg and Bette Greenberg's *The Index of Scientific Writings on Creativity* (Archon, vol. I, 1974; vol. II, 1976). The first volume, *Creative Men and Women*, contains scientific articles on creative people in literature, the visual arts, music, theater, and dance. The second volume, *General, 1566-1974*, is devoted to creativity in general; creativity and psychopathology; creativity in the fine arts, the sciences, engineering, and business; creativity and women; and facilitating creativity through education.

The journal *Literature and Psychology*, psychology here meaning only Freudian psychology, has published a bibliography on literature and Freudian psychology for the years 1966-67, 1968-69, and 1970. Evelyn Perloff's *A Selected Bibliography in Psychology and Literature: Psychological Abstracts, 1960-1969* (MS. #661, *Catalog of Selected Documents in Psychology*, 4, Summer, 1974, 68-69) was "prepared to assist those who seek to understand the nature of behavior by studying the writer and his works." The items listed, along with their annotations, were all gathered from *Psychological Abstracts*.

There are two bibliographies of phenomenology that are not restricted to the literature-phenomenological psychology relationship but are nonetheless worthy of mention: Howard W. Ivey's *Phenomenology: A Bibliography of English Language Writings* (Council of Planning Librarians Exchange Bibliography #885) and Leonard Orr's *Existentialism and Phenomenology: A Guide for Research* (New York: Whitson Publishing Co., 1978). There is no separate Jungian psychology-literature bibliography, although Joseph F. Vincie and Margreta Rathbauer-Vincie's *C. G. Jung and Analytical Psychology: A Comprehensive Bibliography* (New York: Garland, 1977) contains a number of items in this area.

Unlike Kiell, we have restricted our coverage to articles and books in which a fairly recognizeable school or method of psychology is applied to literature. Therefore, many studies indexed by Kiell in his mammoth revised bibliography have not been annotated here because we have discovered them to be in a broad, colloquial domain of psychology which has been prevalent in literary studies before the advent of formal psychology. For instance, studies concerned with "psychological realism," or the "psychology of love or hate or fear," or the "psychology of character motivation," or the "psychology of identity," which do not refer to any specific psychological approach have not been included. We discovered numerous references to "psychology," "dream," "consciousness," "madness," "insanity," "archetype" or "archetypal," "mind," "psyche," "disintegration," and so forth, which made no reference to any formal psychology. It can be argued that literary criticism that deals with characterization or author's intent is in some way "psychological," but, needless to say, such a broad view of psychology ceases to be useful to the scholar seeking a defined approach to literature.

The present work covers the literature and psychology relationship as presented in secondary works (critical and scholarly) from 1969–1982. Following a chapter listing general studies and essay collections, the material is arranged according to the literary periods Ancient and Classical, Medieval, and Renaissance (Fifteenth and Sixteenth centuries), and then simply according to the Seventeenth, Eighteenth, Nineteenth, and Twentieth centuries, since terms like Realism, Romanticism, Naturalism, Symbolism, and so forth do not cover uniform periods in all Western literatures. Each chapter begins with a listing of general articles falling within that period.

Surnames of authors-as-subjects of articles are arranged alphabetically within their appropriate literary divisions, except in the General Studies chapter and sections where items are listed under the names of the authors of those studies. In addition, all authors-as-subjects are listed in the Subject Index. Authors who share equally the subject of an article are cross-listed within the bibliography proper, but when an author is only a peripheral subject of the article, he or she is listed only in the Subject Index. The Author Index lists the authors of the articles and books contained in the bibliography.

In addition to the above cited works, the following sources were used to compile this Bibliography:

Arts and Humanities Citation Index
Book Review Digest
Bulletin Signaletique 390: Psychologie et Psychopathologie, Psychiatrie
Essay and General Literature Index
Excerpta Medica
Humanities Index
Internationale Bibliographie der Zeitschriftliterature
Index to Book Reviews in the Humanities
Library of Congress Catalog: Books: Subjects
MLA International Bibliography and *Abstracts*
Philosopher's Index
Psychological Abstracts
Social Science Citation Index
Social Science Index

Introductory Essay
A SURVEY OF PSYCHOCRITICISM*

This bibliography will be of use to students of literature interested in the application of the tenets of formal psychology to literature. It should also be of use to psychologists interested in literature as a nondiscursive source of human behavior, perceptions, and intentions. Regardless of what theories a psychologically oriented critic may hold, he or she joins with his or her colleagues in recognizing the importance of applying an extra-literary analogue to literature so as to trace psychic determinants. Furthermore, psychologists themselves often view literature as richly illuminating to human behavior. However, the psychological approach adhered to by both psychologist and critic does much to determine purpose, method, and results. In order to give the student some sense of the variety of psychological approaches to literature that will be encountered in this bibliography, we have included discussion of several of them in this introduction. Some of what Norman Holland has referred to as "unorthodox" psychological approaches to literature can be found in the casebook collection *Psychological Perspectives on Literature: Dissident Freudian and Non-Freudian.*[1] This casebook includes psychocriticism based on the work of Carl Jung, Alfred Adler, Wilhelm Reich, Erich Fromm, Jacques Lacan, Karen Horney, Norman Holland, Roy Schafer, and R. D. Laing, as well as on cognitive, behavioral, and phenomenological psychology.**

---

*Portions reprinted from essay by Joseph P. Natoli originally published in *Critical Survey of Poetry*, vol. 8, pp. 3414-3428. By permission of publisher, Salem Press, Inc. Copyright, 1982, by Frank N. Magill.

**Bernard J. Paris is editing a collection of essays entirely devoted to Third Force psychology, *Third Force Psychology and the Study of Literature*, University Presses of Florida.

PSYCHOANALYTIC APPROACHES TO LITERATURE—FREUD

Sigmund Freud's views of the relationship between art and psychoanalysis were presented in his "Delusion and Dreams in Jensen's *Gradiva*" and in "The Relationship of the Poet to Daydreaming." The forbidden wishes of dreams associated with the psychosexual stages (oral, anal, phallic, and genital) appear in the literary work but are disguised by distracting aspects of aesthetic form. The superegos of both reader and author are circumvented, and art serves to release unconscious forces that might otherwise overwhelm the ego. The critic's job is to delve below the surface of a distracting literary facade and point out the lurking fantasies. Freud himself began, in his book on Leonardo da Vinci, a stage of psychoanalytic criticism that has been termed "genetic reductionism," or the discussion of a work in terms of the author's neurosis.

Genetic reductionism has been and remains a primary focus of psychoanalytic criticism in spite of a general recognition that the danger for psychoanalysis is the lure of a simplistic and mechanistic interpretation. The dispute here is between those who hold that literature is autonomous, existing independently of a creator's emotional disposition, and those who hold that a psychoanalytic critic can "show how a writer's public intention was evidently deflected by a private obsession."[2] A psychoanalytic examination of the author's wishes and anxieties, in the view of antipsychoanalytic criticism, ignores the variety and ontology of literature. Crews argues, nevertheless, that there does exist a certain range of problems which psychoanalytic assumptions illuminate.

Freud also initiated a psychoanalytic interpretation of particular characters in his work on Wilhelm Gensen's *Gradiva* (1918) and in his discussion of oedipal complexes displayed by certain characters in Sophocles' *Oedipus Tyrannus* (ca. 429 b.c.) and William Shakespeare's *Hamlet* (1600-1601). While most contemporary psychoanalytic critics deplore genetic reductionism, there is debate regarding the treatment of characters as real people. Critics on one side of the spectrum tend to put a character on the analyst's couch, talk about the character's childhood, and totally neglect other aspects of the literary work. Opposing critics contend that while readers do indeed experience characters as human beings, the critic must use psychoanalysis so as to understand fully the character in relation to other aspects of the work.

In Freud's view, literature was like dream—a symbolic expression of the unconscious whose original meaning could be interpreted. This relationship between the writer and his work, and in the creative process and its importance in interpreting a work, remains an interest of contemporary psychoanalysts and psychoanalytic critics. Freud's original view of creativity has been refashioned in various ways, and psychoanalytic critics now fall into various camps. Freud's view of the work of literature as a product of the author's sublimated desires has been challenged by an emphasis upon the literary work as "the potential space between the individual and the environment," by an emphasis upon the reader whose own "identity theme" fashions meaning from a work of art, and by an emphasis on preconscious and conscious involvement with literary creation (Donald W. Winnicott). These views have been termed, respectively, Object-Relations, Reader-Response (based on the work of Norman Holland), and Ego Psychology. The psychoanalyst Jacques Lacan has also created a unique approach to literature.

PSYCHOANALYTIC APPROACH TO LITERATURE— EGO PSYCHOLOGY

Freud's view of literature-as-symptom emerging from the id is modified by ego psychologists who recognize creativity as a function of the ego. For the ego psychologists, literature in the service of the ego reflects the ego's mission of mediating between self and others, between id and superego. Symbols from the id are therefore shaped in literature so as to be communicable beyond the intrapsychic level. The movement in ego psychology is away from literature as raw wish fulfillment of the author and toward the literary text as a manifestation of id instinct and ego-monitoring. Literary critics utilizing ego psychology seek in the text not the disguised wish or wishes of the author but their transformation by the ego in the direction of something beyond the personality of the author, something of thematic import, communicable and succeeding or not succeeding depending upon the author's gifts or skills.

The ego psychoanalyst analyzing literature emphasizes ego functions rather than id impulses. In what ways, this critic asks, does the piece of literature display the ego's assertion of control by allowing repressed instincts an outlet? A discovery of what instincts are latent does not lead the critic into the entire work, but a study of the work as a manifestation of an ego directing the release of repressed instincts does.

PSYCHOANALYTIC APPROACH TO LITERATURE— READER-RESPONSE

Norman Holland, in *The Dynamics of Literary Response* (1968), emphsizes the instinctual drives of the id rather than the monitoring, controlling powers of the ego, although, unlike early Freudian interpreters of literature, he posits an ego that mediates between the id and the superego and whose mediation is the form of the work itself. The form of a literary work is indeed comparable to the ego defenses against the assault of the id, but it is this assault that is the hidden, determining root of the work. A core fantasy is the base of every literary work, and the writer, through form, defends against it while attempting to shape it in the direction of redeemable social, moral, and intellectual value. The eye of the critic, in Holland's view, is on the core fantasy, on the id, while the eye of the ego psychologist-critic is on the ego's manipulation of the id through literary form. The core fantasy critic seeks out the core fantasy and demonstrates the author's artistry in shaping and disguising it. The reader accepts both the core fantasy, which he or she may share, and the devices employed to contain the fantasy. Thus, the reader achieves pleasure by possession of the fantasy as well as by having it controlled. The reader, in the view of the ego psychologist-critic, attains pleasure primarily through the pattern of ego control expressed in the literary work.

In his later works, *Poems in Persons* and *Five Readers Reading* (both 1975), Holland places the pertinent core fantasy in the mind of the reader rather than in the text. The reader extracts meaning from the text in accordance with his or her "identity theme." That is, the reader may be directed by his or her own desires to seek them in the text he or she reads. Finding them, the reader may deal with them as he or she does in his or her own life. The reader may also attend the author in transforming a core fantasy into something socially acceptable or intellectually significant. Holland believes that through the literary text the reader confronts himself or herself, engaging in an act of self-discovery by analyzing what he or she as a reader has said about a text. Throughout the three faces of psychoanalysis that Holland identifies—psychology of the unconscious (id), of the ego, and of the self—readers have always been structuring the text by means of their own intentions. A realization of this fact enables readers to make use of literature as an opportunity to gain self-knowledge.

A critical approach to literature based on Holland's later work would begin with a description of the critic-reader's own responses to the work. These responses, determined by the critic-reader's "identity theme," direct an analysis of the work. A dialectic then takes place between the objective reality of the work (a common store of shareable realities) and the critic.

PSYCHOANALYTIC APPROACHES TO LITERATURE—OBJECT-RELATIONS

Object-relations theory does not hold, as do traditional psychological and ego psychological theories, that a literary work is the product of psychic conflict. It holds, rather, that a literary work is the place where the writer's wishes and the culture around him or her meet. Rather than emphasizing the literary work as narcissistic wish fulfillment, object-relations critics emphasize those aspects of a literary work that are not the author's self, which lead toward a world outside the writer. This outside world of convention and tradition is transformed by the writer, who has accepted what is outside his or her own self. The literary work as an object is an extension of the writer somewhat as a teddy bear is an extension of a child. Both teddy bear and literary work are invested with illusions; yet they are objects in the world. In the case of the child, the teddy bear is something like the mother's breast, although significantly it is another object. Similarly, the literary work is wish fulfillment and yet an object that is not pure wish fulfillment but a place where wishes and world meet, an object representing a "collective love affair with the world."

A critical approach to literature based on an object-relations theory would not focus on the literary work as an expression of intrapsychic conflict but as the ground in which the writer's wishes and the outside world meet. In what ways does the piece of literature signify the internal desires of the writer? In what ways does it stand as a transformation of those desires into what is outside the writer? The meeting of internal and external is the finished peice.

PSYCHOANALYTIC APPROACHES TO LITERATURE— JACQUES LACAN

Lacanian psychoanalysis once again resurrects the sole supremacy of the id in the creative process. Indeed, the unconscious itself is structured as a language and, therefore, both the conscious and the unconscious are identically rooted. Literary discourse, like ordinary discourse, is symbolical and subjective. Rather than the id being a source of instinctual drives that are disguised in literature, specifically in the language of literature, the Lacanian id is a reservoir of words that determine perceptions.

Lacanian literary interpretation depends upon tracing literary language to a constitutive language of the unconscious. It depends upon relating significant words in the literary text to words signified in the unconscious. The unconscious is structured in childhood not according to innate laws but originally according to the image of another, someone upon whom the child is dependent (usually the mother). This desire to remain secure is fulfilled when the child constructs his unconscious in accordance with the significant other. The "discourse" of the other becomes the discourse of the child's unconscious, which is fictional insofar as it is not the child's but another's.

In Lacan's view, the ego is composed of a *moi*, which is unconscious, overriding the other but determined by it, and the *je*, which is identified with spoken language and culture. The discourse of the *moi* permeates the discourse of the *je*. The symbolic, subjective *moi* permeates the apparently logical discourse of the *je*. The Lacanian literary critic seeks to go from the discourse of the *je* to the discourse of the *moi*, from a symbolical consciousness to a symbolical unconsciousness. The discourse of the *moi*, of the unconscious, is weakly and elusively manifest in the surface of the literary text. Both signifiers and signifieds are available in the surface of the text, and the act of literary interpretation attempts to reconstruct, wherever possible, the connection between signifiers and signifieds. It is an act that seeks to uncover the unconscious desires that determine the details of the literary text.

PSYCHOANALYTIC APPROACHES TO LITERATURE— A CRITICAL OVERVIEW

Alan Roland and Frederick Crews, among others, have provided criticism of various psychoanalytic approaches to literature. Roland objects to the correlation of literary work and daydream. The literary work, in his view, goes far beyond the author's fantasies and the imagery of dream. Poetic metaphor and the structure of paradox are essential components of the literary work but not of dream. According to Roland, literary form must be freed from the notion that it is synonymous with the ego's defenses. Defense is viewed as only part of form. Object-relations critics do not limit the author's fantasies to those of a psychosexual stage, but they fail, in Roland's view, to integrate their exploration of fantasies with what the work may mean on its highest level. In opposition to Holland's view of the reader, Roland feels that, besides a core fantasy, a literary work possesses an abstract meaning, a total vision formally created. The relationship between these two levels should be described by the critic. In Roland's view, the core fantasy within the reader's mind is apparently affected by the critic's efforts.

Frederick Crews sees as reductionistic the views that Holland expresses in *The Dynamics of Literary Response,* although he admits that Holland is sensitive to literary form and very cautious about making "armchair diagnosis of authors." Holland's reductionism lies in his view of literature as subterfuge for forbidden thoughts. Crews also maintains that no one goes to criticism to discover the "identity theme" of the critic but rather to learn more about literature as a meaning-creating enterprise.

In the final analysis, according to Crews, Holland's focus on the reader is yet another example of academic objectivity being attacked by subjectivists, by those who argue that the interpretation of literature is a private affair. Crews finds no real remedy for contemporary psychoanalytic criticism, not even ego psychology. Eventually, all psychoanalytic critics realize that their interpretations say more about themselves than about the text, that "they have reduced literature to the rigid and narrow outlines of their own personalities." A psychoanalytic critic, according to Crews, must bear in mind that his method is reductive and that there are many aspects of a work excluded from his approach.

In an essay entitled "Anaesthetic Criticism," Crews goes beyond a discussion of the dangers of reductionism in psychoanalytic criticism and defends it against antideterministic critics. He considers the "informal taboo" placed on extraliterary theories by many academic critics. Northrop Frye, the most influential antideterministic critic, in Crews's view, advocates an inductive survey of literary works in which no external conceptual framework is considered. Literature, in Frye's archetypal view, is its own progenitor. Crews terms such a belief "a common fantasy among writers, a wish that art could be self-fathered, self-nurturing, self-referential, purified of its actual origins in discontent."[3] Such a "fantasy," of course, is no less common among critics than among writers. In essence, critics who deplore the search for causes and effects are anti-intellectual, preferring a literary approach in which references to extraliterary analogs are at once disclaimed. Finally, in Crews's view, criticism that ignores the affective element of literature and accentuates the role of form over chaos, of genre conventions and the like, is anaesthetic criticism. Crews concludes that regardless of the dangers of reductionism in the application of pyschoanalysis to literature, the approach is more efficacious than that of such antideterministic critics as Frye.

As editor of a special issue of *Yale French Studies* (number 55/56, 1977), Shoshana Felman considers ". . . how the question of the relationship between literature and psychoanalysis might begin to be articulated—*otherwise:* how psychoanalysis and literature might indeed begin to be rethought, both in their otherness and in their common wisdom." She suggests that literature and psychoanalysis traverse each other rather than lie distinctly outside each other's border. Her desire to read this relationship "otherwise" leads to the interesting suggestions that literature is the unconscious of psychoanalysis (reversing the traditional view that psychoanalysis unfolds the unconscious of literature) and that the text is like the psychoanalyst and thus is "the very place where meaning, and *knowledge* of meaning, reside" (reversal of the traditional view that the text is the psychoanalytic critic's "patient"). Felman clarifies these apparent reversals:

Instead of literature being, as is usually the case, submitted to the authority and to the knowledge of psychoanalysis, psychoanalysis itself would then here be submitted to the literary perspective. This reversal of the perspective, however, does not intend to simply reverse the positions of master and slave in such a way that literature would *take over* the place of the master, but rather its intention is to disrupt altogether the position of mastery as such, to try to avoid *both* terms of the alternative, to deconstruct the very structure of the *opposition* master/slavery. (p7)

JUNGIAN CRITICISM

Carl Jung deals specifically with literature in the following essays: "The Type Problem in Poetry," *Psychological Types;* "The Phenomenology of the Spirit in Fairytales," *The Archetypes of the Collective Unconscious;*

"On the Relations of Analytical Psychology to Poetry," *The Spirit in Man, Art, and Literature*; "Psychology and Literature," *Alchemical Studies*.

According to Morris Philipson in his *Outline of a Jungian Aesthetics*, the ". . . link that connects Jung's theory of individual psychology to the considerations of aesthetics, and to the relations between aesthetics and epistemology, is found in Jung's persistent efforts to define and employ the concept of *symbol*."[4] According to Jung, the inexplicable part of the symbol is a manifestation of certain "inherited" structural elements of the human psyche. According to Jung's extensive investigations, these elements or "archetypes" are revealed in dreams, visions, or fantasies that have their ". . . closest analogies in the typical figures of mythology, sagas, and fairytales."[5] Jung's thought remains within the empirical confines since every aspect of it, including the collective unconscious and its archetypes, are hypotheses presented by Jung in response to empirical investigations. It is a fact that sophisticated literature, folklore, mythology, and fairytales have provided substantial data upon which Jung's archetypes were based.

In "Psychology and Literature" Jung mentions those "visionary artists" who seem to allow us ". . . a glimpse into the unfathomed abyss of what has not yet become." Beyond Jung's specific focus on symbol as revealed in literature as a basis for certain hypotheses—and finally, for an entire "depth psychology," which may be applied in turn to literature itself—Jung's study of the specific nature of symbol gives him an especially perceptive understanding of the nature of literature.

However, while Jung has a great deal to say about the visionary artist, the artist in contact with the archetypes, and the symbolic expression of the archetypes in dream, fantasy, and myth, he has no concern for the specific form, the specific presentation of symbols. It is not possible to distinguish the symbolic processes of the poet from those of anyone else, not even from a Jung patient. Therefore, the symbolic richness of a work as illuminated by the Jungian paradigm does not itself make that work successful. However, a Jungian methodology can be said to reinforce the notion of a symbolic unity of a work in the sense that it can make explicit certain image-patterns that may be obscure.

The Freudian attacks upon Jung's view of art are strident and somewhat muddled. Crews believes that invoking the Jungian system ". . . is of course a revealing mark of indifference toward evidence . . ." and offers Glover's *Freud or Jung* as proof positive that Jung's ". . . hypotheses are logically unnecessary and mutually contradictory. . . ."[6] Glover maintains that certain Freudian notions ameliorate Jung's charge that Freud regards art as pathological or neurotic.

The elaborate history of unconscious sublimation, whereby the frustrated energies of infantile libido are profoundly modified and deflected towards a diversity of individual and social ends, the individual origin and function of unconscious phantasy and the intricate evolution therefrom of pre-conscious ideation and expression, the protean manifestations of unconscious conflict and the complicated series of psychic manoeuvres whereby conflict can be assuaged and the harshness of existence rendered more endurable . . . are summarily misrepresented by Jung. . . ."[7]

Glover also states that ". . . Jung cannot understand the difference between conscious and unconscious mental activity. . . ."[8] He further says that Jung's spiritual home is the conscious psychology of the pre-Freudian epoch and that Jung ". . . seeks to get rid of those embarrassing manifestations of unconscious function which call for explanation in terms of individual development by projecting them into an alledged Collective Unconscious. . . ."[9] This misrepresents Jung, however, since acquiring and developing consciousness are the labors of the individual in the first stage of life, or what Jung terms the first stage of Individuation. In this ego differentiation stage, Jung differs from Freud in that Freud assumes the contents of the unconscious to be qualitatively inferior and possibly injurious to the ego. The id represents the ". . . blind, impulsive, irrational . . ." aspects of man's nature. Rather than accent the energies of the personal unconscious through dreams and their attendant images, Freud advocated the channeling of such energies into pursuits that would be compatible with what he called the "reality principle." Jung, on the contrary, called for a direct acceptance of the Shadow, a "being" that encompasses all those traits and proclivities that we have consciously de-emphasized. The energies of this personification of the id must be accepted before the second stage of Individuation can begin. Thus, for Freud an individual could only achieve a development permissable within his society, while for Jung, an individual pursued a development that could only be achieved by encountering energies repressed in the name of any society.

And for Jung, art represents necessary contact with the personal unconscious, as in the case of psychological art, and with the collective unconscious, as in the case of visionary art. While the artist for Freud then is ". . . a man who turns from reality because he cannot come to terms with the demand for the renunciation of the instinctual satisfaction as it is first made, and who then in phantasy-life allows full play to his erotic and ambitious wishes . . . ,"[10] the artist for Jung is not driven to art because of such unfulfilled desires but achieves his art through a natural encountering of energies existing on two levels of the unconscious and through a manifestation of archetypal energy by means of unique symbols.

With Freud, no universal, inherited archetypes exist; therefore no continuum of comparable symbols can be traced in literature except those that refer to the personal unconscious and specifically to repressed energy therein. Symbols in Freud's view represent instinctual needs and are always defined within a limited model of the human personality—one in which no real growth beyond childhood takes place. On the other hand, Jung's consideration of archetype and symbol as emerging from a nonpathological relationship between consciousness and two levels of the unconscious goes beyond Freud's notion that all art is the sublimation of repressed drives.

The Jungian approach has been criticized for reducing the artist to being a mere instrument of the archetype. However, this criticism is based on a confusion between the archetype and the symbol, the observable image representing the archetype, an image that cannot be fully grasped and that does not fully realize the archetype. The archetype may be considered autonomous, since it depends not on the conscious mind. But the symbol that the imagination grasps is manifested in accord with the volitions of the conscious mind. Actual pictorial and verbal images owe their aesthetic aspects not to the uncontrollable forces of the archetypes but to the forming disposition of the conscious mind. A Jungian approach to literature casts light on the symbolic aura of a literary work as well as on the creative process itself. Such revelation in turn, from a psychological view, acquaints us with unconscious levels we ourselves cannot reach and encourages a continuation of our own growth.

A PHENOMENOLOGICAL PSYCHOLOGICAL APPROACH TO LITERATURE

In the case of a phenomenological psychology, a delineation of a *Lebenswelt,* or human life-world of a character, a speaker in a literary work, or an author, is in each case a delineation of consciousness. The phenomenologist's desire is to return to lived experiences and "bracket," or set aside, presuppositions. Such experiences are not understood by an examination of external behavior but by an examination of psychic reality, or consciousness. Since consciousness is always consciousness of something, intentionality with regard to external reality being always implicit, a focus on a person in literature or on the author himself, on various self-revelations, reveals the *Lebenswelt.* To the phenomenological psychologist, literary accounts—poetry, drama, or fiction—are personal records, descriptions of psychic reality that aid in achieving a psychological understanding of both behavior and phenomenal experience. Through a phenomenological approach to literature that emphasizes various portrayals of self by both poetic speakers and the poet, portrayals of others, of objects, and time, it is possible both to define and to reveal meaning in literary work as a whole.

The literary consciousness involves the writer's own intentions, which are tied to his or her own human life-world and his or her own particular arrangement of phenomena. Although such an arrangement is unique to each poet, a patterning presided over by his or her own poetic consciousness, such consciousness, by virtue of its intentionality, is directed to and tied to objects comprising the reader's natural universe. The very process of literary construction and patterning reveals the experiential foundation of the reader's world and illuminates rather than mirrors disparate objects and impressions. The literary critic has little interest in literature as a source of phenomenal experience, as an exploration of psychic-subjective reality. Rather, he utilizes the phenomenological perspective to define the relationship between intentionality and aesthetic patterning or form.

The relationship between intentionality and form cannot be defined until the *Lebenswelt* of each speaker or persona in the literature is defined, leaving the writer's own *Lebenswelt* discernible. Thus, the phenomenological perspective enables the critic to analyze speakers and personae by means of their perceptions of the world and eventually to distinguish aspects of the writing that are derived from intentions, not of any speaker or persona, but of the writer. Nothing less than the entire literary work is revealed.

THIRD FORCE PSYCHOLOGY AND LITERATURE

"There are many works," Bernard Paris writes, "about which I can say very little from a Horneyan perspective; but there are others with which it seems highly congruent."[11] Third Force psychologists are those psychologists who recognize a force operating in people other than that presented by Freudians and Behaviorists, "an evolutionary constructive force." Paris leans most on Karen Horney's theory of self-alienation and Abraham Maslow's theory of the hierarchy of basic needs. There are certainly ties here with Jung's theory of Individuation, that is, the development of the full human personality, the cognitive view that "emphasizes the constructing capacities and processes of human thought," and the existential brand of phenomenology wielded by Carl Rogers and Rollo May.

BEHAVIORAL CRITICISM

While Ingarden derives an aesthetic based on phenomenology which, via intentionality, does not separate either the literary work from conscious experience or aesthetic form from content, much use of literature by psychology focuses on a mimetic view in which what is useful to the psychologist can be extracted by objective and statistical study. Lindauer posits a distinction between literature as art and literature as knowledge. "Literature as art is read for personal enjoyment, literature as knowledge is studied as a source of data."[12]

The implication is that elements of literature are easily separable depending upon the reader's purposes. And the author of fiction, unlike the author of discursive works, is concerned with literary rather than scientific criteria. This fact is disturbing to those who wish to extract data from fiction and who wish to do so by quantitative means. An empirical approach to fiction seeks to explain scientifically, while a phenomenological approach relies only on a psychological understanding of phenomenal experiences. In the former approach, a reductive method is utilized in which what can be quantified is substituted for what seems broader and more complex. Just as the behavioral psychologist interprets behavior in terms of neurophysiological processes (reinforcement is electrical charges in the brain and motivation is a hypothalmic function), those applying similar reductivist methods to literature identify meaning with the particular structure of language itself. Vowels, consonants, gutterals—the phonetic structure of sound as a whole—are looked upon as the physicist looks upon atoms, the building blocks of very sophisticated things indeed, but essentially comprehensible because the basic units are comprehensible. In the case of literary analysis of, say, Dostoevsky, what becomes accessible is meaning that has been scientifically deduced from the quantifiable, analyzable components of language itself.

WILHELM REICH AND ERICH FROMM

Finally, a word about Reichian and Frommian literary criticism. Wilhelm Reich, much maligned, considered brilliant but mad, and mostly ignored in the past, is clearly ascending as an influence on psychological criticism. It seems that some writers of fiction have long known of Reich's work. For instance, one can detect a Reichian influence on Norman Mailer and especially Saul Bellow, whose character, Herzog, in the novel of that name, uses Reichian language at certain crucial emotional moments. Reich, who died in jail, a martyr of official state repression, was, perhaps, ahead of his time. Now that various popular psychologies and treatments—the primal scream therapy comes immediately to mind—have used his ideas, Reich's time has come. Erich Fromm, on the other hand, is perhaps the least represented of the major psychological theoreticians found in this bibliography. However, as it becomes increasingly clear that the entire structure of Western civilization is in danger of collapsing, Fromm's social psychology, his analyses of our social malaise, may well become more influential in the world of literary criticism, perhaps providing needed insights to those people searching for some answers to the problems of today.

Whatever their psychological approaches, all the entries in this bibliography attest to a dynamic and growing relationship between literature and psychology. The meeting ground is human behavior and human consciousness. Thus interaction between the writer and the psychologist would seem inevitable.

NOTES

1. Joseph P. Natoli, ed. (New Haven: Archon, 1984).
2. Frederick Crews, "Reductionism and Its Discontents." *Critical Quarterly*, 1 (1975), 545.
3. Frederick Crews, "Anaesthetic Criticism." *Psychoanalysis and Literary Process.* edited by F. Crews (Cambridge, Mass.: Winthrop, 1970), 5.
4. Morris Philipson, *Outline of a Jungian Aesthetics* (Evanston, Ill.: Northwestern University Press, 1963), 15.
5. Jolande Jacobi, *The Psychology of C. G. Jung* (New Haven: Yale University Press, 1968), 125.
6. Crews, "Anaesthetic Criticism," 8.
7. Edward Glover, *Freud or Jung?* (Cleveland and New York: World, 1956), 170.
8. Ibid., 171.
9. Ibid., 173.
10. Sigmund Freud, "Formulations Regarding the Two Principles in Mental Functioning." *Standard Edition* (London: Hogarth Press, 1953-1974).
11. "Third Force Psychology and the Study of Literature," in *Psychological Perspectives on Literature.* edited by J. Natoli.
12. Martin S. Lindauer, *The Psychological Study of Literature* (Chicago: Nelson-Hall, 1974), 82.

PSYCHOCRITICISM

General Studies and Essay Collections

1. Aarons, Z. Alexander. "Normality and Abnormality in Adolescence: With a Digression on Prince Hal: 'The Sowing of Wild Oats'." Psychoanalytic Study of the Child, 25 (1970), 309-339.

    Includes a critical study of Prince Hal of Henry IV in order to illustrate "the resolution of adolescent ambivalence and conflict between father and son."

2. Axberger, Gunnar. "Arson and Fiction: A Cross-Disciplinary Study." Psychiatry, 36, 3 (1973), 244-265.

    A study of the psychological causes of arson through the examination of literature, with emphasis on the works of Robinson Jeffers. Fascination with fire is a way of dealing with repression, especially sexual repression.

3. Bachelar, Gaston. The Poetics of Reverie. New York: Orion Press, 1969.

    Introduces the dimension of reverie on the reader's part in his or her reading of literature. The phenomenological approach to reverie's affect on poetic images involves a "return to putting the accent on their original quality, grasping the very essence of their originality and thus taking advantage of the remarkable psychic productivity of the imagination."

4. Baird, James. "Jungian Psychology in Criticism: Theoretical Problems." In Strelka, Joseph, ed., Literary Criticism and Psychology. University Park: Pennsylvania State University Press, 1976, 3-30.

    A summary of the aspects of Jungian theory which have affected literary criticism and of various critics and theoreticians who have accepted or dismissed Jungian theory. The author argues for the rejection not only of all determinisms applied to literature but for ". . . all claims made by criticism which deny the subjectivity of the critic."

5. Beck, Samuel J. *The Rorschach Test Exemplified in Classics of Drama and Literature*. New York: Stratton Intercontinental Medical Book Corp., 1976.

Uses the psychological insights of writers and identifies the "Rorschach variables" for the purpose of elucidating the psychological meanings of O'Neill's *The Iceman Cometh*, Ibsen's *Hedda Gabler*, Dostoevsky's *The Brothers Karamozov*, and Shakespeare's *King Lear*.

6. Behrens, Roy R. "Lunatics, Lovers and Poets: On Madness and Creativity." *Journal of Creative Behavior*, 9, 4 (1975), 228-232; 266.

"The character's mind can be characterized as a cognitive flight, making associations that generate new configurations by rearranging previously experienced elements." Stresses Don Quixote as prototype.

7. Berg, Jan Hendrick van den. *A Different Existence: Principles of Phenomenological Psychopathology*. Pittsburgh: Duquesnes University Press, 1972.

In the course of presenting his phenomenological pathography, van den Berg employs fiction in order to illuminate his views.

8. Bersani, Leo. *A Future for Astyanax: Character and Desire in Literature*. Boston: Little, Brown, 1976.

Discusses "the correlations between different ways of conceiving desire and different ways of conceiving character in literature. . . . It is perhaps the role of sublimation, conscience, and character-formation to modify the potentially limitless aggressiveness of desire." Examines Racine, Flaubert, Stendal, H. James, D.H. Lawrence, Rimbaud, and Artaud, among others.

9. Bettelheim, Bruno. *The Uses of Enchantment: The Meaning and Importance of Fairy Tales*. New York: Alfred A. Knopf, 1977.

A psychological study of themes and specific stories in traditional fairy tales. Fairy tales provide sense, meaning, and support to the child in his struggle with the overwhelming outside world he finds himself in. Children's literature should enrich the child's life and show "that a struggle against severe difficulties in life is unavoidable, is an intrinsic part of human existence--but that if one does not shy away, but steadfastly meets unexpected and often unjust hardships, one masters all obstacles and at the end emerges victorious." Traditional fairy tales, unlike most modern children's stories, do not avoid the problems of existence.

10. Bjornson, Richard. "Cognitive Mapping and the Understanding of Literature." *Sub-stance*, 30 (1981), 51-62.

Argues that an epistemological model is needed "to elaborate a generally comprehensible explanation of how the writing and reading of literary texts relate to the more universal problem of how people orient themselves in the world where they are obliged to live." This model Bjornson argues can be found in cognitive mapping. "This model is generally based upon some form of analogy between mental activity and the making or modifying of maplike structures that allow individuals to situate themselves in their environment."

11. Black, Stephen A. "On Reading Psychoanalytically." College English, 39 (1977), 267-274.

"Reading psychoanalytically" is meaningful if there is an "interaction between the reader and the author's compositional processes," between the text and the reader's ability to empathize with it. Scholarship is a step-by-step process of response to the text, not a "completed interpretation" of the text. Contains a discussion of the teaching of Moby-Dick in these terms.

12. Bleich, David. "Emotional Origins of Literary Meaning." College English, 31, 1 (1969), 30-40.

Finding meaning in a literary work is not so much a discovery of something objective, but rather a discovery of "something subjective that others wish to accept." The reader invests his ego into the meaning he finds in the text and calls it "true" just as "the author invests ego into his meaning and calls it 'art'." Pinter's The Caretaker is used in an experiment with a student to demonstrate these ideas.

13. _____. "Psychological Bases of Learning from Literature." College English, 33, 1 (1971), 32-46.

Discusses two cases of response to Death of a Salesman in order to indicate "how the need to derive instruction from the play is connected with an introjected sense of parental authority."

14. _____. Subjective Criticism. Baltimore and London: Johns Hopkins University Press, 1978.

Assails the "myth of objective reading" and argues for the sole determining status of the reader-critic.

15. _____. "The Subjective Paradigm in Science, Psychology, and Criticism." New Literary History, 7 (1976), 313-334.

A demonstration of the importance of the subjective "thought paradigm" in interpreting literature. According to T.S. Kuhn "a paradigm is a model that describes the cognitive state of mind of those systematically observing something in human experience . . . , a world view." With the subjective paradigm the observer creates "new truth . . . by use of language and a new structure of thought . . . . Knowledge is made by people and not found." Thus the subjective paradigm makes knowledge part of a person's psychic make-up.

16. Bloom, Harold. The Anxiety of Influence: A Theory of Poetry. London: Oxford University Press, 1973.

The art of criticism lies in recognizing the hidden roads that go from poem to poem, in recognizing that the meaning of a poem lies in one poet's anxious reaction to another poet-influence.

17. _____. "Poetic Crossing: Rhetoric and Psychology." Georgia Review, 30, (1976), 495-524.

A "trope" is "a turning," and poetry exhibits tropes when it expresses a turning from one thing to another, which is similar to the Freudian "'reaction-formation,' a defensive movement of the spirit that is opposed to a repressed desire and so manifests itself as a reaction against that desire." Rhetorically, reaction-formation is "irony as a figure of speech." Wallace Stevens, William Wordsworth, and S.T. Coleridge are used as examples.

18. _____. Poetry and Repression: Revisionism from Blake to Stevens. New Haven: Yale University Press, 1976.

Employs Freud's views of repression in order to argue for a view of poetic creativity based on repression. "It is only by repressing creative 'freedom,' through the initial fixation of influence, that a person can be reborn as a poet. And only be revising that repression can a poet become and remain strong."

19. Boomslitter, Paul C., et. al. "Perception and English Poetic Meter." PMLA, 88, (1973), 200-208.

The meter of writing or speech establishes a structure for the listener so that he or she then comes to anticipate the metrical pattern, and this activity contributes to the continuance of it as it controls his or her attention.

20. Brantlinger, Patrick. "Romances, Novels, and Psychoanalysis." In Tennenhouse, Leonard, ed., The Practice of Psychoanalytic Criticism. Detroit: Wayne State University Press, 1976, 18-46.

Considers whether romance or realism in literature conveys a truer sense of human psychology. Concludes that " . . . there is no guarantee that the social values expressed in realistic works will not be of the most conservative and retrograde kind, any more than there is that realistic works are less illusory than romances because they seem disillusioned and disillusioning."

21. Brenman-Gibson, Margaret. "Notes on the Study of the Creative Process." Psychological Issues, vol. 9 (4, mono. 36), (1976), 326-357.

A discussion of creativeness in terms of Eastern thought, physical and behavioral sciences, and the arts. Because more information can be gathered, it is easier to study creativeness in well-known people like leaders, scientists, and artists.

22. _____. "The Creation of Plays: With a Specimen Analysis." Psychoanalytic Review, 64, 2 (1977), 237-288.

Discussion of the nature of playwrighting, drawing upon two hypotheses: 1) Whatever the play is about, "it regularly deals at some level of consciousness with the writer's deepest feelings about his own creativity"; 2) the characters in the play represent "a projection of the playwright's identity-elements and fragments, a distribution of the self and its conflicts." The progress of the play represents an attempt by the playwright to achieve personal wholeness. (Contains also a thirty-six page biographical sketch of Clifford Odets.)

23. Briggs, Julia. "Not Without But Within: The Psychological Ghost Story." In <u>Night Visitors: The Rise and Fall of the English Ghost Story</u>. London: Faber and Faber, 1977, 142-164.

"The psychological ghost story could set the perceptions of the child, savage or madman against a more skeptical or reductively scientific attitude, often with an undercurrent of sympathy for the animistic response." Studies F.T.A. Hoffmann, Poe, Maupassant, H. James, De la Mare, and W.F. Harvey, among others.

24. Brink, Andrew. "On the Psychological Sources of Creative Imagination." <u>Queen's Quarterly</u>, 81 (1974), 1-19.

An understanding of the psychological aspects of art is "necessary to give wholeness to any account of" it. In this regard, "object relations theory" is useful because it "brings the artist's ego and his products into a single field of operations." A study of the artist's life and motives can enrich one's own self-understanding and ability to attain health.

25. Burke, Kenneth. "A (Psychological) Fable, with a (Logological) Moral." <u>American Imago</u>, 35 (1978), 203-207.

Speculations on the nature of creativity and its relationship to the conscious. Psychological fantasy is matched with "logological" fantasy, whereby, "any term suggests other terms variously related." Relationships of terms lead to an unfolding of a structure, "a family of terms," so that pursuing the implications of these relationships is "the sheerly <u>logological</u> analogue of delving into a psychological unconscious."

26. Butery, Karen Ann. "Contributions of Horneyan Psychology to the Study of Literature." <u>The American Journal of Psychoanalysis</u>, 42 (1982), 39-50.

Horney's theories contribute "to the humanistic value of literature by helping the reader transfer to real life the deeper understanding of human nature gained through a Horneyan interpretation . . . of characters."

27. Calogeras, Roy, and Alston, Toni M. "On 'Action Language' in Psychoanalysis." <u>Psychoanalytic Quarterly</u>, 49 (1980), 663-696.

Concludes that Schafer's action language is a language game which, brought to a successful resolution, disappears along with the patient's conflicts.

28. Carroll, David. "For Example: Psychoanalysis and Fiction or the Conflict of Generation(s). <u>Sub-stance</u>, 21 (1878), 49-67.

Two concepts of the father of a text--one Freudian and the other Lacanian. Is the author the father of the text, through it expressing his or her interiority? Or, is the text fathered by a law conceived in the name of father? In Lacan's view this law is formal and linguistic.

29. Casey, Edward S. "Comparative Phenomenology of Mental Activity: Memory, Hallucination, and Fantasy Contrasted with Imagination." Research in Phenomenology, 6 (1976), 1-25.

" . . . in this essay I shall concentrate on eidetic differences between imagining on the one hand and memory, hallucination, and fantasy on the other."

30. _____. "Imagination: Imagining and the Image." Philosophy and Phenomenological Research, 31, No. 4 (1971), 475-490.

Imagination is defined as "the conscious projection and contemplation of objects posited as pure possibilities." Creative artists, writers, and thinkers are able to project their imaginative content with the help of their work materials, canvases and paints, writing and speech. This transformation from imagination to material allows their thoughts to move from the private world to the public world.

31. Child, Irving L. "Esthetics." Annual Review of Psychology, 23 (1972), 669-694.

A broad reivew, with bibliography, of the literature from 1965-1971 dealing with the psychologcial aspects of esthetics, part of which is a review of literary esthetics.

32. Chouinard, Timothy. "The Symbol and the Archetype in Analytical Psychology and Literary Criticism. Journal of Analytical Psychology, 15, 2 (1970), 155-164.

Archetypes are symbolic, but a symbol is not necessarily archetypal. An archetype is any symbol that appears with regularity in traditional literature. There are two kinds of symbol. The descending symbol is found in the work of the author who is not consciously aware that he is using something symbolically; an ascending symbol springs from the author who is consciously creating a variation of an archetypal form.

33. Clancier, Anne. "French Literary Criticism and Psychology." In Strelka, Joseph P., ed., Literary Criticism and Psychology. University Park: Pennsylvania State University Press, 1976, 223-248.

A bibliographic essay which discusses Psychobiography, Thematic Criticism, Psychocriticsm, Anthropological Criticism, Structuralist Criticism, and Psychological Criticism.

34. Coles, Robert. "Commentary on 'Psychology and Literature'." New Literary History, 12 (1980), 207-211.

"I think that psychiatrists and psychoanalysts . . . ought for a good while to stop poking into homes next door, if not those located on an extremely different street."

35. Collier, Gary, and Kuiken, Don. "A Phenomenological Study of the Experience of Poetry." Journal of Phenomenological Psychology, 7 (1977), 209-255.

Students read and reread a poem for emotional reaction. Results revealed "a) lack of understanding, b) understanding limited to personal feelings, c) attempts to impose understanding according to a single psychological dimension."

36. Cooper, David. "The Poet as Elaborator: Analytical Psychology as a Critical Paradigm." Critical Inquiry, 6 (1979-80), 51-64.

Argues that the elaboration of experience of analytical psychology (the expression of the unconsciousness through symbol) is identical to creative experience. Analytical psychology views "creative activity as a variety of the existentially relevant" and not as determined by psychopathology.

37. Crews, Frederick. Out of My System: Psychoanalysis, Ideology and Critical Method. New York: Oxford University Press, 1975.

Contains the following essays: "Can literature by Psychoanalyzed?" (originally published in Relations of Literary Study, 1967); "Norman O. Brown: The World Dissolves" (originally published as "Love in the Western World," Partisan Review, 1967); "Anaesthetic Criticism" (originally published in The New York Review of Books, 1970); "Student Protest and Academic Distance" ("The Radical Students" N.Y. Review of Books); "Do Literary Studies Have An Ideology?" (PMLA, 1970); "Offing Culture" (TriQuarterly, 1972); "Anxious Energetics" (Partisan Review, 1974); "Reductionism and Its Discontents" (Critical Inquiry, 1975. "Can Literature be Psychoanalyzed?" contains Crews's responses to objections to psychoanalysis and its application to literature.

38. Crews, Frederick C., ed. Psychoanalysis and Literary Process. Cambridge: Winthrop Publishers, Inc., 1970.

Crews's essay, "Anaesthtetic Criticism," argues against an insular critical view of literature which deplores extra-literary considerations. Crews believes that art is ". . . regression in the service of the ego . . ." in which symbols are manipulated to reconcile competing pressures. The artist makes ". . . a tenuous cultural order where none existed before . . ." and is no longer seen as a sick man. Nor is the work of art, in Crews's view, a symptom of sickness. Crews argues for a non-reductionistic psychoanalytic criticism which is true to the psychoanalytic model but does not distort individual works to coincide with the model. Other essays in the book are: Albert D. Hutter, "Crime and Fantasy in Great Expectations," David Leverenz, "Moby-Dick," Sheldon R. Brivic, "James Joyce: From Stephen to Bloom," Richard L. Stein, "The Private Themes of Pater's Renaissance," Murray A. Schwartz, "Between Fantasy and Imagination: A Psychological Exploration of Cymbeline."

39. Daniels, Marvin. "Pathological Vindictiveness and the Vindictive Character." Psychoanalytic Review, 56 (1969), 169-196.

Briefly uses Paradise Lost, The Scarlet Letter, and Moby-Dick to "suggest an essntial similarity in the etiology of pathological vindictiveness and the manic-depressive personality."

40. David, Michael. "Psychoanalytic Criticism in Italy." *Gradiva*, 1 (1976), 65-75.

"I do seem to sense . . . the beginning of a deliberate interest in and clear signs of progress toward psychoanalytic criticsm as applied to literature."

41. Davis, Judith. "Do Men Need Women's Liberation?" *Psychiatry*, 37 (1974), 387-400.

Uses examples from the writing of G. Flaubert, G. Greer, P. Roth, M. McCarthy, and N. Mailer to show how traditional sex roles, while inhibiting female development, have done the same for male development.

42. Davis, Robert Con. "Critical Introduction: The Discourse of the Father." In Davis, Robert Con., ed, *The Fictional Father: Lacanian Readings of the Text*. Amherst: University of Massachusetts Press, 1981, 1-26.

The Fictional Father "is a book that defines the fictional father according to the operation of the symbolic father in a radical psychoanalysis." Considers *The Odyssey* in order to show "how a complex narrative manifests structural absence and the symbolic authority of the father . . . and, further what Lacanian theory of the father implies about the nature of narrative."

43. Davis, Robert Con., ed. *The Fictional Father: Lacanian Readings of The Text*. Amherst: University of Massachusetts Press, 1981.

The new French Freudianism, based on the work of Jacques Lacan, is the basis of this collection of practical criticism, all of which deals with the symbolic authority of the father.

44. Dervin, Daniel. "Michael Balint's Contributions to the Psychoanalysis of Literature." *Psychoanalytic Review* 66 (1979-80), 553-570.

Considers Balint's neologisms "philobat" and "ocnophil" ("while the ocnophil values his firm bonds with others, the philobat values his freedom and skills and tends to treat objects as interchangeable or part of his gear of equipment") as more useful than older terms describing early human development, and challenges Norman Holland's approach to pyschoanalytic literary criticsm, "an approach which . . . unduly neutralizes and domesticates both literature and psychoanalysis."

45. Dettmering, Peter. "The Development of Studies in Creativity in the German Language Area." In Strelka, J.P., ed., *Literary Criticism and Psychology*. University Park: Pennsylvania State University Press, 1976, 249-259.

A bibliographic essay which focuses on a dichotomy between a traditional psychoanalytic view of art and one presented by writers like Eissler, Kohut, Greenacre and Kris.

46. Di Cyan, Erwin. "Poetry and Creativenss: With Notes on the Role of Psychedelic Agents." *Perspectives in Biology and Medicine*, 14 (1971), 639-650.

Psychedelic agents by themselves will not stimulate creativeness; rather, they may stimulate those who are already creative. Creativeness is the transformation of the material of the mind into transcendent art. Some poets may have been mad, but madness does not necessarily produce poetry. Creativenss "requires discipline, not abandon."

47. Dieckman, Hanns. "The Favourite Fairy-tale of Childhood." Journal of Analytical Psychology, 16, 1 (1971), 18-30.

A review of the use of patients' favorite fairy-tales as a means of therapy in bringing into consciousness, and working with, "the neurotic archetypal fixation of the patient." Basic neurotic patterns and symptoms appear during the major period of exposure to fairy-tales in childhood and, therefore, may reveal in symbolic form various types of psychic growth.

48. Downing, Christine. "Re-visioning Autobiography: The Bequest of Freud and Jung." Soundings, 60 (1977), 210-228.

Freud and Jung have radically reshaped the genre of autiobiography, their entire lifework being really autobiographical.

49. Doyle, Charlotte Lackner. "The Creative Process: A Study in Paradox." In Strelka, J.P., ed., Literary Criticism and Psychology. University Park: Pennsylvania State University Press, 1976, 110-124.

Reviews various psychological theories of creativity and then focuses on the creative episode concluding that the creative process demands freedom, spontaneity, discipline, concentration, a commitment to work, honesty, intelligence, emotion, etc.

50. Dudek, Louis. "The Psychology of Literature." Canadian Literature, 72 (1977), 5-20.

A discussion of the sources of creative writing, critical of the concepts of Northrop Frye. Frye's psychology of literature is a "visionary view," a "psychedelic view" and too restrictive, narrow, and simplistic. On the contrary, "a work of literature is a wonderful, complex, psychological entity."

51. Edel, Leon. "Literature and Psychiatry." In Arieti, S., ed., Amercan Handbook of Psychiatry, I: The Foundations of Psychiatry. New York: Basic Books, 1947, 1024-1033.

A review of the parallels between the aims of the writer and the aims of the psychologist: "The common ground of literature and psychiatry is the world of irrational being." Discusses the "Journey into the Unconscious," "Interdisciplinary problems" between literature and psychology, "Psychiatry and Biography," and "Creative Process."

52. _____. "The Madness of Art." American Journal of Psychiatry, 132 (1975), 1005-1012.

The madness of art is the need to change personal experience by means of writing and other art forms. Perhaps the greatest creative works come from artists who have experienced the dismay of aging and have mastered their rage against it.

53. _____. "The Nature of Literary Psychology." Journal of the American Psychoanalytic Assocation 29 (1981), 447-467.

Works toward a "doctrine" of literary study: 1. literary art is a study of "the metamorphoses of the unconscious materials of literary art into conscious image and symbol"; 2. a study of the artist's personal myth of existence as expressed in his work; a distinction of creator's life from creative work; 4. irrelevance of therapeutic systems and models.

54. Edelson, Marshall. "Two Questions About Psychoanalysis and Poetry." In Smith, J.H., ed., The Literary Freud. New Haven: Yale University Press, 1980, 113-118.

The two questions are: "Why should the psychoanalyst qua psychoanalyst pay any special attention to poetry?" and, "What assumptions are made in some uses of psychoanalysis in literary criticism, which call for examination by the psychoanalyst?"

55. Eder, Doris L. "The Idea of the Double." Psychoanalytic Review, 65 (1978), 579-614.

The double is an "antiself . . . both strange yet familiar, hostile yet sympathetic." The double is examined in a variety of literature, including Dostoevsky, Mann, Joyce, Shakespeare, Conrad, Wilde, R.L. Stevenson, John Barth, and Borges.

56. Edmunds, Lowell, and Ingber, Richard. "Psychoanalytical Writing on the Oedipus Legend: A Bibliography." American Imago, 34, No. 4 (Winter 1977), 374-386.

A bibliography of psychoanalytical writings on the Oedipus legend, exclusive of Freud's. 207 citations.

57. Efron, Arthur. "Beginning A Reichian Approach to Literature." Energy & Character 10 (1979); 11 (1980); 1-12; 82-85.

Argues that Reich's notions of Orgone energy can be used "to illuminate the processes of emotional response. In poems . . . all the words are carefully paid out in sequence, chosen for their cumulative effect. The more we know of such energy patterns and their emotional connections, the more we will understand of the nature of poetic meanings."

58. Ehrenzweig, Anton. "The Creative Surrender." In Tennenhouse, L., ed., The Practice of Psychoanalytic Criticism. Detroit: Wayne State University Press, 1976, 136-151.

A study of the creative process, using the "object-relations theory" from Britain. The unconscious ego looks at things the way an infant does. The artist relates to his art the way an infant relates to his mother. The creative surrender "brings a deepening of the reality sense, but at the same time it possesses a manic quality, a feeling of oceanic, cosmic bliss which strangely contrasts with the imagery of suffering and death."

59. Ehrlich, Victor. "Reading Conscious and Unconscious." College English, 36 (1975), 766-775.

Starting with Aristotle's idea of art as catharsis, the experience of reading is seen as "both conscious and unconscious therapy." A contrast is made between the criticism of Norman N. Holland and Stanley Fish, Holland employing the unconscious mind, Fish the conscious. With this contrast, an "Aristotelian process is accomplished: the complex mental gymnastics, which Fish describes, indirectly express the repressed unconscious, which is described by psychoanalytical criticism such as Holland's." Contains a lengthy discussion of Fish's writing on Francis Bacon.

60. Eissler, Kurt Robert. "Remarks on an Aspect of Creativity." American Imago, 35 (1978), 59-76.

A discussion, concentrating mainly on literature, of the nature of creativity. The creative artist strives to create "a new world, a new cosmos." Creativity takes place when the ego synthesizes the extremes represented by forbidden impulses on the one hand and the control of the superego on the other. Creating art is the forming of an "organic whole" made up of these two extremes.

61. Elliott, Susan M. "A New Critical Epistemology." Hartford Studies in Literature, 7 (1975), 170-189.

A discussion of the writing of David Bleich with emphasis on Reading and Feelings: An Introduction to Subjective Criticism. Bleich calls for a "subjective paradigm" in criticism, as opposed to traditional objectivity. Contains a comparison with the writings of Norman N. Holland.

62. Engstrom, Alfred Garvin. "The Man who Thought Himself Made of Glass, and Certain Related Images." Studies in Philology, 67 (1970), 390-405.

An historical review of literature depicting people who thought they were made of glass, with a discussion of the psychological implications of the syndrome. "The fragile image of glass symbolizes what men and women value most and most fear to lose--their innocence and purity, their beauty, their health, their reputations, their happiness, and brittle life itself."

63. Faber, M.D. "Analytic Prolegomena to the Study of Western Tragedy." Hartford Studies in Literature, 5 (1973), 31-60.

Western tragedy "involves the reactivation of infantile trauma." The infant sees his mother as essential for survival and in moments of danger "splits the maternal image into good and bad object." The "imperfect" organization of Western society tends to cause "pathogenic" mothers whose sons embark on a quest "to solve the mystery of maternal ambivalence." Thus Western tragic heroes are overly involved with mothers or mother figures and threaten a return to matriarchy. Because of this, they must be destroyed by the representatives of patriarchy.

12   Psychocriticism

64. Feder, Lillian. *Madness in Literature*. Princeton: Princeton University Press, 1980.

   A survey of madness in Western literature from ancient Greece to the present day. Demonstrates "how the mad protagonists and personae of literature convey the intricate connections between psychic requirements and the social and cultural milieux in which these, however obliquely, are expressed." Discusses also how writers use madness as a means of self-revelation.

65. Felman, Shoshana. "Turning the Screw of Interpretation." *Yale French Studies*, 55-56 (1977, Special Issue), 94-207.

   An exhaustive study of the nature of psychoanalytical criticism, using Henry James' *The Turn of the Screw* as the anchor of discussion. Looks at the nature of a Freudian reading, the problem of conflicting interpretations, the theory of narrative, and the nature of madness, among other things.

66. Ferguson, Margaret W. "Border Territories of Defense: Freud and Defenses of Poetry." In Smith, J.H., ed., *The Literary Freud*. New Haven: Yale University Press, 1980, 149-180.

   Can Freud's theories regarding the ego and its defenses illuminate "defenses of poetry"? And, can such defenses of poetry illuminate Freud? Focuses upon the defenses of Boccaccio, Sidney, and Shelley. "These defenses . . . occur in a cultural court whose nature is well described by the Jewish founder of a socially offensive science."

67. Fish, Stanley. "Literature in the Reader: Affective Stylistics." *New Literary History*, 2 (1970), 123-162.

   Argues for a method of analysis "which takes the reader, as an actively mediating presence, fully into account, and which, therefore, has as its focus the 'psychological effects' of the utterance."

68. Forrest, David V. "On One's Own Onymy." *Psychiatry*, 36, 3 (1973), 266-290.

   A discussion of onymy, one's personal language, and its relationship to the jargon of political and psychological subgroups, with examples from literature and poetry.

69. Fort, Keith. "The Psychopathology of the Everyday Language of the Profession of Literary Studies." *College English*, 40 (1979), 751-763.

   Only in his oral discussions will a critic or student of literature reveal his unconscious feelings about literature. Such speech reveals the critic's feelings of inferiority to literature, sexual attraction towards literature, desire to seduce the literature, etc. Examples of these feelings are seen in phases about literature like *getting into* or *mastering* the work studied. Furthermore, the study of literature must produce offspring: one must "get something out" of literature. Notes that the title of this essay "is at best an ironic allusion."

70. Foster, Steven. "Eidetic Imagery and Imagistic Perception." Journal of Aesthetics and Art Criticism, 28, 2 (1969), 133-145.

A presentation of Erich Rudolf Jaensch's research into the nature of perception and the insights that that research can give to an examination of the literary image. According to Jaensch, "in very young children ordinary perceptions and memory pictures are both part of an 'undifferentiated unity' which is . . . neither perceptual nor ideation, but 'optical perceptual' or eidetic." This "primitive imaginal" sensibility, lost to most adults, is illustrated in the early work of Wordsworth and the poems of the Imagists.

71. Franz, Marie-Louise von. "Analytical Psychology and Literary Criticism." New Literary History 12 (1980), 117-126. Special issue entitled, Psychological Literature: Some Contemporary Directions.

Discusses the role of the "objective psyche" (Jung's collective unconscious) in literature.

72. Franzosa, John C., Jr. "Criticism and the Uses of Psychoanalysis." College English, 34 (1973), 927-933.

Erik Erikson's methodology may prove better than Norman Holland's or Frederick Crews' approach to interaction between author and reader ("intersubjectivity"). Through Erikson one "must realize the dialectical interaction by re-creating the personal and historical matrix within which the particular author worked."

73. Friedman, Norman. "Psychology and Literary Form: Toward a Unified Approach." Psychocultural Review, 2, 2 (1978), 75-95.

Demonstrates the usefulness of joining psychology and formal criticism. By using a psychological construct in a discussion of literature, the critic can provide "an analysis of the degree of coherence which obtains between the structure of the action and the process of its inner emotional dynamic. Fritz Perls' Gestalt model is seen as the most illuminating model to be applied to literature.

74. Galenbeck, Susan. "Higher Innocence: David Bleich, The Geneva School, and Reader Criticism." College English, 40 (1979), 788-801.

Discusses the common base shared by subjective criticism (as practiced by David Bleich) and phenomenological criticism (the Geneva School--Poulet especially).

75. Gedo, John E. "The Psychoanalyst and the Literary Hero: An Interpretation." Comprehensive Psychiatry, 11, (1970), 174-181.

The psychoanalyst's interest in the literary hero is related to self-analysis. However, to be completely successful the psychoanalyst's insights about the hero must lead to a parallel conscious understanding of himself, or something like analytical transference resistance.

76. Geha, Richard. "For the Love of Medusa: A Psychoanalytic Glimpse into Genocide." Psychoanalytic Review, 62 (1975), 49-77.

An analysis of the fantasy of matricide as seen in clinical studies, mythology, and fiction.

77. Ghiselin, Brewster. "Literary and Psychological Insight." Western Humanities Review, 31 (1977), 31-42.

Notes similarities and differences in the methods and aims of the writer and the psychologist. While both writer and psychologist probe the nature of human behavior, the psychologist is cerebral and scientific in his approach while the writer is emotional, employing "sensation and feeling."

78. Ginn, Robert M. "Psychodrama: A Theatre for Our Time." Group Psychotherapy and Psychodrama, 27, 1-4 (1974), 123-146.

The experience of theater can be a discovery of the power of community among people who have gathered to share the experience of a living performance. The experience can be healing, religious in nature, unlike most contemporary ultracivilized theater which has separated the actor from the audience and from his own inner self.

79. Glenn, Michael L., and Forrest, David V. "Psychological Criticism: Essence or Extract?" Archives of General Psychiatry, 20, 1 (1969), 38-47.

A discussion of the psychological criticism of Kenneth Burke, R.P. Blackmur, and Norman Holland, pointing out that such criticism is broad-based. Furthermore, it is noted that characters in fiction are not real people, authors are not patients, and the work of fiction is not autobiography.

80. Goldstein, Melvin. "La Verita Non E Stata Ancora Inventata: Anglo-American Literary Criticism and Psychology." In Strelka, J.P., ed., Literary Criticism and Psychology. University Park: Pennsylvania State University Press, 1976, 260-293.

A bibliographic essay which focuses on the psychoanalytic approach since it has "generated the greatest variety of psychological literary criticisms" but also includes the existential-phenomenological approach. An enumerative bibliography follows the essay.

81. Gordon, David J. Literary Art and the Unconscious. Baton Rouge: Louisiana State University Press, 1976.

A study written in the belief "that the concept of unconscious mind must be seriously reckoned with in literary criticism." Furthermore, "art is not a kind but a use of language; . . . the self is the organizing agent of artistic structures;" and the importance of forms and conventions "must be appreciated in relation to, and not at the expense of, the importance of originality." Examines Hamlet, Paradise Lost, Billy Budd, and the work of G.B. Shaw, D.H. Lawrence, and Hemingway.

82. Green, André. "Idealization and Catharsis." In The Psychoanalytic Study of Society, vol. 6. New York: IUP, 1975, 11-19.

"In a way, Aristotle and Freud were pursuing the same aim. The release of tension they were attempting to identify was based on an ideal balance: not so much opposing the Apollonian to the Dionysiac, . . . but keeping them together, making them exist alternatively or simultaneously." However, modern "neo-catharsis," derived from Wilhelm Reich, has as its purpose not "purging," but "the awakening of a sleeping body, . . . the revival of violence and vitality once stifled inside it."

83. Greenfield, Jerome. "Wilhelm Reich: A New Approach to Art." *Paunch*, 42-43 (1975), 43-58.

A new esthetic can be developed through Reich's ideas. Orgonomy can throw light on various art forms including literature because it goes beyond the study of the psyche. In literature, orgonomy can provide evaluations that psychoanalysis will not undertake.

84. Grenander, M.E. "Of Graver Import than History: Psychiatry in Fiction." *Journal of Libertarian Studies*, 2 (1978), 29-44.

Suggests Aristotle's notion that poetry is of "graver import than history" and then applies this notion to fiction in order to "see that 'poetry' has indicated rents in the social fabric." This poetic representation of universals is superior to those "singulars" described by the behavioral sciences.

85. Grimaud, Michel. "Critical Notes: Systems Theory, Semiotics, Psychoanalysis, Literature." *Sub-stance*, 20 (1978), 115-118.

Continuation of the bibliography begun in *Sub-stance* 13 (1976), 136-162. (See item 87.)

86. _____. "Hermeneutics, Onomastics and Poetics in English and French Literature." *Modern Language Notes*, 92 (December 1977), 888-921.

A psycholinguistic study of the importance of the use of proper names in literature. Writers use "the peculiar relation of proper names to meaning: they can generalize what is habitually a fleeting fancy and turn it into a standard technique of poetic process." Works by Flaubert, T.S. Eliot, Balzac, Hugo, and Mallarmé are examined in light of onomastics.

87. _____. "Recent Trends in Psychoanalysis: A Survey with Emphasis on Psychological Criticism in English Literature and Related Areas." *Sub-stance*, 13 (1976), 136-162.

A bibliographic essay on the psychoanalytic approach to literature.

88. Grimsley, Ronald. "Psychoanalysis and Literary Criticism in Historical Perspective." In Wolman, B.B., ed., *The Psychoanalytic Interpretation of History*. New York: Basic Books, 1971, 50-78.

A survey of the thought of important figures in the psychoanalytic approach to literature, including orthodox psychoanalytic thinkers (Freud, Jung, Charles Baudouin, Charles Mauron) and those who diverged from orthodoxy (Gaston Bachelard and Sartre). Concludes with a discussion of the value and limitations of psychoanalytical literary criticism.

16   Psychocriticism

89. Grimsley, Ronald R. "Two Philosophical Views of the Literay Imagination: Sartre and Bachelard." Comparaitve Literary Studies, 8 (1971), 42-57.

"Bachelard gives the image a more positive function than Sartre, but both stress the creative, dynamic role of the imagination as a unique aspect of all art."

90. Grossvogel, David I. "Perception as a Form of Phenomenological Criticism." Hartford Studies in Literature, 1 (1969), 83-88.

"The aim of phenomenological criticism is to view the author's writing as a human act representing an existential choice." Focuses on the consciousness of the reader within which narrative becomes experience.

91. Grotjahn, Martin. "Sex and the Mystery Story." Medical Aspects of Human Sexuality, 6, 3 (1972), 126-140.

An analysis of the latent meaning in mystery stories. "Interest in the mystery story is an attempt to solve the riddle of parental sexuality which was not mastered in childhood."

92. Haltresht, Michael. "Interpreting Dreams and Visions in Literature." Journal of English Teaching Techniques, 6, 2 (1973), 1-8.

Argues for the validity and usefulness of applying the theories of psychoanalysis to works of literature which depict dreams and visions. Draws upon the ideas of Emil A. Gutheil, J.A. Hadfield, Wilhelm Stekel, and Calvin S. Hall to propose six steps in a "scientifically sound" procedure for "psychoanalyzing" literature.

93. Hamilton, James W. "Transitional Fantasies and the Creative Process." In The Psychoanalytic Study of Society, vol. 6. New York: IUP, 1975, 53-70.

A study of "the role of the transitional object and transitional phenomena in the creative process" in clinical material and the works of Eugene O'Neill, Ingmar Bergman, Dylan Thomas, and Pablo Picasso. Transitional fantasies may be used by the artist "as a means of mastering various conflicts related to separation-individuation."

94. Hankoff, L.D. "The Hero as Madman." Journal of the History of the Behavioral Sciences, 11 (1975), 315-333.

Shows how Brutus, David, Odysseus, Kaikhosrau, and Solon feigned madness in self-defense, and then went on to successful lives. Pretending madness may have worked as a way of renewing oneself.

95. Hans, James S. "Gaston Bachelard and the Phenomenology of the Reading Consciousness." JAAC (Journal of Aesthetics and Art Criticism), 35 (1977), 315-327.

Bachelard has given us a poetics which: 1) focuses on the image; 2) champions a subjective valuation of poems; 3) elevated poetry and revery through sophisticated readings; 4) left the critic without a function; 5) champions the fragmentary elements of a work rather than the whole; 6) consigns us to a nominalistic universe "where evaluation . . . is meaningless."

96. Hartmann, Geoffrey H. _Psychoanalysis and the Question of the Text_. Baltimore: Johns Hopkins University Press, 1978.

   These essays are not for everyone, in the editor's words, but they do attempt to describe "what kind of event in the history of interpretation psychoanalysis is proving to be."

97. Hayes, Francis. "The Great Dismal Swamp of Amateur Freudian Literary Criticism." _Modern Language Journal_, 58, 7 (1974), 339-342.

   An attack on popular, facile Freudianism, which argues that literary critics without credentials (degrees) in psychology should not presume to present psychological treatments of literature.

98. Hayman, Ronald. "The Art of Being Someone Else." _Encounter_, 49 (July 1977), 77-81.

   A survey of writers' ways of dramatizing their mental anguish by transferring from themselves to something outside of themselves, from "I" to "It." Discussion of Nietzsche, Artaud, Michaux, Plath, and I.A. Richards.

99. Heller, Erich. "The Dismantling of a Marionette Theater; or, Psychology and the Misinterpretation of Literature." _Critical Inquiry_, 4 (1978), 417-432.

   Casts doubt on the validity of psychoanalytic literary criticism, focussing on Margaret Schaefer's "Kleist's 'About the Puppet Theater' and the Narcissism of the Artist." Contains a discussion of Kleist's piece.

100. _____. "Man Guilty and Man Ashamed." _Psychiatry_, 37 (1974), 10-21; 99-103.

   A study of Kafka's _The Trial_. Kafka portrays guilt as an "irreducible phenomenon" having "no legal content nor sufficient psychological causes. It is, for Kafka, part of the anatomy of the soul." Part Two of this essay is a general discussion of the connection between sex and shame, drawing upon, among others, Freud, Homer, Dostoevsky, Goethe, Neitzche, and Genesis.

101. _____. "'Yet There Is Method in It': Psychology and the Misinterpretation of Literature." In _Probleme der Komparatistik und Interpretation_. Bonn: Bouvier, 1978, 280-295.

   Criticizes psychoanalytical literary criticism by citing and disapproving of an unnamed article on Kleist's story "On the Marionette Theater." Said article "is a caricature of 'explaining' poets and poems, artists and their work, by making Victorian taboos into principles of understanding."

102. Helson, Ravenna. "Experiences of Authors in Writing Fantasy: Two Relationships Between Creative Process and Product." _Journal of Altered States of Consciousness_, 3, 3 (1977-1978), 235-248.

Fifty-seven authors of fantasy discuss their experiences in writing their first "best-known" story. The accounts are used to support the idea that a) creativity is associated with inner orientation; b) among creative books, the heroic and comic are written "at a higher level of ego-assertiveness."

103. _____. "Heroic and Tender Modes in Women Authors of Fantasy." *Journal of Personality*, 41 (1973), 493-512.

Creativeness in the works of twenty-seven women writers was measured and found to be parallel to earlier results of creativeness studies of male authors. The findings fit Rank's ideas of the "adjusted, conflicted, and creative types and Jung's conceptions of stages in the relationship between the ego and the unconscious."

104. Hendrickson, Norejane J., *et. al.* "Parent-Daughter Relationships in Fiction." *Family Coordinator* 24 (1975), 257-265.

Suggests a systematic way of examining family life through fiction, noting books which depict parent-daughter relationships.

105. Herd, E.W. "Myth Criticism: Limitations and Possibilities." *Mosaic*, 2, 3 (1969), 69-77.

Argues that it is not sufficient to merely identify myths or archetypes as sources but to comment upon their function, their place, their adaptation to an individual literary work.

106. Herring, Henry. "Constructivist Interpretation: The Value of Cognitive Psychology for Literary Understanding." In Natoli, J.P., ed., *Psychological Perspectives on Literature*. New Haven: Archon, 1983.

"The purpose of this essay . . . is to set out the initial elements of what I will call a constructivist approach to literary criticism--a designation I have chosen to emphasize the role of construction in cognitive processes and that seems justified by the frequent use of terms such as 'construct of thought' or 'construction of reality' by cognitive psychologists." Besides a general discussion of cognitive psychology's literary pertinence, this essay includes a discussion of the "Tomorrow and tomorrow and tomorrow" speech in *Macbeth*.

107. Holland, Norman. "Criticism as Transaction." In Hernadi, P., ed., *What is Criticism?*. Bloomington: Indiana University Press, 1981, 242-252.

"Criticism and psychoanalysis create verbal spaces in which we can externalize and transform inner experiences."

108. _____. *Five Readers Reading*. New Haven: Yale University Press, 1975.

Sam, Saul, Shep, Sebastian, and Sandra read "A Rose for Emily," "Winter Dreams," and "The Battler." "Anyone concerned with the interactions of groups and individuals, may find in the act of reading the basic principles that govern the human activities he studies; for reading ever so curiously mingles person and thing and person and person."

General Studies and Essay Collections   19

109. _____. "Literary Interpretation and Three Phases of Psychoanalysis." In Roland, A., ed., <u>Psychoanalysis, Creativity and Literature</u>. New York: Columbia University Press, 1976, 233-247.

> The three phases according to Holland are the unconscious, the ego, and now, the self. Criticism from "the third phase of psychoanalysis risks intimacy in order to restore individuality."

110. _____. "The New Paradigm: Subjective or Transactive?" <u>New Literary History</u>, 7 (1976), 335-346.

> Counters David Bleich's subjective view with his own transactive one, announcing his "new" paradigm: "one cannot separate subjective and objective perspectives."

111. _____. "Reading and Identity: A Psychoanalytic Revolution." <u>Academy Forum</u>, 23 (1979), 7-9.

> Announcing the new turn toward "transactive" criticism.

112. Holland, Norman N. "How can Dr. Johnson's Remarks on the death of Cordelia Add to My Own Response?" In Hartmann, G.H., ed., <u>Psychoanalysis and the Question of the Text</u>. Baltimore: Johns Hopkins University Press, 1978, 18-44.

> Although readers read in accordance with their unique "identities," shared strategies lead to the success of a literary work." Strategy refers to a matching between reader expectations and author defenses so that fantasy can "be transformed into significance." The diversity of interpretations enables us to "draw empathically on the great and not-so-great critics of the past and present."

113. _____. "Identity: An Interrogation at the Border of Psychology." <u>Language & Style</u>, 10 (1977), 199-209.

> Presents his theory of identity theme, that part of the lifestyle which a reader brings to every new reading. The study of verbal style leads us to the study of lifestyle.

114. _____. "A Letter to Leonard." <u>Hartford Studies in Literature</u>, 5 (1973), 9-30.

> Holland presents his case that reader-response criticism is a fulfillment of psychoanalytic criticism.

115. _____. "Literary Suicide: A Question of Style." <u>Psychocultural Review</u>, 1 (1977), 285-303.

> Suicide is the result of satisfying demands of inner and outer reality. The demands are four: 1) reality demands flux; 2) a basic inertia within the organism; 3) pleasure; 4) internalized intimidations against unrestrained gratifications. Discusses the suicide theme in Poe, Scott Fitzgerald, Yukio Mishima, Hart Crane, Sylvia Plath, and Hemingway.

116. _____. Poems in Persons: An Introduction to the Psychoanalysis of Literature. New York: W.W. Norton, 1973.

"People are the natural habitat of literature. A literary work completely separate from any human mind may be possible, but, by that very definition, we can never know or care about it. The literary work, in this context, is subjective." This book is based on Holland's earlier theoretical work The Dynamics of Literary Response, 1968.

117. _____. The Psychoanalytic Study of Literature. Saratoga Springs: Empire State College, 1975.

A text which parallels the English Open University text designed for independent study. Holland presents his transactional approach and claims that psychoanalysis is the only psychology that has told us much about literature.

118. _____. "A Touching of Literary and Psychiatric Education." Seminars in Psychiatry, 5, 3 (1973), 287-299.

Suggests that literary character, literary work, literary creation, and therapeutic interaction "can all be comprehended by the same interpretative strategy: looking for an invariant center to which the visible details act out different variations and relevancies."

119. _____. "A Transactive Account of Transactive Criticism." Poetics, 7 (1978), 177-189.

A study of tape-recorded comments on short stories indicated that "differences in response are as significant as the sameness of the text." We "transact" texts and experience them "by bringing to bear biological, cultural, and personal schemata, all blended through identity."

120. _____. "Transactive Criticism: Recreation Through Identity." Criticism, 18 (1976), 334-352.

Argues for a criticism "which frankly acknowledges, accepts, and uses the critic's role in his own experience."

121. _____. "The 'Unconscious' of Literature: the Psychoanalytic Approach." In Bradbury, M. and Palmer, D., eds., Contemporary Criticism. New York: St. Martin's, 1970, 131-153.

The function of pyschoanalytic criticism is to explicate the "unconscious content" of the work. The three steps in this process are "traditional explication," the "recognition of a central unconscious fantasy," and "the third step is wholly psychoanalytic--the recognition that the state of being 'rapt' or 'absorbed' . . . takes us back to the original undifferentiated state of being grafted in the oral stage of infancy." Robert Frost's "Mending Wall" is explicated to demonstrate this process.

122. _____. "UNITY, IDENTITY, TEXT, SELF." PMLA, 90 (1975), 813-822.

An amplification of the analogy "unity is to text as identity is to self." Any given person from any given era and culture "can achieve and re-achieve a single literary work, replenishing it by infinitely various additions of subjective to objective." Communication through symbols, writing and reading of literature, is a re-enacting of the "mingling of self and other."

123. _____, and Schwarts, Murray M. "The Delphi Seminar." College English, 36 (1975), 789-800.

Discussion and analysis of a literature-and-psychology seminar which came to terms with using and understanding subjective responses to literature. The Delphic principle Know Thyself was the starting point of an attempt "to explore the feeling of self and others" so that what is being read can be seen in "a more profound, more vital, and more honest way." Excerpts from students' writing are used to demonstrate the procedures of the seminar.

124. _____, and Sherman, L.F. "Gothic Possibilities." New Literary History, 8 (Winter 1977), 279-294.

Attempts to distinguish the singularity and the regularity of literary response to the gothic novel, a genre which has been popular for two centuries and is mostly read by women. "We re-create the text to make it an expression of our own personal style or identity, matching defenses and expectations to the text so as to project fantasies into it and transformation them and it toward significance."

125. Hutter, Albert D. "Dreams, Transformations, and Literature: The Implications of Detective Fiction." Victorian Studies, 19 (December 1975), 181-210.

"I shall describe . . . the pyschoanalytic theory of dreaming and its subsequent revisions, and the implications of the revised theory for constructing a newer model of literary criticism."

126. Ingarden, Roman. "Psychologism and Psychology in Literary Scholarship." New Literary History, 5 (1974), 213-223.

English translation of Ingarden's 1937 article in which he opposes empirical psychology's approach to literature with Husserlian phenomenology, a philosophy "of absolute presuppositionlessness as a fundamental method."

127. Iser, Wolfgang. The Act of Reading: A Theory of Aesthetic Response. Baltimore: Johns Hopkins University Press, 1979.

While Norman Holland opts for the term "transactive" in which the reader or literent begins and creates the response to the text, Iser, who finds his base in phenomenological rather than psychoanalytical theory, opts for a "bi-active" theory in which each text "constitutes its own reader."

128. _____. The Implied Reader: Patterns of Communication in Prose Fiction from Bunyan to Beckett. Baltimore: Johns Hopkins University Press, 1974.

The reader partially determines what he reads, a "bi-active" situation.

129. _____. Indeterminacy and the Reader's Response in Prose Fiction." In Hillis-Miller, J., ed., Aspects of Narrative. New York: Columbia University Press, 1971.

Literary texts do not confirm meanings although they entice us toward meaning.

130. Jacoby, Mario. "The Analytical Psychology of C.G. Jung and the Problem of Literary Evaluation." In Strelka, J., ed., Problems of Literary Evaluation. University Park: Pennsylvania State University Press, 1969, 99-128.

Discusses 1) Jung's disagreements with Freud in regard to the imagination; 2) Jung's three essays which deal directly with literature ("On the Relations between Analytical Psychology and Literature," "Psychology and Literature," "Ulysses"); 3) the "value" archetype and the difficulty of a psychologically-based evaluation of literature. Points out that archetypes are not fixed historic entities but psychic dispositions which are never exhausted by any one literary work, by any one symbol.

131. Jameson, Fredric. "The Imaginary and Symbolic in Lacan: Marxism, Psychoanalytic Criticism, and the Problem of the Subject." Yale French Studies, 55-56 (1978), 338-395.

The Lacanian "doctrine of the decentered subject" offers a model for the "theoretical elaboration of . . . an ideology of the collective."

132. Jayne, Edward. "The Dialectics of Paranoid Form." Genre, 11 (1978), 131-157.

Argues that the value of literature "is simply to be judged by its deceptive use of paranoid distortions which are gratifying to the emotional needs of its audience that arise from their current circumstances." Fiction "has always somehow told us what we like to hear in order to cope with what we don't really want to know."

133. Jones, A. David, Stewart, Abigail J., and Winter, David G. "Socialization and Themes in Popular Drama: An Analysis of the Content of Child-Rearing Manuals and Don Juan Plays in Sixteenth to Twentieth Centuries." European Journal of Social Psychology, 4, 1 (1974), 65-84.

Concludes, through a study of child-rearing manuals and popular plays, that attitudes expressed in the manuals will appear a century later in popular drama using the theme of the Don Juan story.

134. Kahane, Claire. "Comic Vibrations and Self-Construction in Grotesque Literature." Literature and Psychology, 29 (1979), 114-119.

"When I read a grotesque work, I experience that rapid oscillation between the comic and the fearful response, the comic coming to the fore when the artist confirms me in my sense of mastery and superiority over material which was once threatening. But when he undermines that confirmation by perceptual distortions which force me back to a shaky sense of self, the comic yields to those primitive fears against which it has been a defense."

135. Kaplan, Morton, and Kloss, Robert. *The Unspoken Motive: A Guide to Psychoanalytic Literary Criticism*. New York: Free Press, 1973.

Presents the basic aspects of psychoanalytic theory, demonstrates the applicability of the theory to literary texts, and reviews the major practitioners of psychoanalytic literary criticism along with some dissenters. Discusses Conrad's *The Nigger of the Narcissus*, Melville's *Bartleby the Scrivener*, Kafka's *A Hunger Artist*, Shakespeare's *The Tempest*, Sophocles' *Oedipus the King*, and Mary Shelley's *Frankenstein*.

136. Katz, Harvey A., Warrick, Patricia, and Greenberg, Harry. *Introductory Psychology Through Science Fiction*. Chicago: Rand McNally, 1974.

A collection of science fiction stories chosen "to emphasize the main features of general psychology courses." Chapter headings are "Psychobiology," "The Learning Process," "Sensation and Perception," "Social Processes," "Developmental Processes," "Personality," and "Abnormal Processes and Therapy." Contains a bibliography of non-fiction psychological writings which correspond to each chapter.

137. Keppler, C.F. *The Literature of the Second Self*. Tucson: University of Arizona Press, 1972.

An introduction to the double in literature, especially in American and European literature written since the end of the eighteenth century. Analyzes the nature of the double, with examples from literature. Looks at the double from a variety of angles, such as "second self," "twin brother," "pursuer," "tempter," "vision of horror," "saviour," and "beloved."

138. Kernan, Alvin. "Aggression and Satire: Art Considered As a Form of Biological Adaptation." In Brady, F., Palmer, J., and Price, M., eds., *Literary Theory and Structure*. New Haven: Yale University Press, 1973, 115-129.

Satire is "one instance of the way in which man has learned to control aggression and manage it to useful ends." Furthermore, a study of satire may help us to understand and deal with social aggression.

139. Keyes, Margaret F. "Art Processes Evoking Awareness of the Shadow Archetype." *Art Psychotherapy*, 3, 2 (1976), 77-80.

A description of ways of looking for the Jungian personal shadow. Verbal and visual aspects of epic and mythic literature are discussed.

140. Keyishian, Harry. "The Value of Vindictiveness." *The American Journal of Psychoanalysis*, 42 (1982), 21-26.

Horney gives us a fine understanding of vindictiveness but there are also many fine portraits of revengefulness and vindictiveness in literature, suggesting that a congruence of insights is called for.

24 Psychocriticism

141. Khan, Asif Iqbal. "Psychological Criticism and the English Literary Tradition." Explorations, 4, 2 (1977), 26-32.

A general review of the values and history of psychological criticism, with a warning that while such criticism can provide insight, it is dangerous to see the writer's life in all his characters and that most art "violates established norms of psychology."

142. Kiell, Norman. Psychoanalysis, Psychology, and Literature, a Bibliography, a second edition. Metuchen, N.J.: Scarecrow Press, 1982.

143. Kleinschmidt, Hans. "American Imago on Psychoanalysis, Art and Creativity: 1964-1976." American Imago, 35 (1978), 45-58.

An overview of the literature on the study of creativity, concentrating on articles published in American Imago since its inception in 1964. The problem of creativity is multifaceted and often "bewildering" and "vexing."

144. Knapp, Betina. Dream and Image. Troy, New York: Whitson, 1977.

A study of French writers from Descartes to Mallarmé, largely from a Jungian view. Demonstrates "how certain French writers experienced their oneirosphere, how they probed and dissected it, and how . . . they made viable some of the shapes and forms emerging from it."

145. Kohut, Heinz. "Psychoanalysis and the Interpretation of Literature: A Correspondence with Erich Heller." Critical Inquiry, 4 (1978), 433-450.

An exchange of letters between Kohut and Heller, stimulated by Heller's strong criticism of psychoanalytic criticism (item 99).

146. Kolodny, Annette. "The Land-as-Woman: Literary Convention and Latent Psychological Content." Women's Studies, 1 (1973), 167-182.

Traces sexual fantasies and unconscious desires for gratification in the land imagery of early American writing. Concludes that "the initial response to the American continent as woman--be she Mother or Virgin--has restricted us to psychological patterns of response that cannot possibly result in anything other than abuse."

147. Kudszus, Winfried G. "Reflections on the Double Bind of Literature and Psychopathology." Sub-stance, 20 (1978), 19-36.

The paradoxical structures of modern literature "allow for a trans-contextual double bind analysis without resorting to biographical argumentation."

148. Kuenzli, Rudolf. "Interview with Wolfgang Iser." Diacritics. (1980), 57-74.

Questions posed to Iser by Holland, Booth and Fisk. A succinct summary of points of disagreement.

149. Leitch. Vincent B. "A Primer on Recent Critical Theories." College English, 39 (1977), 138-152.

A review of Reception Aesthetics, Geneva Criticism, and Buffalo Criticism. These theories are "subjectivist" and "anti-formalist," and they replace "the sense of history with the sense of 'presence' experienced by the reader-critic engaging the text." However, the Receptionists emphasize the "psycho-sociological," the Geneva Critics the "spiritual," and the Buffalo Critics, the "scientific."

150. Lerner, Laurence. "Psychoanalysis and Art." In Strelka, Joseph, ed., Literary Criticism and Psychology. University Park: Pennsylvania State University Press, 1976, 31-47.

Discusses Freud's view of art as a function of the pleasure principle and concludes that only inferior works can be reduced to wish gratification. Lesser in Fiction and the Unconscious "does full justice to the complexity of artistic experience . . . " and presents overall a better psychoanalytic theory of art than does Freud.

151. Lesser, Simon O. "The Attitude of Fiction." (1956) In Sprich, R., and Noland, R.W., eds., The Whispered Meanings: Selected Essays of Simon O. Lesser. Amherst: University of Massachusetts Press, 1977, 32-43.

Discusses a reader's emotional involvement with a literary text. "If fiction gives us deep satisfaction . . . it must be because what it shows us is to our liking: it must depict our conflicts in a way we find peculiarly satisfying."

152. LeUnes, Arnold. "Psychological Thrillers Revisited: a Tentative List of 'Master Thrillers'." American Psychologist, 29, 3 (1974), 211-213.

A discussion and list of nine "master thrillers" for use in graduate courses in psychology, which adds to McCollom's (1971) list of "psychological thrillers" used to stimulate undergraduate students of psychology. It is suggested that the master thrillers be used as "soft" readings to complement technical psychological readings. Of the nine books, graduate students rated Viscott's The Making of a Psychiatrist the best.

153. Leverenz, David. "Anger and Individualism." Psychoanalytic Review, 62 (1975), 407-428.

Notes the persistence of the individual who avoids close relationships that are threatening, in American literature, most notably Thoreau, Emerson, Melville, and Mailer. This behavior is seen as an adult form of exerting individualism.

154. Levitt, H.N. "Psychoanalyst, Artist and Critic." Contemporary Psychoanalysis, 12 (1976), 140-143.

Psychoanalytic criticism should examine only the work of literature without looking at the possible psychic problems of the author.

155. Lindauer, Martin S. "An Empirical Approach to the Psychology of Literature." In Natoli, J.P., ed., Psychological Perspectives on Literature. New Haven: Archon, 1983.

Argues that an empirical approach may be used to address a variety of psychological aspects of literature: 1. literary content, 2. authors, 3. readers, and, 4. social context.

156. _____. The Psychological Study of Literature: Limitations, Possibilities, and Accomplishments. Chicago: Nelson-Hall, 1974.

Argues that literature can be approached by an empirically-oriented psychology in a fashion acceptable to both litterateurs and psychologists. There are exhaustive references to empirical psychological studies of literature and a detailed discussion of precisely what aspects of literature can be treated by which empirically verifiable, scientific approaches. The literary work, the author, and the reader all supply "factual pools" which the psychologist cannot ignore as data.

157. Lynch, William. "The Imagination of the Drama." Review of Existential Psychology and Psychiatry, 14, 1 (1975-1976), 1-10.

An existential study of the plays of, among others, Aeschylus, Shakespeare, Beckett, and Brecht. Tragedy struggles unsuccessfully with the universe while comedy tends to conform to nature. The dramatist gives us a better understanding of human existence by its profound stimulation of the imagination.

158. Magliola, Robert. Phenomenology and Literature. West Lafayette, Indiana: Purdue University Press, 1977.

An introductory work which considers the two generations of Geneva critics, distinguishes Heideggerians and Husserlians, presents a chapter each on Ingarden and Dufrenne, and discusses phenomenology's confrontation with Parisian structuralism. Traces the psychological offshoots of phenomenology, focusing on Binswanger and Van den Berg.

159. Magliola, Robert R. "The Phenomenological Approach to Literature: Its Theory and Methodology." Language and Style, 5 (1972), 79-99.

In the course of his exposition of phenomenology, Magliola distinguishes the metaphysical speculations of Heidegger and Sartre from the phenomenology based in description of the followers of Husserl. The phenomenological literary critic is metaphysically neutral.

160. Maini, Darshan Singh. "Psychoanalysis and Modern American Criticism." In Chander, J. and Pradhan, N.S., eds., Studies in American Literature: Essays in Honor of William Mulder. Delhi: Oxford University Press, 1976, 1-16.

A review of the wide range of psychological approaches that have been applied to American literature, a literature that has a basic inclination to delve "into the dark, subterranean, atavistic, regions of the American psyche."

161. Manheim, Leonard F. "Newer Dimensions in Psychoanalytic Criticism." CEA Chapbook, 35 (1972), 29-34.

A review of the history and development of psychoanalytical criticism and a look at where it is going.

162. _____. "Newer Dimensions in Psychoanalytic Criticism." Peabody Journal of Education, 50 (October 1972), 29-34.

    See item 161.

163. Marotti, Arthur F. "Countertransference, the Communication Process, and the Dimensions of Psychoanalytic Criticism." Critical Inquiry, 4 (1978), 471-489.

    Suggests that psychoanalytic critics use "a more sophisticated and more widely respected interpretive approach," by returning "to the epistemological basis of psychoanalysis to discover the importance of the countertranference phenomenon," constructing "a model of communication that would facilitate the discussion of literature not only in terms of the psychodynamics of creation or response but also in terms of their relationships" and stressing "the social matrix of aesthetic experience."

164. Marquard, Odo. "On the Importance of the Theory of the Unconscious for a Theory of No Longer Fine Art." In Amacher, R.E., and Lange, V., eds., New Perspectives in German Literary Criticism. Princeton: Princeton University Press, 1979, 260-278.

    A discussion of the relationship between the growth of the theory of psychoanalysis and the growing belief that beauty is no longer the criterian for fine art. "Freud's definition of art as the return of the repressed makes art interchangeable with non-esthetic phenomena, and . . . it also makes art extremely insensitive to any obligation to be fine."

165. Martindale, Colin. "Father's Absence, Psychopathology, and Poetic Eminence." Psychological Reports, 31 (1972), 843-847.

    A study of the "degree of psychopathology and of probability of cross-sexual identification" in poets, from a sampling of forty-two "eminent English and French poets." Thirty percent of these poets came from homes without a father. It was found that "psychopathology and cross-sexual identification were highly related."

166. _____. "Psychological Contributions to Poetics." Poetics: International Review for the Theory of Literature, 7, 2 (1978), 121-133.

    A survey of the trends in the study of psychological aesthetics, emphasizing three approaches: the "psychodynamic," the "psychobiological," and "the cognitive."

167. Massey, Irving. "Escape from Fiction: Literature and Didacticism." Georgia Review, 32 (1978), 611-630.

    A discussion of how guilt is connected to writing and the subsequent didacticism that grows out of this connection. Didacticism may be a "compensation for the strains of aggression and weakness that authors themselves feel to be inherent in the act of producing fiction." Short stories by Chekhov ("Ward 6"), Tolstoy ("The Death of Ivan Ilyich"), and Flaubert ("The Legend of Saint Julian the Hospitaler") are used as illustrations.

168. McAllester, E. Mary. "Gaston Bachelard: Towards a Phenomenology of Literature." *Forum for Modern Language Studies*, 12 (1976), 93-104.

   An exposition of phenomenology and of Bachelard's contribution to the phenomenology of literature. Perceives phenomenology as a rigorous way to handle the "essential subjectivity of experience."

169. McNall, Sally. *Who Is in the House? A Psychological Study of Two Centuries of Women's Fiction in America, 1795 to the Present*. New York: Elsevier, 1981.

   Some reference to Jungian theories, but mostly based on the object-relations school, Melanie Klein specifically. This school focuses "on internalized interpersonal relationships--that is to say, early experiences within the bourgeois nuclear family--in contrast to the Freudian concept of drives." Fiction here refers to popular fiction written by and for women in the United States.

170. Meissner, W.W. "Some Notes on the Psychology of the Literary Character: A Psychoanalytic Perspective." *Seminars in Psychiatry*, 5 (1973), 261-274.

   A look at the connection between psychoanalytic and literary attitudes toward human behavior. Clinical study and literary analysis are beneficial to each other. The analyst "seeks to understand and formulate the characteristics of human psychology, while the writer seeks to create and express the characteristics of human psychic functioning."

171. Menaker, Esther. "Creativity as the Central Concept in the Psychology of Otto Rank." In Roland, A., ed. *Psychoanalysis, Creativity, and Literature: A French-American Inquiry*. New York: Columbia University Press, 1976, 162-177.

   A study of the creative use of the will in the formation of personality and how the artist as a model of this creative use of the will well illustrates everyone's attempt at self-creation. The struggle between mortality and immortality is the root of individual creativeness.

172. Meyers, Jeffrey. "*Angst* and Art." *Critical Quarterly*, 16 (1974), 370-378.

   A review of Kafka's *Letters to Felice*, Douglas Day's *Malcolm Lowry: A Biography*, and T.J. Reed's *Thomas Mann: The Uses of Tradition*, demonstrating that "the lives of Kafka and Lowry and the work of Thomas Mann . . . illustrate Nietzche's idea that genius springs from abnormality and disease, from the tragic personal fate of the artist."

173. Mijuskovic, Ben Lazare. *Loneliness in Philosophy, Psychology, and Literature*. Atlantic Highlands, N.J.: Humanities Press, 1979.

   A study based upon the premise that "all men are activated by a fear of aloneness--loneliness--and that consequently every human thought, passion, and action derives from this one original, ubiquitous source, or fund, of frightened, psychic energy." Gives examples of this loneliness and seeks to answer the question of why man is isolated and alone.

174. Miller, J. Hillis. "Geneva or Paris? The Recent Work of Georges Poulet." <u>University of Toronto Quarterly</u>, 39 (1970), 212-228.

   Assesses Poulet's contribution since 1963 and sets Poulet's criticism "against the challenging new developments in literary criticism appearing now in Paris under the impact of structuralism and current reinterpretations of Nietzsche, Marx, and Freud."

175. Miller, Ralph N. "Associationist Psychology and Stedman's Theory of Poetry." <u>Markham Review</u>, 5 (1976), 65-71.

   A discussion of Stedman's <u>The Nature and Elements of Poetry</u>. Notes parallels in Stedman's ideas on poetry to materialistic theories of the associationist psychologists. Stedman "held to the belief that poetry is fundamentally rational, that it is legitimate only when it seeks to realize high purposes, that it makes emotion serve the reason."

176. Mollinger, Robert N. <u>Psychoanalytic Approach to Literature</u>. Chicago: Nelson-Hall, 1976.

   Reviews various psychoanalytic approaches to literature and summarizes classic Freudian psychology. Chapters on the literary work, the author and the audience.

177. Morris, Humphrey. "The Need to Connect: Representations of Freud's Psychical Apparatus." In Smith, J.H., ed., <u>The Literary Freud</u>. New Haven: Yale University Press, 1980, 309-344.

   Both the reification of psychoanalytic concepts and a Lacanian rereading of Freud are viewed as "actings-out according to principles . . . bearing on approaches to, and reproaches toward, the last object."

178. Morrison, Claudia C. <u>Freud and the Critic: The Early Use of Depth Psychology in Literary Criticism</u>. Chapel Hill: University of North Carolina Press, 1968.

   ". . . I have attempted to trace the introduction of Freudian ideas into the literary world and to study the reaction to them among literary critics of the first quarter of this century." Contains a chapter on D.H. Lawrence and American literature.

179. Morson, Gary. "Literary Theory, Psychoanalysis, and the Creative Process." <u>Poetics Today</u>, 3 (1982), 157-172.

   A review-article of Dalton's <u>Unconscious Structure In The Idiot</u> (item 647) which accepts Fish's "interpretive communities" theory of literary reception and argues that "production and reception are symmetrical and reciprocal processes."

180. Mosak, Harold H., and Mosak, B. <u>A Bibliography for Adlerian Psychology</u>. Washington: Hemisphere Publishing Co., 1975.

181. Mueller, Carl R. "Jungian Analysis." <u>Drama Review</u>, 22 (1978), 73-86.

An exposition of Jungian theory and then an application of it to the plays *Cops* and *Shaggy Dog Animation*. Points out that "the most unique aspect of Jungian psychology in its application to art in general is that it views the artist as the dreamer for the social collective of his time."

182. Müller-Braunschweig, Hans. "Psychopathology and Creativity." *Psychoanalytic Study of Society*, 6 (1975), 71-99.

Psychopathology inhibits the ability of the ego to deal with the unconscious fantasies of the id. Nevertheless, despite the psychopathology, the creative person develops a system of creativeness which allows his or her ego to work with the impulses that would have been repressed. Through symbols, fantasies can be objectified into a new reality.

183. Myerson, Paul G. "How the Psychiatrist Might Relate to the Writer." *Seminars in Psychiatry*, 5, 3 (1973), 245-260.

Some psychiatrists approach a literay work as a representation perhaps of the "neurotic conflicts . . . of a particular society." Others separate the author's neurosis from his observations of society.

184. Nadel, Barbara S., and Altrocchi, John. "Attribution of Hostile Intent in Literature." *Psychological Reports*, 25 (1969), 747-763.

Refers to *Billy Budd*, *Othello*, *The Ginger Man*, *In Cold Blood*, *Crime and Punishment*, *Wuthering Heights*, *Sometimes a Great Notion*, *A Separate Peace*. Hostile intent is attributed to the socially powerful, to those who have qualities we don't have, and to representatives of the devil.

185. Nance, William L. "Eden, Oedipus, and Rebirth in American Fiction." *Arizona Quarterly*, 31 (1975), 353-365.

American fiction illustrates the desire for Eden and the escape from death. This can be seen in the movement towards the wilderness, the escape into the past, and the adolescent's search for a mother and the denial by an oedipal father. James' *The Ambassadors* and Mailer's *An American Dream* illustrate these points.

186. Natoli, Joseph. "Archetypal/Psychological Approach to Poetry." In *Magill's Critical Survey of Poetry*. California: Salem Press, 1983.

Includes a discussion of the Jungian approach to poetry (as an archetypal approach) as well as theory and praxia presentations of the following approaches: Freudian, an Ego-Psychology, Transactional, Object-Relations, Lacanian, and phenomenological psychological.

187. _____. "Introduction." In Natoli, J.P., ed., *Psychological Perspectives on Literature: Freudian Dissidents and Non-Freudians*. New Haven: Archon, 1983.

A survey of "unorthodox" psychological approaches to literature with attendant inevitable categorizations.

General Studies and Essay Collections 31

188. _____. "Phenomenological Psychology and Literary Interpretation." In Natoli, J.P., ed., Psychological Perspectives on Literature: Freudian Dissidents and Non-Freudians. New Haven: Archon, 1983.

"A phenomenological perspective takes us out of the armchair of the psychoanalyst attending only to the words a character speaks, and enables us to reconstruct the phenomenal reality of a character by attending to that character's varied interactions with the world." Includes analyses of Hamlet, Blake's "The Sick Rose," and Didion's Play It As It Lays.

189. Natoli, Joseph, ed. Psychological Perspectives on Literature: Freudian Dissidents and Non-Freudians. New Haven: Archon, 1983.

A casebook of "unorthodox" psychological approaches to literature: Jung, Adler, Reich, Fromm, Lacan, Holland, Schafer, Horney, phenomenological psychology, cognitive, empirical. Each essay presents a theoretical and a praxis section.

190. Nelson, Benjamin, ed. "Psychoanalysis and the Classics of Literature." Psychoanalytic Review, 62, Special Issue (1975), 5-194.

Contains articles on women in Greek myth, Gynecocide, Prometheus Unbound, Socrates' Apology, Shakespeare, Wuthering Heights, The Beast in the Jungle and The Ambassadors, the Grimms' The Table, the Ass, and the Stick, Dickens' "Nurse Stories," and psychoanalysis, literature, and society.

191. Nelson, Cary. "The Psychology of Criticism, or What Can Be Said." In Hartman, Geoffrey, ed., Psychoanalysis and the Question of the Text. Baltimore: Johns Hopkins University Press, 1978, 45-61.

"What is essential now is to begin looking at critical texts themselves with some sensitivity to the psychology of their rhetoric."

192. Nemiah, John C. "The Art of Deep Thinking: Reflections on Poetry and Psychotherapy." Seminars in Psychiatry, 5 (1973), 301-311.

Argues that "the psychiatrist . . . must be both poet and scientist and must be able to encompass the methods of both as he deals with the facts of human life and human experience."

193. Newman, Karen. "Writing the 'Talking Cure': Psychoanalysis and Literature." Poetics Today, 3 (1982), 173-182.

A review-article of Schwartz and Kuhn's Representing Shakespeare and Orlando's Toward a Freudian Theory of Literature. Maintains that Holland's "rhetoric of humility which pretends to abdicate the role of priest and giver of truth is in fact a strategy for justifying solipsism." Orlando's "theoretical model is audacious; it is based on a signifying process, not an allegory of human development."

194. Noland, Richard W. "The Future of Psychological Criticism." Hartford Studies in Literature, 5 (1973), 88-105.

A brief summary of different phases of psychological criticism. Advocates an adherence to the principle of epigenesis (later stages of development are not completely determined by earlier stages), and to a plurality of theories and methods (Freudian, Jungian, behavioral, existential-phenomenological).

195. Ong, Walter J. "Beyond Objectivity: The Reader-Writer Transaction as an Altered State of Consciousness." CEA Critic, 40, 1 (1977), 6-13.

Discusses the contributing role of the reader in the author's writing which Ong maintains is supremely important.

196. Orr, Leonard. Existentialism and Phenomenology: A Guide for Research. New York: Whitson Publishing Co., 1978.

A bibliography.

197. Oughourlian, Jean-Michel, and Lefort, Guy. "Psychotic Structure and Girard's Doubles." Diacritics, 8 (1978), 72-74.

Presents Girard's argument "that the psychotic structure is one of symmetry, of a double, that it is a return to the undifferentiated, pre-sacrificial mimetogony. . . . "

198. Oxenhandler, Neal. "The Horizons of Psychocriticism." New Literary History, 14 (1982), 89-104.

Asks the question, "What are the horizons of psychocriticism?" Looks toward an horizon for psychocriticism in which psychocriticism "would be both intrinsic to the text, yet resonant with its dynamic (affective) life."

199. _____. "Retrieving the Self: the Critic as Existential Psychoanalyst." Boundary, 4 (1975), 299-302.

A discussion of Serge Doubrovsky, an existential psychoanalyst, focusing on his work The New Criticism of France. "Doubrovsky implies that there is a network of emotional and psychological relations in the work that can be decoded by psychoanalytic techniques."

200. Palmer, Richard E. "Phenomenology as Foundation for a Post-Modern Philosophy of Literary Interpretation." Cultural Hermeneutics, 2 (July 1973), 207-222.

Phenomenology "offers the resources for putting literary interpretation back on a more viable philosophical foundation--such a foundation could restore some sense of the deep importance of the historical and ontological dimensions in literary interpretation." Argues for the work of art as an act of perception rather than as an object or organism. Refers to the act of perception as "an event of understanding." "What is needed is a philosophy of interpretation which takes the event of understanding as the starting point for all thinking and theory about literary interpretation: a phenomenology of the event of understanding."

201. Paris, Bernard J. "Horney's Theory and the Study of Literature." American Journal of Psychoanalysis, 38 (1978), 343-353.

Applying Karen Horney's theoretical formulations to criticism suggests that authors of different times and locations have "grasped intuitively and artistically portrayed the same basic patterns of conflict and behavior that Horney described and attempted to explain."

202. _____. *A Psychological Approach to Fiction: Studies in Thackeray, Stendahl, George Eliot, Dostoevsky and Conrad*. Bloomington and London: Indiana University Press, 1974.

Argues that it is valid to treat characters in fiction as real people. Treats *Vanity Fair*, *Red and the Black*, *Mill on the Floss*, and *Lord Jim*. Draws on Karen Horney's writings for a conception of neurosis and Maslow's Third Force psychology for a conception of health.

203. _____. "Third Force Psychology and the Study of Literature." In Natoli, J.P., ed., *Psychological Perspectives on Literature*. New Haven: Archon, 1983.

Thoroughgoing discussion of Third Force psychology and an extensive Horneyan analysis of Hamlet.

204. _____. "Third Force Psychology and the Study of Literature, Biography, Criticism, and Culture." *Literary Review*, 24 (1981), 181-221.

Paris here reviews his use of the "Third Force" psychologists, namely Karen Horney, Abraham Maslow, Carl Rogers and others who maintain that there is an "evolutionary constructive force" which urges man "to realize his given potentialities."

205. Paris, Jean. "The Mortal Sign: Psychological Implications of Linguistic Elements in Literature." In Strelka, J.P., ed., *Literary Criticism and Psychology*. University Park: Pennsylvania State University Press, 1976, 174-197.

Discusses, among other things, "meaning of non-sense," "non-sense of meaning," "retinal rivalry," and "the generative disjunction."

206. Pasotti, Robert N. "The Emotional Plague in Literature." *Journal of Orgonomy*, 10 (1976), 232-249.

On character structure in *Othello*, *Moby Dick*, *The Possessed* and *Nineteen Eighty-Four* from a Reichian view.

207. Payne, Michael. "Do Psychologists and Critics Speak the Same Language?" *Journal of General Education*, 24 (1972), 179-183.

A discussion which joins literary study and psychology, ranging from Prudentius' *Psychomachia* to the work of R.D. Laing. *Othello*, *Hamlet*, *King Lear*, and Burton's *Anatomy of Melancholy*, among other works, are discussed.

208. Pearce, Howard D. "A Phenomenological Approach to the *Theatrum Mundi* Metaphor." *PMLA*, 95 (1980), 42-57.

"The theater-dream metaphor raises fundamental ontological and epistemological questions and treats them in much the same way as phenomenological thought does." David Storey's <u>The Contractor</u>, Shakespeare's <u>A Midsummer-Night's Dream</u>, Cyril Tourneur's <u>The Revenger's Tragedy</u>, Ibsen's <u>The Wild Duck</u>, Calderón's <u>Life Is a Dream</u>, Chekhov's <u>The Sea Gull</u>, Alexander Ostrovsky's <u>The Forest</u>, are discussed in terms of the <u>theatrum mundi</u> metaphor.

209. Peckham, Morse. "Psychology and Literature." In Strelka, Joseph P., ed., <u>Literary Criticism and Psychology</u>. University Park: Pennsylvania State University Press, 1976, 46-68.

Psychology and literary criticism should interact, but they do not, owing to basic deficits in both. Psychology can supply much needed generalizations for literary criticism, and literary criticism can aid the psychologist in offering itself as a sophisticated model of language use.

210. Petrosky, Anthony R. "The Effects of Reality Perception and Fantasy on Response to Literature: Two Case Studies." <u>Research in Teaching English</u>, 10 (1976), 239-258.

A clinical study demonstrating the uniqueness of individual responses to literature. The reader's fantasies and perception of reality determine the responses.

211. Porter, Laurence M. "Do Literary Dreams Have a 'Latent Content?' The Jungian View." <u>Journal of Altered States of Consciousness</u>, 4 (1978-79), 37-42.

Jungian psychology pursues latent meaning in a literary text by paying attention to the "undetermined" elements--"sudden changes of setting, time, or identity or subject . . . " which may be "momentary failures to understand the message of the archetype of spirit, or the collective nature of the <u>anima</u>."

212. Porter, Peter. "Poetry and Madness." <u>Southerly</u>, 36 (1976), 385-405.

A survey of "mad" writers and writing, demonstrating some connections between madness and the process of creating literature.

213. Purdy, Strother B. "On the Psychology of Erotic Literature." <u>Literature and Psychology</u>, 20 (1970), 23-29.

A discussion of the fantasy of the big penis, the "phallic fallacy" of "the bigger the better." Argues that we "have a male-dominated erotica" and an erotica which perpetuates physiological misconceptions. Cites Fowles 1965 <u>The Magus</u> as a sign of a more balanced erotica.

214. Ragland-Sullivan, Ellie. "Explicating Jacques Lacan: An Overview." <u>Hartford Studies in Literature</u>, 11 (1979), 140-156.

Summarizes Lacan's theories and their relevance to literary criticism. Focuses on the mirror-stage, division of the ego, the Other, the Oedipal structure, the structural-linguistac nature of the unconscious and Lacan's attacks on American ego psychology.

215. _____. "Jacques Lacan--Ecrits: A Selection." (review article) Gradiva, 2 (1979), 58-63.

"Whatever one may think of specific aspects of Lacanian thought, in reading him one cannot escape his challenge to scholars and critics above all to submit to new scrutiny our received ideas on truth, knowledge, and language. . . . "

216. _____. "Lacan, Language and Literary Criticism." The Literary Review, 24 (1981), 562-577.

A review-essay of Sherry Turkle's Psychoanalytic Politics. Ragland-Sullivan presents a summary of Lacan's views as well as a discussion of his impact on literary theory.

217. _____. "The Language of Laughter." Sub-stance, 13 (1976), 91-106.

"In this essay, I shall discuss the psycho-dynamics of laughter first in terms of Freudian theory and then, using Lacan as a referent, I shall interpret Freud's findings within a structural framework."

218. Rahv, Philip. "Freud and the Literary Mind." In Literature and the Sixth Sense. Boston: Houghton Mifflin, 1969, 150-167.

A discussion of the important relevance of Freud to an understanding of the workings of the writer's mind and a comment on some of the vulgarizations and excesses of Freudian literary criticism.

219. Richmond, Hugh M. "Personal Identity and Literary Personae: A Study in Historical Psychology." PMLA, 90 (1975), 209-221.

Historical psychology is the study of the evolution of the collective human personality. In this psychic history, it is noted that in the Renaissance there was a growth of awareness of the individual self, perhaps because of social alienation, as seen, for example, in Petrarch and Montaigne. The recognition of historical psychology can aid in the understanding of historical literary developments. Milton and Shakespeare, among others, are also examined in the light of self-awareness.

220. Roberts, Patrick. The Psychology of Tragic Drama. London and Boston: Routledge & Kegan Paul, 1975.

"Psychoanalysis shows man's capacity for love struggling constantly against his envious and destructive impulses; tragedy is born out of nothing so much as the waste of one by the other." Essays on Euripides, Strindberg, Pinter, Ionesco, Weiss, Aeschylus, O'Neill, Eliot, Sartre, Shakespeare and Ibsen.

221. Rogers, Robert. "Amazing Reader in the Labyrinth of Literature." Poetics Today, 3 (1982), 31-46.

Postulates yet another kind of reader--Amazing Reader. "A paradoxical feature of Amazing Reader's position is that he experiences the interpretive process as determinate in some ways and indeterminate in others." Discusses Amazing Reader's response to Stevens' "The Snow Man."

222. _____. "A Gathering of Roses." *Hartford Studies in Literature*, 5 (1973), 61-76.

> A psychoanalytic study of rose imagery in literature. Besides traditional iconography of rose symbolism, Rogers points out " . . . the primary process potentialities of rose image . . . , " including " . . . that which is oral-nourishing, oral-sadistic, masochistic--and, of course, thornily phallic."

223. _____. *Metaphor: A Psychoanalytic View*. Berkeley: University of California Press, 1978.

> A study of the "psychological aspects of the metaphoric process." Looks at "the relationship of metaphor to sexuality, to creativity, and to what psychoanalysis . . . calls 'object relations'."

224. _____. "On the Metapsychology of Poetic Language: Modal Ambiguity." *International Journal of Psycho-Analysis*, 54 (1973), 61-74.

> Converts Pound's definition of an image into a description which considers " . . . the full range of mental activity. . . . " Speaks of primary process mentation and secondary process mentation. Pound's definition however is unsurpassed.

225. _____. *A Psychoanalytic Study of the Double in Literature*. Detroit: Wayne State University Press, 1970.

> A wide-ranging discussion of latent and manifest doubles, the "multiple representation" of the self, in Western literature. Distinguishes subject doubles from object doubles, the Mirror Image, The Secret Sharer (theme), The Opposing Self, fragmentation of the mind, and Psychomachia.

226. Roland, Alan. "Psychoanalytic Literary Criticism--Promise and Problems." *Book Forum*, 1 (1974), 275-284.

> Discusses the analogy of dream to the work of art as well as "certain basic assumptions by psychoanalysts on aesthetic form and processes of creativity. Discusses the criticism of Frederick Hoffman and Norman Holland, creators of new aesthetics based on psychoanalysis.

227. _____. "Toward a Reorientation of Psychoanalytic Literary Criticism." In Roland, A., ed., *Psychoanalysis, Creativity and Literature*. New York: Columbia University Press, 1976. 248-270.

> Argues that the analogy of a work of art with the dream is a fundamental cause of reductionism. Considers the work of Simon O. Lesser, Frederick Hoffman, and Norman Holland. Finally, considers "very recent explorations into the creative process and primary process thinking" and their relation to literary criticism.

228. Roland, Alan, and Rizzo, Gino. "Psychoanalysis in Search of Pirandello: *Six Characters* and *Henry IV*." In Roland, Alan, ed., *Psychoanalysis, Creativity and Literature*. New York: Columbia University Press, 1976, 323-351.

A review of the psychoanalytic work on Pirandello done by Charles Kligerman, Theodore Jacobs, Eric Bentley, and Martin Wangh. Six Characters "is ultimately concerned with the most primal form of repudiation a human being can experience, the repudiation of a child by his mother." In Henry IV, Henry is a narcissist whose behavior is compensation for, and defense against, his "wounded narcissism."

229. _____. "Psychoanalysis in Search of Pirandello: Six Characters and Henry IV. Psychoanalytic Review, 64 (1977), 63-99.

See item 228.

230. Rollman-Branch, Hilda S. "Psychical Reality and the Theatre of Fact." American Imago, 26 (1969), 56-70.

Unlike tragedy in which the audience is free of individual responsibility, the theatre of fact is a threatre of individual responsibility. The viewer reacts based on his or her own psychical reality, conscious and unconscious. "The Theatre of Fact faces us with the responsibility for our own fate and our responsibility for the fate of others." Cites the work of Brecht, Grass, Weiss and Miller.

231. Rosenblatt, Louise. The Reader, The Text, The Poem: The Transactive Theory of the Literary Work. Carbondale: Southern Illinois University Press, 1978.

"The reader-critic savors as fully as possible his personal evocation during the lived-through transaction with the text . . . the work envisaged is a product of the reverberations between what he has brought to the text and what the text offers."

232. Rothenberg, Albert. "The Process of Janusian Thinking in Creativity." Archives of General Psychiatry, 24, 3 (1971), 195-205.

"'Janusian thinking'--the capacity to conceive and utilize two or more opposite or contradictory ideas, concepts, or images simultaenously-- is discussed in relation to its role in the creative process in art, literature, architecture, music, science and mathematics."

233. _____. "The Unconscious and Creativity." In Roland, A., ed., Psychoanalysis, Creativity and Literature. New York: Columbia University Press, 1976, 144-161.

Distinguishes unconscious, primary processes from cognitive and linguistic processes involved in creativity in both literature and science.

234. Rothenberg, Albert, and Greenberg, Bette. The Index of Scientific Writings in Creativity. New Haven: Archon Books, 1974.

See Introduction to this bibliography.

235. Rycroft, Charles. "Freud and the Imagination." New York Review of Books, (3 April 1975), 26-30.

A discussion of Freud's concept of primary and secondary modes of thinking as related to creativeness. The "idea that artists and writers are neurotic" comes from the fallacious belief that the primary and secondary processes of thinking are antagonistic to each other. On the contrary, creative people may exhibit a healthy co-existence of the two processes.

236. Sardello, Robert. "An Empirical-Phenomenological Study of Fantasy, with A Note on J.R.R. Tolkien and C.S. Lewis," Psychocultural Review, 2 (1978), 203-220.

States that phenomenology has taken an empirical turn in this century and then proceeds to consider fantasy, from an experimental as well as a phenomenological perspective. Refers to Tolkien's and C.S. Lewis's comments on fantasy.

237. Schafer, Roy. "Action and Narration in Psychoanalysis." New Literary History, 12 (1980), 61-86.

On the action-language view of narration. Both psychoanalyst and literary critic encounter narration.

238. _____. "Narration in the Psychoanalytic Dialogue." Critical Inquiry, 7 (1980), 29-54.

Pursues his belief that literary interpretation and psychoanalytic interpretation face similar problems.

239. _____. Narrative Actions in Psychoanalysis: Narratives of Space and Narratives of Time. The Heinz Werner Lectures. Worcester, Mass.: Clark University Press, 1981.

A discussion of psychoanalytic narrative which has qualities similar to fictional narrative since the analysand faces the same problems in "situating" in time and space his or her "story."

240. Scheff, Thomas J. "Audience Awareness and Catharsis in Drama." Psychoanalytic Review, 63 (1976-77), 529-554.

Argues that " . . . discrepant awareness is a device used to control the amount of identification by the audience with the characters, and that the amount of identification, in turn, helps to determine whether the audience experiences catharsis."

241. Schmidl, Fritz. "Problems of Method in Applied Psychoanalysis." Psychoanalytic Quarterly, 41 (1972), 402-419.

Includes a general discussion of psychoanalytic criticism: use of biography to discuss a work, use of the work to discuss an author, use of psychoanalysis to analyze a character.

242. Schor, Naomi. "Female Paranoia: The Case for Psychoanalytic Feminist Criticism." Yale French Studies, 62 (1981), 204-219.

"I shall propose a psychoanalytic feminist thematics which turns to account the specific contribution of women to contemporary theory, that is, their militant materialism." Illustrates her approach through a reading of Poe's "The Mystery of Marie Roget."

243. Schroeder, Fred E.H. "The Development of the Super-Ego on the American Frontier." Soundings, 57 (1974), 189-205.

Using Freud's ideas on acculturation and civilization, Schroeder notes that the writing of Frederick Jackson Turner, Hector St. John de Crèveçoeur, and Bret Harte demonstrates that "a new and historically unique super-ego . . . has developed out of the shared guilt and primal sin of the frontier."

244. Sears, Robert R., and Lapidus, Deborah. "Episodic Analysis of Novels." Journal of Psychology, 85 (1973), 267-276.

"Episodic analysis is the separation of a novel into its component episodes--i.e., into short stories each of which has a unitary theme in order to provide equivalent units for content analysis."

245. Shupe, Donald R. "Representation versus Detection as a Model for Psychological Criticism." The Journal of Aesthetics and Art Criticism, 34 (1976), 431-440.

"Representational criticism is the mapping of a work of literature into a framework as illuminated by a particular set of assumptions and underlying theory. . . . In the case of psychological studies of literature its special merit is to distinguish and differentiate between the representation and the theoretical model which serves as its basis."

246. Silberger, Julius. "Using Literary Materials to Teach Psychiatry." Seminars in Psychiatry, 5, 3 (1973), 275-285.

Discusses an elective seminar, "The Psychology of Characters in Fiction," taught at the Massachusetts Mental Health Center. The purpose is to expose students to "the individuality and uniqueness of others."

247. Silverman, Hugh J. "Dufrenne's Phenomenology of Poetry." Philosophy Today, 20 (Spring 1976), 20-24.

"The common reader enters into the world of the poem seeking meaning. What he finds is an expression of the very world which he can know more thoroughly having entered the realm of the poetic." The common reader "is every reader who is prepared to take himself to the poem with his corporeal presence, activating the sensuous, which in turn reveals meaning."

248. Simon, Bennett. "Mental Life in Greek Tragedy." In Mind and Madness in Ancient Greece: The Classical Roots of Modern Psychiatry. Ithaca: Cornell University Press, 1978, 89-121.

Looks at modern and ancient ideas on the connection between creativeness and madness, and explores the idea of the theater as therapy.

249. Siomopoulos, Gregory. "Poetry As Affective Communication. Psychoanalytic Quarterly, 46 (1977), 499-513.

A discussion of the experience of poetry as "an act of affective communication," using T.S. Eliot's The Waste Land as an example. "The capacity for flexible language behavior of the participants in the poetic experience makes possible . . . empathic communication."

250. Siomopoulos, V. "The Existential Hero: Schizophrenic or the Forerunner of a New Affectivity?" The Psychoanalytic Review, 62 (1975), 429-436.

Argues that " . . . the affectivity of the existential hero contains elements of severe psychopathology as well as the rudiments of a new mode of feeling--a new affectivity--which transcends the abstractions of the existential philosopher." The existential hero like the schizophrenic patient does not have any affective ties with reality.

251. Skura, Meredith. The Literary Use of the Psychoanalytic Process. New Haven: Yale University Press, 1981.

Argues throughout that the "analyst's work can . . . be both different and relevant, provided that it is not taken as a substitute for the critic's investigations but rather as a separate investigation that can supplement the critic's work in various ways."

252. _____. "Revisions and Rereadings in Dreams and Allegories." In Smith, J.H., ed., The Literary Freud. New Haven: Yale University Press, 1980, 345-379.

Discusses how Freud's view of wish and censorship was broadened in his own practice to "imply a much wider conflict in dreams." In her second section, the author finds this wider conflict in a Freudian dream analysis. The final section discusses the relationship between dream conflict and literary texts.

253. Slaby, Andrew E., and Tancredi, Laurence. "Literary Insights and Theories of Passion." In Peschel, E.R., ed., Medicine and Literature. New York: Watson, 1980, 113-119.

Discusses the function of literature "as the cutting edge for psychiatric theory." Literature increases a psychiatrist's "intellectual and emotional understanding of patients."

254. Slochower, Harry. "Contemporary Psychoanalytic Theories on Creativity in the Arts." In Strelka, J.P., ed., Literary Criticism and Psychology. University Park: Pennsylvania State University Press, 1976, 223-248.

Discusses methodological pitfalls in the psychoanalytic approach to the arts as presented in the work of Barchillon, Kove, Kris, Eissler, Kohut, Weissman, Greenacre, Niederland, Ehrenzweig, Kanzer. Havelka, Ammon, Ricoeur and Bloch are among the few who consider the social-historical determinants of the artist's social milieu.

255. _____. "The Psychoanalytic Approach to Literature: Some Pitfalls and Promises." Literature and Psychology, 21 (1971), 107-111.

Argues that " . . . the artist's symbolic and formal powers are more than defense-reactions and substitute gratification, that they are first of all ego powers which seek out conflict free spheres, or at least, keep conflicts etc. in control."

256. _____. "Suicides in Literature: Their Ego Function." American Imago, 32 (1975), 389-416.

There is a difference between the suicide of a real person and the suicide of a character in literature. Fictional suicide is a symbolic act of rebellion and a product of the whole ego in a character who knows that he or she will be defeated. Among other characters, Anna Karanina, Emma Bovary, and Hedda Gabler are examined.

257. Smith, Joseph H., and Parloff, Gloria H., eds., The Literary Freud: Mechanisms of Defense and the Poetic Will. Psychiatry and the Humanities, vol. 4. New Haven: Yale University Press, 1980.

Essays by Bloom (whose theories set the tone of the collection), Susan and Leslie Brisman, Morris Dickstein, Marshall Edelson, Shoshana Felman, Margaret Ferguson, David Gordon, Geoffrey Hartman, John Irwin, William Kerrigan, Humphrey Morris and Meredith Skura.

258. Snider, Clifton. "C.G. Jung's Analytical Psychology and Literary Criticism: I." Psychocultural Review, 1 (1977), 96-108.

A discussion of Jung's theories of archetypes and creativity as related to literature. Literature is not neurosis; it is man's rising above himself to speak to mankind. An appendix of Jungian definitions is included.

259. _____. "C.G. Jung's Analytical Psychology and Literary Criticism (II): Jung's Psychology of the Conscious and the Unconscious." Psychocultural Review, 1 (1977), 216-242.

A continuation of the author's exposition of a Jungian approach to literature (see item 258). Discusses psychological types, function of consciousness, anima/animus archetypes, shadow archetype, mandala, God-archetype, the Self.

260. _____. "C.G. Jung's Analytical Psychology and Literary Criticism (III): The Archetypal Self in Swinburne's 'Tristram of Lyonesse.'" Psychocultural Review, 1 (1977), 371-396.

Argues that the "achievement of psychological wholeness (of what Jung calls the Self) in the poem makes its structure aesthetically pleasing." (See items 258 and 259.)

261. Spivey, Ted R. The Journey Beyond Tragedy: A Study of Myth and Modern Fiction. Orlando: University Press of Florida, 1980.

Identifies the postmodern with an age of high comedy, one replacing the tragedy of the modern age, and one in which the visionary and mythic powers which lead to our spiritual development have been sustained. Jung has done much to reveal the creative power of myth and rite, the power that will lead to a renewed creativity.

262. Sprich, Robert. "Pressed Flowers/Fresh Flowers: New Directions in Psychoanalytic Criticism." *Colby Library Quarterly*, 13 (1977), 67-72.

A review which registers both practical and theoretical problems in the psychoanalytic approach to literature and discusses and defends Holland's concern with the psychology of the reader.

263. Steig, Michael. "The Intentional Phallus: Determining Verbal Meaning in Literature." *JAAC (Journal of Aesthetics and Art Criticism)*, 36 (1977), 51-61.

A study of the problem of discovering--and distinguishing between--intension and meaning in literature. Discusses the theories on literary interpretation of E.D. Hirsch. Uses examples from Dickens' *The Old Curiosity Shop* and *Martin Chuzzlewit* and Hardy's *Jude the Obscure*. Hirsch's ideas are useful, "but if it is essntial, in the interpretation of literary works where implied meanings must be brought to light, to distinguish between meaning and significance, then one must employ a concept of intention that fully accommodates the known biographical facts about an author as well as the full picture of the occasion of composition, and which combines, in its application to the text, an awareness of linguistic and historical boundaries with an openness to the possibility that an author may have violated the critic's preconceptions about generic or cultural limitations."

264. Stockholder, Katharine. "Fictions, Phantasies, and 'Reality': A Reevaluation." *Literature and Psychology*, 26, 1 (1976), 17-30.

Argues for the propriety and value of a psychoanalytic approach to literature and attempts to reconcile that approach "to more traditional conceptions of meaning and value."

265. Stone, Albert E. "Psychoanalysis and American Literary Culture." *American Quarterly*, 28 (1976), 309-323.

An overview of psychoanalytic criticism, with emphasis on criticism of American literature. "Psychoanalytic critics are united by a fact often underrated by other kinds of critics: people write poems, other people read poems, and there is a self in the poem on the page." However, psychoanalysts do not always agree with each other when interpreting literature. Nevertheless, psychoanalysis has changed the way we read literature.

266. Stott, Jon. "Midsummer Night's Dreams: Fantasy and Self-Realization in Children's Fiction." *Lion and Unicorn*, 1 (1977), 25-39.

Traces the circular patterns of personal growth in three children's books: Virginia Hamilton's *Zeely*, Mordecai Richler's *Jacob Two-Two Meets the Hooded Fang*, and Madeleine L'Engle's *A Wrinkle in Time*. In each story, "the central character does return from his or her fantasy world, does complete the circular journey." Each character "must face the reality of his inner situation."

267. Styan, J.L. "Psychology in the Study of Drama: The Negative and the Positive." *College Literature*, 5 (1978), 77-93.

An historical survey of the various psychological perspectives towards characterization directors and actors have taken when doing plays and portraying characters of Shakespeare and Chekhov, among others.

268. Suleiman, Susan, and Grosman, Inge, eds. <u>The Reader in the Text: Essays on Audience and Interpretation</u>. Princeton: Princeton University Press, 1980.

Audience-oriented criticism is "not one field but many, not a simple widely trodden path but a multiplicity of crisscrossing, often divergent tracks that cover a vast area of the critical landscape in a pattern whose complexity dismays the brave and confounds the faint of heart."

269. Swan, Jim. "Giving New Depth to the Surface: Psychoanalysis, Literature, and Society." <u>Psychoanalytic Review</u>, 62, 1 (1975), 5-28.

Presents Norman Holland's <u>The Dynamics of Literary Response</u> and Enrenzweig's <u>The Hidden Order of Art</u> as two studies which present a "dialectical and historical method of interpetation, in which the interpreter and his interpretive principle, his hermeneutic, are themselves subjected to analysis and interpretation."

270. Taubenheim, Barbara Wiese. "Erikson's Psychosocial Theory Applied to Adolescent Fiction: A Means for Adolescent Self-Clarification." <u>Journal of Reading</u>, 22 (1979), 517-522.

A discussion of Erik Erikson's fifth stage of human development, the "sense of Identity," and how it is relevant to choosing reading material for adolescents. Contains an annotated bibliography of books which might help adolescents "in their search for self-clarification."

271. Townsend, Dabney W., Jr. "Phenomenology and the Form of the Novel: Toward an Expanded Critical Method." <u>Philosophy and Phenomenological Research</u>, 34 (1974), 331-338.

"A book must be read to be a book; therefore both book and reader must occupy our attention. The act of reading is an extremely complex conscious awareness, and that consciousness is our true 'object' of study."

272. Tsur, Reuven. "Emotion, Emotional Qualities, and Poetry." <u>Psychocultural Review</u>, 2 (1978), 165-180.

A discussion of the nature of emotion and what qualities in a poem make it emotional. "A poem is <u>not</u> an emotion. It <u>may</u> be . . . an <u>imitation</u> of an emotion."

273. Vincie, Joseph F. and Rathbauer-Vincie, Margreta. <u>C.G. Jung and Analytical Psychology: A Comprehensive Bibliography</u>. New York: Garland, 1977.

274. Wasiolek, Edward. "The Future of Psychoanalytic Criticism." In Malone, D.H., ed., <u>The Frontiers of Literary Criticism</u>. Los Angeles: Hennessey and Ingalls, 1974, 149-168.

Suggests that some psychoanalytical criticism is bad and notes some of its excesses, concluding: "If psychoanalytic criticism can live up to the promise of Freud's brilliance and can divest itself of its own defenses and enter the main stream of literary criticism, it may have an important part to play in the future of criticism."

275. Weiss, Allen. "Merleau-Ponty's Concept of the 'Flesh' as Libido Theory." Sub-stance, 30 (1981), 85-95.

"1) I wish to unpack the complex metaphorical implications to the term 'flesh,' which is the central ontological term of Merleau-Ponty's The Visible and the Invisible; and 2) in doing so I wish to show how the theory of the 'flesh' served as a nascent libido theory, thus providing one of the roots of post-Structuralist thought."

276. Weissman, Judith. "Vision, Madness and Morality: Poetry and the Theory of the Bicameral Mind." Georgia Review, 33 (1979), 118-148.

Applies Julian Jaynes's theory of the bicameral mind (early man's behavior was determined more by code and ritual than by consciousness and morality) to British poetry of the last four centuries. Milton was a bicameral poet; the nineteenth century poets doubted the supernatural and thus such inspiration was not always available to them. Twentieth century poets demystify the experience of hallucination and possession and focus on madness.

277. Weissman, Philip. "Psychoanalyzing the Critic." Canadian Theatre Review, 8 (1975), 17-23.

Critics do not have the urge to be creative. However, the critic "may have a greater capacity than the artist for awareness of relatedness among sensory stimuli which reside in and emanate from works of art. . . . The critic's noncreativity may be rooted in psychological determinants, since critics are often childless in their adult lives."

278. Wijsen, Louis. "From Text to Symbol: The Cognitive and Affective Response to Literature." Psychocultural Review, 2, 3 (1978).

Information processing theory (based on Piaget's model of the working mind) emphasizes "the dynamic interactions of individual and environment and of perception and cognition." The author believes this approach is a needed improvement of psychoanalysis and is of interest to the study of aesthetics. Argues that a theory must deal with a literary text's cognitive and affective influence on a reader. "It will have to include the subjective response in its examination and focus on the illusion of an experience that occurs in the synthesis of the stimuli of the text and the imagination of the reader."

279. Withim, Philip M. From Symptom to Process: The Movement of Psychoanalytic Criticism." Journal of General Education, 25 (1973), 173-183.

An overview of trends in psychoanalytic criticism. Taking their cue from Freud's idea that the nature of art is pathological, the early critics emphasized the negative. Norman Holland reduces Freud's views to the idea that literature springs from a child's "primal scene" when first seeing his parents in sexual intercourse. However, the psychologists of the ego, as opposed to the psychologists of the id, believe that the psyche tends to be "creatively autonomous." The phenomenologists and Sartre go along with this view, believing that a person is the sum of his choices and that psychological criticism must be tempered by "common sense and discrimination."

280. _____. "The Psychodynamics of Literature." Psychoanalytic Review, 56 (1969-1970), 556-585.

Discusses the interaction between literature and psychoanalysis as disciplines dealing with the nature of the psyche. Uses "psychoanalysis to explain how the work affects the reader and how the author is able to manipulate and guide his audience through a particular emotional, psychological and esthetic experience." Discusses, among other works, Beowulf and Jane Austen's Emma.

281. _____. "Tragic Catharsis and the Resources of the Ego." Psychoanalytic Review, 60 (1973-4), 497-518.

Aristotle's notion of catharsis was an attempt to define the interaction between the dynamics of tragedy and the dynamics of the reader's psyche. Withim utilizes a psychoanalytic viewpoint to examine catharsis, recognition, peripety and hamartia.

282. Ziolkowski, Theodore. "The Telltale Teeth: Psychodontia to Sociodontia." PMLA, 91 (1976), 9-22.

Traces the psychological attitudes towards teeth in history as reflected in literature. Movement is from teeth as symbols of potency, to symbols of psychic pain and disease, to healthy teeth as representative of social health. "Hence the dentist enters contemporary fiction as psychic healer and social analyst."

Ancient and Classical Literature

General Studies

283. Caldwell, Richard S. "The Blindness of Oedipus." *International Review of Psycho-Analysis*, 1 (1974), 207-218.

   The myth of Oedipus is found often to be interpreted similarly by the classicist and the psychoanalyst.

284. Ekstein, Rudolf. "Psychoanalytic Precursors in Greek Antiquity." *Bulletin of the Menninger Clinic*, 39 (1975), 246-267.

   Uses Greek literature and drama to discover how Greeks in need of psychiatric help and care may have found such care, around 400 B.C.

285. Farber, Ada. "Segmentation of the Mother: Women in Greek Myth." *Psychoanalytic Review*, 62 (1975), 29-47.

   The female characters in Greek myths often depict segments of the mother, rather than the whole mother, thus illustrating the infantile sexual desires connected with the Oedipus complex.

286. Glenn, Justin. "Psychoanalytic Writings on Greek and Latin Authors, 1911-1960." *Classical World*, 66, (1972), 129-145.

   An annotated bibliography of books and articles.

287. Howard, Stephen. "Oedipus of Thebes: The Myth and Its Other Meanings." *American Journal of Psychoanalysis*, 36 (1976), 147-154.

   Unlike Freud's interpretation of the myth, Howard sees Oedipus' life as symbolic of what is necessary for a person's psychic development: suffering and courage and final transcendence.

288. Rubinstein, L.H. "The Theme of Electra and Orestes: A Contribution to the Psychopathology of Matricide." *British Journal of Medical Psychology*, 42, 2 (1969), 99-108.

A psychological analysis of the literary uses of the Electra/Orestes myth, with emphasis on matricide in reality and fantasy.

Aeschylus

289. Caldwell, Richard S. "The Psychology of Aeschylus' *Supplices*." *Arethusa*, 7 (1974), 45-70.

> The imagery of the *Supplices* shows that "the Danaids are preoccupied not with acquiring the male organ but with the wound they have suffered and its possible recurrence; not with becoming men themselves, but rather with reducing men to their own mutilated state." The Danaids also "typify the oedipal situation."

290. Devereux, George. *Dreams in Greek Tragedy: An Ethno-Psycho-Analytical Study*. Berkeley: University of California Press, 1976.

> Demonstrates "the psychological credibility of the dreams Aischylos, Sophokles, and Euripides had devised for certain of their personages," that the dreams in the work of these writers "are authentically dreamlike."

291. Tolpin, M. "Aeschylus: *Oresteia*: A Cure in Fifth Century Athens." *Journal of the American Psychoanalytic Association*, 17 (1969), 511-527.

> "Aeschylus transformed and exalted the Orestes legend to dramatize what appear to be hitherto unachieved resolutions of ancient psychological and cultural conflicts."

Aristotle

292. Arvanitakis, M.D. "Aristotle's *Poetics*: The Origins of Tragedy and the Tragedy of Origins." *American Imago*, 39 (1982), 255-268.

> "What I propose to attempt in this paper is to examine a number of key concepts in Aristotle's seminal treatise and to develop their psychoanalytic significance."

"Beauty and the Beast"

293. Mintz, Thomas. "The Meaning of the Rose in 'Beauty and the Beast'." *Psychoanalytic Review*, 56 (1969-1970), 615-620.

> Discusses the rose in the fairy tale "Beauty and the Beast" as symbolic of both masculinity and femininity.

48   Psychocriticism

The Bible

294. Medlicott, R.W. "The Akedah (The Binding of Isaac)." <u>Journal of Evolutionary Psychology</u>, 2 (1981), 71-82.

   A discussion of Genesis 22:1-19. "The <u>Akedah</u> firstly dramatizes the parent-child relationships and is a variant of the Oedipal myth. Secondly, it raises the problem of good and evil. Thirdly, it highlights the problem of obedience; blind obedience versus individual responsibility. Finally, sacrifice and the sadomasochistic element of the <u>Akedah</u> give ground for concern."

295. Stein, Calvert. "Psychotherapy in the Bible." <u>Journal of the American Academy of Psychiatry and Neurology</u>, 1, 2-3 (1976), 67-70.

   Illustrates various modern psychological theories and methods that are suggested in the Old and New Testaments, such as group therapy, dream interpretation, psychosomatic disease, and psychodrama.

Euripides
(See also item 290.)

296. Abood, Edward F., and Harris, Phyllis. "The Splintered Personality in Euripides." <u>Psychological Perspectives</u>, 8 (1977), 60-75.

   A Jungian study of Euripides' plays. In <u>Medea</u>, <u>Hippolytus</u>, and <u>Bacchantes</u>, there is a similar theme of an ego-dominated man in conflict with a passionate woman. This conflict symbolizes the male's inability to accept the female part of himself and is Euripides' political and psychological comment on his times.

297. McConaghy, N. "Drama and Psychiatry: Some Insights of Euripides." <u>The Australian and New Zealand Journal of Psychiatry</u>, 4 (1970), 109-112.

   Euripides' plays challenge and go beyond "the psychodynamic viewpoint" of psychiatry; they are "in harmony with neo-organic psychiatry." Euripides indicates "the belief that many processes, while not part of the mind, can act upon it to determine resultant behaviour."

298. Perry, Ruth. "Madness in Euripides, Shakespeare, and Kafka: An Examination of <u>The Bacchae</u>, <u>Hamlet</u>, <u>King Lear</u> and <u>The Castle</u>." <u>Psychoanalytic Review</u>, 65 (1978), 253-279.

   "All three writers imagine madness as being locked inside a nightmare perpetuated unwillingly and despairingly by characters who are unable to mediate between the self and the world." Madness however is used differently in the works discussed.

299. Sale, William. "The Psychoanalysis of Pentheus in <u>The Bacchae</u>." <u>Yale Classical Studies</u>, 22 (1972), 63-82.

   Pentheus is mad. Traces Pentheus' self-revelation as his defenses break down in the course of the play. Draws parallels to a clinical study of transvestism.

Ancient and Classical Literature   49

Gilgamesh

300. Luke, J. Tracy and Pruyser, Paul W. "The Epic of Gilgamesh." American Imago, 39 (1982), 73-94.

The Gilgamesh epic "is notably a liturgical drama in which youthful erotic preoccupations become overtaken by thoughts of death, first leading to fierce narcissistic protest, and then to acceptance in sober resignation that still leaves room for living-on with periodic renewal."

Homer

301. Lesser, Simon O. "The Hidden Dreams." (1967) In Sprich, R., and Noland, R., eds., The Whispered Meanings: Selected Essays of Simon O. Lesser. Amherst: University of Massachusetts Press, 1977, 113-127.

There is indeed latent meaning in the Odyssey and that meaning has to do with the poem's satisfaction of ultimate human wishes: to be omnipotent, to be immortal, and to be the center of one's own universe.

302. Reid, Stephen. "The Iliad: Agamemnon's Dream." American Imago, 30 (1973), 33-56.

A psychoanalytic discussion of Agamemnon's dream in Book II of The Iliad. The dream reveals Agamemnon's unconscious desires to free himself from the guilt and deception within him surrounding his argument with Achilles.

303. Simon, Bennett. "The Hero As an Only Child: An Unconscious Fantasy Structuring Homer's Odyssey: A Reply to the Discussion by Leonard Shengold." International Journal of Psycho-Analysis, 56 (1975), 377.

Restates the idea that the Odyssey can be seen as unconscious fantasy. Notes similarity of psychoanalytic interpretation of literature to the unique interpretations which spring from any given analyst-patient pairing.

304. _____. "Mental Life in the Homeric Epics." In Mind and Madness in Ancient Greece: The Classical Roots of Modern Psychiatry. Ithaca, N.Y.: Cornell University Press, 1978, 53-77.

Looks at Homeric manifestations of psyche, dreams, mental disorder, and the therapeutic aspects of epic. "Homer has elaborated a complex picture of what is needed to resolve the turmoil and sorrow of the human heart."

Ovid

305. Becker, Michael. "The Narcissus Myth in Ovid." American Journal of Psychoanalysis, 37 (1977), 259-261.

50   Psychocriticism

In the metamorphosis of Narcissus, the destruction of the self is caused by introversion and inability to see outer reality.

306. Danelius, Gerhard. "Ovid's Metamorphoses: The Great Poem of Neurotic Suffering." In Kirsch, H., ed., The Well-Tended Tree. New York: Putnam, 1971, 351-362.

A Jungian discussion of Ovid's "psychological insights, his feeling-side, his deep compassion for human suffering." Concentration is on the stories of "Narcissos" ("narcism"), "Myrrha" ("Electra-complex"), and "Medea" ("sorceress"). Note is made of the importance for Jungian analysts of studying Ovid.

Plato

307. Brenkman, John. "The Other and the One: Psychoanalysis, Reading, the Symposium." Yale French Studies, 55-56 (1977), 396-456.

Discusses the ideas of Jacques Derrida and Jacques Lacan and the interaction between literature, philosophy, and psychoanalytic theory, using Plato's Symposium as a model. "Our reading of the Symposium . . . makes it possible to argue that the psychoanalytic theory of desire emerges from the subversion that literary writing performs on the discourse of philosophy."

308. Reid, Stephen A. "The Apology of Socrates." Psychoanalytic Review, 62 (1975), 97-106.

Socrates does not need love, and thus is seen as a saint because he is free of responsibility to others, which is what we all desire.

Plautus

309. MacCary, W. Thomas. "The Significance of a Comic Pattern in Plautus and Beaumarchais." Modern Language Notes, 88 (1973), 1262-1287.

Discusses Plautus' Casina and Beaumarchais' Figaro from a psychoanalytic point of view, focusing on the relations between Figaro and Count Almavira.

Sophocles
(See also item 290.)

310. Aufhauser, Marcia C. "On the Guilt of Oedipus." Psychoanalytic Review, 64 (1977), 135-145.

Sophocles' Oedipus Rex illustrates psychoanalytic discovery of self, the "dissolution of Oedipus' pretensions to omnipotence; i.e., the narcissism that characterizes him at the beginning." Just as Oedipus has to deal with crimes he was not aware of, so also does the patient in psychoanalysis who must deal with "crimes" of his unconscious.

311. Faber, M.D. "Oedipus Rex: A Psychoanalytic Interpretation." Psychoanalytic Review, 62 (1975), 239-268.

   The strongest psychological significance of Sophocles' play is the destructiveness caused by Oedipus' confusion about the identity of his mother. Fate is seen as similar to the impact of infant and childhood relationships. Oedipus' ability to go on living after he discovers his identity is a sign of his strength.

312. _____. "Self-Destruction in Oedipus Rex." American Imago, 27 (1970), 41-51.

   A psychoanalytical, textual discussion of Oedipus' and Jocasta's respective self-destruction. Both characters suffer from "displaced aggression," but they direct it differently: "For the son it is the mother who is the significant object, the one toward whom the emotions overwhelmingly cathect; for the mother, however, the son is not the object, and can never be, for it is the father upon whom her marriage oedipally rests."

313. Harshbarger, Karl. "The Report of the Bedroom Scene in Sophocles' Oedipus." Hartford Studies in Literature, 6 (1974), 197-220.

   A discussion of Oedipus' childhood trauma of exile and the feeling of being emasculated by his mother. Oedipus' behavior in Jocasta's bedroom is a manifestation of his anger towards his mother and symbolic of his desire "to prove himself a man by both killing her and raping her."

314. Hoey, Thomas F. "On the Theme of Introversion in Oedipus Rex." Classical Journal, 64 (1969), 296-299.

   Notes the "complex system of imagery" that supports the idea that "Oedipus is a symbol of . . . intellectual inturning on the part of man." Oedipus represents the human intellect reflecting on itself.

315. Lesser, Simon O. "Oedipus the King: The Two Dramas, the Two Conflicts." (1967) In Sprich, R., and Noland, R., eds., The Whispered Meanings: Selected Essays of Simon O. Lesser. Amherst: University of Massachusetss Press, 1977, 149-180.

   Scene-by-scene analysis of Oedipus' quest to establish the circumstances of his birth and to identify the person responsible for the Theban plague.

316. Lester, David. "Comment on Faber's Analysis of Jocasta's Suicide in Oedipus Rex." Psychological Reports, 34 (1974), 182.

   Disagrees with M.D. Faber's (item 312) seeing Jocasta's suicide in Freudian terms. Rather than anger towards Laius as the cause of her suicide, the case may be the feeling of loss and a wish to be with him again.

317. Medlicott, R.W. "Oedipus." Australian and New Zealand Journal of Psychiatry, 10 (1976), 229-236.

Demonstrates the validity of Freud's theory of the Oedipus complex, with an analysis of the important developments in the course of the life of Sophocles' Oedipus.

318. Noland, Richard W. "The Theory of the Crisis of Generativity in Sophocles' *Oedipus the King*." *Hartford Studies in Literature*, 11 (1979), 83-93.

A study of *Oedipus the King* in terms of Erikson's ego psychology and life cycle concepts. The play is Sophocles' "highly self-conscious dramatic work . . . expressing his personal vision of the human condition." It portrays three crises: "an adult growth crisis, an infantile developmental crisis, and a cultural crisis."

319. Rosenman, Stanley. "The Legend of Oedipus: Victimizing Implantations." *American Imago*, 39 (1982), 119-132.

Oedipus is "described as a victimizer seeking to place into other persons the harmful experiences and bad introjects that he had extensively suffered in an anguished infancy and early childhood."

320. Werman, David. "Methodological Problems in the Psychoanalytic Interpretations of Literature: A Review of Studies on Sophocles' *Antigone*." *Journal of the American Psychoanalytic Association*, 27 (1979), 451-478.

Psychoanalytic criticism often distorts the text, and a piece of literature "is often used to corroborate an author's theoretical bias or advance some special interest." Furthermore, over-emphasis on the life of a writer deflects attention from the main object, the text itself. The major problem with psychoanalytic criticism is "the inherent difficulty that the interpretation . . . is unable to benefit from the process of the analytic situation." It would be better "to analyze our emotional response to a work as affording a valuable source of insight into the work itself."

Medieval Literature

General Studies

321. Adolf, Helen. "Personality in Medieval Poetry and Fiction." Deutsche Vierteljahrsschrift für Literaturwissenschaft und Geistesgeschichte, 44 (1970), 9-19.

>Refers to numerous psychologists and theories in order to answer the question, "Is there a medieval personality, comparable to the modern one that emerged in the days of the Renaissance?"

322. Leclercq, Jean. "Modern Psychology and the Interpretation of Medieval Texts. Speculum, 48 (1973), 476-490.

>The psychological approach is a necessary complement to other traditional methods of exploring medieval texts.

Beaumanoir, Philippe de

323. Fenster, Thelma. "Beaumanoir's La Manekine: Kin D(r)ead: Incest, Doubling, and Death." American Imago, 39 (1982), 41-58.

>Argues that part of the meaning and interest of La Manekine is in its psychosexual aspects.

Beowulf

324. Foley, John M. "Beowulf and the Psychohistory of Anglo-Saxon Culture." American Imago, 34 (1977), 133-154.

>A discussion of archetypal patterns in Beowulf. The structure of the story parallels the development to manhood.

Chaucer, Geoffrey

325. Brown, Eric. "Transformation and the 'Wife of Bath's Tale': A Jungian Discussion." The Chaucer Review, 10 (1976), 303-316.

"The skeletal structure of the 'Wife of Bath's Tale,' that is, the background of a seasonal myth and of a myth of personal, physical transformation, can usefully be examined for its archetypal implications." Perceives transformation, "a basic change in appearance and/or condition," to be the essential motive in this tale.

326. Corsa, Helen. "Dreams in Troilus and Criseyde." American Imago, 27 (1970), 52-65.

Examines the three dreams in Troilus and Criseyde in order to show the "greater psychological and dramatic meaning" in Chaucer's poem when compared with Bocaccio's Il Filostrato.

327. Haskell, Ann. "The Doppelgängers in Chaucer's Troilus." Neuphilologische Mitterlungen, 72 (1971), 723-734.

"The 'double Variacioun' of Troilus and Criseyde complements the broad opposite themes of the poem, such as earthly love versus heavenly love, or temporality versus eternity."

328. Kinney, Thomas. "The Popular Meaning of Chaucer's 'Physician's Tale'." Literature & Psychology, 28 (1978), 76-84.

The popularity of the "Physician's Tale" is based on a normal social attitude of the time toward reproduction (as a good) and death (as an evil).

329. Kloss, Robert J. "Chaucer's The Merchant's Tale: Tender Youth and Stooping Age." American Imago, 31 (1974), 65-79.

Discusses the effects Chaucer's variations on fabliaux literature have on his readers.

330. Mais, M. "Troilus: A Medieval Psychoanalysis." Annuale Mediaeviale, 11 (1970), 81-88.

Argues that as much emphasis must be placed on the interior factors of Troilus' personality as on the destinal forces operating on him. In medieval terms, Troilus suffered from a love melancholy.

331. Pearlman, E. "The Psychological Basis of the Clerk's Tale." Chaucer Review, 11 (1977), 248-257.

Asserts that an application of Freudian psychology to this tale is warranted only if "we can demonstrate that Walter's psychological structure was liable to be similar to that of Freud's patients." Chaucer's psychological reality, however foreign to us, "is not inhuman."

332. Rudat, Wolfgang E.H. "The Canterbury Tales: Anxiety Release and Wish Fulfillment." American Imago, 35 (1978), 407-418.

"By composing the springtime ritual which is presented in the Canterbury Tales, Chaucer the poet/pilgrim is able to release the concern that the satirist feels for his fellow men."

333. ──────────. "The Misdirected Kisses in the Miller's Tale." Journal of Evolutionary Psychology, 3 (1982), 103-108.

A psychoanalytical study of Absolom's kissing of Alison. "Chaucer poetically punishes the ladies' man Absolom by representing his love for Alison as a regression wish, a fantasy in which Alison becomes a mother figure."

Hartmann von Aue

334. Endres, Rolf C. "Understanding the Lifestyle of a Medieval Literary Character." Journal of Individual Psychology, 30 (1974), 251-264.

Medieval behavior was only partly conditioned by society, as seen in an Adlerian study of the poem Der Arme Heinrich, by H. von Aue.

335. Neumarkt, Paul. "Hartmann von Aue: The Psychologism of a Medieval Poet." American Imago, 30 (1973), 157-176.

A study of the "crime, incest, catatonic delusions, expiations of guilt" in Hartmann's epic Der arme Heinrich. Hartmann's Gregorius is also touched upon in this context.

Malory, Thomas

336. Kimball, Arthur Samuel. "Merlin's Miscreation and the Repetition Compulsion in Malory's Morte d'Arthur." Literature and Psychology, 25, No. 1 (1975), 27-33.

Contrary to Freud's view, Morte d'Arthur is reality-oriented. It is not an imaginary garden nor a neurotic fantasy but a manifestation of Malory's concern "with the problem of a miscreated world."

Sir Gawain and the Green Knight

337. Brewer, Derek. "The Interpretation of Dream, Folktale and Romance with Special Reference to Sir Gawain and the Green Knight." Neuphilologische Mitteilungen, 77 (1976), 569-581.

The plot of Sir Gawain is seen "as a symbolic representation of the emergence of the young adult in reaction against and partial reconciliation with his parents."

338. Butturf, Douglas R. "Laughter and Discovered Aggression in <u>Sir Gawain and the Green Knight</u>." <u>Literature and Psychology</u>, 22, 3 (1972), 139-150.

>Argues that the author undermines "what is potentially comic in order to compel us to feel more deeply. . . . "

Renaissance Literature

General Studies

339. Benson, Morris. *Renaissance Archetypes: The Long Shadows*. London: Coleman, 1977.

>Traces the *shadow* archetype, that other self emerging from the personal unconscious which according to Jung must be assimilated on the road to Individuation, in Renaissance literature.

340. Kerrigan, William. "The Articulation of the Ego in the English Renaissance." In Smith, J.H., and Parloff, G.H., eds., *The Literary Freud: Mechanisms of Defense and the Poetic Will*. New Haven: Yale University Press, 1980, 261-300.

>"A highly integrated and essentially anthropormophic symbolism encouraged the expansive poet to feel that his *parole* might encompass the *langue* of world-order, just as the contractive poet might hope to retain, enfolded within his firmer boundaries, an epitome of the whole design."

Jonson, Ben

341. Mahony, Patrick. "Ben Jonson's 'best piece of poetrie'." *American Imago*, 37 (1980), 68-81.

>Explication of Jonson's "On My First Sonne" and "On My First Daughter."

Kyd, Thomas

342. Willbern, David P. "Thomas Kyd's *The Spanish Tragedy*: Inverted Vengeance." *American Imago*, 28 (1971), 247-267.

Argues that the true subject of The Spanish Tragedy is as much sex and marriage as death and revenge.

Marlowe, Christopher

343. Herring, Henry. "The Self and Madness in Marlowe's Edward II and Webster's The Duchess of Malfi." Journal of Medieval and Renaissance Studies 9 (Fall 1979), 307-323.

Employs the ideas of Bateson, Laing and others as a psychological model for interpretation.

344. Roy, Emil. "Faustus' Dream of Punishment." American Imago, 34 (1977), 158-169.

Analyses in classic Freudian fashion Scene XIX. 11. 133-190 and concludes that "Faustus' dream vision operates at every level by the process of wish-fulfilling reversal."

More, Thomas

345. Bleich, David. "More's Utopia: Confessional Modes." In Tennenhouse, L., ed., The Practice of Psychoanalytic Criticism. Detroit: Wayne State University Press, 1976, 46-74.

A discussion of form in Utopia, drawing upon Norman Holland's idea of form being a defense. In Utopia, More was able to voice his desire for power while at the same time, through its form, renouncing those desires and his fantasies of murder.

346. Wolfenstein, Martha. "Looking Backward from A Clockwork Orange." Psychoanalytic Study of the Child, 31 (1976), 535-553.

A discussion of fantasies of childhood as the beginnings of fantasies of utopia. In utopian works, there is often a conflict between romantic love and society. Burgess' A Clockwork Orange, Orwell's 1984, Huxley's Brave New World, and More's Utopia are examined.

Rabelais, Francois

347. Ragland, Mary E. Rabelais and Panurge: A Psychological Approach to Literary Character. Amsterdam: Rodop, 1976.

"Twentieth century findings from psychology provide critical support for the interpretation of Panurge as child-like man as well as for the idea that readers respond to certain literary characters through the emotions as well as through the intellect."

Shakespeare, William
(See also item 298.)

348. Andreasen, Nancy J.C. "The Artist as Scientist: Psychiatric Diagnosis in Shakespeare's Tragedies." <u>Journal of the American Medical Association</u>, 235 (1976), 1868-1872.

    Details Shakespeare's accurate pictures of insane people in <u>Macbeth</u>, <u>Hamlet</u>, and <u>King Lear</u>, and suggests that Shakespeare anticipated later clinical observations. Furthermore, in his plays, "one finds portrayals of psychiatric syndromes far more sophisticated than those seen in medical treatises of his time."

349. Aronson, Alexander. <u>Psyche and Symbol in Shakespeare</u>. Bloomington: Indiana University Press, 1972.

    A Jungian interpretation of Shakespeare which focuses on the ego--the Shakespearean hero in terms of his conscious mind only; the Anima--the gradual domination of the ego by the unconscious; and the Self--from conflict to resolution.

350. Bachmann, Susan. "'Daggers in Men's Smiles': The 'Trust Issue' in <u>Macbeth</u>." <u>International Review of Psycho-Analysis</u>, 5 (1978), 97-104.

    Macbeth is without trust, fearing division and loss as does a child who has experienced premature or unanticipated weaning. Refers to the work of Erikson.

351. Barroll, J. Leeds. <u>Artificial Persons: The Formation of Character in the Tragedies of Shakespeare</u>. Columbia: University of South Carolina Press, 1974.

    A psychological study. Chapter headings: "Psychology and Psychiatry in Renaissance England," "The Motivations of Men," "Man and His Reflection," "The Shakespearean Approach," "The Human Image in Renaissance Drama," "Shakespeare's Material Men," "Shakespeare's Lovers," "Tragic Actors," "Shakespeare's Villains," "The Concept of Character in Shakespearean Tragedy."

352. Burke, Kenneth. "<u>King Lear</u>: Its Form and Psychosis." <u>Shenandoah</u>, 21 (1969), 3-18.

    Argues that in <u>King Lear</u>, Shakespeare has chosen to write about "the paradox of substance." "Insofar as a man's person gains substance from social powers which are not intrinsic to him yet with which, by reason of his vocation or role in life, he becomes associated, what can he essentially be, once these extrinsic underpinnings are removed?" Lear asks, "Now that I have given up my office, who am I?"

353. Byles, Joan. "Macbeth: Imagery of Destruction." <u>American Imago</u>, 39 (1982), 149-164.

    "This essay will explore the relationship between fear and guilt in Macbeth's character, expressed through imagery of destruction." Argues that in tragic action there are links between the protagonist's suffer-

60 Psychocriticism

ing and death, "and the destructiveness of his superego and that of the community he exists in."

354. Byles, Joan M. "*The Winter's Tale,* Othello, and Troilus and Cressida: Narcissism and Sexual Betrayal." American Imago, 36 (1979), 80-93.

"Troilus is an idealistic lover, Othello is both an idealistic and narcissistic lover, whereas Leontes is a wholly narcissistic lover." Furthermore, "the relative power and scope of the protagonists' idealism and/or narcissism provides a basic pattern of psychological conflict which is dramatized as a struggle between intense hate and intense love."

355. Byles, Joan Mary. "The Basic Pattern of Psychological Conflict in Shakespearean Tragic Drama." Hartford Studies in Literature, 11 (1979), 58-71.

A study of the "rejection of Eros" as a major contributor to the fate of Shakespeare's tragic heroes. These heroes illustrate the Freudian concepts of "defusion of the dual instincts of Eros and Death" and "superego aggression."

356. Calef, V. "Lady Macbeth and Infanticide: Or 'How Many Children Had Lady Macbeth Murdered?'" Journal of the American Psychoanalytic Association, 17 (1969), 528-548.

Since childlessness may unconsciously be perceived as parallel to infanticide, and Lady Macbeth is childless, Macbeth can be read as an illustration of similar ideas on childlessness in both Shakespeare and Freud.

357. Chaplin, William H. "Form and Pscyhology in King Lear." Literature and Psychology, 19, 3-4 (1969), 31-46.

King Lear is a daring work "because it is the most inclusive, the most radical: it drives to the heart of man's psychic kingdom, and exposes him to his own elements--the primitive, bestial, and god-like forces of his nature."

358. Cox, Marjorie K. "Adolescent Process in Romeo and Juliet." Psychoanalytic Review, 63 (1976), 379-392.

Rather than an Aristotelian tragedy, Shakespeare's play is a tragedy of adolescence in which Romeo and Juliet come to terms with the problems typical of their age group.

359. Desai, Rubin W. "Freudian Undertones in the Isabella-Angelo Relationship of Measure for Measure." Psychoanalytic Review, 64 (1977), 487-494.

Psychoanalytic focus on Isabella. The severity of her relationship with Angelo hides opposite emotions.

360. Dickes, Robert. "Desdemona: An Innocent Victim?" American Imago, 27 (1970), 279-297.

Rather than a passive victim, Desdemona is "a somewhat domineering woman who works actively to obtain her ends." Demonstrates the internalization of Desdemona's motivations and her unconscious desire for death.

361. Durham, Mildred O. "Drama of the Dying God in *Julius Caesar*." *Hartford Studies in Literature*, 11 (1979), 49-57.

The play contains "the elements of ancient rituals of communion, cannibalism, and initiation."

362. Ebel, Henry. "Caesar's Wounds: A Study of William Shakespeare." *Psychoanalytic Review*, 62 (1975), 107-130.

Although Shakespeare and Freud approached the subject differently, they both felt that the situation in *Julius Caesar* was oedipal and erotic.

363. Edgar, Irving. *Shakespeare, Medicine and Psychiatry: An Historical Study in Criticism and Interpretation*. New York: Philosophical Library, 1970.

The psychiatry and Shakespeare sections of this work are restricted to general discussions of *King Lear* and *Hamlet*, focusing on the psychoanalytic interpretations of *Hamlet*.

364. Eissler, Kurt Robert. *Discourse on Hamlet and "Hamlet."* New York: International Universities Press, 1971.

An exhaustive study of *Hamlet* from the standpoint of Freud's ego psychology.

365. Ellrodt, Robert. "Self-consciousness in Montaigne and Shakespeare." *Shakespeare Survey*, 28 (1975), 37-50.

Shakespeare's creation of self-conscious characters like Hamlet, for instance, is typical of a trend in many writers toward the end of the sixteenth century. This trend can be seen earlier than Shakespeare in Marlowe. Like Montaigne, Hamlet's self-consciousness destroys character and motivation. However, when he created Lear, Shakespeare was different from Montaigne because he was not self-centered.

366. Erlich, Avi. *Hamlet's Absent Father*. Princeton: Princteon University Press, 1977.

Follows the weaving of conscious and unconscious creativity in *Hamlet*. Believes that "we are closer to the beginning than the end of an attempt to understand the ways in which the play grips our unconscious, our imagination, and our intellect."

367. Faber, M.D. "The Adolescent Suicides of Romeo and Juliet." *Pscyhoanalytic Review*, 59 (1972), 169-181.

Romeo and Juliet have immature egos because of their family and social situation. This explains their impulsiveness and inability to cope. While there is love within their families, it does not go beyond causing a narcissistic situation. As a result, they are not able to move normally into a world outside their famiilies or to understand fully that which represses their freedom.

368. _____. "Hermia's Dream: Royal Road to A Midsummer Night's Dream." Literature and Psychology, 22, 4 (1972), 179-190.

Argues that A Midsummer Night's Dream "is a comic remark upon the mind of man, particularly with regard to causality."

369. _____. "On Jacques: Psychological Remarks." (I and II) University Review, 36 (1970), 89-96; 179-182.

Uses Joseph Slap's theories on the nature of sarcasm for a psychological analysis of Jacques in As You Like It. Jacques is infantile, orally fixated, dependent on "the Good Mother," and in search of an authority figure.

370. _____. "Othello: Symbolic Action, Ritual, and Myth." American Imago, 31 (1974), 159-205.

A demonstration of the "regressive, indeed oral affects that lie behind Othello's marriage. . . . Othello is vulnerable to the power of women harboring maternal qualities." Unconsciously, Othello views Desdemona as a parent about whom he has a great deal of ambivalence.

371. _____. "Othello: The Justice of It Pleases." American Imago, 28 (1971), 228-246.

Discusses the analytic significance of Iago's suggestion that Othello strangle Desdemona in her bed and Othello's enthusiastic reception of this idea.

372. Fineman, Joel. "Fratricide and Cuckoldry: Shakespeare's Doubles." Psychoanalytic Review, 64 (19-7), 409-413.

A study of As You Like It, Twelfth Night, Hamlet, and Troilus and Cressida, analyzing "the transition from Shakespeare's comedies to his tragedies by examining structural development of cuckoldry, fratricide, and androgyny." Shakespeare uses "doubling formulas and mirroring relationships to generate psychologically plausible categories of difference."

373. Fliess, Elenore Stratton, and Fliess, Robert. "Shakespeare's Juliet and Her Nurse." American Imago, 33 (1976), 244-260.

An analysis of Act II, scene v, in Romeo and Juliet, demonstrating the unconscious and anxiety-ridden sexual content of the Nurse's speech.

374. Fyler, Anson C., Jr. "Self-Unification: An Archetypal Analysis of Prospero in The Tempest." Hartford Studies in Literature, 3 (1971), 45-50.

Argues that The Tempest," if analyzed in terms of Jungian archetypal patterns, can be seen as a process of the self-unification of the central consciously functioning figure of the play, Prospero." Focuses on Magna Mater, the shadow, anima and animus, wise old man archetype and the mandala as a symbol of the self.

375. Ganim, Carole. "The Divided Self: Caliban from Shakespeare to Auden." *Kentucky Philological Association Bulletin*, 1975, 9-15.

A discussion of Shakespeare's *The Tempest*, Robert Browning's "Caliban Upon Setebos; Or, Natural Theology In the Island," Ernest Renan's *Caliban suite de la Tempête*, and W.H. Auden's *The Sea and the Mirror*. These authors all recognize "the human condition we clinically call schizophrenia today, which R.D. Laing describes as a contrast between 'a basic existential position of ontological security and one of ontological insecurity'."

376. Gerenday, Lynn de. "Play, Ritualization, and Ambivalence in *Julius Caesar*." *Literature and Pscyhology*, 24 (1974), 24-33.

Julius Caesar well illustrates the nature of ambivalence, as seen in Brutus. Brutus, through the use of play-acting and ceremony, masks and holds in his "love and hostility" towards Caesar. Brutus must hide his emotions in order to destroy Caesar. "His final denial of feelings is not in the service of practical action but of death."

377. Goldstein, Melvin. "Identity Crises in a Midsummer's Nightmare: Comedy as Terror in Disguise." *Psychoanalytic Review*, 60 (1973), 169-204.

A study of **A** *Midsummer Night's Dream*. The characters in the play "have chosen to flee the sufferings of the savage sleep called madness in order to confront the pleasures and the pains of reality." The play succeeds in ending in marriage "through the process of stripping away defenses, defenses in the manifest and dramatic form of an endless variety of disguises."

378. Gottschalk, Paul A. "The Universe of Madness in *King Lear*." *Bucknell Review*, 19, 3 (1971), 51-68.

A discussion of the "dramatic inner world" as seen in Lear's madness. "Lear's regal world betraying him, he creates a world to express his new identity." Notes the audience's willingness to enter the world of a play and the parallel but further willingness to enter Lear's world, a world within the world of the play.

379. Grinstein, Alexander. "King Lear's Impending Death." *American Imago*, 30 (1973), 121-141.

With the imminence of death, Lear faces old conflicts emerging from prior levels of development; but now his ego is weakened and he has been abandoned by a protecting superego.

380. Handelman, Susan. "*Timon of Athens*: The Rage of Disillusion." *American Imago*, 36 (1979), 45-68.

Timon of Athens portrays the loss of "primary narcissism" without redemption, and that is probably why it is unfinished. It does not contain "the magic of art" which transforms loss "into life-affirming energies." Rather, it depicts "the rage which refused to accept loss."

381. Hnderson, Joseph. "Symbolism of the Unconscious in Two Plays of Shakespeare." In Kirsch, H., ed., *The Well-Tended Tree*. New York: Putnam, 1971, 284-299.

64 Psychocriticism

A Jungian study of the "inter-relationship of the conscious rational mind of man and the imagery of the unconscious" in A Midsummer Night's Dream and The Tempest. These plays illustrate Jung's idea of awareness developed through the inward movement of consciousness to unconscious archetypal images, bringing forth individual awareness.

382. Herbert, Edward T. "Myth and Archetype in Julius Caesar." Psychoanalytic Review, 57 (1970), 303-308.

A Freudian perspective on Shakespeare's play, drawing upon Totem and Taboo. If the play is read as myth, it coheres as the story of Caesar and not the tragedy of Brutus as some critics would like.

383. Hofling, Charles K. "Notes on Shakespeare's The Winter's Tale." Psychoanalytic Review, 58 (1971), 90-110.

The Winter's Tale, written shortly after Shakespeare had returned to a normal life with his wife, is an example of sublimation because it suggests that he had come to terms with his libidinal desires for his daughter and was moving into the happy and adjusted years of his later life.

384. _____. "Psychological Aspects of Shakespeare's Tempest." Psychoanalytic Review, 61 (1974), 375-395.

Identifies Prospero's problem of re-connecting himself with the world of ordinary human beings without the support of his special art, and Shakespeare's problem at the last stage of his life.

385. Hogan, Patrick Colm. "King Lear: Splitting and Its Epistemic Agon." American Imago, 36 (1979), 32-44.

"Lear's three daughters represent split ambivalence: Cordelia is the benevolent mother; Reagan is the withdrawing, and Goneril the devouring, thanatic mother. The less important father figure is split, again through inversion (son as father, father as son)."

386. Holland, Norman N. "Hermia's Dream." In The Annual of Psychoanalysis, vol. vii/1979. New York: IUP, 1980.

Presents a "level-by-level exegesis" which works "out the implications of the dream through such schemes as Erikson's for analyzing the interaction of manifest and latent content or the classic psychoanalytic scheme of developmental levels." Also presents an analysis which demonstrates how "we would use this airy nothing to symbolize ourselves to ourselves." Here "airy nothing" refers to Hermia's dream.

387. _____. "Transactive Teaching: Cordelia's Death." College English, 39 (1977), 276-285.

"Here is a sample of . . . responses in which students--and faculty-- are trying to get at feelings, associations, persons (and selves and societies) they brought to mind as they transacted the death of Cordelia in King Lear."

388. Hyman, Stanley Edgar. "Iago Psychologically Motivated." Centenial Review, 14 (1970), 369-384.

Iago acts like a person who is "motivated by strong latent homosexuality." He "unconsciously loves both Othello and Cassio, and that love is repressed and, by the defense mechanism called 'reaction formation,' turned into hate."

389. Jaarsma, Richard J. "The 'Lear Complex' in The Two Gentlemen of Verona." Literature and Psychology, 22, 4 (1972), 199-202.

There are hints of Lear's psychology in that of the Duke of Two Gentlemen of Verona.

390. Jeske, Jeffrey M. "Macbeth, Ahab, and the Unconscious." American Transcendental Quarterly, 31 (1976), 8-12.

A largely Jungian study of Shakespeare's and Melville's portrayals of "the results of a psyche divided against itself." Macbeth and Moby-Dick depict "a numinous atmosphere" which suggests that "the unconscious encloses the action of both works."

391. Jiji, Vera M. "Portia Revisited: The Influence of Unconscious Factors upon Theme and Characterization in The Merchant of Venice." Literature and Psychology, 26, 1 (1976), 5-15.

Concentrates on Portia's darker side, as a necessary corrective to previous views.

392. Kanzer, Mark. "Shakespeare's Dog Images--Hidden Keys to Julius Caesar." American Imago, 36 (1979), 2-31.

A study of dog imagery to demonstrate Freud's idea of "the unconscious of the one being transmitted through his art to the unconscious of the other." The major dog images are the "candy-licking-dog" and "the hunter." A free association method is used to examine audience, unconscious reaction to the iamges and to come to conclusions about the mind of Shakespeare.

393. Kirsch, Arthur. "Hamlet's Grief." ELH, 48 (1981), 17-36.

Argues that "it is Hamlet's experience of grief, and his recovery from it, to which we ourselves respond most deeply."

394. Kuriyama, Constance Brown. "The Mother of the World: A Psychoanalytic Interpretation of Shakespeare's Antony and Cleopatra." English Literary Renaissance, 7 (1977), 324-351.

Antony and Cleopatra is viewed as "a richly elaborated rendering of a basic human sexual fantasy (liebestod) which also explores and mediates the psychological conflicts attending that fantasy." The fantasy is "double-edged: pleasure and punishment, gratification and frustration."

395. Lacan, Jacques. "Desire and the Interpretation of Desire in Hamlet." Yale French Studies, 55-56 (1978), 11-52.

Attempts to show, in Lacanian enigmatic fashion, "the tragedy of desire as it appears in Hamlet, human desire, that is, such as we are concerned with in psychoanalysis."

66   Psychocriticism

396. Lesser, Simon O. "Act One, Scene One, of Lear." College English, 32 (1970), 155-171.

   Argues that "the critic must devote much of his effort and energy to recapturing his own understanding and responses to whatever work he proposes to deal with."

397. _____. "Freud and Hamlet Again." (1955) In Srprich, R. and Noland, R.D., eds., The Whispered Meanings: Selected Essays of Simon O. Lesser. Amherst: University of Massachusetts Press, 1977, 20-31.

   Re-affirms the Freud-Jones interpretation of Hamlet as opposed to the objective view of Karl Werder. Also opposes the view that "psychoanalysis tends to align itself with the defense of the status quo."

398. _____. "Macbeth: Drama and Dream." In Strelka, J.P., ed., Literary Criticism and Psychology. University Park: Pennsylvania State University Press, 1976, 150-173.

   The flaws and inconsistencies of the play do not annoy its readers because Shakespeare "induces a regression so deep that we read Macbeth as though it were our account of a dream." In this way, it appeals to "our most primitive desires and conflicts."

399. _____. "Macbeth: Drama and Dream." In Sprich, R. and Noland, R.D., eds., The Whispered Meanings: Selected Essays of Simon O. Lesser. Amherst: University of Massachusetts Press, 1977, 212-234.

   See item 398.

400. Leverenz, David. "The Woman in Hamlet: An Interpersonal View." Signs, 4 (1978), 291-308.

   "The woman in Hamlet is the source of his most acute perceptions about the diseased, disordered patriarchal society that tries to 'play upon this pipe' of Hamlet's soul. . . . "

401. Lichtenberg, Joseph and Charlotte. "Prince Hal's Conflict, Adolescent Idealism, and Buffoonery." Journal of the American Psychoanalytic Association, 17 (1969), 873-887.

   "The play reveals a point suggested by Freud--that the grandeur of humor lies in the persistence in the ego ideal of the same ideals we jest about."

402. Lickorish, John R. "The Casket Scenes from The Merchant of Venice: Symbolism or Life Style." Journal of Individual Psychology, 25 (1969), 202-212.

   The casket scenes are used to illustrate differences between Adlerian and Freudian interpretations of literature.

403. Lidz, Theodore. Hamlet's Enemy: Madness and Myth in Hamlet. New York: Basic Books, 1975.

   Not only pursues the theme of madness in order to clarify certain dilemmas in the play, but also considers "the implications of Hamlet, and of the myths that it encompasses, to psychoanalytic psychiatry."

404. Lindauer, M.S. "Quantitative Analyses of Psychoanalytic Studies of Shakespeare." Journal of Psychology, 72 (1969), 3-9.

Demonstrates that Shakespearean psychoanalytical critics concentrate on: 1) "plays, character, and traits," 2) "trends of time," and 3) "similarities and distinctions between Freud and other analysts." Why these aspects are chosen while others are omitted is discussed.

405. Mahony, Patrick. "Shakespeare's Sonnet Number 20: Its Symbolic Gestalt." American Imago, 36 (1979), 69-79.

A line-by-line study of Sonnet 20, demonstrating that "a homosexually motivated castration anxiety gives rise to linguistically expressed derivatives of absence and overcompensating excess; the upshot is a beautiful Symbolic Gestalt manifest in the poem's lexical, syntactical, logical and prosodical structures."

406. Mairet, Philip. "Hamlet as a Study in Individual Psychology." Journal of Individual Psychology, 25, 1 (1969), 71-88.

Attempts to employ Adler's theories in order to resolve the Hamlet "problem"--why can't Hamlet, intelligent, courageous, ambitious, revenge his father's death? Hamlet suffers from a "goal of godlikeness."

407. Markert, John. "Shakespeare's Neurotic Persona: Sonnets 71-74." Journal of Evolutionary Psychology, 2 (1981), 101-111.

A psychological and objective, non-biographical, approach to the Sonnets, demonstrating that the persona in Sonnets 71-74 suffers from a neurosis. He is depressed and is thinking about his death; he "becomes neurotic when the depression becomes excessive or when indulged in vindictively in an attempt to elicit guilt from the love object."

408. McGuire, Jerry. "Shakespeare's Tempest: Poetics and Rhetoric." American Imago, 39 (1982), 219-239.

Discusses "the way in which Shakespeare 'uses' gender to affirm patriarchal authority in The Tempest" and "the relationship between Shakespeare's treatment of gender and his attitudes toward the creative and manipulative use of language--his psychosexual poetics and rhetoric."

409. McLaughlin, Ann L. "The Journeys in King Lear." American Imago, 29 (1972), 384-399.

King Lear portrays "journeys into madness," the most significant one being Lear's. The beginning of Lear's journey is his breaking the tie of kinship with Cordelia. Cordelia's repetition of the word "nothing" suggests what Lear has come to in the chaos of losing contact with family and society. Cordelia and Edgar represent sanity, and Lear's final love for Cordelia brings him back to sanity.

410. McLaughlin, John J. "The Dynamics of Power in King Lear: An Adlerian Interpretation." Shakespeare Quarterly, 29 (1978), 37-43.

Lear, his three daughters and Edmund "are driven by the need to achieve social, personal, and sexual power." Cordelia expresses a "weak social interest;" Lear is motivated erotically; Goneril and Regan display the "masculine protest;" and Edmund suffers from an inferiority complex.

411. Moglen, Helene. "Disguise and Development: The Self and Society in Twelfth Night." Literature and Psychology, 23, 1 (1973), 13-20.

Shakespeare "reinterpreted conventional techniques and incorporated them into an apparent theory of the development of personal and therefore sexual identity."

412. Moss, A.E. "Hamlet and Role-Construct Theory." British Journal of Medical Psychology, 47 (1974), 253-264.

"My aim is to put forward an interpretation of Hamlet in terms of roles and constructs, and on this basis to discuss the possibility of an integrated role-construct theory."

413. Moss, A.E. St. G. "Shakespeare and Role-Construct Theory." British Journal of Medical Psychology, 47 (1974), 235-252.

Uses "personal construct psychology . . . from a dramaturgical viewpoint" in a discussion of Shakespeare's plays and poems. Analyzes Shakespeare's obsessive sexual disgust, and shows "how he attempted to sweeten his imagination through his art."

414. Muir, Kenneth. "Some Freudian Interpretations of Shakespeare." In The Singularity of Shakespeare and Other Essays. New York: Barnes and Noble, 1977, 110-123.

A survey of some of the contributions to Freudian interpretations of Shakespeare, with some comments on the validity of said interpretations. Looks at Freud, Ernest Jones, and Ella Freeman Sharpe.

415. Muller, John. "Psychosis and Mourning in Lacan's Hamlet." New Literary History, 12 (1980), 147-165.

An explication of Lacan's essay, "Desire and the Interpretation of Desire in Hamlet."

416. Neiditz, Minerva. "Primary Process Mentation and the Structure of Timon of Athens." Hartford Studies in Literature, 11 (1979), 24-35.

A study of the dream quality of the play, showing that its structure "is strongly influenced by primary process mentation which ignores consideration of time, space, and logical consistency, fulfilling wishes magically; and employs symbolism in a crudely associative manner."

417. Noland, Richard W. "Psychoanalysis and Hamlet." Hartford Studies in Literature, 6 (1974), 268-281.

Reviews various psychoanalytic interpretations of Hamlet and concludes that psychological criticism needs to deal more completely with the whole structure of the play.

418. Padel, J.H. "'That the Thought of Hearts Can Mend': An Introduction to Shakespeare's Sonnets for Psychotherapists and Others." London Times Literary Supplement, 3849 (December 19, 1975), 1519-1521.

Points out "one or two identifications made by the transference of past relationships." For example, William Herbert, elder son of the Earl and Countess of Pembroke, was identified by Shakespeare with his son, Hamnet.

419. Paris, Bernard J. Bargains with Fate: A Psychological Approach to Shakespearean Tragedy. Forthcoming.

"I argue that the central characters are in a state of psychological crisis, which leads to their destruction, because of a breakdown of their predominant solutions, with the accompanying value systems, world views, conceptions of human nature, and bargains with fate."

420. _____. "Bargains with Fate: A Psychological Approach to Shakespeare's Major Tragedies." The Aligarh Journal of English Studies, 5 (1980), 144-161.

A Horneyan approach to Shakespeare in which tragedy results from the dissolution of a variety of "bargains with fate" made by the protagonists.

421. _____. "Bargains with Fate: The Case of Macbeth." The American Journal of Psychoanalysis, 42 (1982), 7-20.

Macbeth "precipitates his own psychological crisis by violating his dominant set of shoulds in order to act out the arrogant-vindictive trends which are reinforced by his wife." According to Karen Horney a "bargain with fate" is a strategy of defense "in which if a person lives up to his shoulds, his claims are supposed to be honored."

422. _____. "Hamlet and His Problems: A Horneyan Analysis." Centennial Review, 21 (1977), 36-66.

Applies a Horneyan perspective to Hamlet in order to analyze the conscious material of the play. Horney's theories "focus upon inter-personal and intra-psychic strategies of defense which have very clear connections with a person's conscious attitudes and beliefs."

423. _____. "The Inner Conflicts of Measure for Measure." The Centennial Review, 25 (1981), 266-276.

"Though the play is thematically puzzling, we can make sense of it, I believe, if we see it as the manifestation of a system of psychological conflicts, such as is described in the theories of Karen Horney, in which contradicting attitudes are generated by different trends within the personality."

424. Payne, Michael. "Phenomenological Criticism of Shakespeare." Shakespearean Research Opportunities, 7-8 (1972-74), 75-77.

Discusses possibilities of a phenomenological criticism of Shakespeare, but restricts that criticism to the reader's perceptions. "Unlike extraliterary contextual approaches--such as the psychoanalytic . . .--existential and phenomenological criticism works directly with the reader's perception of the felt content of a work in its precise temporal specificity, rather than with the work processed through a modular theory."

425. Pearlman, E. "Shakespeare, Freud, and the Two Usuries, or, Money's a Meddler." English Literary Renaissance, 2 (1972), 217-236.

Traces the connection in The Merchant of Venice and Measure for Measure between bearing children and moneylending, and the "psychoanalytic idea that money and children are both fecal symbols." Also discussed is the "medieval trope in which the womb of the Virgin is thought of as producing a child of infinite wealth" as another connection between bearing children and moneylending.

426. Pinder, Donna. "The Normalcy of Suffering and Artistic Survival." Paunch, 38 (1974), 66-78.

Discusses Shakespeare's Henry IV, Part One, Brecht's Baal, and D.H. Lawrence's Women in Love, showing "characteristics and qualities of suffering and survival . . . as a progression in awareness of suffering, and of what suffering does to the characters and to others around them." Draws upon Erik Erikson's Childhood and Society.

427. Rabkin, Leslie Y., and Brown, Jeffrey. "Some Monster in His Thought: Sadism and Tragedy in Othello." Literature and Psychology, 23 (1973), 59-67.

An understanding of sadism gives insight into the characters of Iago and Othello and the nature of the play. "To understand that Othello's and Iago's desire to remove their feeling of helplessness is a driving force in their lives, the reader must be willing to see that the same may be true of himself." Othello is not completely innocent, and in some ways he is like Iago.

428. Reid, Stephen. "Desdemona's Guilt." American Imago, 27 (1970), 245-262.

Argues that Desdemona resented her father's preference for her mother and retaliated by encouraging her father's friend, Othello, to declare his love for her.

429. _____. "Hamlet's Melancholia." American Imago, 31 (1974), 378-400.

Argues that for two months out of two and a half months, "Hamlet's condition requires the label melancholia."

430. _____. "'I Am Misanthropos': A Psychoanalytic Reading of Shakespeare's Timon of Athens." Psychoanalytic Review, 56 (1969), 442-452.

Perhaps the reason Shakespeare could not complete the play was that Timon's extreme hatred was too dominating.

431. _____. "In Defense of Goneril and Regan." American Imago, 27 (1970), 226-244.

> A psychoanalytical study focusing on Goneril and Regan's motives for wanting their father dead. In Goneril and Regan, "Edmund becomes the instrument of their revenges against Lear and Cordelia, but in doing so he inevitably becomes the replacement of their father. . . . Having exhausted their hatred for Cordelia, Goneril and Regan . . . return to their earlier rivalry for their father's love and reenact it in their jealous possession of Edmund."

432. _____. "Othello's Occupation: Beyond the Pleasure Principle." Psychoanalytic Review, 63 (1976-1977), 555-570.

> Argues that once Othello is no longer a soldier he uses Desdemona as a new means of diverting his "innate self-injuring impulses."

433. _____. "A Psychoanalytic Reading of Troilus and Cressida and Measure for Measure." Psychoanalytic Review, 57 (1970), 263-282.

> In Troilus and Cressida, Shakespeare saw that complete sexual gratification was unlikely, which explains the bitterness of the play. Later, however, in Measure for Measure he turned the bitterness of sexual frustration into compromise, showing that partial sexual satisfaction is for the good.

434. _____. "The Winter's Tale." American Imago, 27 (1970), 263-278.

> Views the play allegorically: Mamillius is "Leontes' masculine self. Perdita is Leontes' feminine self." Furthermore, "Polixenes has resolved his homosexual attachment to Leontes," but Leontes "has not resolved his homosexual love for Polixenes." Jealousy in Leontes is caused by "boyhood homosexual attachment" and "oedipal guilt."

435. Ricciardelli, Rachel M. "King Lear and the Theory of Disengagement." Gerontologist, 13 (1973), 148-152.

> A discussion of Lear's "retirement" in terms of gerontological findings. "Lear emerges as a credible old man whose life cycle traces a model pattern: activity--differential disengagement--total disengagement--death."

436. Rogers, Robert. "Endopsychic Drama In Othello." Shakespeare Quarterly, 20 (1969), 205-215.

> Endopsychic conflict exists between Othello and Iago. "The main action of the play represents an antagonism between two inseparable components of a single psychological configuration."

437. Rose, Gilbert J. "King Lear and the Use of Humor in Treatment." Journal of the American Psychoanalytic Association, 17 (1969), 927-940.

> "The relationship of King Lear and his Fool might be viewed as an analytic therapy in which humor is an essential vehicle."

438. Rothenberg, Alan B. "Infantile Fantasies in Shakespearean Metaphor: I. The Fear of Being Smothered." *Psychoanalytic Review*, 60 (1973), 205-222.

>   In *Titus Andronicus*, Shakespeare attempts to express a deeply repressed infantile emotion--"the pre-Oedipal fear of being smothered, buried alive, and eaten by the breast or mouth of a cannibalist mother."

439. _____. "Infantile Fantasies in Shakespearean Metaphor: II. Scopophilia and Fears of Ocular Rape and Castration." *Psychoanalytic Review*, 60 (1973), 533-556.

>   Shakespeare's imagery gives expression to "wishes, fears, and anxieties that derive from the early infant psyche." It is noted that "the scopophilic eye is . . . an organ that is pierced by dazzling light reflected by woman's beauty, by her naked body . . . by the sight of her vagina, with results that blind, destroy, or in other ways profoundly disturb the visual apparatus of the beholder."

440. _____. "Infantile Fantasies in Shakespearean Metaphor: III. Photophobia, Love of Darkness, and 'Black' Complexions." *Psychoanalytic Review*, 64 (1977), 173-202.

>   "Shakespeare uses metaphor and symbol to achieve the expression of scopophilic fantasies of infancy and early childhood. . . . Also, by directing the libidos of . . . characters from what they must not see to what they cannot see, Shakespeare arrives at love objects for them that satisfy the photophobic requirements." This may explain Shakespeare's paradoxical "praise of both brightness and darkness in beauty."

441. _____. "The Oral Rape Fantasy and Rejection of Mother in the Imagery of Shakespeare's 'Venus and Adonis'." *Psychoanalytic Quarterly*, 40 (1971), 447-468.

>   Notes that in the relationship of mother and child in Shakespeare's poem a typical pattern is developed: the fear that the offspring has of "being killed by an outwardly loving but deeply aggressive mother or nurse."

442. Rubin, Samuel S. "Hamlet: A Psychoanalytic Reinterpretation." *Psychoanalytic Review*, 57 (1970-1971), 660-670.

>   "The thesis of this paper is that Hamlet's behavior can best be understood by focusing on the pre-Oedipal aspects of his problem, his depression resulting--not from an unresolved Oedipal struggle--but from the reactivation of a disappointment in the oral period." An overly frustrating mother generates helplessness in the child.

443. Rudat, Wolfgang E.H. "Ernest Jones' *Hamlet* Interpretation and Nevile's Translation of Seneca's *Oedipus*." *American Imago*, 38 (1981), 369-387.

>   While "the *Historia Danica* is the source for the plot of *Hamlet*, the Oedipus myth is the source for that play's oedipal theme." Shakespeare was familiar with Nevile's 1581 rendering of Seneca's *Oedipus*.

444. Sanders, Kenneth. "Shakespeare's The Winter's Tale--And Some Notes on the Analysis of a Present-Day Leontes." International Review of Psycho-Analysis, 5 (1978), 175-178.

Compares the avoidance of repentance and mental anguish in The Winter's Tale and a modern psychoanalytic case.

445. Sasaki, M.S. "Influence Structure of Julius Caesar." Psychological Reports, 39 (1976), 1191-1195.

A discussion of mathematical techniques as a way of understanding emotional involvements of characters. Using such techniques reveals that Brutus is a "natural leader" with the most "political influence" in the play.

446. Schlesinger, Kurt O. "Thoughts on King Lear and the Current Generation Gap." In Lindon, J.A., ed., The Psychoanalytic Forum, vol. 4. New York: IUP, 1972, 63-99.

A discussion of the Oedipal situation and Lears' libidinal desires in the play, as related to parent-child relationships. Lear's problem "lies in his conflict with this incestuous feelings. The motivation of the three daughters can also be clarified around the organizing concept of Lear's incestuous strivings." Concludes with comments on the article, by Eric Solomon, John Donnelly, Joseph M. Natterson, and Gerald H.J. Pearson, with the author's response.

447. Schneiderman, Stuart. "The Saying of Hamlet." Sub-stance, 8 (1974), 77-88.

Follows Lacan's interpretation of Hamlet and argues that Hamlet can only flee responsibility since he is "faced with his signifier in the act of his uncle. . . . " And Hamlet's signifier is the phallus.

448. Schwartz, Murry M. "Between Fantasy and Imagination: A Psychological Exploration of Cymbeline." In Crews, F., ed., Psychoanalysis and Literary Process. Cambridge, Mass.: Winthrop, 1970, 219-283.

"Shakespeare activates a range of characteristic threats to sexual, familial, and national integrity" with the events in Cymbeline. He "has not yet found the psychic courage to admit that the fears and aggressions he evokes . . . reside in a father, and that their object is an unconsciously harbored mother-imago."

449. _____. "Leontes' Jealousy in The Winter's Tale." American Imago, 30 (1973), 250-273.

Leontes' jealousy reflects both his fear of, and desire for, the powers of women.

450. _____. "Leontes' Jealousy in The Winter's Tale." In Tennenhouse, L., ed., The Practice of Psychoanalytic Criticism. Detroit: Wayne State University Press, 1976, 202-225.

See item 449.

74 Psychocriticism

451. _____. "Shakespeare Through Contemporary Psychoanalysis." Hebrew University Studies in Literature, 5 (1977), 182-198.

"I want to offer some broad formulations of the Shakespearean use of play space in tragic and comic modes during the 'mature' period, starting about 1600." Applies Winnicott's view of "potential space" and "transitional object."

452. _____. "The Winter's Tale: Loss and Transformation." American Imago, 32 (1975), 145-199.

The play represents the renewal of social and personal wholeness despite the possibility of tremendous loss. In the course of the play, Shakespeare creates scenes which re-enact Leontes' madness as well as finally coming to both denial and understanding of loss.

453. Schwartz, Murray, and Kahn, Coppelia. Representing Shakespeare: New Psychoanalytic Essays. Maryland: Johns Hopkins University Press, 1980.

Revisionary Freudian essays which refer to the work of Erik Erikson, G.S. Klein, R.D. Laing, Heinz Lichtenstein, Margaret Mahler, D.W. Winnicott and others. Identity and object-relations theory support the revisionary stance.

454. Semour-Smith, Martin. "Shakespeare's Sonnets 1-42: A Psychological Reading." In Landry, H., ed., New Essays on Shakespeare's Sonnets. New York: AMS Press, 1976, 21-39.

A discussion of how Shakespeare dealt with his discovery of homosexual feelings of love for a friend and his conflicting lustful desires for women.

455. Seward, R.C., and Faber, M.D. "A Note on Stephen Reid's Essay '"I Am Minsanthropos": A Psychoanalytic Reading of Shakespeare's Timon of Athens'." Psychoanalytic Review, 58 (1971-1972), 617-623.

Timon equates money with love and feels he cannot have love until he goes bankrupt. This causes both his generosity and developing misanthropy. (See item 430.)

456. Shupe, Donald R. "The Wooing of Lady Anne: A Psychological Inquiry." Shakespeare Quarterly, 29 (1978), 28-36.

Applies Richard Christie's Mach scale (based on Machiavelli's The Prince and the Discourses) to Richard III, specifically the wooing scene, Act I, to assess its psychological credibility.

457. Stetner, S.C.V. "Baptista and His Daughter." Psychoanalytic Review, 60 (1973), 223-237.

A study of Baptista's "subliminal conflict" in The Taming of the Shrew. Discusses Baptista's buried incestuous fantasies which cause his reluctance to marry off his daughters.

458. Stockholder, Katherine. "Hamlet: Between Day and Night." Literature and Psychology, 21, 1 (1971), 7-20.

"The combination of the revenge motif . . . and the Oedipal configuration . . . provides a . . . framework for exploring . . . the murky and agonizing process of mediating between the demands of the past and the present."

459. Stuart, Simon. New Phoenix Wings: Reparation in Literature. London: Routladge and Kegan Paul, 1980.

Explores the theories of Melanie Klein in the work of Blake, Wordsworth, Dostoevsky, and Shakespeare. Symbol formation and creativity are the products of reparation, a rebuilding of a shattered internalized fantasy to accord with a growing awareness of a different, outside reality.

460. Teplitz, Zelda. "King Lear and Macbeth in Relation to Shakespeare." Bulletin of the Philadelphia Association of Psychoanalysis, 20 (1970), 196-211.

A discussion of Macbeth and King Lear in light of Shakespeare's biography and Freud's comments on Shakespeare's work. The "factor of the frustration of single, legitimate male inheritance" links the two plays. Behind Macbeth's "childlessness was hidden the repudiated incestuous and hostile impulses towards girls and daughters." Lear also has "conflictful wishes for love of his daughters."

461. Wall, John N. "Suffering and Charity: Similarities Between Rank's View of Illness and Shakespeare's Christian Humanism." Journal of Otto Rank Association, 11 (1976), 29-32.

"What I hope to do . . . is to explore Dr. Rank's thoughts on Illness and Healing, and to comment on them from the perspective of my understanding of the Gospel, and what they both say to me about what happens in King Lear."

462. Weisberg, Richard. "Hamlet and Ressentiment." American Imago, 29 (1972), 318-337.

Opposes Eissler's "Freudian' humanistic-existentialist" interpretations with a "ressentiment-aristocratic-heroic" one.

463. West, Fred. "Iago the Psychopath." South Atlantic Bulletin, 43, 2 (1978), 27-35.

A.C. Bradley's description of Iago as a psychopath is very much like the analysis of the psychopath presented by the psychiatrist Hervey Cleckley in his 1941 The Mask of Sanity.

464. Wheeler, Richard P. "Poetry and Fantasy in Shakespeare's Sonnets 88-96." Literature and Psychology, 22 (1972), 151-162.

These sonnets can be divided into two categories: "poems of self-negation and poems of self-assertion." On the one hand, the poet relinquishes his individual self for his ideal love; on the other hand, the poet needs to deal with his love as an individual person.

76 Psychocriticism

465. Willbern, David P. "Paranoia, Criticism, and Malvolio." *Hartford Studies in Literature*, 11 (1979), 1-23.

> "Writing criticism is a bit like talking to oneself, too, but teaching and publishing are communicative gestures toward real audiences. If we as critics must sometimes seem to be Malvolios obsessed with letters, at least we can try to be Malvolios who know we're on stage."

466. _____. "William Shakespeare: A Bibliography of Psychoanalytic and Psychological Criticism, 1964-1975." *International Review of Psychoanalysis*, 5 (1978), 361-372.

467. Wolf, Ernest S. "What Method This Madness: An Inquiry Into Hamlet's Antic Disposition." *Comprehensive Psychiatrist*, 14 (1973), 189-195.

> Hamlet is an adolescent. "I submit that Hamlet forms . . . a 'secret society' with Horatio; together, after swearing secrecy, they set out on the common plan to avenge the injustice."

Sidney, Philip

468. Turner, Myron. "Distance and Astonishment in the old *Arcadia*: A Study of Sidney's Psychology." *Texas Studies in Literature and Language*, 20 (1978), 303-329.

> Considers the consciousness of Sidney's characters and argues that they possess "common psychological patterns and structures which I call Arcadian consciousness." Differs from Poulet who considers all that occurs in a literary work to be the product of a single literary consciousness.

Spenser, Edmund

469. Gerenday, Lynn de. "The Problem of Self-Reflective Love in Book III of *The Faerie Queene*." *Literature and Psychology*, 26 (1976), 37-48.

> "This essay will focus on Spenser's multiple exposition of love in its negative extremes of self-love or self-immolation, extremes which find emblematic expression in the tapestry at the House of Busirane."

470. Hughes, Felicity A. "Psychological Allegory in *The Faerie Queene* III.xi-xii." *Review of English Studies*, 29 (May 1978), 129-146

> Takes the view that only a psychology which existed during an author's time can be applied to that author's work. Therefore, only Elizabethan humoral psychology can be applied to Spenser, Freud, Jung and existential psychology being anachronistic.

471. Okerlund, Arlene N. "Spenser's Wanton Maidens: Reader Psychology and the Bower of Bliss." *PMLA*, 88 (1973), 62-88.

> Spenser forces his readers to confront and to discover the true nature

of their basic desires because they find that they much prefer the
lure of the attractive wanton maidens in the Bower of Bliss over the
abstractions of virtue stated in the initial eleven cantos of Book II
of the Fairie Queen.

472. Price, John. "Phedon's Fury: Some Psychoanalytic Notes on The
Faerie Queene II, Canto iv." Literature and Psychology, 26, 4 (1976),
167-171.

Freud's idea of "projective delusional jealousy" is seen as the reason
that Phedon picks Pryene on whom to vent his anger. Pryene's offense
is stealing away Phedon's friend Philemon. Phedon is jealous.

Seventeenth-Century Literature

General Studies

473. Levernnz, David. *The Language of Puritan Feeling: An Exploration in Literature, Psychology, and Social History*. New Brunswick, N.J.: Rutgers University Press, 1980.

   A largely Freudian look at Puritanism "as an ambivalent psychological response, expressed in theological language, to various tensions and conflicts in an age of dislocation." Emphasis is on "dislocations in male roles and male authority." Studies English and American family tracts and Puritan sermons as well as the writing of Jonathan Edwards and Benjamin Franklin.

Calderón (de la Barca), Pedro

474. Feal, Gisèle, and Feal-Deibe, Carlos. "Calderón's *Life Is a Dream*: From Psychology to Myth." *Hartford Studies in Literature*, 6 (1974), 1-28.

   At the beginning of the play, Segismundo "lives a purely instinctual life" while Basilio and Clotaldo "repress their instincts." Thus their fathers "evolve in a direction counter to that of their children. . . . In each one of them there is a final reconciliation of opposing forces within a person, the unconscious and the conscious."

Crashaw, Richard

475. Tytell, John. "Sexual Imagery in the Secular and Sacred Poems of Richard Crashaw." *Literature and Psychology*, 21, 1 (1971), 21-27.

   Reveals an ambiguity in Crashaw's poetry in which theme is not supported by the formal qualities of the poetry. He was "unaware of the larger implications of the sexual terms integral to his celebration of a union with God."

Donne, John

476. Steig, Michael. "Donne's Divine Rapist: Unconscious Fantasy in Holy Sonnet XIV." Hartford Studies in Literature, 4 (1972), 52-58.

   Argues that this poem appeals on a fundamental psychological level and that the childhood experiences or fantasies kindled by this poem must be considered.

Herbert, George

477. Wilson, Raymond J., III. "George Herbert's 'A Parodie': Its Double Meanings." American Imago, 34 (1977), 154-157.

   "Herbert's poem gains power from his, probably unconscious, use of words that could as well imply fear of premature interruption of the sex act."

Marvell, Andrew

478. Swan, Jim. "At Play in the Garden of Ambivalence: Andrew Marvell and the Green World." In Tennenhouse, Leonard, ed., The Practice of Psychoanalytic Criticism. Detroit: Wayne State University Press, 1976, 189-201.

   According to the editor of this collection, Swan's essay is indebted to object-relations theory. Swan concentrates on stanzas V through VII of Marvell's "The Garden."

479. _____. "History, Pastoral, and Desire: Andrew Marvell's Mower Poems." International Review of Psychoanalysis, 3, 2 (1976), 193-202.

   All conflicts experienced by Marvell's Mower are displaced onto the man and woman conflict, a conflict which does not lead to security or nurture.

Middleton, Thomas

480. Jordan, Robert. "Myth and Psychology in The Changeling." Renaissance Drama, 3 (1970), 157-165.

   Myth and poetic pattern create this play's "haunting power" rather than its psychological subtlety.

481. Roy, Emil. "Sexual Paradox in The Changeling." *Literature and Psychology*, 25 (1975), 124-132.

A psychoanalytical study demonstrating the oral anxieties, fears of castration, and conflict between social forces and passionate desires in the characters of the play.

482. Wiglar, Stephen. "Penitent Brothel Reconsidered: The Place of the Grotesque in Middleton's A Mad World, My Masters." *Literature and Psychology*, 25, 1 (1975), 17-26.

"The juxtaposition of the eschatological with the mundane yields . . . the 'grotesque': a mixture of styles which produces feelings of bemusement and perhaps of anxiety because our expectations have been violated and our reality-testing momentarily impaired."

483. _____. "Thomas Middleton's A Chaste Maid in Cheapside: The Delicious and the Disgusting." *American Imago*, 33 (1976), 197-215.

A Chaste Maid is often distasteful because it is a comic-grotesque, one in which unconscious conflicts "between archaic appetites and powerful inhibitions in its language and its auditors" take place.

Milton, John

484. Bell, Barbara C. "'Lycidas' and the Stages of Grief." *Literature and Psychology*, 25 (1975), 166-174.

The elegy for Edward King is said to "recreate for the reader a realistic response to loss" that parallels the structure of the four main stages of grief. Images in the poem reflect symptoms of various stages.

485. van den Berg, Sara. "Describing Sonnets by Milton and Keats: Roy Schafer's Action Language and the Interpretation of Texts." In Natoli, J.P., ed., *Psychological Perspectives on Literature*. New Haven: Archon, 1983.

"A critic who attempts to describe a poem using the interpretive methodology Schafer has developed for psychoanalytic narratives must distinguish in the text four separate actions: the action recorded in the poem, the action of recording that is the poem, the act of reading recorded in the interpretation of the poem, and the action that is the interpretation."

486. Zimmerman, Shari. "Milton's Paradise Lost: Eve's Struggle for Identity." *American Imago*, 38 (1981), 247-267.

Argues that within Paradise Lost is a story of Eve's desire for a separate and secure self. "We find a woman who is in search of her identity, something she 'surrenders' almost from the outset and tries to regain throughout the poem."

Molière, Jean Baptiste Poquelin

487. Knutson, Harold. *Molière: An Archetypal Approach*. Toronto: University of Toronto Press, 1976.

   Attempts to persuade the reader "that archetypal theory provided a useful and fitting tool for the analysis of Molière's comedies." Divides Molière's work into three basic archetypal patterns: romantic comedies, romances, and ironic comedies.

Quevedo, Francisco de

488. Neumann, Dwight K. "Excremental Fantasies and Shame in Quevedo's Buscòn." *Literature and Psychology*, 28 (1878), 186-191.

   A study of the five scatological episodes in *Buscòn* and their relationship to the picaresque tradition. Some of the episodes are attacks on pride or greed, and "the excremental vision . . . distinguishes itself by an intimate relation with shame and fear."

Racine, Jean

489. Cloonan, William J. "Father and Son in *Mithridate*." *French Review*, 49 (1976), 514-521.

   " . . . I wish to explore the disparity between the king's self-image and actions, between his aims and his means, in order to achieve a fuller understanding of the meaning of *gloire* in this play. . . . "

490. _____. "Love and *Gloire* in Bérénice: A Freudian Perspective." *Kentucky Romance Quarterly*, 22 (1975), 517-526.

   Explores "the similarities between Eros and love on one hand and the Death Wish and *gloire* on the other." Focuses on Bérénice and argues that Titus represents the desires of the Death Wish/*gloire* and Bérénice represents those of Eros/love.

491. Meyrowitz, J. "The Legitimization of Hippolytus." *Psychoanalytic Review*, 64 (1977), 531-538.

   Argues "that a hidden Oedipal fantasy in the *Hippolytus* is the source of both the play's ambiguity and its popularity."

492. Orlando, Francesco. *Toward a Freudian Theory of Literature with an Analysis of Racine's Phèdre*. Baltimore: Johns Hopkins University Press, 1978.

   Argues throughout that it is quite legitimate to expect a semiotic benefit rather than a strictly psychological one from a psychoanalytic approach to literature. Is poetic language a language "through which the unconscious manifests itself and is recognizable?" Selects

Racine's _Phèdre_ in order to bring out the semiotic component of psychoanalysis.

Traherne, Thomas

493. Dauber, Antoinette. "Thomas Traherne and the Poetics of Object Relations." _Criticism_, 23 (1981), 103-125.

In Traherne's poetry we can discern a three-part view of human development, one whose outlines can be seen "in the psychoanalytic theories of the object relations school, if we allow for the displacement of God by the mother figure." Main source is D.W. Winnicott, _Playing and Reality_, 1971.

Tristan L'Hermite, François

494. Braga, Thomas J. "Madness in the Theater of Tristan l'Hermite." _French Review_, 48 (1975), 539-547.

Madness in Tristan L'Hermite's theater emerges from a poignant realization that reason does not encompass either death or fate.

Webster, John
(See also item 343.)

495. Mitchell, Giles, and Wright, Eugene. "Duke Ferdinand's Lycanthropy as a Disguise Motive in Webster's _The Duchess of Malfi_." _Literature and Psychology_, 25 (1975), 117-123.

The play demonstrates the psychoanalytical connection between incest and lycanthropy. Ferdinand is lycanthropic because of his incestuous feelings for his sister.

496. Whiteside, George. "John Webster: A Freudian Interpretation of His Two Great Tragedies." In Pope, R.D., ed., _The Analysis of Literary Texts_. Ipsilanti, Michigan: Bilingual Press, 1980, 201-211.

Searches for oedipal feelings in _The White Devil_ and _The Duchess of Malfi_, hoping to prove that certain men in Webster's plays "feel toward some women as a little boy feels toward his mother."

497. Wilkinson, Charles. "Twin Structures in John Webster's _The Duchess of Malfi_." _Literature and Psychology_, 31 (1981), 52-65.

The underlying unity of this play emanates from the Doppleganger motif. "Doubling is the phenomenon of the projection of identity, in which the subject perceives himself to be part of a duality."

Eighteenth-Century Literature

General Studies

498. Hershey, Jane. "Female Playwrights of the Eighteenth Century: Shaping the Marketplace of Love." <u>American Journal of Psychoanalysis</u>, 35 (1975), 69-74.

    Socially conscious women playwrights of the Restoration in England often depicted a "sexual marketplace" in which the ritual of flirtation with men led to a relationship of status and security, but not usually love. Among others, the works of Aphra Behn and Susanna Centlivre are studied.

<u>Blake, William</u>
(See also item 459.)

499. Beck, Michael. "William Blake and Psychological Integration." <u>Psychoanalytic Review</u>, 66 (1979), 245-251.

    "If there is a healthy interface between the mental and the material, energy will express itself constructively. If the connection is distorted or corrupted, the outcome will not be as favorable. This is the message that Blake sought to transmit in his poem 'A Poison Tree'."

500. Dickstein, Morris. "The Price of Experience: Blake's Reading of Freud." In Smith, J.H., ed., <u>The Literary Freud</u>. New Haven: Yale University Press, 1980, 67-111.

    Dickstein adheres to Bloom's view of intertextuality--that writers influence their precursors as well as their successors. Thus, he attempts to show how Blake was influenced by Freud. Predominantly a study of the <u>Songs</u>. Dickstein believes that Blake's importance in our own day parallels the growth of Freudianism and that when the prestige of Freud is replaced by other models of the human mind, Blake will move "from the status of an exemplary moralist to a ready niche in the academic pantheon as an English romantic poet."

501. Gallant, Christine. Blake and the Assimilation of Chaos. New Jersey: Princeton University Press, 1978.

A Jungian reading of Blake's poetry which tries to avoid "translating" Blake into a Jungian system. Equates the unconscious and the irrational with the romantic sensibility and finds a parallel not only in the basically romantic nature of Blake's and Jung's thought but also in their "methodological assumptions."

502. George, Diana. Blake and Freud. Ithaca, N.Y.: Cornell University Press, 1980.

Argues that Blake anticipated Freud and that Blake's "mapping of psychic processes actually subsumes Freud's in several identifiable respects." Blake's work in fact goes beyond Freud to certain Freudian revisionists: Reich, Marcuse, and N.O. Brown. The author finds the closest correspondence between Blake and Marcuse.

503. _____. "Malignant Fires and the Chain of Jealousy. Blake's Treatment of Oedipal Conflict." Hartford Studies in Literature, 11 (1979), 197-211.

Blake knew what Freud knew and Blake may have had the better analytical mind. Focuses on the development of the Oedipus complex in the male child as presented by Blake and by Freud.

504. Helms, Randel. "Blake at Felpham: A Study in the Psychology of Vision." Literature and Psychology, 22, 2 (1972), 57-68.

Argues that by a recourse to the research of Freud and Anton Boisen and to the life, letters and poetry of Blake, Blake's life at Felpham (1800-1803) can be reconstructed.

505. _____. "Orc: The Id in Blake and Tolkien: Literature and Psychology, 20, 1 (1970), 31-36.

Suggests that a common literary stance toward Orchood on the part of Blake and Tolkien, involves "a correlative political stance and implicit political doctrine."

506. Marcus, Steven. "Madness, Literature, and Society." In Representations: Essays on Literature and Society. New York: Random House, 1975, 137-160.

Notes parallels in the writing of William Blake and Samuel Beckett to modern studies of madness.

507. Singer, June. The Unholy Bible: A Psychological Interpretation of of William Blake. New York: Putnam, 1970.

A Jungian interpretation of Blake and his work which stays closely with Blake--the man--and moves less surely with the work he produced.

508. Stepto, Michele. "Mothers and Fathers in Blake's 'Songs of Innocence'." Yale Review, 67 (1978), 357-370.

> Focuses on mothers and fathers in the Songs so as to reveal "the genesis . . . of Tirzah, goddess of sexual reproduction, and her association in the fallen world with Satan-Unizen, prince of men and nations."

509. Storch, Margaret. "Blake and Women." American Imago, 38 (1981), 221-246.

> Argues that Blake "had personal and partly unconscious feelings about women that shaped his conception of the fall of humankind, and determined the destructive function he often gave to women."

Brown, Charles Brockden

510. Beranger, Jean. "Charles Brockden Brown's Wieland: A Psychoanalytical Approach to Structure." In Sienicka, M., ed., Proceedings of a Symposium on American Literature. Poland: Adam Mickiewicz University Press, 1979.

> "It is the object of this study to suggest the existence of a central network by relying on family structures and the sexual relationship of several key members of the group and related persons with special emphasis on brother and sister."

511. Hughes, Philip R. "Archetypal Patterns in Edgar Huntly." Studies in the Novel, 5 (1973), 176-190.

> Argues that Edgar Huntly "utilizes archetypes to work out a rebellion --and--initiation process for the hero, one that ends with ambiguous success."

Burke, Edmund

512. Kaufman, Pamela. "Burke, Freud, and the Gothic." Studies in Burke and His Time, 13 (1972), 2178-2192.

> The Gothic enjoyed acclaim in the 18th century but is today criticized because it is equated with death, a fact our society denies.

Defoe, Daniel

513. Brown, Homer. "The Displaced Self in the Novels of Daniel Defoe." Studies in Eighteenth-Century Culture, 4 (1975), 69-94.

> There is a "game of names" in Defoe's work which may be caused by a "strong fear of the menace of other wills," or by "the way the self becomes somebody else in conversion."

514. Castle, Terry J. "Amy, Who Knew My Disease: A Psychosexual Pattern in Defoe's *Roxana*." *Journal of English Literary History*, 46 (1979), 81-96.

> "It is not possible that Roxana, enacting an obscured version of what Freud calls the 'phantastic repetition,' attempts to place Amy, her ubiquitous companion, in the posture of the female parent, while she herself assumes the role of a child in the scene?"

515. Hartog, Curt. "Aggression, Femininity, and Irony in *Moll Flanders*." *Literature and Psychology*, 22, 3 (1972), 121-138.

> By adopting a feminine point of view in *Moll Flanders*, Defoe is able to express aggression while seeming not to, while pretending to disapprove of it.

516. Kavanaugh, Thomas. "Unraveling Robinson: The Divided Self in Defoe's *Robinson Crusoe*." *Texas Studies in Literature & Language*, 20 (1978), 416-432.

> "*Robinson Crusoe*, it is our contention, must be read through this optics of compensation--an obsessive repetition of the claim to a unity and identity of the self coming to grips with the obvious proofs of its arbitrariness and insufficiency."

517. Olshin, Toby. "'Thoughtful of the Main Chance': Defoe and the Cycle of Anxiety." *Hartford Studies in Literature*, 6 (1974), 117-128.

> Views Defoe as a typical aggressive product of this period. "Those infants who did not die of starvation remained to create, because of their internal terror, a period of intense commercial ruthlessness."

Fielding, Henry

518. Park, William. "Tom and Oedipus." *Hartford Studies in Literature*, 7 (1975), 207-215.

> In Henry Fielding's *Tom Jones*, Tom is a comic Oedipus who, it is claimed, desires the death of his "father" Allworthy. Furthermore, his sexual relationships are mostly with motherly women.

Franklin, Benjamin

519. McLaughlin, John J., and Ansbacher, Rowena R. "Sane Ben Franklin: An Adlerian View of His Autobiography." *Journal of Individual Psychology*, 27 (1971), 189-207.

> Discusses the social development of Ben Franklin. At first Franklin's actions "were misdirected toward self-centered goals." Later he became more socially oriented.

Gerstenberg, Heinrich Wilhelm von

520. Duncan, Bruce. "'Ich Platze!' Gerstenberg's Ugolino and the Mid-Life Crisis." Germanic Review, 53 (1978), 13-19.

The "logic of the unconscious" gives structure and meaning to Gerstenberg's play, which "presents a metaphorical configuration strikingly similar to what modern psychiatric literature calls 'the mid-life syndrome'." Viewing the play in these terms explains the "anomalies" that other critics have not explained.

Goethe, Johann Wolfgang

521. Bragg, Marvin. "The Psychological Elements of 'Werther'." South Central Bulletin, 36 (1976), 132-137.

Werther contains Goethe's psychological theories, which were a "total refutation of the psychology of the Enlightenment." Werther is "a symbolic representation of the life of a poet," and the book presents "a total picture of the island universes of individual human consciousness and their interaction."

522. Faber, M.D. "The Suicide of Young Werther." Psychoanalytic Review, 60 (1973), 239-276.

". . . my chief purpose in this essay is to analyze the hero's behavior in such a way as to shed light upon the motivational dynamics of self-destruction as they are presented in the novel, as well as upon Goethe's achievement as a writer."

523. Tiberia, Vincenza. "A Jungian Interpretation of Goethe's Alchemical Allegory: The Marchen." International Journal of Symbology, 6, 2 (1975), 24-36.

A study of symbolism in Goethe's The Marchen in order to achieve an understanding "of the artistic creative process . . . through a view of the work as expressive of a priori archetype forms, accessible to consciousness through the guise of recurrent universal symbols."

Gray, Thomas

524. Hartog, Curt. "Psychic Resolution in Gray's Elegy." Literature and Psychology, 25, 1 (1975), 5-16.

"What psychic processes involve the reader so intimately with the poem, and if they can be described, do they explain why the ending has posed such a challenge to critics, especially those seeking a principle of unity in the text?"

Johnson, Samuel

525. Gorss, Gloria. "Sanity, Madness and the Family in Samuel Johnson's Rasselas." Psychocultural Review, 1 (1977), 152-160.

> Johnson may be one of the first social psychiatrists. "In Rasselas, he scrutinizes what is currently labeled family process and child outcome theory, namely that schizophrenia and other personality disorders could be best understood and treated as the product of specific patterns of family interaction."

MacKenzie, Henry

526. Gilman, Sander L. "Seeing the Insane: MacKenzie, Kleist, William James." Modern Language Notes, 93 (1978), 871-887.

> MacKenzie's The Man of Feeling, Kleist's letter of 1800 to Wilhelmine von Senge, and James' The Varieties of Religious Experience demonstrate "the individual use of . . . root-metaphors." A study of the "root-metaphors" in each work brings a greater understanding "of the insane in the past two centuries."

Moritz, Karl-Philipp

527. Boulby, Mark. "Karl-Philipp Moritz and the 'Psychologcial' Study of Language." German Life and Letters, 29 (1975), 15-26.

> A discussion of Moritz's writing on structure, etymology, and semantics, and his idea that certain linguistic structures stem from the psychological emphases of the speaker.

Novalis

528. Breugelmans, René. "Novalis' Gewissen and the Relevance of the Basic Jungian Concepts to the Understanding of His Work and World-view." Preceedings of the Pacific Northwest Conference on Foreign Languages, 28 (1977), 17-21.

> Novalis' Die Lehrlinge and Heinrich von Ofterdingen suggest Jung's theory of Individuation; Hymnen an de Nacht and Ofterdingen suggest Jung's collective unconscious; and the Great Mother and anima archetypes are suggested in Ofterdingen.

529. Delphendahl, Renate. "Self-Identity and Subject-Doubling in Dreams and Mirror Images in Novalis' Heinrich von Ofterdingen. Journal of Evolutionary Psychology, 3 (1982), 76-85.

> In Heinrich von Ofterdingen, "doubling occurs within a group of related

characters in form of fragmentation that is not only dual but multiple," and "the Doppelgänger motif . . . is a divided double projection, or a mirroring of the self." Furthermore, "a textual analysis reveals that attainment of self is not finite but rather infinite."

Pope, Alexander

530. Meyers, Jeffrey. "The Personality of Belinda's Baron: Pope's 'The Rape of the Lock'." American Imago, 26 (1969), 71-77.

"The Baron's perverse behavior suggests hair-fetishism, and he is a hair despoiler."

Richardson, Samuel

531. Eldredge, Patricia. "Karen Horney and Clarissa: The Tragedy of Neurotic Pride." The American Journal of Psychoanalysis, 42 (1982), 51-59.

"With Horney, I affirm . . . impulses toward growth and self-realization, even as I point to the very human conflicts that make this great novel a tragedy of neurotic pride."

532. Lesser, Simon O. "A Note on Pamela." (1952) In Sprich, R., and Noland, R.W., eds., The Whispered Meanings: Selected Essays of Simon O. Lesser. Amherst: University of Massachusetts Press, 1977, 14-19.

Although Pamela is so obviously a "dated" work, it has given pleasure and continues to give pleasure because readers apprehend unconsciously the rightness of Pamela's actions.

533. Levin, Gerald. "Lovelace's Dream." Literature and Psychology, 20, 3 (1970), 121-127.

Argues that Lovelace's pursuit of Clarissa in Richardson's Clarissa is the result of what Freud called moral masochism in which "morality becomes sexualized afresh and the Oedipus complex reactivated."

534. _____. "Richardson's Pamela: 'Conflicting Trends'." American Imago, 28 (1971), 319-329.

Both Pamela and B. exhibit masochistic traits.

Sade, marquis de

535. Chasseguet-Smirgel, Janine. "Reflexions on the Connexions Between Perversion and Sadism." International Journal of Psycho-Analysis, 59 (1978), 27-35.

Demonstrates, primarily through a discussion of A.D. De Sade's The 120 Days of Sodom and a clinical example, that "the pervert's world becomes confused . . . with the anal-sadistic world." Emphasis is on the symbolic importance of Sade's settings.

536. Perkins, M.L. "The Psychoanalytic Merveilleux: Suspense in Sade's Florville et Courval." Sub-stance, 13 (1976), 107-119.

Using concepts of Freud and Lacan, this study of Florville et Courval ou le fatalisme seeks "to uncover underneath the external, unverisimilar action of the story the hidden metaphoric and metonymic threads."

Schiller, Friedrich von

537. Sellner, Timothy F. "The Lionel-Scene in Schiller's Jungfrau von Orleans: A Psychological Interpretation." German Quarterly, 50 (1977), 264-282.

A psychological study of Johanna's behavior, noting how she deals with her instinctual sexual drives to achieve a "degreee of freedom over the demands of her body."

Steele, Richard

538. Paulissen, Mary N. "Richard Steele's The Conscious Lovers: The Use of the Doppelganger." American Imago, 35 (1978), 419-430.

"Steele in fulfilling his own need as a self-adulating sentimentalist, delved into the shadowy, unconscious side of his own psyche to bring up the one-sided image of all the qualities which the conscious Steele did not have."

Sterne, Laurence

539. Parks, A. Franklin. "Yorick's Sympathy for the 'Little': A Measure of His Sentimentality in Sterne's Sentimental Journey." Literature and Psychology, 28 (1978), 119-124.

"I argue that Yorick's language embodies the conflict between the 'real' and 'false' selves by simultaneously representing to the reader real and false meanings."

540. Swearingen, James E. Reflexivity in "Tristram Shandy:" An Essay in Phenomenological Criticism. New Haven: Yale University Press, 1977.

The thesis that is argued in this book is "that Sterne's novel is an incipient phenomenology which clarifies the processes of human be-ing in the person of the protagonist."

Swift, Jonathan

541. Dervin, Daniel A. "Breast Fantasy in Barthelme, Swift, and Philip Roth: Creativity and Psychoanalytic Structure." *American Imago*, 33 (1976), 102-122.

Discusses basic types of fantasy, using clinical and literary examples, and relating them to imagery associated with primal scene and oedipal situations.

542. Gilmore, J.B., Jr. "Freud and Swift: A Psychological Reading of *Strephon and Chloe*." *Papers on Language and Literature*, 14 (Spring 1978), 147-151.

"If Freud's view of man is no more complete than that of the Augustans and if it tends toward Swift's pessimism about the possibilities of sexual delight, it is, at least, like Swift's view, less insulting to man's complexity than the messages of *Playboy* magazine or the infantile dreams of Norman O. Brown."

543. Rothman, Irving N. "The Execution Scene in *Gulliver's Travels*." *Journal of Evolutionary Psychology*, 3 (1982), 56-75.

A psychoanalytical discussion of the "psychosexual symbolism" of Chapter Five of Swift's satire. "Expands upon the arguments of Greenacre and Karpman who demonstrate Gulliver's loss of stature in the land of Brobdingnag and his sense of impotency," and focusses on Gulliver's anxiety and guilt and "psychological castration and impotency."

544. Steig, Michael. "Dickens' Excremental Vision." *Victorian Studies*, 13 (1970), 339-354.

Both "Swift and Dickens achieve profound artistic insights into the ineradicability of the biological and psychological sources of civilization, and their works at least leave open the possibility . . . of human liberation taking place through man's ceasing to deny, and seeking to affirm, his basic nature."

545. Stillman, Claudia R. "Swift in Wonderland: The Language of Dream in the *Journal to Stella*." *Literature and Psychology*, 25, 3 (1975), 108-116.

The predominant tone of the *Journal* is dream-fantasy, a tone supported by the little language and verbal play of the *Journal*.

Nineteenth-Century Literature

General Studies

546. Beja, Morris. *Psychological Fiction*. Glenview, Ill.: Scott, Foresman, 1971.

> An anthology of literature which focusses on "the inner lives of human beings." A brief introduction reviews the area of psychological fiction and how modern psychological thought has influenced the writer and his work. The literature is by major nineteenth and twentieth century American, English, and Continental writers, and categorized under "The Family," "Eros," "Stream of Consciousness," "Obsessive-Compulsive Reactions," "Dissociation," and "Insanity."

547. Bickman, Martin. "Occult Traditions and American Romanticism: A Jungian Perspective." In Frank, L., ed., *Literature and the Occult*. Arlington, Texas: University of Texas, 1977, 54-64.

> A movement toward interiorization in American Romanticism "reaches a culmination in Jung's theory of the development of consciousness." Considers Jungian theory a modern version of the illuminist tradition which Meyer Abrams presents in *Natural Supernaturalism*. Discusses Poe's "To Helen" and Whitman's "Chanting the Square Deific."

548. _____. *The Unsounded Centre: Jungian Studies in American Romanticism*. Chapel Hill: University of North Carolina Press, 1980.

> An approach to American Romanticism via Jungian psychology *and* vice versa. Chapters on Whitman, Emerson, Dickinson, Poe.

549. Castelnuovo-Tedesco, Pietro. "Stealing, Revenge, and the Monte Cristo Complex: A Reply to the Discussion by Charles Kligerman." *International Journal of Psycho-Analysis*, 56 (1975), 231-232.

> A psychoanalytic study, showing that in the tale of Monte Cristo the hero's behavior as a destructive thief springs from his traumas of childhood.

550. Finholt, Richard. *American Visionary Fiction: Mad Metaphysics as Salvation Psychology*. Port Washington, New York: Kennikat, 1978.

A study of Edgar Allan Poe, Herman Melville, Norman Mailer, Ralph Ellison, and James Dickey, whose works, in Mailer's own words, "have a touch of the grandiose, even the megalomaniacal" because they must fit everything into a "comprehensive vision of existence."

551. Gilbert, Sandra M., and Gubar, Susan. *The Madwoman in the Attic: The Woman Writer and the Nineteenth-Century Literary Imagination*. New Haven: Yale University Press, 1979, 1980.

An analysis of nineteenth century women writers and their work, in terms of their social position and their own reading. "Both in life and in art . . . the artists . . . were literally and figuratively confined" in a "male-dominated society." Studies Jane Austen, Mary Shelley, Emily Bronte, Charlotte Bronte, George Eliot, and Emily Dickinson, among others.

552. Hill, James L. "Defensive Strategies in Nineteenth- and Twentieth-Century Criticism." *Journal of Aesthetics and Art Criticism*, 28 (1969), 177-185.

A review of critical attitudes, including a discussion of psychological criticism.

553. Kauvar, Gerald B. "The Psychological Structure of English Romantic Poetry." *Psychoanalytic Review*, 64, No. 1 (1977), 21-40.

Argues that the "typical Romantic poem . . . embodies Oedipal conflicts, defended against by intellectualization on the manifest level and by castration or regression on the unconscious level." Sees the Romantics as courageous voyagers from the isle of consciousness to the horrors of the unconscious. As readers we take these imaginative voyages with them.

554. Lange, Jean. "Mental Illness as Writer's Motif." *Menninger Perspective*, 3, 5 (1972), 24-28.

Examines pictures of life in mental hospitals in the writing of Dostoevsky, F.S. Fitzgerald, Hannah Green, and William Gibson.

555. Levine, M. Herschel. "Oedipal Views of the Jew in American Literature." *Journal of Psychology and Judaism*, 3 (1978), 102-108.

A discussion of anti-semitism in Hawthorne, James Russell Lowell, Jack London, Wharton, F. Scott Fitzgerald, and Hemingway. These writers hated their fathers, and their "Oedipal animosity was redirected to the Jews as a result of displacement."

556. McSweeney, Kerry. "Melville, Dickinson, Whitman and Psychoanalytic Criticism." *Critical Quarterly*, 19, 1 (1977), 71-82.

A review of Frederick Crews' *Out of My System: Psychoanalysis, Idology and Critical Method* and *The Sins of the Fathers: Hawthorne's Psychological Themes*, Edwin Haviland Miller's *Melville*, John Cody's *After*

Psychocriticism

<u>Great Pain: The Inner Life of Emily Dickinson</u>, and Stephen A. Black's <u>Whitman's Journeys into Chaos: A Psychoanalytic Study of the Poetic Process</u>. While psychoanalytic criticism does provide insights into the literature it studies, the "disengaged coldness" and sometime superior attitudes of the critics are somewhat unpleasant.

557. Myer, John C. "The Romantic Response." <u>Psychology</u>, 6, 2 (1969), 40-47.

A study of the Romantic movement from the point of view of behaviorism and cognitive dissonance. The idealism, the naturalism, the interest in revolution, and the need for fantasy are reactions to the inconsistencies in the Neo-Classical period.

558. Porter, Laurence M. <u>The Literary Dream in French Romanticism: A Psychoanalytical Interpretation</u>. Detroit: Wayne State University Press, 1979.

Relies upon Freud for an explanation of the mechanisms of dream and fantasy, Jung for a discussion of dream narratives and Erikson for a definition of the dynamics of personality development.

559. Rigney, Barbara Hill. <u>Madness and Sexual Politics in the Feminist Novel: Studies in Brontë, Woolf, Lessing and Atwood</u>. Madison: University of Wisconsin Press, 1978.

A study which "attempts to reconcile feminism and psychology in the area of literary criticism, to find examples in . . . feminist writers of the relationship between madness and the female condition." Concludes that the protagonists in the novels studied attain "a superior sanity based on personal order and the discovery of at least the potential for an authentic and integrated self." Discusses <u>Jane Eyre</u>, <u>Mrs. Dalloway</u>, <u>The Four-Gated City</u>, and <u>Surfacing</u>.

560. Rovit, Earl. "The American Literary Ego: An Essay in Psychohistory." <u>Southern Review</u>, 14 (1978), 409-427.

A study of individualism as seen through American writers of the nineteenth and twentieth centuries. There is a lack of strong filial bond between American writers and their fathers; at the same time women are dominant in American families. This leads in the Lost Generation to writers with a strident "contempt for figures of authority." Concentration is on nineteenth century American writers.

561. Ryan, Judith. "The Vanishing Subject: Empirical Psychology and the Modern Novel." <u>PMLA</u>, 95 (1980), 857-869.

A study of writers' presentations of "consciousness in fiction" and their attempts "to abolish the 'self' as a discrete entity." Notes that "Empirical psychology, as developed by William James and Ernst Mach, unmasked the traditional concept of 'self' as a delusion, replacing it by a new emphasis on the intentionality of consciousness." Discusses, among others, Henry James, Robert Musil, Hermann Broch, Alfred Doblin, and Virginia Woolf.

562. Sterrenburg, Lee. "Psychoanalysis and the Iconography of Revolution." Victorian Studies, 19 (1975), 241-264.

" . . . Freud's Interpretation of Dreams serves as a reductive gloss in the nineteenth century tradition of revolutionary symbolism." Argues that the works of Carlyle, Dickens and H.G. Wells re-establish revolutionary symbolism de-politicized by Freud.

563. Stoll, John E. "Psychological Dissociation in the Victorian Novel." Literature and Psychology, 20, 2 (1970), 63-73.

Argues that from a socially oriented novel, the psychological novel emerged.

564. Taylor, Gordon O. The Passages of Thought: Psychological Representation in the American Novel, 1870-1900. New York: Oxford University Press, 1969.

Discusses the shift in the American novel to psychological analysis of characters and life, "the author's premises concerning the nature of the mind, and his embodiment of these premises in fictive art." Studies the work of Henry James, Stephen Crane, William Dean Howells, Theodore Dreiser, and Frank Norris.

565. Terras, Rita. "The Doppelgänger in German Romantic Literature." In Deguise, P., and Terras, R., eds., Symposium on Romanticism. New London: Connecticut College, 1977, 13-20.

A survey of the use of the doppelgänger, with emphasis on the work of Goethe and Hoffmann.

566. Woodman, Ross. "Shaman, Poet, and Failed Initiate: Reflections on Romanticism and Jungian Psychology." Studies in Romanticism, 19 (1980), 51-82.

"The theory of analytical psychology . . . is grounded in the idea of apocalypse as was Romanticism before it." The Jungian Self is a new anthropos, an expansion of consciousness through the assimilation of the "gods" of the unconscious. The Romantic attempt was likewise directed toward restoring "to nature and to man the fixed and dead content of religious dogma which had . . . been the instrument of a growing consciousness but was now functioning to arrest it." For Jung, "their vision was prophetic rather than rational, though as prophetic it contained the seeds . . . of a future understanding."

567. Wright, Elizabeth. "The New Psychoanalysis and Literary Criticism." Poetics Today, 3 (1982), 89-105.

"I would like to see if the new method can be made to work on an individual text in a way that neither reduces the text to clinical material nor robs it of all referential status." Makes use of Lacan's theory of the Subject and Derrida's "method of treating language as a decentered system that can have no univocal meaning." Discusses "Young Goodman Brown" and "Benito Cereno."

Andersen, Hans Christian

568. Mishler, William. "H.C. Andersen's 'Tin Soldier' in a Freudian Perspective." Scandinavian Studies, 50 (1978), 389-395.

Suggests using psychoanalytic literary criticism as a means of focusing the reader's awareness. Discusses the sexual anxiety and the ironic use of the theme of the romantic quest in Andersen's story.

Austen, Jane

569. Chabot, C. Barry. "Jane Austen's Novels: The Vicissitudes of Desire." American Imago, 32 (1975), 288-308.

Adheres to Heinz Lichtenstein's identity theme and argues that all of an author's text "must evidence the shaping influence of his or her identity theme."

570. Corsa, Helen S. "A Fair But Frozen Maid: A Study of Jane Austen's Emma." Literature and Psychology, 19, 2 (1969), 101-123.

The riddle scene is an important example of what Simon O. Lesser has termed "over-determination in fiction."

571. Paris, Bernard J. Character and Conflict in Jane Austen's Novels: A Psychological Approach. Detroit: Wayne State University Press, 1979.

Applies Third Force psychology in order to illustrate Jane Austen's mimetic achievement-characterization and her authorial personality. Maintains that there is a reciprocal relationship between psychological theory and literary representation, the former helping us uncover the latter. Ultimately, the "student of human behavior will be able to understand psychological phenomena in a much fuller way if he avails himself of the richness of artistic presentation."

572. _____. "'Creations Inside a Creation': The Case of Emma Woodhouse." Psychocultural Review, 2, 2 (1978), 119-138.

"By seeing Emma as a 'creation inside a creation,' we shall at once account for the novel's inner tensions and enhance our appreciation of Jane Austen's genius in mimetic characterization." Employs the theories of Karen Horney in order to treat Emma as an "imagined human being whose problems have deep psychological sources."

573. Steig, Michael. "Psychological Realism and Fantasy in Jane Austen: Emma and Mansfield Park." Hartford Studies in Literature, 5 (1973), 126-134.

Emma's character is governed by realism, by mimeticism while Fanny Price's character is a fantasy creation, a character of romance. Emma is a representation of ego development whereas Fanny is a fixed surrogate of the superego. Steig suggests that the superego " . . . is closer than the ego to the irrational, to the id."

Balzac, Honoré de

574. Champagne, Roland A. "The Architectural Pattern of a Literary Artifact: A Lacanian Reading of Balzac's Jesus-Christ en Flandre." Studies in Short Fiction, 15 (1978), 49-54.

> A "Lacan-assisted reading can help us to decipher a 'deep structure' commenting on the nature of writing." A similarity between the deep structure of the Bible and this story "suggests relationships between the Bible ('les Ecritures') and the literary artifact ('ecriture')."

575. Felman, Shoshana. "Women and Madness: The Critical Phallacy." Diacritics, 5, 4 (1975), 2-10.

> A review of Phyllis Chesler: Women and Madness, Luce Irigary: Speculum De L'Autre Femme, and Balzac: "Adieu." "Adieu" is examined in light of feminism, madness, and its critical reputation. Concludes that "the challenge facing the woman today is nothing less than to 're-invent' language, to re-learn how to speak."

576. Jameson, Fredric. "Balzac and Lacan: Imaginary and Symbolic in La Rabouilleuse." Social Science Information, 16 (1977), 59-81.

> Argues that Lacan's Imaginary, Symbolic and Real orders of human existence provide "a model for distinguishing between . . . the subjective (what is private, projective, purely fantasized) and the objectively true."

Baudelaire, Charles

577. Bersani, Leo. Baudelaire and Freud. Berkeley: University of California Press, 1977.

> "A psychoanalytic theory of fantasy can be most profitably brought into analyses of literary texts not in terms of specific sexual content, but rather in terms of the mobility of fantasy, of its potential for explosive displacements."

578. Mehlman, Jeffrey. "Baudelaire with Freud: Theory and Pain." Diacritics, 4 (1974), 7-13.

> A review of Charles Mauron's Le Dernier Baudelaire and an interpretation of Baudelaire through Nietzsche and Freud.

Bierce, Ambrose

579. Dimeo, Steven. "Psychological Symbolism in Three Early Tales of Invisibility." Riverside Quarterly, 5 (1971), 20-27.

> A study of Fitz-James O'Brien's "What Was It? A Mystery," Ambrose Bierce's "The Damned Thing," and Guy de Maupassant's "The Horla."

These stories can be seen "as disguised autobiographical accounts, specifically of the writers' artistic throes." Explores each author's "psychological association with his main character" and analyzes the "symbolic role of the monster" in each story.

Bjørnson, Bjørnstjerne

580. Sehmsdorf, Henning K. "The Self in Isolation: A New Reading of Bjørnson's *Arne*." *Scandinavian Studies*, 45 (1973), 310-323.

Like other Bjørnson peasant stories, *Arne* is a novel of initiation. However, Arne's problem is that he is psychologically "arrested at the second stage" of growing up: "isolation." Although Arne is superficially adjusted to society, "internally he remains separated by deep-seated anxiety and guilt feelings." Arne's unconscious reveals his problems. This is a reading of the 1859 version of *Arne*.

Brontë, Charlotte
(See also item 559.)

581. Burkhart, Charles. *Charlotte Brontë: A Psychosexual Study of Her Novels*. London: Gollancz, 1973.

A survey of Brontë's writing, discussing the reasons for her being considered "vulgar and in bad taste" by her contemporaries, and why she has such great appeal today. Discusses her "sexuality" and "Victorianness," her desire for Eden on Earth and her conscious and unconscious use of her heritage.

582. Butery, Karen. "Jane Eyre's Flights From Decision." *The Literary Review*, 24 (1981), 222-251. A Special Issue entitled *Third Force Psychology and the Study of Literature*.

Through the use of Karen Horney's psychology, attempts to "show that Jane neither matures nor proves herself right from the beginning but . . . ultimately, her conflicting needs are all fulfilled through Bronte's manipulation of the plot."

583. Cowart, David. "Oedipal Dynamics in *Jane Eyre*." *Literature and Psychology*, 31 (1981), 33-38.

Examines the symbolism of primal scenes and the "strategy for circumventing the incest inhibitions of the superego" in order to answer the question of whether the oedipal fixation in this work is merely documented or resolved.

584. Pratt, Branwen. "Charlotte Brontë's 'There was once a little girl': The Creative Process." *American Imago*, 39 (1982), 31-39.

"Charlotte Brontë's earliest surviving story is, like all art, an intrinsic part of actual life which changes the reality in which child and adult, writer and reader, live."

Bronte, Emily

585. Burns, Wayne. "In Death They Were Not Divided: The Moral Magnificence of Unmoral Passion in Wuthering Heights." Hartford Studies in Literature, 5 (1973), 135-159.

Wuthering Heights carries "a particular ideal--the ideal of immaculate love--to such uncompromising extremes that it not only becomes magnificent in itself but also serves to undercut the pretensions of nearly all our other ideals."

586. Carson, Joan. "Visionary Experience in Wuthering Heights." Psychoanalytic Review, 62, 1 (1975), 131-151.

"My procedure has been first to study the text of the the novel, and secondly to attempt to show a relationship between what the novel reveals and the conclusions established by C.G. Jung's empirical method." On the deepest level Wuthering Heights reflects an archetypal experience of the night sea journey.

587. Efron, Arthur. "Reichian Criticism: The Human Body in Wuthering Heights." In Natoli, J.P., ed., Psychological Perspectives on Literature. New Haven: Archon, 1983.

Lists ten basic Reichian perspectives and discusses them with illustrations from literature and literary criticism. Employs this Reichian perspective in order to answer the perennial questions of Wuthering Heights.

588. Mitchell, Giles. "Incest, Demonism and Death in Wuthering Heights." Literature and Psychology, 23, 1 (1973), 27-36.

Argues that Cathy represses material she cannot tolerate, that her feelings and Heathcliff's are ruled by incestuous desire and guilt, and that Heathcliff's Satanism is related to both incest and lycanthropy.

589. Paris, Bernard J. "'Hush, hush! He's a human being': A Psychological Approach to Heathcliff." Women and Literature, 2 (1982), 101-117.

Argues that via the theories of Karen Horney, we can see that Heathcliff "does have 'continuity of character' and a 'described self'." Furthermore, "both his vindicitiveness and his devotion to Cathy will make sense when we see them as defensive reactions to the severe deprivation and abuse to which he was subjected to in childhood."

590. Reed, Michael. "The Power of Wuthering Heights: A Psychoanalytical Examination." Psychocultural Review, 1 (1977), 21-42.

Explains the "power" of the novel by referring to Holland's view of a core fantasy. The core fantasy in Wuthering Heights is "the fearful desire of aggressive oral fusion, an aggressive return to the original at-oneness with mother that will prevent denial, betrayal, and intrusion." Readers objected to the work because this core fantasy was "weakly defended," though not formally.

Byron, George Gordon

591. Rapf, Joanna. "The Byronic Heroine: Incest and the Creative Process." *Studies in English Literature*, 21 (1981), 637-645.

>Byron's ideal woman, the Byronic heroine, is a Jungian "anima," the indispensable female half of the complete human personality. Byron's problem was that he "is unable to face his creative unconscious since she is his sister."

Carroll, Lewis

592. Baum, Alwin L. "Carroll's *Alices*: The Semiotics of Paradox." *American Imago*, 34 (1977), 86-108.

>A discussion of the paradoxes contained in dreams and language and the relationship of dreams and language in Carroll's work. Basic to these paradoxes is Freud's idea "that the 'either-or' relation cannot exist in dreams. Whenever an alternative is presented within the dream, even when the terms are mutually exclusive, the relation may be read as one of conjunction."

593. Deleuze, Gilles. "The Schizophrenic and Language: Surface and Depth in Lewis Carroll and Antonin Artaud." In Harari, J.V., ed., *Textual Strategies*. Ithaca, N.Y.: Cornell University Press, 1979, 277-295.

>Maintains that psychoanalysis should be "geographic before being anecdotal." It should be concerned with "irreducible structures" which enable the critic to perceive the fundamental distinctions in, say, Lewis Carroll and Antonin Artaud. "Psychoanalysis should not be content with designating cases, analyzing personal histories, or diagnosing complexes."

594. Graham, Neilson. "Sanity, Madness and Alice." *Ariel*, 4 (1973), 80-89.

>Alice's rectitude (linguistic and philosophical) diminishes her as a person, but it does "provide the necessary foil to the dangerous aberrations of the creatures."

595. Johnson, Paula. "Alice Among the Analysts." *Hartford Studies in Literature*, 4 (1972), 114-122.

>Surveys various psychological approaches to *Alice in Wonderland* and *Through the Looking-Glass*.

596. Phillips, Robert. *Aspects of Alice*. New York: Vanguard Press, 1971.

>Section VII contains reprints of various Freudian interpretations: A.M.E. Goldschmidt, "*Alice in Wonderland* Psychoanalyzed"; Paul Schilder, "Psychoanalytic Remarks on *Alice in Wonderland* and Lewis Carroll"; John Skinner, from "Lewis Carroll's *Adventures in Wonderland*"; Martin

Grotjahn, "About the Symbolization of Alice's <u>Adventures in Wonderland</u>"; Phyllis Greenacre, from "The Character of Dodgson as revealed in the writings of Carroll"; Kenneth Burke, from "The Thinking Body"; William Empson, "Alice in Wonderland: The Child as Swain." Section VIII is "Jungian and Mythic"--Judith Bloomingdale, "Alice as <u>Anima</u>: The Image of Woman in Carroll's Classic"; Donald Rackin, "Alice's Journey to the End of Night."

Chekhov, Anton

597. Schneck, Jerome M. "Anton Chekhov: Psychiatrist Manqué." New York State Journal of Medicine, 78 (1978), 1130-1135.

   An overview of the psychological content of Chekhov's work, noting that Chekhov said that if it were not for his work as a writer he would have become a psychiatrist to go along with his medical practice.

598. Sperber, Michael A. "The 'As If' Personality and Anton Chekov's 'The Darling'." Psychoanalytic Review, 58 (1971), 14-21.

   Olenka, in <u>The Darling</u>, is an example of an "as if" personality, exhibiting "a defective capacity for love, . . . a defective ability to invest emotional interest in others due to deprivation during the period of most intense dependency."

Chopin, Kate

599. Girgus, Sam B. "R.D. Laing and Literature: Readings of Poe, Hawthorne, and Kate Chopin." In Natoli, J.P., ed., Psychological Perspectives on Literature. New Haven: Archon, 1983.

   Analyzes a number of Poe stories using Laing as a gloss. Combines a Laingian perspective and a Freudian one in order to discuss <u>The Scarlet Letter</u> and <u>The Awakening</u>.

600. Wolff, Cynthia G. "Thanatos and Eros: Kate Chopin's <u>The Awakening</u>." American Quarterly, 25 (1973), 449-471.

   Rather than being the product of her rigid society, Edna's problems come from within herself. "Her willingness to compromise the dream of ecstacy--of total fulfillment, sensuous union with the world about her--leads . . . to a denial of the constrictions of that world and the sensuous fulfillment of death."

Clemens, Samuel

601. Girgus, Sam B. "Conscience in Connecticut: Civilization and Its Discontents in Twain's Camelot." New England Quarterly, 51 (1978), 547-560.

A Freudian discussion of Mark Twain's "model of the conscience and its relationship to culture." Studies Mark Twain's fiction as an anticipation of Freud's ideas on the development of the super-ego, conscience, and the sense of guilt.

602. Karpowitz, Stephen. "Tom Sawyer and Mark Twain: Fictional Women and Real in the Play of Conscience with the Imagination." Literature and Psychology, 28 (1978), 85-92.

A discussion of The Adventures of Tom Sawyer in terms of Mark Twain's many fantasies and daydreams about women and his actual relationships with women, especially with his mother and his wife.

603. May, Charles E. "Literary Masters and Masturbators: Sexuality, Fantasy, and Reality in Huckleberry Finn." Literature and Psychology, 28 (1978), 85-92.

Huckleberry Finn illustrates Mark Twain's "conflict between sexuality and purity" and "fantasy and reality." The sexuality "lies latently concealed in the drawing-room Tom Sawyer frame" of the novel.

604. Patterson, Robert G. "Death on the Mississippi: Mark Twain's Huckleberry Finn." Psychological Perspectives, 7 (1976), 9-22.

A Jungian study of Mark Twain's novel, noting parallels in Huck's life to rituals of initiation and the cycles of death and rebirth. Similar thematic material is found in Longfellow's The Song of Hiawatha.

605. Robinson, Virginia P. "The Double Soul: Mark Twain and Otto Rank." Journal of the Otto Rank Association, 6, 1 (1971), 32-53.

Notes that Rank discovered Mark Twain at a time of crisis in his life, and demonstrates similarities between the two writers.

606. Sears, Robert R. "Episodic and Content Analysis of Mark Twain's Novels: A Longitudinal Study of Separation Anxiety." In Strelka, J.P., ed., Literary Criticism and Psychology. University Park: Pennsylvania State University Press, 1976, 198-206.

An episodic analysis of Mark Twain's novels, examining his fantasies and anxiety pertaining to his fears about losing love. His anxiety is traced to his youth, and his youthful suffering shows up "unwittingly in his novels."

Coleridge, Samuel Taylor

607. Goldiamond, Israel. "Literary Behavior Analysis." Journal of Applied Behavior Analysis, 10 (1977), 527-529.

A discussion of Coleridge's "Kubla Kahn" and "The Rime of the Ancient Mariner," with reference to John Livingston Lowes' The Road to Xanadu. Coleridge's two poems are a product of a mind in complete control of itself.

608. King, Billie. "Coleridge's Mandala." Southwest Review, 66 (1981), 404-410.

   Coleridge used his "poetry as a vehicle for his attempted realization of his potential self." Employs Jung's theory of individuation as a gloss to "Kubla Khan."

609. Lupton, Mary. "'The Rime of the Ancient Mariner': The Agony of Thirst." American Imago, 27 (1970), 140-159.

   Opposes the neo-Freudian revisionist view that the downward movement of the poem is balanced by a "movement upward and outward--an expansion or outburst of activity, a transition toward reintegration and life-renewal."

610. Sloane, Eugene H. "Coleridge's 'Kubla Khan': The Living Catacombs of the Mind." American Imago, 29 (1972), 97-122.

   Argues that "Kubla Khan" is an elaborate development of a birth dream.

611. Twitchell, James. "'Desire and Loathing Strangely Mixed': The Dream Work of Christabel." Psychoanalytic Review, 61 (1974), 33-44.

   Contends that in "Christabel," Coleridge was "consciously reworking a dream vision of his own." Presents an Oedipal reading of the poem and suggests that Coleridge did not finish the poem because he was getting too close to its Oedipal source.

612. Waldoff, Leon. "The Quest for Father and Identity in The Rime of the Ancient Mariner." Psychoanalytic Review, 58 (1971), 439-453.

   Argues that the father-son theme "is central to the meaning the Mariner finds in his experience and in the point at which the frame and the narrative converge."

Constant, Benjamin

613. Morrison, Ian R. "Emotional Involvement and the Failure of Analysis in Adolphe." Neophilologus, 60 (1976), 334-341.

   Focuses on Adolphe's lapses of insight into his psychological state and the connection of these lapses to the emotional involvement in the events of his life.

Crane, Stephen

614. Begiebing, Robert J. "Stephen Crane's Maggie: The Death of the Self." American Imago, 34 (1977), 50-71.

   Maggie depicts "three patterns of annihilation of the self, represented by Maggie, Jimmie, and Pete and Mrs. Jackson." The book's "complex subjective fantasy . . . reveals a vision of a chaotic reality external to the self, and the activity of this external disorder makes for the disintegration of the self and absorption into chaos."

Darwin, Charles

615. Franzosa, John. "Darwin and Melville: Why a Tortoise?" *American Imago*, 33 (1976), 361-379.

An analysis of the unconscious suggestiveness in descriptions of Galapagos tortoises by Darwin and Melville. While both passages reveal "anal" and "oral" content, they are also different in that they reflect the different ages, social positions, strivings, and nationalities of their respective authors.

De Quincey, Thomas

616. Haltresht, Michael. "The Meaning of De Quincey's 'Dream Fugue on . . . Sudden Death'." *Literature and Psychology*, 26, 1 (1976), 31-36.

Applies his six-step procedure for the analysis of dreams in literature to De Qunicey's "Dream-Fugue Founded on the Preceding Theme of Sudden Death" in *The English Mail Coach*.

Dickens, Charles
(See also item 544.)

617. Brown, Arthur Washburn. *Sexual Analysis of Dickens' Props*. New York: Emerson Books, 1971.

A psychoanalytic approach to Dickens' works. Studies "the language of the props and the mythology of unconscious sexual meaning which they reveal," as a reflection of Dickens' "profound psychic struggle."

618. Cohan, Steven. "'They Are All Secret': The Fantasy Content of *Bleak House*." *Literature and Psychology*, 26, 2 (1976), 79-92.

"The action of this novel generates from a disguised fantasy of sexual guilt, which determines the imaginative logic behind Dickens' fictional world."

619. Eldredge, Patricia. "The Lost Self of Esther Summerson: A Horneyan Interpretation of *Bleak House*." *The Literary Review*, 24 (1981), 252-278.

Applies Horneyan psychology to Esther Summerson and proposes that she "has adopted a self-effacing solution as her major defensive strategy."

620. Frank, Lawrence. "Dickens' *A Tale of Two Cities*: The Poetics of Impasse." *American Imago*, 36 (1979), 215-245.

Argues that Charles Darnay symbolizes a conflict between generations as he struggles to free himself from the father's tyranny.

621. Grove, T.N. "The Psychological Prison of Arthur Clennam in Dickens' Little Dorrit." *Modern Language Review*, 68 (October 1973), 750-755.

    Describes Dickens' depiction in Chapter 28 of Clennam's psychological prison.

622. Grundy, Dominick. "Growing Up Dickensian." *Literature and Psychology*, 22, 2 (1972), 99-106.

    Argues that "love alone is insufficient to reconstruct the individual in Dickens' fiction, to help him achieve freedom from the destructive patterns of the past."

623. Hanzo, Thomas. "Paternity and the Subject in *Bleak House*." In Davis, R.C., ed., *The Fictional Father*. Amherst: University of Massachusetts Press, 1981, 27-47.

    John Jarndyce is seen as the absent, symbolic father, a Lacanian metaphor of paternity which signifies a system which "is independent of reality, an autonomous construct that cannot be bound in a natural way to reality. . . ."

624. Hirsch, Gordon D. "Charles Dickens' Nurse's Stories." *Psychoanalytic Review*, 62, 1 (1975), 173-179.

    The "Nurse's Stories" shed some light on early influences on the mind of Dickens.

625. _____. "The Mysteries in *Bleak House*: A Psychoanalytic Study." In Partlow, R.B., ed., *Dickens Studies Annual*, vol. 4. Carbondale: Southern Illinois University Press, 1975, 132-152.

    The novel can be clarified when it is viewed as a parable concerning three vicissitudes of infantile sexual curiosity: curiosity may be inhibited, partially converted or fully expressed.

626. Hutter, Albert D. "Crime and Fantasy in *Great Expectations*." In Crews, F., ed., *Psychoanalysis and Literary Process*. Cambridge, Mass.: Winthrop, 1970, 25-65.

    In order to explain the continued potency of the Pip-Magwitch relationship, the author argues that Magwitch must be seen as Pip's father, "or more specifically, as that aspect of the father that both threatens and terrifies the child."

627. _____. "The High Tower of His Mind: Psychoanalysis and the Reader of *Bleak House*." *Criticism*, 14 (1977), 296-316.

    Presents a psychoanalytic reading of *Bleak House* which analyzes "both an individual reader's response to a text and the common text that many readers share." Thus, the author attempts to find a middle ground between psychoanalytic criticism which "ignores differences among readers and explores only the text's latent content," and psychoanalytic criticism which focuses on the experience of reading by an individual reader (Norman Holland's view).

628. _____. "Psychoanalysis and Biography: Dickens' Experience at Warren's Blacking." Hartford Studies in Literature, 8 (1976), 23-37.

    Argues that Dickens used his experience at Warren's in order to manage and resolve earlier crises "and that he continued to use his adult memory of Warren's to preserve a sense of his own boyishness, his own identity as a child. . . . "

629. Kligerman, Charles. "The Dream of Charles Dickens." Journal of the American Psychoanalytic Association, 18 (1970), 783-799.

    "In the present study, I shall investigate a leading motif in Dickens' love life--his tendency to idealize a certain ethereal kind of young girl and the consequence of a series of narcissistic disappointments in relation to such idealized objects."

630. Lelchuk, Alan. "Self, Family and Society in Great Expectations." Sewanee Review, 78 (1970), 407-426.

    Through various family associations (Gargery, Havisham, Magwitch, Wemmicks and Pockets), Pip learns about the reality of society and about the ideal--"the road away from society altogether." Pip eventually understands the conflict between real and ideal forces.

631. Manheim, Leonard F. "The Law as 'Father': An Aspect of the Dickens Pattern." Hartford Studies in Literature, 9 (1977), 100-109.

    Examines some of the subjective elements behind Dickens's attack on certain legal institutions in Bleak House and Little Dorrit.

632. _____. "The Personal History of David Copperfield." In Tennenhouse, Leonard, ed., The Practice of Psychoanalytic Criticism. Detroit: Wayne State University Press, 1976, 75-94.

    The author maintains that Dickens's own life was deeply intertwined with that of his hero, David Copperfield, who failed to become a modern hero because Dickens himself was unable or unwilling to come to terms with his own unconscious. Rather than delve deeply, Dickens spreads his psychological portraits over innumerable characters.

633. _____. "A Tale of Two Characters: A Study in Multiple Projection." In Partlow, R.B., ed., Dickens Studies Annual, Vol. 1. Carbondale: Southern Illinois University Press, 1970, 225-237.

    In A Tale of Two Cities, Dickens embodies an ideal of himself, his own "Fantasy-Hero," in several characters--"multiple projection." The author adheres to Holland's view that a literary work is "good" if it "can please many and please long" by embodying a fantasy which is provocative but also by embodying a defense mechanism to be used by the reader to enable the reader to master that fantasy. In A Tale of Two Cities, Dickens fantasizes an acceptable love for Ellen Ternan, a rosy future following Sydney Carton's noble sacrifice.

634. Neary, John. "The Dickens Child: From Infantilism to Wholeness." Psychological Perspectives, 13 (1982), 138-158.

Argues that the child image in Dickens' work does not represent regression "to a dull, primitive comfort" but rather emerges from the Jungian child archetype, an archetype which expands and enriches consciousness.

635. Pearlman, E. "David Copperfield Dreams of Drowning." In Tennenhouse, L., ed., The Practice of Psychoanalytic Criticism. Detroit: Wayne State University Press, 1976, 105-117.

Presents David's dream of drowning as a path into David's two complementary figures in the novel, Uriah Heep and Steerforth. While Heep represents a fear David has of being socially unacceptable, Steerforth is the epitomy of success and respectability.

636. Spilka, Mark. "Kafka and Dickens: The Country Sweetheart." In Tennenhouse, Leonard, ed., The Practice of Psychoanalytic Criticism. Detroit: Wayne State University Press, 1976, 95-104.

Parallels the Rosa Dortle episode in David Copperfield with the Clara Pollunder episode in Amerika. Kafka's treatment of a youth's first "sexual" encounter is aided by Freudian psychology. Karl Rossmann advances from bisexual to oedipal love to sexual maturity.

637. Steig, Michael. Dickens' Characters and Psychoanalytic Criticism." Hartford Studies in Literature, 8 (1976), 38-45.

Discusses a variety of psychoanalytic approaches to character analysis: 1. the biographical; 2. the archetypal; 3. the projective; 4. the mimetic.

638. Thomson, David. "Pip: The Divided Self." Psychoanalytic Review, 1 (1977), 49-67.

Applies Laing's views to Pip and concludes that although Pip began life as a rebel, he ended up completely compliant.

Dickinson, Emily

639. Faber, M.D. "Psychoanalytic Remarks on a Poem by Emily Dickinson." Psychoanalytic Review, 56 (1969), 247-264.

"A classical Freudian analysis" of "My life closed twice before its close," demonstrating Dickinson's "full-blown Oedipus complex."

640. Morey, Frederick L. "The Four Fundamental Archetypes in Mythology, as Exemplified in Emily Dickinson's Poems." Emily Dickinson Bulletin, 24 (1973), 196-206.

A study of Dickinson's poetry in which "the four stages of archetypes of birth, life, death, and immortality" are equated with Jung's "three stages of consciousness."

641. Patterson, Rebecca. "Emily Dickinson's 'Double' Tim: Masculine Identification." American Imago, 28 (1971), 330-362.

A detailed discussion of Dickinson's life and poetry, in terms of her masculine alter ego, as seen in her own descriptions of herself as a boy "possessed . . . by an unappeasable desire to return to the mother."

642. Shands, Harley C. "Malinowski's Mirror: Emily Dickinson as Narcissus." Contemporary Psychoanalysis, 12 (1976), 300-334.

Notes anticipation of Freud's ideas in the work of Dickinson and Kierkegaard. Concentrates on Dickinson. She desired a patient-psychoanalyst relationship with T.W. Higginson, with her as a patient. In her poetry, she was able to objectify her unhappiness, which helped her in self-analysis and let her create imaginary selves in her lonely existence.

Dostoevsky, Feodor
(See also items 459, 680.)

643. Anderson, Roger B. "Crime and Punishment: Psycho-Myth and the Making of a Hero." Canadian-American Slavic Studies, 11 (1977), 523-538.

Raskolnikov is not merely determined by his past, by an Oedipal conflict, but actually duplicates an internal journey of psycho-myth in which he goes through stages of personality development. His claim to being a hero lies in his ability to go beyond his legacy of neurosis and toward a new knowledge of himself.

644. _____. "Raskolnikov and the Myth Experience." Slavic and East European Journal, 20 (Spring, 1976), 1-17.

A study, using myth theory, of Raskolnikov's "developing pattern of thought and behavior, his 'stepping over'" the limits imposed upon him by society. Raskolnikov "reaches back into the human inventory of unconscious thought, images and actions to create his own special meaning and sense of purpose."

645. Chaitin, Gilbert. "Religion as Defense: The Structure of The Brothers Karamazov." Literature and Psychology, 22, 2 (1972), 69-88.

Uses Holland's view of fictional characters and the reader's response to them in order to study the character and role of Father Zossima.

646. Dalton, Elizabeth. "Myshkin's Epilepsy." Partisan Review, 45 (1978), 595-610.

"In The Idiot the epileptic seizure itself appears as the violently condensed expression of that intimate, equivocal relationship between the most debased and the most exalted aspects of human experience."

647. _____. Unconscious Structure in The Idiot: A Study in Literature and Psychoanalysis. Princeton, N.J.: Princeton University Press, 1979.

"In literary criticism the text has priority over the life. Biographical material should be used, therefore, not to arrive at an interpretation, but only to support and confirm what is first discovered in the work itself." Refers to New Criticism and Structuralism.

648. Fernandez, Ronald. "Dostoevsky, Traditional Domination, and Cognitive Dissonance." Social Forces, 49, 2 (1970), 299-303.

By reaffirming the Russian Messianic traditions, Dostoevsky resolved his conflicting attraction for both traditional and modern forces.

649. Geha, Richard. "Dostoevsky and The Gambler: A Contribution to the Psychogenesis of Gambling: II." Psychoanalytic Review, 57 (1970), 289-302.

Dostoevsky and his novel, The Gambler, reinforce primary psychoanalytic studies on gambling. The Gambler presents a pre-oedipal mother, the Grandmother.

650. Hoffmeister, Charles C. "'William Wilson' and The Double: A Freudian Insight." Coranto, 9, 2 (1974), 24-27.

Both Poe and Dostoevsky used the double in their writing. In Poe's "William Wilson," one finds "an unbalanced psyche, the ego of which fails to reconciliate the id and superego. . . . Dostoevsky's The Double depicts a victim of acute schizophrenia . . . who projects a double out of failure and inadequacy."

651. Hutzler, Jeffrey. "Family Pathology in Crime and Punishment." American Journal of Psychoanalysis, 38 (1978), 335-342.

Examines the family pathology in this novel according to four basic schizophrenia theories: (1) Theodore Lidz's; (2) Palo Alto Group's; (3) Wynne and Singer's; (4) Bowen's.

652. Justman, Stuart. "The Strange Case of Dostoevsky and Freud: A Lesson in the Necessity of Imagination." Gypsy Scholar, 2 (1975), 94-101.

Although Freud was only minimally acquainted with The Brothers Karamazov, and Dostoevsky did not know Freud, this novel "must be understood in terms of the head-to-head contention of these men."

653. Kiremidjian, David. "Crime and Punishment: Matricide and the Woman Question." American Imago, 33 (1976), 403-433.

"Raskolnikov's psychology is examined from the standpoint of pre-oedipal dynamics leading to matricidal impulses and generalized patterns of infantile dependencies upon women and aggression toward women."

654. _____. "Dostoevsky and the Problem of Matricide." Journal of Orgonomy, 9 (1975), 69-81.

A Reichian interpretation of the murders in Dostoevsky's Crime and Punishment.

655. Kravchenko, Maria. Dostoevsky and the Psychologists. Amsterdam: Hakkert, 1978.

Discusses 1. Dostoevsky's psychological insights by examining his letters, his *Diary of a Writer*, his novels and biographical details; 2. early analyses of his novels and stories; 3. the Freudian treatment of Dostoevsky and his work; and, 4. a variety of opinions regarding the source and quality of Dostoevsky's psychological opinions.

656. Lesser, Simon O. "Saint and Sinner: Dostoevsky's *Idiot*." (1958) In Sprich, R., and Noland, R., eds., *The Whispered Meanings: Selected Essays of Simon O. Lesser*. Amherst: University of Massachusetts Press, 1977, 54-67.

Prince Myshkin's "fatal flaw is an undeveloped ego: a sense of reality so deficient that it not only prevents him from doing good, but causes him to fail everyone, himself included. . . . "

657. Lower, R.B. "On Raskolnikov's Dreams in Dostoevsky's *Crime and Punishment*." *Journal of the American Psychoanalytic Association*, 17 (1969), 728-742.

Raskolnikov's dreams show that his murder of the pawnbroker is "the defensive acting-out of an unconscious sadomasochistic oedipal fantasy." This is related to Dostoevsky's own unconscious conflict over patricide.

658. Magretta, Joan. "Radical Disunities: Models of Mind and Madness in *Pierre* and *The Idiot*." *Studies in the Novel*, 10 (1978), 234-250.

A discussion of the two novels in light of nineteenth century psychological perceptions: "disunity of personality, . . . manifestations of the unconscious, and . . . the limits of reason." Melville and Dostoevsky see madness as "essentially tragic, a haunting reminder of human limitation."

659. Meissner, W.W. "A Case in Point." In *The Annual of Psychoanalysis*, Vol. 5. New York: IUP, 1977, 405-436.

A clinical analysis of Yakov Petrovich Golyadkin, the hero of Dostoevsky's "The Double." Golyadkin is "a weak, petty, ingratiating, obnoxious, entitled, and quite schizoid man." Furthermore, his self "is structured around severely pathogenic introjects--primarily the victim-introject."

660. Neuhauser, Rudolf. "Social Reality and the Hero in Dostoevskij's Early Works: Dostoevskij and Fourier's Psychological System." *Russian Literature*, 4 (1973), 18-36.

"Dostoevsky's creative use of Fourier's psychological interpretation of social relationships in the modern world" gives structural coherence to his early works.

661. Paris, Bernard J. "*Notes from the Underground*: A Horneyan Analysis." *PMLA*, 88 (1973), 511-535.

Attempts to account for the bizarre behavior of the underground man by applying Karen Horney's theories of neurosis.

662. _____. "The Two Selves of Rodion Raskolnikov: A Horneyan Analysis." Gradiva, 1 (1978), 316-328.

Raskolnikov is shown "to be moving away from a failed neurotic solution toward one which is better adapted to his situation." Argues that there is a certain similarity between Dostoevsky's own spiritual development and Raskolnikov. Dostoevsky's "need to glorify the self-effacing solution is such that he is unable to recognize its limitations, though he presents a faithful picture of its destructive effects in characters like Marmeladov and Sonya." Interpretation based on Horney's three basic strategies of defense employed by neurotics.

663. Pratt, Branwen E.B. "The Role of the Unconscious in The Eternal Husband." Literature and Psychology, 21 (1971), 29-40.

Dostoevsky's feelings about psychic life are illustrated in The Eternal Husband." The novel presents the "psychological truth" that "out of evil, illness, and madness grow the 'fleurs du mal' of understanding and Christian forgiveness of both the self and the other."

664. Reid, Stephen. "Dostoevski's Kirilov and Freedom of the Will." Hartford Studies in Literature, 3 (1971), 197-208.

Argues that in his fiction, Dostoevsky "understands freedom of the will to be an illusion."

665. Sperber, Michael A. "The Daimonic: Freudian, Jungian, and Existential Perspectives." Journal of Analytic Psychology, 20, 1 (1975), 41-49.

Includes a discussion of the dysdaimonia (state of being controlled by one function) of Ivan Karamazov of The Brothers Karamazov from a Freudian, Jungian and Existential perspective.

666. _____. "Symptoms and Structure of Borderline Personality Organization: Camus' The Fall and Dostoevsky's Notes from Underground." Literature and Psychology, 23, 3 (1973), 102-113.

Argues that Jean-Baptiste Clamence of The Fall and the protagonist in Dostoevsky's "Notes from the Underground" are borderline personalities as defined by Kernberg.

667. Wasiolek, Edward. "Raskolnikov's Motives: Love and Murder." American Imago, 31 (1974), 252-269.

Points out the important contribution to the understanding of Raskolnikov's motives made by W.D. Snodgrass, but feels that the "repressed eroticism and hostility that Raskolnikov feels for his mother is expressed more fully and in finer structural detail than Snodgrass suspected."

668. _____. "Raskolnikov's Motives: Love and Murder." In Tennenhouse, Leonard, ed., The Practice of Psychoanalytic Criticism. Detroit: Wayne State University Press, 1976, 118-135.

See item 667.

669. Wilson, Raymond J., III. "Raskolnikov's Dream in Crime and Punishment." Literature and Psychology, 26, 4 (1976), 159-166.

Raskolnikov's horse-beating dream presents actions and reactions which will be demonstrated by Raskolnikov in the novel.

Doyle, Arthur Conan

670. Rosenberg, Samuel. "'The Red-Headed League' As a Freudian Parable." In Naked Is the Best Disguise. Indianapolis: Bobbs-Merrill, 1974, 150-158.

"Though, on the conscious level, 'The Red-Headed League' is a fantasy about a man who is prevented by Sherlock Holmes from stealing real money from a real bank, on its subconscious level it may be read as the parable of a man who is acting out his passionate desire to perform an act of sodomy."

Eichendorff, Joseph

671. Hubbs, Valentine C. "Metamorphisis and Rebirth in Eichendorff's Marmorbild." Germanic Review, 52 (1977), 243-259.

A Jungian interpretation of Marmorbild, concentrating on parallels between romantic ideas of metamorphosis and rebirth, and the idea of individuation.

672. Wijsen, Louk. "Cognition and Synthetic Text: An Interpretation of Eichendorff's 'Waldgesprach'." Literature and Psychology, 29 (1979), 185-192.

It is the task of the interpreter to elucidate "different levels of affective and cognitive responses."

Eliot, George

673. Paris, Bernard J. "The Inner Conflicts of Maggie Tulliver: A Horneyan Analysis." Centennial Review, 13 (1969), 166-199.

"In order to understand the character that George Eliot has actually presented (rather than the one she thinks she has presented) it is necessary to employ not thematic, but psychological analysis."

Emerson, Ralph Waldo

674. Clendenning, John. "Emerson's 'Days': A Psychoanalytic Study." American Transcendental Quarterly, 25 (1975), 6-11.

Uses psychoanalysis to suggest why Emerson wrote "Days" in such a protracted way and why, when he finished the poem, it was "buried beneath consciousness and beyond recall." "Days" is a product of Emerson's unconscious, telling "a truth the conscious could not accept, . . . a poem of identity." It is an acceptance of the loss of "the Edenic 'morning' of his life."

675. Hutch, Richard A. "Emerson and Incest." Psychoanalytic Review, 62 (1975), 320-332.

Emerson's plea for a truly American art is viewed as similar to his moving away from dependence on the maternal breast. His 1842 trip to New York City is important to his identity and his vocational crisis and the activating of infantile fantasies.

676. Young, Gloria. "'The Fountainhead of All Forms': Poetry and the Unconscious in Emerson and Howard Nemerov." In DeMott, R.J., and Marovits, S.E., eds., Artful Thunder. Kent, Ohio: Kent State University Press, 1975, 241-267.

Studies Emerson's "intuition of the unconscious as a source of inspiration" and sees him as anticipating "theories of the unconscious in poetry." Discusses Emerson in terms of the "psychological, linguistic, and aesthetic theories of Carl Jung . . . and Howard Nemerov."

Flaubert, Gustave

677. Bart, Benjamin F. "Psyche into Myth: Humanity and Animality in Flaubert's Saint-Julien." Kentucky Romance Quarterly, 20 (1973), 317-342.

A study of the relationship of Flaubert's dreams to Légende de Saint-Julien l'Hospitalier, illustrating Flaubert's projection of "fundamental, normally unconscious, aspects of the psyche" into fiction. Discusses "our conscious understanding of the dream and the mythic elements of Saint-Julien," especially in the two hunting scenes and the ending of the novel.

678. Baudry, Francis D. "On the Problem of Inference in Applied Psychoanalysis: Flaubert's Madame Bovary." In The Psychoanalytic Study of Society, vol. 8. New Haven: Yale University Press, 1979, 331-358.

A close study of a passage at the end of Chapter Ten, Section Two, of Madame Bovary, to gain a greater understanding of the character of Emma, and "combine certain aspects of the analytic situation between a work of art and its creator."

679. Kovel, Joel. "On Reading Madame Bovary Psychoanalytically." Seminars in Psychiatry, 5 (1973), 331-345.

A discussion of the uses of psychoanalysis in interpreting literature and an analysis of Emma Bovary's eroticism and narcissism through the imagery in the novel.

680. Lesser, Simon O. "The Role of Unconscious Understanding in Flaubert and Dostoevsky." (1963) In Sprich, R., and Noland, R., eds., The Whispered Meanings: Selected Essays of Simon O. Lesser. Amherst: University of Massachusetts Press, 1977, 86-104.

Focuses on the bisexuality of both authors and addresses the question as to why Dostoevsky achieved greater success than Flaubert in representing bisexuality in his fiction.

681. Williams, D.A. Psychological Determinism in 'Madame Bovary'. Occasional Papers in Modern Languages, No. 9. Hull: Hull University Press, 1973.

Investigates "the sources of the strong impression of inevitability that Madame Bovary creates" by examining Flaubert's ideas on determinism and the various stages that the novel went through as Flaubert was writing it. Concludes that "Madame Bovary does not invoke an oppressive fatality driving Emma to her destined end. . . . Flaubertian determinism is not . . . reductive or mechanistic." Psychologically, the portrait of Emma is complex rather than simplistic.

Galdós, Benito Pérez

682. Allison, George. "The Intuitive Psychoanalytic Perspective of Galdós in Fortunata and Jacinta: A Reply to the Discussion by José Rallo." International Journal of Psycho-Analysis, 56 (1975), 219-220.

Benito Pérez Galdós' creativeness sprang from frustrated parenting. His work is sublimation for both fatherhood and his unconscious desires for motherhood. Emphasis is on Fortunata and Jacinta.

683. Allison, George, and Ullman, Joan C. "The Intuitive Psychoanalytic Perspective of Galdós in Fortunata and Jacinta." International Journal of Psycho-Analysis, 55 (1974), 333-343.

An appreciation of Galdós' perceptive understanding of psychosis and Freudian theory, noting especially the psychological truth demonstrated in the portrayal of Maximiliano in Fortunata and Jacinta.

684. Penuel, Arnold M. "Galdós, Freud, and Humanistic Psychology." Hispania, 55 (1972), 66-75.

Benina, the protagonist of Misericordia (1897) is "a character with an affirmative thrust in life" which is illustrative of recent humanistic psychological theories. Maslow, Rogers, Allport and Frankl are cited among others.

Gilman, Charlotte Perkins

685. MacPike, Loralee. "Environment as Psychopathological Symbolism in 'The Yellow Wallpaper'." American Literary Realism, 1870-1910, 8 (1975), 286-288.

Gilman is seen as anticipating R.D. Laing's idea "that in an insane world only the mad are sane."

Goncourt, Edmund (Hout) de, and Jules (Hout) de

686. Duncan, Jennifer. "Self and Others: The Pattern of Neurosis and Conflict in Germinie Lacerteux." Forum of Modern Language Studies, 13 (1977), 204-218.

"The parallels between the Goncourts' insights into the psychology of their heroine and the conclusions drawn by Laing and others from their extensive observation of schizophrenics . . . suggest that . . . the Goncourts hit on some very astute perceptions, almost a century before . . . the psychologists."

Grillparzer, Franz

687. Mahlendorf, Ursula. "Franz Grillparzer's The Poor Fiddler." American Imago, 36 (1979), 118-146.

Grillparzer's novella is an attempt to deal with his own problems with creativeness. The story is about a fiddler who uses his art to separate himself from the world and a dramatist who accepts the world. Both characters are part of Grillparzer, himself.

Grimm, Jakob, and Wilhelm

688. Huss, Roy. "Grimms' The Table, the Ass, and the Stick: A Drama of the Phallic Stage." Psychoanalytic Review, 62 (1975), 165-171.

Freud's concepts of the stages of psychosexual development provide a fuller understanding of the story than do Adler's or Jung's concepts.

Hardy, Thomas

689. Edwards, Carol, and Edwards, Duane. "Jude the Obscure: A Psychoanalytic Study." Hartford Studies in Literature, 13 (1981), 78-90.

Jude "is the victim of too much thought, too much reason, too much conscious control. This, not passion, is his affliction."

690. Efron, Arthur. "'A Bluer, Moister, Atmosphere': Life Energy in Thomas Hardy's Jude the Obscure." International Journal of Life Energy, 1 (1979), 175-184.

Offers a reading of the opening chapters in relation to Reichian life-energy.

691. Jordan, Mary Ellen. "Thomas Hardy's Return of the Native: Clym Yeobright and Melancholia." American Imago, 39 (1982), 101-118.

> Argues that Hardy's depiction of depression as Clym Yeobright's natural state "points to a blow to early narcissism, resulting in a deficiency in the libidinal investment of the self and consequent impairment of the internalization process by which the self is structured."

692. Levy, Lenore. "Armoring and Human Potential in Jude the Obscure." Paunch, 42-43 (1975), 149-152.

> A Reichian interpretation.

693. Ordway, J.A. "Psychoanalytic Comments on Thomas Hardy's The Return of the Native." Journal of the Maine Medical Association, 65 (1974), 65-68.

> "If one loses one's objectivity in the reading, one may become identified with the general depression, implicit hopelessness, and continually thwarted purpose of the helpless humans and half-humans that inhabit Egdon Heath."

694. Paris, Bernard J. "'A Confusion of Many Standards': Conflicting Value Systems in Tess of the D'Urbervilles." Nineteenth Century Fiction, 24 (1969), 57-79.

> Attempts "to analyze more thoroughly than has yet been done the nature of the novel's incoherence . . . to discuss some of the implications of its lack of thematic unity . . . and . . . to show that many of the novel's strengths and weaknesses go hand in hand."

695. Steig, Michael. "Sue Bridehead." Novel: A Forum on Fiction, 1 (1968), 260-266.

> Analyzes Sue Bridehead from a Reichian perspective.

696. Trail, George Y. "The Consistency of Hardy's Sue: Bridehead becomes Electra." Literature and Psychology, 26, 2 (1976), 61-68.

> "This paper may . . . be seen as an exploration of the similarities between Freudian patterns and patterns in Jude the Obscure, with no more claim made for them than they are similar."

Hawthorne, Nathaniel
(See also item 599.)

697. Baldessarini, Ross. "Literary Technique and Psychological Effect in Hawthorne's 'The Minister's Black Veil'." Literature and Psychology, 24 (1974), 115-123.

> An appreciation of Hawthorne's understanding of the complexity of human motives. The story is "about a vision of psychological reality, of ambivalent attitudes, largely unconscious, communicated in the only way appropriate to that vision--indirectly and obliquely, through a central symbol, a black veil."

698. Bales, Kent. "Allegory and the Radical Romantic Ethic of The Blithedale Romance." American Literature, 46 (1974), 41-53.

> Blithedale Romance is an analysis of the psychological needs of the main characters, especially Miles Coverdale, with a discussion of how these characters view and react to a "radical romantic ethic." Although Hawthorne was ambivalent towards romantic radicalism, he did put these ideas at the center of his romance, which suggests that he was more attracted to the radicals than is his character Miles Coverdale.

699. Benoit, Raymond. "Hawthorne's Psychology of Death: 'The Minister's Black Veil'." Studies in Short Fiction, 8 (1971), 553-560.

> The story is about facing death. The minister faces death and thus leads a meaningful life "through a sense of one's uniqueness that only death reveals." The other people in the story do not face death and "live half lies." Thus the "power of blackness" in Hawthorne "adds up to something quite other than gloom."

700. Brown, Dennis. "Literature and Existential Psychoanalysis: 'My Kinsman, Major Molineux' and 'Young Goodman Brown'." Canadian Review of American Studies, 4 (1973), 65-73.

> Argues that existential psychology, especially R.D. Laing's work, "is more favourable to an understanding of Hawthorne's psychological emphases" than Freudian psychology. Hawthorne is concerned with "being" in its totality.

701. Campbell, Harry M. "Freudianism, American Romanticism, and 'Young Goodman Brown'." CEA Critic, 33 (1971), 3-6.

> Cautions restraint in applying Freudian ideas to literature. Freudianism is connected to Romanticism in two ways: 1) "over-emphasis on the supremacy of the individual," and 2) use of "extravagent metaphors and symbols." Objects to the Freudian studies of "Young Goodman Brown," by Roy Male, Daniel G. Hoffman, and Frederick C. Crews, because they oversimplify Hawthorne.

602. Cook, Reginald. "The Forest of Goodman Brown's Night: A Reading of Hawthorne's 'Young Goodman Brown'." New England Quarterly, 43 (1970, 473-481.

> Brown's journey from the town to the forest is a trip from the conscious to the subconscious. The story demonstrates the diabolism that D.H. Lawrence said was below the surface of American writing.

703. Dennis, Carl. "The Blithedale Romance and the Problem of Self-Integration." Texas Studies in Literature and Language, 15 (1973), 93-110.

> The four main characters in The Blithedale Romance, Hollingsworth, Senobia, Coverdale, and Priscilla, face the problem of attaining fully developed personalities. They fail in this because none of them can "express the individuating qualities of their beings while incorporating the complementary qualities of those protagonists with whom they are opposed."

704. Franklin, Benjamin, V. "Aylmer's Lovely Plant and Colorless Liquor; or The 'Birth-Mark' Reconsidered." *Journal of Evolutionary Psychology*, 2 (1981), 125-136.

 A study of the "sexual incompatibility" of Aylmer and Georgiana in Hawthorne's short story. "Aylmer cannot respond, as both he and Georgiana truly desire, to her sexuality; she must therefore die and he must forever stand apart from the human community."

705. Franzosa, John. "A Psychoanalysis of Hawthorne's Style." *Genre*, 14 (1981), 383-409.

 Seeks "to reconstruct Hawthorne's personal style as it emerged from his family and social situation and determined and was in turn shaped by his literary style."

706. Grant, William E. "Hawthorne's *Hamlet*: The Archetypal Structure of The Blithedale Romance." *Rocky Mountain Review of Language and Literature*, 31 (1977), 1-15.

 An archetypal pattern gives structure to Hawthorne's novel. *Blithedale* is "clearly within the great tradition of the Oedipal archetype" and thus is related to Shakespeare's *Hamlet*. Discusses Hawthorne's novel in terms of the ideas on literary structure of Freud, Kenneth Burke, Maud Bodkin, Ernest Jones, and Jung.

707. Herndon, Jerry A. "Hawthorne's Dream Imagery." *American Literature*, 46 (1975), 538-545.

 Hawthorne uses nightmare imagery to suggest that certain of his characters have become obsessed with evil, and because of this they can no longer love other people. Love allows people to overlook human imperfection and thus render evil an illusion. Hawthorne's short stories are concentrated upon.

708. Holsberry, John E. "Hawthorne's 'The Haunted Mind," the Psychology of Dreams, Coleridge and Keats." *Texas Studies in Literature and Language*, 21 (1979), 307-331.

 Places Hawthorne's aesthetic in the tradition of the philosophical/psychological beliefs of the English Romantics, Hawthorne is seen, along with Coleridge, as a precursor of later theory of the unconscious.

709. Jayne, Edward. "Pray Tarry with Me Young Goodman Brown." *Literature and Psychology*, 29 (1979), 100-113.

 Focuses on Hawthorne's "paranoid manipulation of experience," seeing "Young Goodman Brown" as an example of "paranoid consciousness." The story is "a remarkable case history of paranoid aberration and . . . a 'negative' example of the wilderness consciousness."

710. Kushen, Betty. "Love's Martyrs: The Scarlet Letter as Secular Cross." *Literature and Psychology*, 22 (1972), 109-120.

 The Scarlet Letter is both a religious allegory and a psychological romance. Psychologically, the scarlet "A" represents Dimmesdale's guilt arising from "his incapacity to resolve those anxieties experienced during his childhood oedipal conflict." For Hester, the "A" represents, psychologically, the "suppression of her exhibitionistic and erotic drives."

711. Lefcowitz, Allan. "Apologia pro Roger Prynne: A Psychological Study." Literature and Psychology, 24 (1974), 34-43.

In The Scarlet Letter, Roger Chillingworth's oedipal problems force him to focus his jealousy on Dimmesdale instead of on Hester. This behavior "indicates homosexual longings reduplicating earlier compulsion brought on by rejecting mother figures."

712. Lesser, Simon O. "Hawthorne's 'My Kinsman, Major Molineux'." (1957) In Sprich, R., and Noland, R., eds., The Whispered Meanings: Selected Essays of Simon O. Lesser. Amherst: University of Massachusetts Press, 1977, 44-53.

Robin laughs at Major Molineux at the story's end because the Major is connected in Robin's unconscious with repressive paternal authority.

713. Manheim, Leonard F. "Outside Looking In: Evidences of Primal-Scene Fantasy in Hawthorne's Fiction." Literature and Psychology, 31 (1981), 4-15.

Primal-scene fantasy, a recollection of an early sexual experience, is a pattern which pervades the "literary work of the mature artist."

714. Micklus, Robert. "Hawthorne's Jekyll and Hyde: The Aminadab in Aylmer." Literature and Psychology, 29 (1979), 148-159.

Hawthorne's "The Birthmark" is placed in the tradition of doppelganger stories. "Aminadab is . . . the repressed, 'lower' half of Aylmer's composite nature."

715. Mollinger, Shernaz. "The Divided Self in Nathaniel Hawthorne and D.H. Lawrence." Psychoanalytic Review, 66 (1979), 79-102.

A discussion of dualism in Hawthorne and Lawrence, drawing upon "psychoanalytic object-relations theory" to show that the psychic identity of both authors "involves . . . the mechanism of ego-splitting." Both authors are united in "the necessity . . . to describe experience in terms of antitheses, of irreconcilable opposites that nevertheless must somehow be reconciled or transcended." Uses letters, literary criticism, and fiction of Lawrence and Hawthorne.

716. Predmore, Richard. "'Young Goodman Brown': Night Journey into the Forest." Journal of Analytical Psychology, 22 (1977), 250-257.

A Jungian interpretation of Hawthorne's story. Brown's trip into the forest is compared to the mythological hero's journey into the unconscious. Brown fails in his archetypal quest to rescue the princess from the terrible mother.

717. Quinn, James, and Baldessarini, Ross. "'The Birth-Mark': A Death Mark." *Hartford Studies in Literature*, 13 (1981), 91-98.

   The birthmark is a central symbol which elicits different responses from different viewers, responses which reveal neurosis. The symbol goes beyond sin and death and is connected with sexuality and new life.

718. _____. "Literary Technique and Psychological Effect in Hawthorne's 'The Minister's Black Veil'." *Literature and Psychology*, 24, 3 (1974), 115-123.

   Through various psychological symbols and his general style of writing, Hawthorne sets up a situation whereby the readers can project their own psychological states onto the Minister.

719. Rahv, Phillip. "Hawthorne in Analysis." In *Literature and the Sixth Sense*. Boston: Houghton Mifflin, 1969, 422-429.

   A review of Frederick C. Crews' *The Sins of the Fathers: Hawthorne's Psychological Themes*. Crews is commended for counteracting the genteel, academic Hawthorne critics by revealing Hawthorne's fantasies.

720. Ross, Donald. "Dreams and Sexual Repression in *The Blithedale Romance*." *PMLA*, 86 (1971), 1014-1017.

   An expansion of Sprague's discussion (item 722). Miles Coverdale's dreams and thoughts reveal his confusion about his world and his attempt to understand his unconscious mind and come to terms with the sexual attraction he has for Zenobia.

721. Small, Michel. "Hawthorne's *The Scarlet Letter*: Arthur Dimmesdale's Manipulation of Language." *American Imago*, 37 (1980), 113-123.

   The conflict between Dimmesdale's ideal and libidinal selves is revealed in his dual use of language.

722. Sprague, Claire. "Dream and Disguise in *The Blithedale Romance*." *PMLA*, 84 (1969), 596-597.

   "The central dream of Miles Coverdale . . . is a compelling and heretofore unnoticed sample of the dream as discovery and wish fulfillment. . . . It also illuminates the structurally unconvincing elements" in the novel. The dream is discussed in terms of Coverdale's disguises and wish fulfillment.

723. St. Armand, Barton Levi. "Hawthorne's 'Haunted Mind': A Subterranean Drama of the Self." *Criticism*, 13 (1971), 1-25.

   A study of Hawthorne's "The Haunted Mind," showing parallels to Jung's idea that the hypnagogic state can be useful in attaining individuation. However, while Hawthorne "comes very close to the kind of understanding which is the desideratum of Jung's therapeutic method," he feels that "the price of experiencing the full cathartic effect of this hypnagogic morality play would seem to border too closely on the sheer edge of absolute uncontrol and madness."

724. Todd, Robert E. "The Magna Mater Archetype in The Scarlet Letter." New England Quarterly, 45 (1972), 421-429.

    Hester Prynn's "duality or ambivalence" (she is both saint and sinner) is "typical of that which Jung identified with the 'anima' or Magna Mater archetype, as it is called in its reflected or projected form." Hester, representing the Magna Mater archetype, has an ultimate influence on Roger Dimmesdale's fate.

Heine, Heinrich

725. Roth, Nathan. "The Porphyria of Heinrich Heine." Comprehensive Psychiatry, 10, 2 (1969), 90-106.

    Heine's porphyria, causing him to be hysterical, and his consequent sexual frustrations can be seen as assimilated trauma in his poetry.

Hoffmann, E.T.A.

726. Hertz, Neil. "Freud and the Sandman." In Harari, J.V., ed., Textual Strategies: Perspectives in Post-Structuralist Criticism. Ithaca, New York: Cornell University Press, 1979, 296-319.

    A study of Freud's reading of E.T.A. Hoffmann's "The Sandman," as found in Freud's essay "The Uncanny." Includes some biographical detail on Freud.

727. Mahlendorf, Ursula. "E.T.A. Hoffmann's The Sandman: The Fictional Psycho-biography of a Romantic Poet." American Imago, 32 (1975), 217-239.

    Hoffmann accomplishes the following in The Sandman: 1. he links Nathaniel's oedipal phase of development with his creativity; 2. he portrays the interpersonal dynamics which enter into the creative process.

Holmes, Oliver Wendell

728. Fryer, Judith. "Elsie Venner: The Literary Convention with Psychological Trappings." In The Faces of Eve: Women in the Nineteenth Century American Novel. New York: Oxford University Press, 1976, 29-40.

    Discusses Holmes' psychological insight into the character of Elsie Venner, a "temptress" whose relationship with her father is problematical because her father avoids her "perhaps because of sexual jealousy." Furthermore, "Elsie has grown up as what one would today call an autistic child."

Howells, William Dean

729. Crow, Charles L. "Howells and William James: 'A Case of Metaphantasmia' Solved." American Quarterly, 27 (1975), 169-177.

> Howells had reviewed James' The Principles of Psychology, and some of his later stories reveal an interest in James' theories, as seen, for instance, in Howells' recurring character Wanhope, who may be based on James himself. Howells' "A Case of Metaphantasmia" is a prototype of the stream-of-consciousness story.

730. Crowley, John W. "The Oedipal Theme in Howells's Fennel and Rue." Studies in the Novel, 5 (1973), 104-109.

> A study of the Oedipal aspects of the relationship between Philip Verrian and his mother. Mrs. Verrian skillfully blinds Philip to the Oedipal nature of her possessiveness towards him.

731. Crowley, John W., and Crow, Charles L. "Psychic and Psychological Themes in Howells' 'A Sleep and a Forgetting'." ESQ, 23 (1977), 41-51.

> Traces Howells' interest in the theories of French psychologists and William James, and his own experience with the psychiatric treatment of his daughter, as manifested in "A Sleep and a Forgetting."

Hugo, Victor

732. Gatti-Taylor, Marisa. "The Child As an Archetypal Image in the Poetry of Victor Hugo." Michigan Academician, 10 (1978), 249-263.

> Uses Jungian concepts in a discussion of the relationship of the descriptions of children in Hugo's peotry to Hugo's psychological needs. The "archetypal dimensions" of his images of children illustrate his "heightened paternal sentiments," his "desire to embody the characteristics of childhood himself," and "his confidence in intuition and . . . his implicit belief in a type of collective unconscious."

Ibsen, Henrik

733. Binswanger, Ludwig. "Ibsen's The Masterbuilder (1892)." Gras, V.W., trans. In Gras, European Literary Theory and Practice. New York: Dell, 1973, 185-216.

> A study, not mainly of Ibsen's "purely artistic purposes nor even his secondary social ones but rather with the visible and tangible manifestation of his basic 'symbol-idea' viewed anthropologically."

734. Carr, Joan. "'The Forest's Revenge': Subconscious Motivation in The Wild Duck." Modern Language Review, 72 (1977), 845-856.

> An explanation of the bewildering behavior in Ibsen's play. "The ac-

tion of The Wild Duck is . . . the playing out of a subconscious drive in both Gregers and Hjalmar to revenge themselves upon Håkon Werle by visiting his sins upon his child."

735. Davis, D. Russell. "The Death of the Artist's Father: Henrik Ibsen." British Journal of Medical Psychology, 46 (1973), 135-141.

A discussion of Peer Gynt, The League of Youth, Ghosts, and The Wild Duck in terms of what effects the death of Ibsen's father had on their contents.

736. d'Heurle, Adma, et. al. "Lost Children: The Role of the Child in the Psychological Plays of Henrik Ibsen." Psychoanalytic Review, 63 (1976), 27-47.

Application of E. Erikson's theories of the stages of generativity and intimacy in children to Ibsen's plays. The inability of parents to perform the tasks needed for the development of the child relates to the idea of death in childhood found in Ibsen's plays. Little Eylof, The Wild Duck, and Lady from the Sea, among others, are analyzed.

737. Ferris, Lesley K. "TA and Drama." Transactional Analysis Journal, 5 (1975), 158-160.

Applies transactional analysis to the directin of Ibsen's A Doll's House. Transactional analysis allows for greater communication between director and actors, a better understanding of the characters in the play, and greater actor spontaneity. "Egograms" are drawn for the characters.

738. Grain, Frances. "The Interpersonal Psychology of Some of Ibsen's Later Plays." Ibsenårbok, 1974, 127-147.

Traces Ibsen's psychological insights which are parallel to the ideas of R.D. Laing, especially the idea of the "'violation' of one human being to another."

739. Little, Margaret I. "Notes on Ibsen's Peer Gynt." International Journal of Psychoanalytic Psychotherapy, 6 (1977), 403-414.

Peer's personality change is seen as "the breakdown of a psychopath into a psychosis, against which psychopathy had been a defence." Clinical studies are introduced to suggest Peer Gynt's relevance to the modern world.

740. Mancini, Joseph. "'Bird of Prey' or 'Dawning Day': Hilda as Anima Figure in Henrik Ibsen's Master Builder." Journal of Evolutionary Psychology, 3 (1982), 41-55.

A Jungian study. "If Hilda can realize her highest function as the anima, she will frustrate Solness' attachment to negative anima carriers like Aline, help him retrieve his female aspect, and finally lead him back to his alienated, suprapersonal Godlikeness, the ultimate source of his creativity and his power to face death with integrity.

741. Norris, Margot. "Myth and Neurosis in Ibsen's Mature Plays." Comparative Drama, 10 (1976), 3-15.

Ibsen portrays "a highly structured world in the process of unraveling." He "forces his protagonists into crises when their myths are challenged. The crises take the form of a ritual which re-enacts the guilt myth--a process essentially therapeutic in nature." Levi-Strauss' ideas on myth are used "to overcome the dichotomy of myth and the real in Ibsen's last twelve plays."

742. Szalita, Alberta B. "Some Questions for Psychoanalysts: Reflections on Ibsen's The Wild Duck." Psychoanalytic Review, 57 (1970-71), 587-598.

Sees works of literature like The Wild Duck as useful for giving psychoanalysts insights into their relationships with their patients, specifically in learning "to maintain the necessary distance, scan expressions of the various participants and demonstrate enough empathy to identify the accessible and crucial conflict for a particular situation and open a possibility for change and integration."

Irving, Washington

743. Devlin, James E. "Irving's 'Adventure of a German Student'." Literature and Psychology, 29 (1979), 120-122.

A discussion of the "disguised sexual allusions" in Irving's story.

744. Kann, David J. "Reading One's Self and Others: Holland's Approach to Interpretive Behavior." In Natoli, J.P., ed., Psychological Perspectives on Literature. New Haven: Archon, 1983.

Reviews Holland's controversial critical approach and deals with "Rip Van Winkle" in his "version of the Hollandaise manner."

745. _____. "'Rip Van Winkle': Wheels Within Wheels." American Imago, 36 (1979), 178-196.

A discussion of the structure of "Rip Van Winkle." "The interplay of paratactic and syntactic structure, of fantasy and irony controlled through the form of the story, both reveals and conceals, confirms and denies, the core fantasy."

James, Henry, Sr.

746. Feinstein, Howard. "The Double in The Autobiography of the Elder Henry James." American Imago, 31 (1974), 293-315.

A study of James' autobiography, Immortal Life, Illustrated by a Brief Autobiographical Sketch of the Late Stephen Dewhurst. Dewhurst is James' Swedenborgian alter ego, reflecting James' struggling with his vocation, self-hood, and his inability to finish his autobiography.

James, Henry

747. Armstrong, Paul B. "Knowing in James: A Phenomenological View." Novel: A Forum on Fiction, 12 (1978), 5-20.

>An introduction to phenomenology, drawing upon the work of Henry and William James, and a discussion of the "meanings and implication of the 'impression' . . . as a way of knowing" for Henry James.

748. Bleich, David. "Artistic Form as Defensive Adaptation: Henry James and The Golden Bowl." Psychoanalytic Review, 58 (1971), 223-244.

>A discussion of Freud's "author psychology" and Norman N. Holland's "reader's psychology" as approaches to literary analysis, leading to specific application to The Golden Bowl, using the work of Leon Edel on James.

749. Crowley, Francis E. "Henry James' The Beast in the Jungle and The Ambassadors." Psychoanalytic Review, 62 (1975), 153-163.

>Both works illustrate the hero's romantic quest of escape from anxiety and fulfillment of the libido.

750. Deans, Thomas R. "Henry James' The Ambassadors: The Primal Scene Revisited." American Imago, 29 (1972), 233-256.

>The "unconscious traumatic primal scene" evoked by Chad and Marie de Vionnet on the river destroys Strether's self-image and reveals the oedipal aspects of his fantasies, showing the true nature of Chad and Marie's relationship. Thus Strether renounces "his genital sexual striving" in favor of "a secondary erotic gratification from oral scoptophilic impulses by visually incorporating the forbidden scene" of Chad and Marie on the river.

751. Gargano, James W. "Washington Square: A Study in the Growth of an Inner Self." Studies in Short Fiction, 13 (1976), 355-362.

>A discussion of Catherine Sloper's "expanding consciousness" and evolving psyche. Catherine is "an early portrait--without the later nuance and depth-psychology--of the Jamesian protagonist transformed . . . by the discovery of selfhood and an inner life."

752. Gotti, Richard. "Love and Neurotic Claims." The American Journal of Psychoanalysis, 42 (1982), 61-70.

>In "The Beast in the Jungle," "John Marcher's claims reflected some of the characteristics described by Karen Horney as basic to neurotic claims: their unrealistic and egocentric nature, the assumption that no personal effort is necessary for their fulfillment, and their vindictiveness."

753. Green, André. "The Double and The Absent." In Roland, A., ed., Psychoanalysis, Creativity, and Literature. New York: Columbia University Press, 1978, 271-291.

A close textual analysis of Henry Jame's "Private Life" focusing on a writer's concern with his own creativity.

754. Haddick, Vern. "Fear and Growth: Reflections on 'The Beast in the Jungle'." *Journal of the Otto Rank Association*, 9, 2 (1974-75), 38-42.

A Rankian discussion of "The Beast in the Jungle," dealing with the theory of fear as being the first part of consciousness and the importance of the will for individual development.

755. Houghton, Donald E. "Attitude and Illness in James' *Daisy Miller*." *Literature and Psychology*, 19 (1969), 51-60.

A discussion of the relationship of illness to mental states. James' characters become sick in Europe because of "culture shock." Furthermore, James suggests that "anyone who ignores or defies society to the extreme that Daisy did is 'sick' . . . in the psychological sense, sick even unto death."

756. Hovey, Richard. "*Washington Square*: James and 'The Deeper Psychology'." *University of Hartford Studies in Literature*, 14 (1982), 1-10.

The narcissistic Doctor Sloper of *Washington Square* is "both a sadist and a masochist."

757. Huntley, H. Robert. "James' *The Turn of the Screw*: Its 'Fine Machinery'." *American Imago*, 34 (1977), 224-237.

The Governess' "double" experiences demonstrate James' great ability to show the balance of the real world and the fantastic world, which makes complete understanding of "reality" impossible to explain completely.

758. Johnson, Lee Ann. "The Psychology of Characterization: James's Portraits of Verena Tarrant and Olive Chancellor." *Studies in the Novel*, 6 (1974), 295-303.

A discussion of Verena and Olive in *The Bostonians*, in terms of James' attempt to move from romance to realism in his writing. The characterization of Verena is romantic and does not fit the realistic setting. Olive becomes the real heroine because of James' "sympathetic yet critical" portrayal of her complex and ambivalent feelings.

759. Kaston, Carren Osna. "Houses of Fiction in *What Maisie Knew*." *Criticism*, 18 (1976), 27-42.

The houses in James' fiction are "parental structures in which family dramas show us what it means to be a child and what it means to grow up." Maisie's Oedipal situation is seen in her fondness for her stepfather and competitiveness with her stepmother. Connection is also made between the structure of a house and the structure of art.

760. Nance, William. "'The Beast in the Jungle': Two Versions of Oedipus." *Studies in Short Fiction*, 13 (1976), 433-440.

James' story is like a dream because "it is abstracted from the real world yet connected with it through the deeper realities of the unconscious." The story is given a psycho-mythic interpretation. May Bartram's "mythic function" is of a sphinx inviting Marcher "to be the heroic Oedipus." But Marcher's life is without myth, and thus ultimately purely subjective and empty.

761. Norton, Rictor. "The Turn of the Screw: Coincidentia Oppositorum." American Imago, 28 (1971), 373-390.

A study of the "union of opposites" (as opposed to mere unity of opposites) in The Turn of the Screw. The governess "acts like a phallic 'screw'." Allegorical, symbolic, and sexual aspects of the work, as developed in the relationships of the characters, revolve around the image of the screw and its suggestion of the concept of union.

762. Schneider, Daniel J. "The Divided Self in the Fiction of Henry James. PLMA, 90 (1975), 447-460.

A study of how the pressures of external reality on the individual cause a divided self in James' work. James develops "obsessive imagery" as a means of demonstrating the anxieties caused by a world that threatens to overcome the individual self. James' insights have parallels in the findings of clinical psychology.

763. Shinn, Thelma J. "A Question of Survival: An Analysis of 'The Treacherous Years' of Henry James." Literature and Psychology, 23 (1973), 135-148.

A discussion of the novels written by James after the poor critical reception of his plays. The failure of his dramatic works brought on depression, and James wrote the novels under discussion as a means of returning to good health. These novels "deal with the developing consciousness of representative children at different ages." The Other House, The Spoils of Poynton, What Maisie Knew, In the Cage, and The Awkward Age are discussed.

764. Tatar, Maria M. "From Science Fiction to Psychoanalysis: Henry James' Bostonians, D.H. Lawrence's Women in Love, and Thomas Mann's Mario and the Magician." In Spellbound: Studies on Mesmerism and Literature. Princeton: Princeton University Press, 1978, 230-271.

A discussion of "how mesmerism came to be stripped of its magical powers and the human psyche revealed" to show its devine and diabolical elements.

765. Tremper, Ellen. "Henry James' Altering Ego: An Examination of His Psychological Double in Three Tales." Texas Quarterly, 19, 3 (1976), 59-75.

"The Aspen Papers," "The Beast in the Jungle," and "The Jolly Corner" are viewed as a group of stories dealing with the "ability to love." All three contain "a hunt . . . by an egoist which brings him face to face with his alter ego."

766. Vann, Barbara. "A Psychological Interpretation of Daisy Miller." In Penninger, F.E., ed., A Festschrift for Professor Marguerite Roberts. Richmond: University of Richmond Press, 1976, 205-208.

A Jungian view of <u>Daisy Miller</u>, the theme of which is "Winterbourne's gradual loss of inner freedom in a society of constraints and the subordination of the consciousness to false values." Daisy and Randolph are "aspects of Winterbourne's personality, which he needs to integrate to achieve self-actualization."

767. Wolf, Howard R. "The Psychology and Aesthetics of Abandonment in <u>The Ambassadors</u>." <u>Literature and Psychology</u>, 21, 3 (1971), 133-147.

The character of Strether gives insight into the mind of the abandoned child. Strether is ambivalent towards his mother and can only act as a spectator.

<u>Keats, John</u>
(See also item 485.)

768. Bernstein, Gene. "Keats' 'Ode on a Grecian Urn': Individuation and the Mandala." <u>Massachusetts Studies in English</u>, 4 (1973), 24-30.

The paradoxes of this poem "can be genuinely reconciled by showing that the poem represents a manifestation of what C.G. Jung calls 'individuation' through the projection of a 'mandala,' the urn itself."

769. Hamilton, James W. "Object Loss, Dreaming and Creativity: The Poetry of John Keats." <u>Psychoanalytic Study of the Child</u>, 24 (1969), 488-531.

Focuses on Keats' poetry in order "to gain some further understanding of the relationship between creative activity and intrapsychic functioning." Emphasizes the dreaming and mourning processes, REM research, and children's responses to object loss.

770. Jacobs, Edward. "Further Reflections on 'La Belle Dame Sans Merci' as Anima Archetype." <u>Journal of Altered States of Consciousness</u>, 4 (1978-79), 291-296.

"La Belle Dame" can be read as "dramatizing the failure of the knight to achieve the wholeness Jung would call individuation."

771. Leavy, Stanley A. "John Keats' Psychology of Creative Imagination." <u>Psychoanalytic Quarterly</u>, 39, 2 (1970), 173-197.

"The making of poems is the poet's way of completing the process of internalization of the world of experience." This process of internalization is dependent upon "Negative Capability."

772. Reid, Stephen. "Keats' Depressive Poetry." <u>Psychoanalytic Review</u>, 58 (1971), 395-418.

Presents a view of Keats based on Melanie Klein's discussion of the "depressive position."

773. Simpson, David E. "Keats' Lady, Metaphor, and the Rhetoric of Neurosis." <u>Studies in Romanticism</u>, 15 (Spring 1976), 265-288.

Explores the structure of indeterminacy in "La Belle Dame Sans Merci" in the light of Freud's theory of mind in order to "suggest some profitable directions which an anatomy and theory of metaphor might follow."

774. Stephenson, William. "Applications of Communication Theory: Interpretation of Keats' 'Ode on a Grecian Urn'." Psychological Record, 22 (1972), 177-192.

"Using Keats' 'Ode on a Grecian Urn' as an example, the paper outlines the objectivity that is substructure to the arts and humanities, paralleling the subjectivity that is substructure of science."

775. Twitchell, James. "Levels of Consciousness in Keats' 'Endymion'." Journal of Altered States of Consciousness, 3 (1977-78), 309-323.

Presents a pattern of organization in Endymion "by detailing the various states of consciousness referred to in Keats' 'Pleasure Thermometer' and then applying this to changes in the protagonist."

Kleist, Heinrich von
(See also item 526.)

776. Crosby, Donald H. "Psychological Realism in the Works of Kleist: Penthesilea and Die Marquise von O." Literature and Psychology, 19, 1 (1969), 3-18.

"Kleist's realism is often observed to be of a non-literal kind, specifically of an inner-oriented, psychological nature which transcends the artificial situations and circumstances of his plays and tales."

777. Mahlendorf, Ursula R. "The Wounded Self: Kleist's Penthesilea." German Quarterly, 52 (1979), 252-272.

Argues that Heinz Kohut's work on the psychology of narcissism is a more rewarding orientation to Kleist's work than structural Oedipal theory. The characters in this play regress to preverbal states of human development.

778. Ryder, Frank G. "Kleist's Findling: Oedipus Manqué?" Modern Language Notes, 92 (1977), 509-524.

Kleist has created "a complex of psychological action," which is made clear by comparing it to the Oedipus myth. "The chronology and other details of the story . . . permit the crucial assertion of outward identity. And . . . nothing within Nicolo requires explanation, because he is blind to deeper meaning."

779. Tatar, Maria M. "Psychology and Poetics: J.C. Reil and Kleist's Prinz Friedrich von Homburg." Germanic Review, 48 (1973), 21-34.

Kleist adapted Reil's studies of mental diseases to his play. Homburg's sickness and cure are similar to those described in Reil's Rhapsodieen.

Mallarmé, Stéphane

780. Oxenhandler, Neal. "The Quest for Pure Consciousness in Husserl and Mallarmé." In Hardison, O.B., ed., The Quest for Imagination. Cleveland: Case Western Reserve University Press, 1971, 149-166.

Asks the question, "How can Husserlian phenomenology help us to understand poetic consciousness?" Focuses on Mallarmé, "whose poetic quest seems . . . to parallel the spiritual discipline of Husserl's own effort to move from the 'natural attitude' to transcendental subjectivity."

Maupassant, Guy de
(See also item 579).

781. Artinian, Robert Willard. "'Then, Venom, To Thy Work': Pathological Representation in Pierre et Jean. Modern Fiction Studies, 18 (1972), 225-229.

Pierre et Jean is a novel of obsessions. Furthermore, Maupassant skillfully keeps himself out of the novel while he has his characters analyze themselves. He anticipates Proust, Camus, and Robbe-Grillet.

Melville, Herman
(See also items 390, 615, 658.)

782. Abrams, Robert E. "'Bartleby' and the Fragile Pageantry of the Ego." English Literary History (ELH), 45 (1978), 488-500.

A discussion of Bartleby's aloof personality in terms of Freud's essay on "The Uncanny" and the relationship of horror to humor. "The uncanniness of Bartlebyian horror . . . becomes more fully explicable once comic variations of the catatonic innocent are explored."

783. Beja, Morris. "Bartleby and Schizophrenia." Massachusetts Review, 19 (1978), 555-568.

A discussion of Bartleby's schizophrenic and catatonic personality, drawing especially on the ideas of R.D. Laing.

784. Blake, Nancy. "Mourning and Melancholia in 'Bartleby'." Delta, 7 (1978), 155-168.

"The story of Bartleby is the story of the ritual murder of the son, the murder of the other in oneself in order to pay a debt to the divinity." Thus, "Bartleby actualizes the pain of the loss of self. And as the narrator merges with Bartleby, . . . he discovers that the damaged soul of the victim of melancholia is not to be consoled: he must remain 'incurably forlorn'."

785. Bollas, Christopher. "Melville's Lost Self: Bartleby." *American Imago*, 31 (1974), 401-411.

"Bartleby's arrival at the office and his subsequent breakdown into negativity is a mimetic representation of a need to find a nurturant space where he can regress toward the healing of a 'basic fault' in the self." Bartleby is the other side of Melville's questing heroes, the "true self finally existentially revealed."

786. _____. "Melville's Lost Self: 'Bartleby'." In L. Tennenhouse, ed., *The Practice of Psychoanalytic Criticism*. Detroit: Wayne State University Press, 1976, 226-236.

See item 785.

787. Brodtkorb, Paul, Jr. *Ishamel's White World: A Phenomenological Reading of Moby Dick*. New Haven: Yale University Press, 1965.

A reading which employs phenomenological psychiatrist J. van den Berg's "pathography" approach, one in which self, others, time and objects provide a descriptive view of consciousness.

788. Chabot, C. Barry. "Melville's *The Confidence-Man*: A 'Poisonous' Reading." *Psychological Review*, 63 (1976-77), 571-585.

"Issues of trust and autonomy increasingly concerned Melville, until with the writing of this novel he can no longer find anything or anyone, not even himself, worthy of confidence, a revelation which leaves him bereft of his world."

789. Costello, Jacqueline A., and Kloss, Robert J. "The Psychological Depths of Melville's 'The Bell-Tower'." *Emerson Society Quarterly*, 73 (1973), 254-261.

Bannadonna's obsession with building the (phallic) tower and uniting it with a clock-works (a female symbol) all on his own suggests his desire to out-do Mother Nature and ignore the female as necessary for procreation. For this "sin" symbolic of incest, he is "symbolically castrated." Phallic imagery is used in a similar fashion in Melville's "I and My Chimney," "The Paradise of Bachelors and the Tartarus of Maids," and "The Lightning Rod Man."

790. Durand, Regis. "'The Captive King': The Absent Father in Melville's Text." In Davis, R.C., ed., *The Fictional Father*. Amherst: University of Massachusetts Press, 1981, 48-72.

In *Pierre*, "the return to narcissism is effected through a complex and painful ritual of introjection and rejection of the dead father and of the doomed fantasy of wholly incestuous origin." The essay attempts to "trace some aspects of this intricacy."

791. Edinger, Edward F. *Melville's 'Moby Dick': A Jungian Commentary-- An American Nekyia*. New York: New Directions, 1978.

Undertakes the following: 1. to discuss the psychological significance of *Moby-Dick*; 2. to display the uses of analytical psychology in work-

132 Psychocriticism

ing with symbols; 3. to present "the basic orientation, or <u>Weltanschaung</u>, which underlies the therapeutic approach of analytical psychology."

792. Emery, Allan Moore. "The Alternatives of Melville's 'Bartleby'." <u>Nineteenth Century Fiction</u>, 31 (1975), 170-187.

An analysis of the narrator and Bartleby as psychological opposites, drawing upon the writings of Jonathan Edwards and Joseph Priestly on free will.

793. Faber, M.D. "The Painted Breast: A Psychological Study of Melville's <u>Pierre</u>." <u>Psychoanalytic Review</u>, 66 (1979-80), 519-551.

Pierre is an example of "the deepest urge of the Western tragic hero . . . <u>to resolve the mystery of maternal ambivalence</u>" and to deal with a patriarchal society that produces the ambivalence. "He ingests 'mother's' poison in 'father's' jail."

794. Fisher, Marvin. "'Bartleby,' Melville's Circumscribed Scrivener." <u>Southern Review</u>, 10 (1974), 59-79.

"Bartleby" is a story of a society which has failed in "community, communication, and communion." Bartleby reacts to this failed soceity with "the pathology of schizophrenia."

795. Floyd, Nathaniel M. "<u>Billy Budd</u>: A Psychological Autopsy." <u>American Imago</u>, 34 (1977), 28-49.

Answers the question of why Billy attacks Claggart. Underneath Billy's pleasantness is his "stuttering, impulsivity, suggestibility, dissociation of early memories, lack of awareness of his own sexually provocative behavior, and generalized attitutde of dependency toward senior men." Billy has characteristics of an hysteric who can express anger only in sudden outbursts.

796. Grenander, M.E. "<u>Benito Cereno</u> and Legal Oppression: A Szaszian Interpretation." <u>Journal of Libertarian Studies</u>, 2 (1978), 337-342.

An analysis of Melville's novella, using Szasz's studies of oppression and slavery. Discusses the psychological results of slavery on both Babo, the victim, and Cereno, the victimizer, who is, nevertheless, also a victim of his society, which demands that he oppress blacks.

797. Haberstroh, Charles. "<u>Redburn</u>: The Psychological Pattern." <u>Studies in American Fiction</u>, 2 (1974), 133-144.

<u>Redburn</u> reflects Melville's chronic suicidal desires and is "probably . . . the end product of a suicidal crisis." The novel is the "successful use of his fiction to quiet his rage, to tell himself that endurance and control were still possible."

798. Hennelly, Mark. "Ishmael's Nightmare and the American Eve." <u>American Imago</u>, 30 (1973), 274-293.

A "psychoallegorical" analysis "in terms of the uniquely American consciousness and unconsciousness that Moby Dick dramatizes, especially with regard to the American male's 'flight from woman'."

799. Justman, Stewart. "Repression and Self in 'Benito Cereno'." Studies in Short Fiction, 15 (1978), 301-306.

Delano represses his self and thus is "immune to reality." He is "a prisoner of his own repressions, unable to see farther than his own self."

800. Kellner, R. Scott. "Sex, Toads, and Scorpions: A Study of the Psychological Themes in Melville's Pierre." Arizona Quarterly, 31 (1975), 5-20.

As the subtitle of Pierre (The Ambiguities) suggests, Pierre is ambivalent about his sexual role. His sexuality disgusts him and causes him to attempt the suppression of his libido. This brings about an idealization of his love which conflicts with his erotic desires and feelings of incest, leading to symptoms of homosexuality.

801. Leverenz, David. "Moby-Dick." In Crews, F.C., ed., Psychoanalysis and the Literary Process. Cambridge, Mass.: Winthrop, 1970, 66-117.

A psychological study of characters, symbols, and events in Moby-Dick, with focus on the sexual associations with the whale and Melville's problematical relationship with his mother.

802. Miner-Quinn, Paula. "Pierre's Sexuality: A Psychoanalytic Interpretation of Herman Melville's Pierre, or, The Ambiguities." Hartford Studies in Literature, 13 (1981), 111-121.

Argues that impotency and homosexuality underlie all other sexual problems in Pierre and not fornication and incest.

803. Pops, Martin Leonard. The Melville Archetype. Kent, Ohio: Kent State University Press, 1970.

A Jungian study of "the quest for the Sacred, for the realization of soul" in Melville's writing. This quest took Melville's "heroes outside the boundaries of formal worship, toward the sacramental modes of romanticism, primitivism, and, ultimately, that archetypal experience C.G. Jung called individuation."

804. Rubin, Larry. "Billy Budd: What Goes on Behind Closed Doors?" American Imago, 37 (1980), 65-67.

Suggests that a "homosexual encounter" took place between Billy and Captain Vere.

805. Schneck, Jerome M. "Hypnagogic Hallucinations: Herman Melville's Moby Dick." New York State Journal of Medicine, 77 (1977), 2145-2147.

When he was a child, Ishmael had a "tactile hypnagogic hallucination" of a supernatural hand being placed in his. The hallucination is a portent of Ishmael's being saved from death at the end of the novel.

806. _____. "Karl Kahlbaum's Catatonia and Herman Melville's Bartleby the Scrivener." Archives of General Psychiatry, 27 (1972), 48-51.

   A discussion of Melville's psychological problems and how they are related to his accurate picture of catatonia in "Bartleby the Scrivener." The story, published twenty-one years before Kahlbaum's study of catatonia, contains "seminal material of personality psychodynamics."

807. Smith, Henry Nash. "The Madness of Ahab." In Democracy and the Novel: Popular Resistance to Classic American Writers. New York: Oxford University Press, 1978, 35-55.

   Notes that Melville was aware of the new theory of monomania and that he used Ahab's madness to draw a picture of an insightful hero of a mythic level.

808. Strauch, Carl F. "Ishmael: Time and Personality in Moby-Dick." Studies in the Novel, 1 (1969), 468-483.

   Discusses the interfusing of personalities, archetypal relationships, and the curing of Ishmael's suicidal neurosis in Moby-Dick.

809. Sullivan, William P. "Bartleby and Infantile Autism: A Naturalistic Explanation." Bulletin of the West Virginia Association of College Teachers, 3 (1976), 43-60.

   Bartleby manifests "infantile autism in the adult phase." He "fits the pattern of a reasonably successful, coping, autistic adult, whose tragedy is that he almost succeeded in finding the structured environment and understanding personal supervisor he needed."

810. Vernon, John. "Melville's 'The Bell-Tower'." Studies in Short Fiction, 7 (1970), 264-276.

   A discussion of the bell-tower in terms of its symbolic significance to creativeness and sex. An artist is reluctant to complete his work because completion kills it. The "endless ringing of the bell in the Tower could be called a projection of Bannadonna's wish for a constant, self-enclosed orgasm."

Meredith, George

811. Baker, Robert. "Sir Willoughby Patterne's Inner Temple: Psychology and Sentimentalism in The Egoist." Texas Studies in Language and Literature, 16 (1975), 691-703.

   Argues that Meredith's work "does point toward the twentieth-century novelists' preoccupation with psychological analysis and both individual and social irrationality."

Mörike, Eduard

812. Mahlendorf, Ursula. "Mörike's <u>Mozart on the Way to Prague</u>: Stages and Outcomes of the Creative Experience." <u>American Imago</u>, 33 (1976), 304-327.

>Notes Mörike's "insights into the different motivations, stages, and results of creativity." Mörike identified with Mozart, but his story of the composer reveals his own ideas about the creative process. He describes scenes in Mozart's life which reflect different levels of creativity, "oral, phallic, oedipal, resulting in a different mode of expression (lyrical-idyllic-intimate; festive-social-humorous; tragic-elegiac-sublime)."

Morris, William

813. Reed, Michael. "Morris' 'Rapunzel' as an Oedipal Fantasy." <u>American Imago</u>, 30 (1973), 313-322.

>William Morris's "Rapunzel" is a rite of passage myth supported by a "fulfilled oedipal fantasy that allows the son to possess the mother totally and sexually."

814. Wyrick, Deborah. "The Hieros Gamos in William Morris' 'Rapunzel'." <u>Victorian Poetry</u>, 19 (1981), 367-380.

>Reference "to alchemy can help illuminate the psychological movement of 'Rapunzel' and demonstrate another instance of Morris' apparently spontaneous ability to produce archetypally symbolic images and actions."

Nodier, Charles

815. Porter, Laurence M. "The Forbidden City: A Psychoanalytical Interpretation of Nodier's <u>Smarra</u>." <u>Symposium</u>, 26 (1972), 331-348.

><u>Smarra ou les démons de la nuit; songs romantiques</u> has a dream structure that depicts the psyche which "anticipates the theories of modern psychoanalysis." The structure of <u>Smarra</u> "corresponds . . . to Jung's description of dream-plot."

Pater, Walter

816. Schroeder, Natalie. "The Oedipal Triangle in Pater's 'Hippolytus Veiled'." <u>University of Hartford Studies in Literature</u>, 14 (1982), 67-76.

>Not only did Pater, like Hippolytus, will his father's death but Pater also displayed Oedipal desires for his mother.

Poe, Edgar Allan
(See also items 599, 650.)

817. Babener, Liahna Klenman. "The Shadow's Shadow: The Motif of the Double in Edgar Allan Poe's 'The Purloined Letter'." Mystery and Detection Annual, 1 (1972), 21-32.

>Poe presents Dupin as identifying psychologically with the Minister D___. "The Prominant pattern of doubles suggests that the protagonist and his foil are moral duplicates and may ultimately be two phases of the same mind."

818. Butler, David W. "Usher's Hypochondriasis: Mental Alienation and Romantic Idealism in Poe's Gothic Tales." American Literature, 48 (1976), 1-12.

>Physicians in Poe's time saw a connection between a romantic imagination like Usher's and madness, but denied the possibility that such madness could lead to a true understanding of a higher reality. However, in "The Fall of the House of Usher" Poe indicates that the dichotomy between true creativeness and madness is not necessarily discreet. Often, in Poe's stories "the natural and the supernatural, or the scientific and the romantically idealistic, are deliberately paralleled rather than cautiously distinguished."

819. Carlson, Eric W. "'William Wilson': The Double as Primal Self." Topic: A Journal of the Liberal Arts, 16 (1976), 35-40.

>"William Wilson" is an "embodiment of the Double and the glimpsed essential Self that it symbolizes." It is a tale of "psychic conflict" detailing the deterioration of Wilson's soul as he ignores the warning of his central self. Reference is made to Jung's ideas on the "anima" and "individuation" in this regard.

820. Coskren, Robert. "'William Wilson' and the Disintegration of Self." Studies in Short Fiction, 12 (1975), 155-162.

>The psyche of human beings is split. On one hand, man wants to be pure spirit; on the other hand, he wants to be a definite individual, "a distinct being in the mass of humanity." In Poe's story, the symbol of this split psyche is the wall, suggesting "both restriction and defense." Wilson's psyche disintegrates because of the "opposition of contrary wills."

821. Felman, Shoshana. "On Reading Poetry: Reflections on the Limits and Possibilities of Psychoanalytical Approaches." In Smith, J.H., ed., The Literary Freud. New Haven: Yale University Press, 1980, 119-148.

>Argues that "the critical contradictions to which Poe's poetry has given rise are themselves indirectly significant of the nature of poetry." Argues that Poe's text is subject to psychoanalytic study because "of its strong 'effects,' of the reading-acts that it provokes. . . . " Surveys Krutch's, Bonaparte's and Lacan's psychoanalytic approaches to Poe.

822. Fraiberg, Louis. "Poe's Intimations of Mortality." Hartford Studies in Literature, 5 (1973), 106-125.

   Examines "the manifestations of psychic conflict in Poe's writings," his "love and fear of death," and "his infatuation with and horror of suicide." Poe's biography and writing demonstrate that he "suffered from a conflict between his unconscious wish to join his mother in death and his fear of dying."

823. Girgus, Sam B. The Law of the Heart: Individualism and the Modern Self in American Literature. Austin: University of Texas Press, 1979.

   Pages 24-36 provide an extended discussion comparing R.D. Laing and Poe.

824. _____. "Poe and R.D. Laing: The Transcendent Self." Studies in Short Fiction, 13 (1976), 299-309.

   The use of Laing's existential psychology gives insight into Poe's characters' "divided, disembodied and false selves." Poe anticipates the Laingian view that schizophrenia is the means of attaining a transcendent self to escape an insane society.

825. Halliburton, David. Edgar Allan Poe: A Phenomenological View. Princeton: Princeton University Press, 1973.

   Follows the phenomenological work of Brodtkorp and J. Hillis Miller in order to present a phenomenological view of Poe. The literary interpreter does not seek the intentions of the author but of signifying intentions within the text. The literary interpreter identifies with these signifying intentions in order to "determine 'where it goes'--to ascertain . . . its aim and final purpose."

826. Holland, Norman. "Re-covering 'The Purloined Letter'." In Suleiman, S., and Grosman, I., eds., The Reader in the Text: Essays on Audience and Interpretation. Princeton: Princeton University Press, 1980, 350-370.

   A reading of Poe's story by means of "transactive criticism, a criticism in which the critic works explicitly from his transaction to the text." Seeks to open up criticism by exploring the fact that every reader reads the same text differently, and thus, in a sense, the text is not really the same text for each reader.

827. Johnson, Barbara. "The Frame of Reference: Poe, Lacan, Derrida." Yale French Studies, 55-56 (1977), 457-505.

   Proceeds to discover a "stable sequence" in the acts of analysis present in Poe's "The Purloined Letter," Lacan's "Seminar on 'The Purloined Letter'," and Derrida's "The Purveyor of Truth."

828. Lacan, Jacques. "Seminar on The Purloined Letter." Yale French Studies, 48 (1972), 38-72.

   Attempts to illustrate "that is is the symbolic order which is constitutive for the subject--by demonstrating in a story the decisive orientation which the subject receives from the itinerary of a signifier."

138 Psychocriticism

829. Ligocki, Llewellyn. "Poe and Psychoanalytic Criticism." Poe Studies, 4, 2 (1971), 54-55.

   A review of Arthur Lerner's Psychoanalytically Oriented Criticism of Three American Poets: Poe, Whitman, and Aiken. The book "has no consistent point" and is superficial. The inability to produce "a total assessment of the value of psychoanalytic criticism of poetry in general . . . is the most significant failing in the book."

830. Martindale, Colin. "Archetype and Reality in 'The Fall of the House of Usher'." Poe Studies, 5 (1972), 9-11.

   The story is a tale of an "attempt to escape from a regressive state of consciousness." However, for Usher, the attempt ultimately fails, and "the tale ends with the catastrophic breakdown of his repressions and the overwhelming of the ego by the unconscious."

831. Mollinger, Robert N. "Edgar Allan Poe's 'The Oval Portrait': Fusion of Multiple Identities." American Imago, 36 (1979), 147-153.

   Poe's story suggests that "the universe consists of infinite, individualized variations of an original primordial particle which both encompasses the variations and is contained in them." This, however, conflicts with Poe as an artist who wished "to impose on the world an individual version of reality."

832. Reeder, Roberta. "'The Black Cat' As a Study in Repression." Poe Studies, 7 (1974), 20-22.

   The narrator of "The Black Cat" is trying to destroy his anima, as symbolized by his wife and cat. However, he destroys himself, showing how his negative feelings towards his anima, his instincts, are nonproductive and a denial of creativeness.

833. Schwaber, Paul. "On Reading Poe." Literature and Psychology, 21, 2 (1971), 81-99.

   "The Fall of the House of Usher" illustrates the struggle between reason and logic, which leads to a feeling of horror. "Horror rationally ordered and mundanely experienced forms the staple of Poe's fiction."

834. Smith, Allan. "The Psychological Context of Three Tales by Poe." Journal of American Studies, 7 (1973), 279-292.

   A study of "The Black Cat," "Berenice," and "The Murders in the Rue Morgue."

835. St. Armand, Barton Levi. "The Dragon and Uroboros: Themes of Metamorphosis in Arthur Gordon Pym." American Transcendental Quarterly, 37 (1978), 58-71.

   Uses two "alchemical symbols, the Dragon and the Uroboros, as a means of exploring imagistic clusters that appear to define two opposite poles of archetypal metamorphosis" in Poe's Narrative of Arthur Gordon Pym. "The metamorphosis . . . is of two kinds: sacred and profane, general and particular, cosmic and quotidian, sublime and grotesque, Uroboric and Draconic."

836. Sullivan, Ruth. "William Wilson's Double." Studies in Romanticism, 15 (1976), 253-263.

"William Wilson's superego tells the story of William Wilson's id. More precisely, part of his ego dominated by the superego tells the story of the part of the ego dominated by the id."

837. Thompson, G.R. "The Face in the Pool: Reflections on the Doppelgänger Motif in 'The Fall of the House of Usher'." Poe Studies, 5 (1972), 16-21.

A study of the growing subjectivity of the narrator in Poe's story. Because of this subjectivity, as the tale develops, the reader becomes increasingly unsure as to what actually has happened. "Usher" is an example of Poe's idea that the mind can never know anything for sure.

838. _____. "'Proper Evidences of Madness': American Gothic and Interpretation of 'Ligeia'." Emerson Society Quarterly, 66 (1972), 30-49.

American gothic fiction illustrates "ambiguously explained" supernatural events. Thus the mind is portrayed as never knowing for sure that anything has definitely happened. Consequently, "the narrator is a totally unreliable reporter of events" in "Ligeia."

Pushkin, Aleksandr Sergeyevich

839. Katz, Michael. "Dreams in Pushkin." In Riasanovsky, N.V., Struve, G., and Eekman, T., eds., California Slavic Studies, vol. XI. Berkeley: University of California Press, 1980, 71-103.

"For Pushkin the dream . . . contains the truth, inasmuch as it shows the dangers inherent in pursuing one's dreams. . . . "

840. Schwartz, Murray M., and Schwartz, Albert. "The Queen of Spades: A Psychoanalytic Interpretation." Texas Studies in Literature and Language, 17 (1975), 275-288.

A Freudian discussion of the dream logic of the language and imagery in Pushkin's book. "We find the psychological unity of The Queen of Spades in the breakdown of obsessional defenses against a megalomaniacal wish to possess a child's imagination of parental powers."

Rimbaud, Arthur

841. Chaitin, Gilbert D. "Psychoanalysis and Literary Interpretation." Literature and Psychology, 27, 4 (1977), 174-182.

Considers a set of competing interpretations of Rimbaud's "Vowels" in order to "isolate the trends underlying all of them." "Then I will attempt to show how the same procedures and standards can be applied in the specific area of psychoanalytic criticism."

Rossetti, Christina Georgina

842. Golub, Ellen. "Untying Goblin Apron Strings: A Psychoanalytic Reading of 'Goblin Market'." <u>Literature and Psychology</u>, 25 (1975), 158-165.

"Goblin Market" is seen as "a portrayal of the conflict between regressive oral sadism and the reality-testing anal stage that battles for prominence in normal development." Temptation as the fruit of the Goblins produces split ego.

Rossetti, Dante Gabriel

843. Warner, Janet. "D.G. Rossetti: Love, Death and Art." <u>Hartford Studies in Literature</u>, 4 (1972), 228-240.

"An attempt will be made here to indicate how Rossetti tries to synthesize the conflicting elements in his work, and make an aesthetic experience of them."

Ruskin, John

844. Joseph, Robert J. "John Ruskin: Radical and Psychotic Genius." <u>Psychoanalytic Review</u>, 56 (1969), 425-441.

Argues that Ruskin's life and work can be described as severely sadomasochistic, and that introjection, incorporation, projection, reaction formation and denial are prominently displayed in his writing.

Scott, Walter

845. Meisel, Martin. "<u>Waverly</u>, Freud, and Topographical Metaphor." <u>University of Toronto Quarterly</u>, 48 (1979), 226-244.

Argues that Walter Scott "opened the century from which Marx and Freud emerged . . . " by uniting the interiorities of character with the externalities of society.

Senancour, Etienne

846. Evans, Martha. "Dream Sequences in Senancour's <u>Oberman</u>." <u>Symposium</u>, 32 (Spring 1978), 1-14.

This novel is "vivified by the secret sense of primordial desire and danger that floats behind its austere surface. . . . "

Shelley, Mary Wollstonecraft

847. Hill, J.M. "Frankenstein and the Physiognomy of Desire." *American Imago*, 32 (1975), 335-358.

> Argues that the central theme of *Frankenstein* is promethean sin. "The dominant incestuous root for Promethean sin seems to take hold in uncompromising psychic wishes for exclusive love, and in possession of the mother--the source of first love."

848. Hirsch, Gordon D. "The Monster Was a Lady: On the Psychology of Mary Shelley's *Frankenstein*." *Hartford Studies in Literature*, 7 (1975), 116-153.

> When Victor Frankenstein's "feelings and behavior are scrutinized more closely from a psychoanalytic perspective, they tend to reveal important similarities with the emotions and strivings of the author as expressed in her introduction, and they conform to characteristic patterns which Freudian psychoanalysis attributes especially to the psychology of women."

849. Joseph, Gerhard. "Frankenstein's Dream: The Child as Father of the Monster." *Hartford Studies in Literature*, 7 (1975), 97-115.

> "Frankenstein's Prometheanism may be interpreted as the frenzy of the aspiring soul to rid itself of the debilitating encumbrances of the flesh through the twin strategies of spiritualized affection and scientific experiment."

850. Rubenstein, Mark A. "'My Accursed Origin': The Search for the Mother in *Frankenstein*." *Studies in Romanticism*, 15 (Spring 1976), 165-194.

> Freud's view regarding the "architecture" of fantasies derived from childhood primal scene memories and "its relationship to the reworking of personal myth is particularly useful in considering Mary Shelley and what she did with the impressions she had of her dead mother as they evolved over the years of her youth."

851. Sherwin, Paul. "*Frankenstein*: Creation as Catastrophe." *PMLA*, 96 (1981), 883-903.

> A reading of the Oedipal drama of the novel in the hope of "a recentering of the novel's unresolved intellectual and emotional turmoil."

852. Spector, Judith. "Science Fiction and the Sex War: A Womb of One's Own." *Literature and Psychology*, 31 (1981), 21-32.

> "Theoretically, it would be as unsuitable for a man to create a 'baby,' as it would be for a woman to create a work of art. Hence, Victor Frankenstein produces a 'monster'."

Shelley, Percy Bysshe

853. Waldoff, Leon. "The Father-Son Conflict in Prometheus Unbound: The Psychology of a Vision." Psychoanalytic Review, 62 (1975), 79-96.

    A psychoanalytic reading of Shelley's work, focusing on the conflict between Prometheus and Jupiter, and coming to the conclusion that the poet's hope of utopia is psychologically valid.

Shevchenko, Taras

854. Holovinsky, Ivan Z. "Psychological Interpretation of Profound Emotions in Selected Writings of Taras Shevchenko." The Ukranian Review, 23, 3 (1976), 30-38.

    The psychological content of Shevchenko's poems falls into three areas: 1) "mother-child dynamics," 2) "psycho-sexual conflicts," and 3) "personal tragedies within the framework of political conflicts."

Stendhal

855. Chaitin, Gilbert D. The Unhappy Few: The Psychological Novels of Stendahl. Bloomington: Indiana University Press, 1972.

    Argues that the psychic content of Stendhal's novels remains the same and that they depict the rich emotional life of Stendhal.

856. Ragland-Sullivan, Ellie. "Julien's Quest for 'Self': Qui Suis-je?" Nineteenth Century French Studies, 8 (1979-80), 1-13.

    Applies basic Lacanian notions to Julien in order to show "that the ending evolves naturally, not from Julien's duality, but from his misconceptions and illusions in regard to . . . his 'self'."

857. Yalom, Marilyn K. "Triangles and Prisons: A Psychological Study of Stendhalian Love." Hartford Studies in Literature, 8 (1976), 82-97.

    The prison of love is an apt metaphor for the man whose passion is "embedded within a compulsion to steal from and aggress against another male. . . ."

Stifter, Adalbert

858. Sjögren, Christine. "Klotilde's Journey into the Depths: A Probe into a Psychological Landscape in Stifter's Der Nachsommer." Germanic Notes, 2 (1971), 50-52.

    A discussion of Klotilde's erotic attachment to her brother, Heinrich. Klotilde's love is not pathological, "but only a misdirected expression of her awakening erotic impulses, which are not permitted to seek other objects in a wider arena." Klotilde's mountain journey is "psychoanalytical therapy" which leads her to understand her libido and her growing maturity.

Stoker, Bram

859. Bentley, C.F. "The Monster in the Bedroom: Sexual Symbolism in Bram Stoker's Dracula." Literature and Psychology, 22, 1 (1972), 27-34.

Although the sexual elements of normal human sexual relationships are repressed on a conscious level, they appear "in a covert and perverted form through" the apparatus of the vampire superstition.

860. Bierman, Joseph S. "Dracula: Prolonged Childhood Illness, and the Oral Triad." American Imago, 29 (1972), 186-198.

The oral triad refers to the wish to eat, be eaten and sleep.

861. Demetrakopoulos, Stephanie. "Feminism, Sex Role Exchanges, and Other Subliminal Fantasies in Bram Stoker's Dracula." Frontiers: Journal of Women Studies, 2 (1977), 104-113.

Discusses Dracula in terms of popular art, or, "collective dreaming." It reflects "our wish to allow our most deeply repressed psychic and societal desires to surface in fantasy form." Specifically, although Mina is a "liberated" woman, she is sexually repressed.

862. Henderson, D. James. "Exorcism, Possession and the Dracula Cult: A Synopsis of Object-Relations Psychology." Bulletin of the Menninger Clinic, 40 (1976), 603-628.

"By examining the popular Dracula mythology, I shall try to synthesize a fuller understanding of human psychology." Includes a psychobiography of Bram Stoker.

863. Roth, Phyllis A. "Suddenly Sexual Women in Bram Stoker's Dracula." Literature and Psychology, 27 (1977), 113-121.

The fantasies in Dracula have a pre-oedipal focus, "specifically the child's relation with and hostility toward the mother." These fantasies "are managed in such a way as to transform horror into pleasure." The book also illustrates "hostility toward female sexuality."

Strindberg, August

864. Anderson, E.W. "Strindberg's Illness." Psychological Medicine, 1 (1971), 104-117.

A psychological discussion of Strindberg's life and mental sickness, drawing upon his family life and opinions of psychiatrists. His psychic life was very complex, with elements of schizophrenia.

865. Burnham, Donald L. "Restitutional Functions of Symbol and Myth in Strindberg's Inferno." The Sixteenth Annual Frieda Fromm-Reichman Memorial Lecture. Psychiatry, 36 (1973), 229-243.

   Strindberg's uses of myth and symbols enabled him to bring order to his experience and to deal with his serious mental problems.

866. _____. "Strindberg's Inferno and Sullivan's 'Extravasation of Meaning'." Contemporary Psychoanalysis, 9 (1973), 190-208.

   A biographical discussion of Strindberg's mental problems in terms of his "extravasation of meaning," a schizophrenic characteristic. Strindberg called his near schizophrenia his "Inferno," in which he wavered back and forth from a desire for dependency to a desire for self-sufficiency.

Swinburne, Algernon Charles

867. Levin, Gerald. "Swinburne's 'End of the World' Fantasy." Literature and Psychology, 24, 3 (1974), 109-114.

   Swinburne's "The Triumph of Time" is a barely transformed fantasy which is "delusional" in structure, making use of a recurring "end of the world" fantasy which Freud encountered in paranoics.

868. Ober, William B. "Swinburne's Masochism: Neuropathology and Psychopathology." Bulletin of the Menninger Clinic, 39 (1975), 501-555.

   "In this essay my intent is to demonstrate that Swinburne's psychopathology had its root in neuropathology. . . . "

869. Wilson, F.A.C. "Swinburne's 'Dearest Cousin': The Character of Mary Gordon." Literature and Psychology, 19, 2 (1969), 89-99.

   Swinburne hoped to progress beyond flagellation to a fuller sexual life through his love for his cousin Mary. She, however, was also a masochist.

Tennyson, Alfred

870. Joseph, Gerhard. "Tennyson's Three Women: The Thought Within the Image." Victorian Poetry, 19 (1981), 1-18.

   Concentrates on the "major poems that have alluded to a triadic view of woman," employing a Jungian conception of woman to gloss The Princess and a Freudian one to gloss the Idylls.

Thackeray, William Makepeace

871. Paris, Bernard J. "The Psychic Structure of Vanity Fair." Victorian Studies, 10 (1967), 389-410.

Attempts a thematic analysis of the novel which proves unsatisfactory and then turns to Karen Horney's theories in order to grasp the psychich structure of the novel. Concludes that the novel fails to depict the nature and condition of man since Thackeray fails to go beyond neurotic values, solutions and characters.

Thoreau, Henry David

872. Bigelow, Gordon E. "Thoreau's Melting Snowbank: Birth of a Symbol." International Journal of Symbology 2, 3 (1971), 7-13.

An analysis of how the mind creates symbols, using an excerpt from Walden. In his imaginative development of symbols, Thoreau parallels "the organicism of Goethe and Coleridge, the occultism of the French Symbolists, and the idea of imagination later exploited by Wallace Stevens."

873. Dillman, Richard H. "The Psychological Rhetoric of Walden." ESQ, 25 (1979), 79-91

Demonstrates how the writing in Walden is in the tradition of psychological rhetoric whose "practitioners attempted to analyze an audience's reactions to discourse strategies by applying a theory of mental psychology from David Hume's notion of the lively idea and from associationist philosophers Thomas Reid and Dugald Stewart."

874. Jacobs, Edward C. "Thoreau and Modern Psychology." Thoreau Society Bulletin, 127 (1974), 4-5.

"The Pond in Winter" section of Walden anticipates Carl Jung. "For Thoreau the conscious mind develops as it separates itself from the unconscious mind." This suggests Jung's idea that the conscious mind must become independent of the unconscious mind, or "individuation." Thoreau uses various images of weather, water, and the shore to symbolize consciousness and unconsciousness.

875. Lebeaux, Richard. "'Sugar Maple Man': Middle-Aged Thoreau's Generativity Crisis." Studies in American Renaissance, (1981), 359-377.

Employs Erik Erikson's "generativity vs. stagnation" view of middle age to Thoreau's own mid-life crisis.

Tieck, Ludwig

876. Rippere, Victoria. "Ludwig Tieck's Der blonde Eckbert: A Psychological Reading." PMLA, 85 (1970), 473-486.

"My interpretation is basically typological-psychological, that is, concerned with establishing the patterns of human behavior that underlie the characters' actions, the areas of human experience to which these patterns refer, and the manner of their relevance."

877. Sellner, Timothy. "Jungian Psychology and the Romantic Fairytale: A New Look at Tieck's Der blonde Eckbert." Germanic Review, 55 (1980), 89-97.

   A thoroughgoing application of Jungian views to this fairytale. Sellner points out the inadequacies of all previous readings.

Tolstoy, Leo

878. Bartell, James. "The Trauma of Birth in The Death of Ivan Ilych." Psychocultural Review, 2 (1978), 97-117.

   Argues that this novella is powerful because "it is structured by the most fundamental fact of life, our birth, and the insistent need to reexperience this crucial event." Ilych's resurrection is one which transcends age and culture and thus the reader intuitively identifies with it.

879. Johnson, Doris V. "The Autobiographical Heroine in Anna Karenina." Hartford Studies in Literature, 11 (1979), 111-122.

   Notes the similarities of Levin to the female characters in Anna Karenina and speculates if "much of Tolstoy's ambivalence toward women could not be explained by an unresolved conflict between the masculine and feminine sides of his nature."

880. Lee, C. Nicholas. "Dreams and Daydreams in the Early Fiction of L.N. Tolstoj." In Terras, V., ed., American Contributions to the 7th International Congress of Slavists. Vol. 2. Literature and Folklore. The Hague: Mouton, 1973, 373-392.

   Traces Tolstoy's interest in dreams in his early fiction and diaries. He was fascinated with dreams as a source for his literature. "Psychology and physiology came to the fore in Tolstoj's dream sequences precisely for motivational purposes, in the sense that they provide the pretext as well as the medium for presenting conditions of incomplete consciousness."

Trollope, Anthony

881. Corsa, Helen S. "'The Cross-Grainedness of Men': The Rev. Josiah Crawley--Trollope's Study of a Paranoid Personality." Hartford Studies in Literature, 5 (1973), 160-172.

   Trollope does not present any reasons for Crawley's character nor does he cure him or change him. Trollope's gift is an accurate portrayal, in having a good ear for the resonances of character. In the portrait of Josiah Crawley, Trollope "created with notable accuracy and compassion one of fiction's most interesting paranoid personalities."

Whitman, Walt

882. Abrams, Robert E. "The Function of Dreams and Dream-Logic in Whitman's Poetry." *Texas Studies in Literature and Language*, 17 (1975), 599-616.

Whitman's early and continuing interest in dreams and his use of dream imagery as a way of providing insight into the unconscious anticipate twentieth century art and psychology.

883. Black, Stephen A. "Journeys into Chaos: A Psychoanalytic Study of Whitman, His Literary Processes, and His Poems." *Literature and Psychology*, 24, 2 (1974), 47-57.

Traces Whitman's emotional development through the stages of his writing. His poems illustrate his neuroses, depression, and anxiety.

884. _____. "Whitman and Psychoanalytic Criticism: A Response to Arthur Golden." *Literature and Psychology*, 20 (1970), 79-81.

Disagrees with Golden. Whitman is analyzing himself through autobiography. This self-analysis leads to "regressive imagery, fantasy, and the reactivation of infantile longings." Rather than seeing Freudian narcissism in Whitman, it may be more useful to see Marcusean narcissism, which, paradoxically, leads to a "oneness with the universe" and a "new depth of conception."

885. _____. *Whitman's Journey into Chaos: A Psychoanalytic Study of the Poetic Process*. Princeton: Princeton University Press, 1975.

Studies Whitman's "poetic processes as they developed between 1855-1865." The "chaos . . . existed in Whitman's unconscious, where his fantasies and poetic impulses originated; the journeys into this chaos are his poems." Contains a Whitman "Chronology" from 1819 to 1892.

886. Cook, Harry James. "The Individuation of a Poet: The Process of Becoming in Whitman's 'The Sleepers'." *Walt Whitman Review*, 21 (1975), 101-110.

A Jungian study focusing on the primary symbols of darkness, soul, unity, mother, and sea in "The Sleepers." Traces the "implied cyclical process: implied innocence or oneness, psychic fragmentation or incompleteness, despair, and then a unifying process in the last section."

887. Doherty, Joseph F. "Whitman's 'Poem of the Mind'." *Semiotica*, 14 (1975), 345-363.

A linguistic analysis of "There Was a Child Went Forth," detailing the child's "evolution of consciousness" as he grows up. Draws upon the linguistic theories of Roman Jakobson.

888. Fein, Richard J. "Whitman and the Emancipated Self." *Centennial Review*, 20 (1976), 36-49.

Whitman expressed an ego that was "able to set its own goals," and that ego is "the justification of life." Uses sociologist Georg Simmel's ideas to give insights into Whitman: "Simmel goes to the heart of the matter in describing the potent tension of the self as we find it in Whitman's poetry." Notes the paradox of seeking the self while at the same time having a self.

889. Kramer, Maruice. "Whitman's Journeys into Chaos." Literature and Psychology, 26 (1976), 124-130.

A review of Stephen A. Black's book on Whitman (item 885). The work is flawed because Black assumes that Whitman's writing was like talking to an analyst. Furthermore, he does not pay enough attention to Whitman's consciousness and tends to ignore Whitman's ego.

890. Miller, Tracey R. "The Boy, the Bird and the Sea: An Archetypal Reading of 'Out of the Cradle'." Walt Whitman Review, 19 (1973), 93-103.

After a review of the criticism on Whitman's poem, it is studied "as a vehicle for the re-presentation of the unconscious, collective racial experience." The narrative of the poem is cyclical, and at the end the boy is reconciled "with the Eternal Mother."

891. Rusch, Frederik L. "Of Eidólons and Orgone." Walt Whitman Review, 13 (1967), 11-15.

A discussion of Walt Whitman and Wilhelm Reich, showing parallels to each other in their lives and thought.

Wilde, Oscar

892. Green, Bernard. "The Effects of Distortion on the Self: A Study of the Picture of Dorian Gray." In The Annual of Psychoanalysis, Vol. III/1979. New York: IUP, 1980.

Hopes to demonstrate "that the novel is a remarkably astute description of the consequences of representational distortion. . . . I shall show that the novel illustrates the way in which a person accepts as his own representations the distorted representations of himself by others, and then subsequently struggles to rid himself of the effects of these distorted perceptions."

Wordsworth, William
(See also item 459.)

893. Beauchamp, Gorman. "Wordsworth's Archetypal Resolution." Concerning Poetry, 7 (1974), 13-19.

Jung's archetype of the Wise Old Man is an illuminative paradigm in an interpretation of Wordsworth's "Resolution and Independence." "The poet--at least in this poem--attains the psychic unity of his symbol."

894. Beyette, Kent. "Wordsworth's Medical Muse: Erasmus Darwin and Psychology in 'Strange Fits of Passion I Have Known'." Literature and Psychology, 23, 3 (1973), 93-101.

> Wordsworth displayed a clinical interest in psychogenic disturbances based on his knowledge of Erasmus Darwin's Zoonomia, or The Laws of Organic Life.

895. Griska, Joseph M. "Wordsworth's Mood Disturbance: A Psychoanalytic Approach to Three Poems." Literature and Psychology, 24, 4 (1974), 144-152.

> Argues that Wordsworth was a neurotic depressive whose moods had probable causes which were observable in the tensions in his poetry.

896. Hartman, Geoffrey. "Diction and Defense in Wordsworth." In Smith, J.H., ed., The Literary Freud. New Haven: Yale University Press, 1980, 205-215.

> Focuses on Wordsworth's 1816 poem beginning with the quotation "A little onward lend thy guiding hand / To these dark steps, a little further on!" and considers the intricate connections between this quotation and an "inner voice." "Poetry . . . is the working-through of such 'voices,' which are often projected as coming from the outside, or attributed to supernatural agency."

897. Mazzeno, Laurence. "Of Fathers, Children, and Poets: Wordsworth's 'Anecdote For Father'." Psychocultural Review, 1 (1977), 421-433.

> Reviews the personality of the young Wordsworth in order to comment on Wordsworth's revisions of his poem "Anecdote For Father," changes which "show the poet moving away from poetry as dramatic projection of his own subconscious dilemmas toward poetry as dramatic expression of the problems of the artistic consciousness reacting with the natural world."

898. Waldoff, Leon. "Wordsworth's Healing Power: Basic Trust in 'Tintern Abbey'." Hartford Studies in Literature, 4 (1972), 147-166.

> In "Tintern Abbey" Wordsworth "defines the essential task of the Romantic and modern poet, which is to create through his imagination and vision a new basis for metaphysical trust."

Zola, Emile

899. Chaitin, Gilbert. "The Voices of the Dead: Love, Death and Politics in Zola's Fortune des Rougon," (parts I and II). Literature and Psychology, 26 (1976), 131-144; 148-158.

> The theme of death unifies the novel and gives it both social and personal meaning. Socially, death represents the past and the old social/power structure; personally, it represents parents and the primal scene.

Twentieth-Century Literature

General Studies

900. Carruth, Hayden. "The Act of Love: Poetry and Personality." Sewanee Review, 84 (1976), 305-313.

   Sees the modern reaction to New Criticism as moving from a responsibility to life as well as art to an "existentialist ethic" leading to solipsism. This produces an "autonomy of isolation" and a poetry of words and images that are so private it cannot be understood. The poet must regain his objectivity and his links with the community.

901. Feder, Lilliam. "Myth as Self-Revealing Instrument." Books Abroad, 48 (1974), 7-14.

   A discussion of contemporary playwrights and poets in terms of myth. Greek myth "is a narrative and dramatic expression of the inner fears, drives and conflicts that determine the course of human life." Furthermore, contemporary writers have recreated the essential aspects of myth which unites twentieth century man with his ancient past.

902. Grosholz, Emily. "The Interpretation of Dream-Poems: Freud, Surrealism and Contemporary American Freud." New England Review, 4 (1981), 292-310.

   Utilizes Freud's explanation as to why a dream-text cannot be viewed as a poem in order to criticize contemporary neo-surrealist poetry and to achieve a better understanding of the relationship between dream and poetry.

903. Heller, Erich. "Observations on Psychoanalysis and Modern Literature." Salmagundi, 31-32 (1975), 17-28.

   Points out that psychoanalysis is our own age's systematic consciousness of its own character and soul, and that literature is "the esthetic form assumed by the self-awareness of an age." They are thus closely linked. Argues that psychoanalysis would not exist if modern man had not lost all certain beliefs concerning the nature of human being.

904. _____. "Observations on Psychoanalysis and Modern Literature." In Smith, J.H., ed., Psychiatry and the Humanities, vol. 1. New Haven: Yale University Press, 1976, 35-50.

See item 903.

905. Hendin, Josephine. "Vulnerable Men, Invulnerable Women: Excerpt from Vulnerable People: A View of American Fiction Since 1945." Psychology Today, 12 (1978), 21-23.

A discussion of the changing roles of men and women in modern American fiction. "Our fictional heroes seem to save their lives by giving up their masculinity, by playing the roles once assigned to women." However, "the new hero is not achieving the strengths of women but merely parodying 'female faults'." Works of Bellow, Updike, Mailer, Philip Roth, and Pynchon are discussed.

906. Irvine, Lorna. "A Psychological Journey: Mothers and Daughters in English-Canadian Fiction." In Davidson, C.N. and Broner, E.M., eds., The Lost Tradition: Mothers and Daughters in Literature. New York: Unger, 1980, 242-252.

A study of the mother-daughter relationships depicted in modern English-Canadian fiction by women. "The psychological journey that appears in so much of this fiction reveals the ambivalence that characterizes the daughter's feelings about her mother." Uniquely Canadian characteristics of the daughters' struggles for autonomy are noted. Works by Margaret Atwood, Sylvia Fraser, Margaret Laurence, and Alice Munro, among others, are studied.

907. May, Keith M. Out of the Maelstrom: Psychology and the Novel in the Twentieth Century. New York: St. Martins, 1977.

A survey of psychological approaches to the novel from Freud to the existentialists. The individual separated from his or her world is the "maelstrom" which existentialists can overcome through their notion of "being-in-the-world." Psychology has also moved from a fractured view of conscious and unconscious mind to a Sartrean refutation of the unconscious. Contemporary fiction does not, however, display a unified view of man and world but is itself fractured into a journalistic-realism and imaginative fantasies.

908. Mazlish, Bruce. "Autobiography and Psycho-analysis." Encounter, 35 (October, 1970), 28-37.

Traces the influence of psychoanalysis on autobiography, and studies the autobiographies of Freud and Ernest Jones. Notes also the importance of the theories of psychic development of Freud and Erikson. Because of psychoanalysis, the core of autobiography has become "the interplay of the truth of fact and feeling, of the actual and psychic reality." Concludes with four points: 1) Autobiography before and after Freud has always been "a consciously shaped literary production;

2) psychoanalysis may hamper the writing of autobiography; 3) psychoanalysis does, however, give a new vocabulary to the genre; 4) "the most meaninfgul impact of psycho-analysis on autobiography is probably in terms of the reader, not the writer."

909. Sellery, J'nan Morse. "The Inner Landscapes of Contemporary Fiction." Psychological Perspectives, 13 (1982), 167-189.

"Contemporary fiction includes heroines or heroes who find growth through projecting on material objects or parts of nature. Prose narratives enable imaginatively oriented readers to suspend the notion that landscapes are only in the outer world and to discover through fantasy experiences, through the incapes of the mind, the psychic realities of love, health, and personal transformation."

910. Sobel, Dava. "Schizophrenia in Popular Books: A Study Finds Too Much Hope." The New York Times, (2/17/81), C1-C2.

Warns of the dangers of a facile diagnosis of schizophrenia in some popular writing. Such diagnoses cause grave misunderstanding of a serious disease. Discusses, among others, Hannah Green's I Never Promised You a Rose Garden and Mark Vonnegut's The Eden Express. Cites the clinical research of Remi Cadoret and Carol North.

911. Stein, Karen F. "Reflections in a Jagged Mirror: Some Metaphors of Madness." Aphra, 6 (1975), 2-11.

"Mad" women in contemporary fiction function "to question and to challenge societal norms and sex roles." Often the mirror is a recurring symbol for these women. Deals with the symbolic aspects of the mirror and its relationship to madness in Plath's The Bell Jar, Charlotte Perkins Gilman's "The Yellow Wallpaper," Lessing's The Summer Before the Dark and The Four-Gated City, and Margaret Atwood's Surfacing.

912. Vernon, John. The Garden and the Map: Schizophrenia in Twentieth Century Literature and Culture. Urbana: University of Illinois Press, 1973.

The "map" is schizophrenic structure, a structure where experience is separate and discrete and often in opposition each to each. The "garden" is the opposite of the map; it represents the accessibility of all experience, the conjoining of each to each and the reconciliation of opposites. Vernon uses a phenomenological method based on Husserl, Heidegger, Merleau-Ponty, Sartre, Minkowski, Straus, Binswanger. Mentions Blake's effect on psychology.

913. Woolf, Michael P. "The Madman As Hero in Contemporary American Fiction." Journal of American Studies, 10 (1976), 257-269.

The modern writer has two choices: he can create anti-heroes, or he can create heroes who "refuse to behave in fashions that are appropriate, who are profound non-realists defying the recognized limits of the possible." Works by Joseph Heller, Philip Roth, Norman Mailer, and Ken Kesey, among others, are examined. "The central characteristic of the mad hero is . . . a refusal to accept the immoral anti-humanistic structure of the imagined reality."

Aiken, Conrad

914. Kloss, Robert. "The Secret of Aiken's Snow." <u>Hartford Studies in Literature</u>, 12 (1980), 29-38.

    A discussion of the sexual imagery in "Silent Snow, Secret Snow." Paul's secret is his sexual urges and masturbation.

915. Slap, Laura R. "Conrad Aiken's 'Silent Snow, Secret Snow': Defenses Against the Primal Scene." <u>American Imago</u>, 37 (1980), 1-11.

    A psychoanalytic study demonstrating the reasons for Paul's psychotic breakdown. Paul is reacting to his awareness of the sexual activity of his parents. "He responds in a variety of ways: humiliation, rage at his mother for her betrayal, grandiose fantasies of successful competition with his father, ideas of vengeance, and extreme withdrawal." Parallels to the story of Oedipus are noted.

916. Spivey, Ted R. "Archetypal Symbols in the Major Poetry of T.S. Eliot and Conrad Aiken." <u>International Journal of Symbology</u>, 2, 3 (1971), 16-26.

    An analysis in terms of "the archetypes of Jung's depth psychology." While different in many ways, Eliot and Aiken can be brought together because of their use of similar patterns of archetypes. Parallel mythic patterns are traced in Eliot's <u>Four Quartets</u> and Aiken's <u>Preludes</u> and <u>Ushant</u>. "Both poets . . . employ archetypal images of the shadow, the wise old man, and the self or cosmic man."

917. _____. "Conrad Aiken's Fusion of Freud and Jung." <u>Studies in the Literary Imagination</u>, 13 (1980), 99-112.

    The journeys of Jung and Aiken "were similar because they were based on a similar vision." Argues that Aiken expressed an overt debt to Freud because he felt Freud's pragmaticism and his analytical bent were more amenable to the American mentality than Jung's European-based erudition and poeticism.

918. Waterman, Arthur. "The Evolution of Consciousness: Conrad Aiken's Novels and <u>Ushant</u>." <u>Critique: Studies in Modern Fiction</u>, 15 (1973), 67-81.

    Aiken saw the "evolution of consciousness" as necessary for the resolution of conflict between psychological drives and outer reality. Aiken's characters employ Freudian "dream-confessions" as a means of moving from mental chaos to love and reconciliation to reality. His autobiography, <u>Ushant</u>, deals more explicitly with these themes.

Albee, Edward

919. Anderson, Mary Castiglie. "Staging the Unconscious: Edward Albee's <u>Tiny Alice</u>." <u>Renascence</u>, 32 (1980), 178-192.

A largely Jungian study of Julian: "His conscious spirituality has been based all along on a subconscious carnality." The play reveals his psyche "from the exposure of his repressed sexuality to the disclosure of the Oedipal drive and the father-son conflict."

920. Avery, Nicholas C. "The Exorcism of a Tabooed Wish: An Analysis of Who's Afraid of Virginia Woolf?" Seminars in Psychiatry, 5 (1973), 347-357.

A discussion of past traumas, present guilt, and a fantasized son in the marriage of George and Martha, "a sadomasochistic relationship in which the partners are compelled to hurt one another to feel safe." However, George and Martha are heroic in their suffering and perseverance.

921. Blum, H.P. "A Psychoanalytic View of Who's Afraid of Virginia Woolf?" Journal of the American Psychoanalytic Association, 17 (1969), 888-903.

A discussion of the fantasy of adoption as a unifying element in the play.

922. Dollard, John. "The Hidden Meaning of Who's Afraid of Virginia Woolf?" Connecticut Review, 7 (1973), 24-48

In Who's Afraid of Virginia Woolf?, Albee is "a genius in the use of deep psychological motives." Despite the mutual hostility between George and Martha, George wishes to protect Martha. First, he tries to protect her by preventing her from proclaiming she has a child (her fantasy). Such a proclamation would deem her insane and isolate her from the community. Later, George helps her purge herself of her fantasy.

923. Glenn, Jules. "The Adoption Theme in Edward Albee's Tiny Alice and The American Dream." The Psychoanalytic Study of the Child, vol. 29. New Haven: Yale University Press, 1974, 413-429.

Artists who have been adopted may project their fantasies in their work. "Moreover, the adopted child's wishes and defenses may serve as the wellspring of his artistic activity." Albee was adopted when he was two weeks old. In Tiny Alice, the adoption theme is disguised; in The American Dream, it is not.

924. Morrison, Kristin. "Pinter, Albee, and 'The Maiden in the Shark Pond'." American Imago, 35 (1978), 259-274.

An examination of Pinter's No Man's Land and Albee's Tiny Alice "to see what sort of sexually-related fantasy seems to be present." Both plays demonstrate hostility towards women. In each play, the male character victimizes women. "And in the physical and psychological violence of his sexual act, he catches sight of his own final moment, his own death, which both attracts and repels him."

Arrabal, Fernando

925. Lyons, Charles R. "The Psychological Base of Arrabal's L'Architecte et l'Empereur d'Assyrie." French Review, 45, Special Issue, 4, Spring (1972), 123-136.

Drawing upon Jung's ideas on parental imagery and child symbolism, it is suggested that "the perspective of the play seems to be the child consciousness, and the play projects a notion of the self as helplessly infantile." Furthermore, "the overt ritual strategy in this play is obviously a metaphor for the destructive act of regression."

Auden, W.H.
(See also item 375.)

926. Callan, Edward. "W.H. Auden's First Dramatization of Jung: The Charade of the Loving and Terrible Mothers." Comparative Drama, 11 (1977), 287-302.

A study of Auden's Paid on Both Sides: A Charade, noting that much of its content comes from Jung's Symbols of Transformation. Paid on Both Sides illustrates "the notion of a divided libido energizing both conscious activity and natural instincts that . . . finds archetypal expression in the myths of the questing hero and the loving and terrible mothers."

927. Snider, Clifton. "Auden's Quest Poems: 'Lady Weeping at the Crossroads' and 'Atlantis'." American Imago, 39 (1982), 95-100.

In these two quest poems, "Auden draws on archetype, fairy tale, and myth to illustrate aspects of the modern personal search for what Jung calls individuation."

Awoonor, Kufi

928. Ojo-Ade, Femi. "Madness in the African Novel: Awoonor's This Earth, My Brother." African Literature Today, 10 (1979), 134-152.

Amamu becomes mad because he cannot adjust to his inhuman society. Although he is an admired professional, he is possessed with guilt for living in a society that is impoverished and brutal. "He becomes an observer of his own life," and as he goes mad he begins to understand himself.

Ballard, J.G.

929. Perry, Nick and Wilkie, Roy. "The Undivided Self: J.G. Ballard's The Crystal World." Riverside Quarterly, 5 (1973), 268-277.

The characters in The Crystal World can be viewed as representing various aspects of the individual psyche as they try to unify in a single whole which represents self-realization of the individual. However, Ballard is pessimistic about such self-realization because he links this unity to leprosy.

Baraka, Imamu Amiri

930. Reck, Tom S. "Archetypes in LeRoi Jones' Dutchman." Studies in Black Literature, 1 (1970), 66-68.

Traces seduction and Adam and Eve myths in Dutchman.

931. Weisgram, Dianne H. "LeRoi Jones' Dutchman: Inter-racial Ritual of Sexual Violence." American Imago, 29 (1972), 215-232.

"Fantasies of an interracial primal scene and ritual revenge lynching inform the political impact of Dutchman." The play focuses on psycho-sexual and racial themes along with "orally focused feeling of separation rage."

932. _____. "LeRoi Jones's Dutchman: Inter-racial Ritual of Sexual Violence." In Tennenhouse, L., ed., The Practice of Psychoanalytic Criticism. Detroit: Wayne State University Press, 1976, 170-188.

See item 931.

Barnes, Djuna

933. Gunn, Edward. "Myth and Style in Djuna Barnes' Nightwood." Modern Fiction Studies, 19 (1973-74), 545-555.

The novel deals with sacred initiation rites which suggest Jungian ideas. It "presents characters who act out their unconscious personal myth in terms of given cultural and religious myths."

934. Nadeau, Robert L. "Nightwood and the Freudian Unconscious." International Fiction Review, 2 (1975), 159-163.

Djuna Barnes' novel Nightwood is a dream world where the characters represent various levels of the personality which are parallel to Freud's ideas on the make-up of the subconscious. Although civilization is repressive, it keeps us from acting like animals. Robin, who throws off civilized rules, becomes animalistic.

Barrie, James Matthew

935. Alston, Edwin F. "James Barrie's 'M'Connachie': His 'Writing Half'." American Imago, 29 (1972), 257-277.

Focuses on Barrie's relationship with his creative demon, M'Connachie, an example of a Rankian "double motif."

936. Hallman, Ralph J. "The Archetypes in Peter Pan." Journal of Analytical Psychology, 14 (1969), 65-73.

A Jungian study of Barrie's Peter Pan, a fantasy with two themes: 1) "the external child," and 2) the "reluctance we experience in sacrificing the magic and charm of . . . infantile existence in the interests of the more demanding claims of the external world." The characters in the play represent Jungian archetypes, and the setting "repeats the primordial images which Jung and his followers have identified."

937. Meisel, Frederick L. "The Myth of Peter Pan." In The Psychoanalytic Study of the Child, vol. 32. New Haven: Yale University Press, 1977, 545-563.

The Peter Pan myth deals with "the fear of adult sexuality as well as the fear of losing 'the nursery'" and the consequent problem of "narcissistic damage" as related to growing up.

Barth, John

938. Martin, Dennis M. "Desire and Disease: The Psychological Pattern of The Floating Opera." Critique: Studies in Modern Fiction, 18 (1976), 17-33.

Barth's novel "is a dramatization of Todd's consciousness of his sexual impotency and his endeavor to conceal from both the reader and himself the significance of his carefully delineated and pointedly emphasized symptoms of subacute bacteriological endocarditis."

939. Morris, Christopher. "Barth and Lacan: The World of the Moebius Strip." Critique: Studies in Modern Fiction, 17 (1975), 69-77.

The world described by Barth in Lost in the Funhouse is no longer an existential world but one which "resembles the universally neurotic one described by the French post-structuralist Jacques Lacan." Notes that "Lacan uses the Moebius strip as a figure for what he calls the 'signifying chain,' that autonomous world of discourse which is to be distinguished from the theoretical constructs of structuralism by the fact that in it the binary opposition fundamental to modern linguistics is challenged."

Barthelme, Donald
(See also item 541.)

940. Davis, Robert Con. "Post-Modern Paternity: Donald Barthelme's The Dead Father." In The Fictional Father: Lacanian Readings of the Text. Amherst: University of Massachusetts Press, 1981, 169-182.

158   Psychocriticism

Barthelme's novel is located between two fictional possibilities: the father in fiction and "a blissful state of unintelligible rapture, a lyric gesture."

Beauvoir, Simone de

941. Keefe, Terry. "Psychiatry in the Postwar Fiction of Simone de Beauvoir." Literature and Psychology, 29 (1979), 123-133.

An examination of Beauvoir's and Sartre's ambivalent attitudes toward psychoanalysis, as seen especially in Beauvoir through her fiction. Beauvoir anticipates R.D. Laing in her "attempts to break wholly new ground in both the theory and practice of psychiatry."

Beckett, Samuel
(See also item 506.)

942. Culik, Hugh. "Samuel Beckett's Molloy: Transformation and Loss." American Imago, 39 (1982), 21-30.

"Ehrenzweig's work can help to clarify the relationships between the imagery of Molloy and the novel's three quests: Molloy for his mother, Moran for Molloy, and the novel itself for a language that minimizes the losses of transforming the primary process vision into creative art."

943. Meares, Russell. "Beckett, Sarraute, and the Perceptual Experience of Schizophrenia." Psychiatry, 36, 1 (1973), 61-69.

"The works of Beckett and Sarraute include descriptions of emotional and perceptual states which may be successive stages in the development of schizophrenia, and, as such, are complementary to formulations in the psychiatric literature."

944. Riva, Raymond T. "Beckett and Freud." Criticism, 12 (Spring 1970), 120-132.

Both Freud and Beckett shared similar ideas concerning Man. Beckett focuses not on conscious man but "rather with the unseen, and . . . consciously unknowable one." Argues that both Freud and Beckett describe a pitiable condition of modern man which our subconscious recognizes as true.

945. Rose, Gilbert J. "On the Shores of Self: Samuel Beckett's Molloy-- Irredentism and the Creative Impulse." Psychoanalytic Review, 60 (1973-1974), 587-604.

Maintains that art is an instrument for improving on perceptions and apprehension of the world, and that "Beckett's art does this by providing the opportunity to resample the primary union of mother and child and separate out anew."

946. Shapiro, Barbara. "Toward a Psychoanalytic Reading of Beckett's Molloy: I." Literature and Psychology, 19, 2 (1969), 71-86.

It is argued "that Beckett's double narrator is unwittingly engaged in a profound internal struggle against unconscious homosexuality, a necessary if fearful mode of loving given the problematic intensity of his involvement with his mother."

Bellow, Saul

947. Alhadeff, Barbara. "The Divided Self: A Laingian Interpretation of Seize the Day." Studies in American Jewish Literature, 3 (1977), 16-20.

Wilhelm Adler is a "literary embodiment of the notion of the 'divided self'" because he "is the classic example of Laing's schizoid individual." However, at the end of the novel "Wilhelm has completed a cycle which has enabled him to transcend R.D. Laing's notion of ontological insecurity."

948. Hull, Byron D. "Henderson the Rain King and William James." Criticism, 13 (1971), 402-414.

Notes parallels in Bellow's novel to James' The Principles of Psychology. "All the chapters dealing with Henderson, Dahfu, and Atti are explicable in terms of Jamesian psychology." Dahfu is a Jamesian psychotherapist.

949. Moss, Judith P. "The Body as Symbol in Saul Bellow's Henderson the Rain King." Literature and Psychology, 20, 2 (1970), 51-61.

Henderson's psychological problems are hysterically manifested in oral and anal psychosomatic symptoms. His "coming to terms with himself is mirrored in his coming to terms with his own body." His ego is dominated by his id, and he cannot control his aggressiveness.

950. Paris, Bernard J. "Herzog the Man: An Analytic View of a Literary Figure." American Journal of Psychoanalyis, 36 (1976), 249-260.

Using the theories of Karen Horney, discusses Herzog in conflict: he wants love from, and communion with, others, while also desiring mastery of others. This explains his inconsistent behavior.

951. Rodrigues, Eusebio L. "Reichianism in Henderson the Rain King." In Tennenhouse, L., ed., The Practice of Psychoanalytic Criticism. Detroit: Wayne State University Press, 1976, 252-274.

Henderson's "quest for humanness" has a "Reichian thrust." Demonstrates how Bellow has taken Wilhelm Reich's ideas and images, and integrated them into Henderson's mode of expression and perceptions of things.

952. Steig, Michael. "Bellow's Henderson and the Limits of Freudian Criticism." Paunch, 36-37 (1973), 39-46.

Freudian criticism is inadequate as an approach to Henderson the Rain King because Bellow was employing Reichian ideas in the novel as illustrated by the suggestion of Reichian therapy with King Dahfu and scenes suggesting Reich's experiments in weather control.

Bernanos, Georges

953. Keane, Susan M. "Dream Imagery in the Novels of Bernanos." In Frohock, W.M., ed., Image and Theme: Studies in Modern French Fiction. Cambridge: Harvard University Press, 1969, 11-37.

Suggests that Bernanos' imagery often comes to him involuntarily. Furthermore, there is a strong connection "between image and metaphor." Notes repeating metaphors of children, animals, light and darkness, sickness and death in the creation of Bernanos' dream world.

954. Vineberg, Elsa. "Journal d'un curé de campagne: A Psychoanalytical Reading." Modern Language Notes, 92 (1977), 825-829.

In Georges Bernanos' Journal, "the priest, instead of hearing confession, actually delivers his own. His is a confession, not in a religious sense, but in a psychoanalytic sense, and it closely resembles the monologue involved in the psychoanalytic treatment Jacques Lacan describes in his Ecrits." The result is that the priest better understands himself because he is able to uncover things he has been unconsciously repressing.

Berryman, John

955. Mazzaro, Jerome. "John Berryman and the Yeatsian Mask." Review of Existential Psychology and Psychiatry, 12 (1973), 141-162.

A discussion of Berryman in terms of Yeat's idea that masks both hide and reveal personality. Various Freudian aspects of Berryman's language are also discussed.

956. Thornbury, Charles W. "The Significance of Dreams in The Dream Songs." Literature and Psychology, 25 (1975), 93-107.

The logic of dreams gives coherency to the seemingly disorganized Dream Songs. Henry's dreams suggest the unconscious selectivity of his mind.

Blais, Marie-Claire

957. Coldwell, Joan. "Mad Shadows as Psychological Fiction." Journal of Canadian Fiction, 2, 4 (1973), 65-67.

A discussion of Mad Shadows as "a psychological novel of inner states through fantastic actions," with emphasis on "an adolescent girl in her response to sexuality."

Bloom, Harold

958. Bassett, Sharon. "*Tristes Critiques*: Harold Bloom and the Sorrows of Secular Art." Literature and Psychology, 27, 3 (1977), 106-112.

"Like Virgil, Bloom derives from the exigencies of his melancholy the blueprint of a golden age, a prelapsarian-kingdom of entropic balance and unselfconscious utterance. . . . "

Bly, Robert

959. Atkinson, Michael. "Robert Bly's Sleepers Joining Hands: Shadow and Self." Iowa Review, 7, 4 (1976), 135-153.

A discussion of the Jungian aspects of Sleepers Joining Hands, with emphasis on "dream archetypes--the shadow and the Self."

Bombal, Maria Luisa

960. Adams, Michael I. Three Authors of Alienation: Bombal, Onetti, Carpentier. Austin: University of Texas Press, 1975.

Employs the social psychology of Erich Fromm (The Sane Society and Man For Himself) and specifically Fromm's view of alienation in order to discuss the novels of Maria Luisa Bombal, Juan Carlos Onetti, and Alejo Carpentier.

Borchert, Wolfgang

961. Nelson, Donald F. "To Live or Not to Live; Notes on Archetypes and the Absurd in Borchert's Draussen vor der Tür. German Quarterly, 48 (1975), 343-354.

Incidents, situations and figures in Borchert's play can be interpreted on a mythic and psychoanalytic plane.

Borges, Jorge Luis

962. Chrzanowski, Joseph. "Psychological Motivation in Borges' 'Emma Zunz'." Literature and Psychology, 28 (1978), 100-104.

Describes Emma Zunz as a character suffering from a neurotic love-hate conflict "with incestuous overtones, that characterizes Emma's relationship with her father."

963. Gyurko, Lanin A. "Borges and the Theme of the Double." Ibero-Amerikanisches Archiv, Neue Folge, 2 (1976), 193-226.

A study of Borges' great range of uses of "character doublings" and "situational doublings." In Borges' stories, the double "attests to the ironic fulfillment of the protagonists and to the futility of their existence; it is both a means of freedom of expanding and enriching the original self, and one of fate, as it denies their vaunted individuality."

Brecht, Bertold
(See also item 426.)

964. Hernadi, Paul. "The Actor's Face as the Author's Mask: On the Paradox of Brechtian Staging." In Strelka, J.P., ed., Literary Criticism and Psychology. University Park: Penn State University Press, 1976, 125-136.

A discussion of Brecht's theories of acting, noting especially the actor's "dual consciousness" whereby the actor plays the part of an actor as well as the part of the character he is portraying.

965. White, John J. "A Note on Brecht and Behaviourism." Forum for Modern Language Studies, 7 (1971), 249-258.

Demonstrates Brecht's indebtedness to behaviorists Watson and Pavlov.

Breton, André

966. Balakian, Anna. "André Breton and Psychiatry." In Peschel, E.R., ed., Medicine and Literature. New York: Watson, 1980, 160-170.

" . . . what Breton had learned from his experience of psychiatry was that the dream need not be considered merely as a channel of escape from reality but rather as an expansion and transfiguration of the real world" Janet and Freud were major influences.

967. Davis, Frederick B. "Three Letters from Sigmund Freud to Andre Breton." Journal of the American Psychoanalytic Association, 21 (1973), 127-134.

Notes use of psychoanalytic ideas by Breton in his surrealistic writing. Breton first read Freud when he was a medical aide at a psychiatric center in 1916. He began correspondence with Freud in 1919. The letters from Freud reprinted are dated from Vienna, 12/13/32, 12/14/32, and 12/26/32, responding to Breton's sending a copy of his Les Vases communicants to Freud. Breton's book, while embracing Freud's ideas, implied plagiarism on Freud's part.

968. Ladimer, Bethany. "Madness and the Irrational in the Work of André Breton: A Feminist Perspective." Feminist Studies, 6 (1980), 175-195.

The surrealists wanted to liberate the psyche, with the consequent liberation of society. It was in women that they saw the most hope for a revolution in society. Breton "valorized Woman and the experience of love above all other potentially 'revolutionary' forces" because he saw women as possessing "extralogical or extrarational modes of thought, including, as an extreme form, madness itself."

969. Morel, Jean-Pierre. "Breton and Freud." <u>Diacritics</u>, 2, 2 (1972), 18-26.

A review of André Breton's <u>Les Vases Communicants</u>. Discusses Breton's indebtedness to Freud's <u>The Interpretation of Dreams</u> and notes that the theories of dream interpretation have caused controversy among the surrealists.

<u>Broch, Hermann</u>

970. Hardin, James. "Hermann Broch's Theories on Mass Psychology and <u>Der Versucher</u>." <u>Germanic Quarterly</u>, 47 (1974), 24-33.

Demonstrates how "Broch's emphasis on the disintegration of values and the anguish produced by the fear of death," as promulgated in his <u>Massenpsychologie</u> can be seen in his novel <u>Der Versucher</u>.

<u>Burroughs, William S.</u>

971. Vernon, John. "William S. Burroughs." <u>Iowa Review</u>, 3 (1972), 107-123.

Discusses Burroughs' imagery and cutups as portraying "schizophrenic atomism, living in pieces, in a world of pieces," and exhibiting "the rhythm of isolation and merging which, according to R.D. Laing is the final stage of schizophrenia."

<u>Camus, Albert</u>
(See also item 666.)

972. Albrecht, Joyce. "<u>The Stranger</u> and Camus' Transcendental Existentialism." <u>Hartford Studies in Literature</u>, 4, 1 (1972), 59-80.

Attempts to make explicit the transcendental aspect of Camus' existentialism and relate it to both Heidegger and Merleau-Ponty while distinguishing it from Sartre.

973. Barchilon, José. "A Study of Camus' Mythopoeic Tale <u>The Fall</u> with Some Comments about the Origin of Esthetic Feelings." <u>Journal of the American Psychoanalytic Association</u>, 19 (1971), 193-240.

Because of his discovery of the infidelity of his mother and his own sexual problems, Jean Baptiste Clamence attempts "to unite superego and ego" and be a "judge-penitent."

164   Psychocriticism

974. Knoff, William. "A Psychiatrist Reads Camus' *The Stranger*." *Psychiatric Opinion*, 6 (1969), 19-21; 24.

Meursault is corrupted into "making meaninglessness itself meaningful."

975. Sachs, Erich. "*The Fall* by Albert Camus: A Study in Adlerian Psychology." *Journal of Individual Psychology*, 28, 1 (1972), 76-80.

The hero of *The Fall* reflects Adler's ideas of the neurotic character--lack of social feeling tied to a goal of personal superiority. The author acknowledges that the absurdist dimensions of Clamance, the hero, far exceed his Adlerian interpretation.

976. Scherr, Arthur. "Albert Camus: Revolt Against the Mother." *American Imago*, 34 (1977), 170-178.

Camus' *The Wrong Side and the Right Side*, *A Happy Death*, and *The Stranger* reveal the unconscious conflicts caused by his rebellion against his mother. "He atoned for his guilt through a catharsis by writing his great novels and through his courageous protagonist Meursault."

977. Slochower, Harry. "Camus' *The Stranger*: The Silent Society and the Ecstasy of Rage." *American Imago*, 26 (1969), 291-294.

A supplementary essay to Stamm's (item 979), examining the imagery which brings forth the meaning of Camus' novel.

978. Sperber, Michael A. "Camus' *The Fall*: The Icarus Complex." *American Imago*, 26 (1969), 269-280.

Examines Jean-Baptiste Clamence, the hero of *The Fall*, in the light of the Icarus Complex which involves a craving for immortality, and a conception of woman as an object to be used for narcissistic gains.

979. Stamm, Julian L. "Camus' *Stranger*: His Act of Violence." *American Imago*, 26 (1969), 281-290.

An analysis of the murder by Meursault. Meursault's "acts were unconsciously motivated, and . . . he seized upon certain events to act out his conflict." He has "an inordinate sense of guilt and an excessively punitive superego, a guilt feeling for his hidden death wishes towards his mother and his desire for the father-brother figure."

Castaneda, Carlos

980. Faber, M.D. "Don Juan and Castaneda: The Psychology of Altered Awareness." *Psychoanalytic Review*, 64 (1977), 323-379.

An analysis of Castaneda's relationship with Don Juan in *A Separate Reality* and *The Teachings of Don Juan*. Through drugs, Castaneda loses his repressions about his negative early relationship with his mother. For Castaneda, Don Juan then becomes representative of Castaneda's mother. Because of this, Don Juan fails to lead Castaneda to a higher consiousness.

Celan, Paul

981. Glenn, Jerry. "Nightmares, Dreams and Intellectualization in the Poetry of Paul Celan." *World Literature Today*, 51 (1977), 522-525.

There are three important aspects of Celan's poetry, regarding his world of dreams: 1) as a victim of the Holocaust, "reality had become a nightmare; 2) his early poetry contained dreams that were nightmares; 3) his "dream imagery did not remain constant." Suggests that the dream lost its "creative force" for Celan, and, ultimately, "the expectation of a new beginning, based on the creative and healing power of the dream . . . was not fulfilled."

Conrad, Joseph

982. Armstrong, Robert M. "Joseph Conrad: The Conflict of Command." *Psychoanalytic Study of the Child*, 26 (1971), 485-534.

In his work, Conrad reactivated past difficult situations in order to reassert mastery. "Impulses opposed to the passive, masochistic ones in the novels . . . are exposed and integrated in the short stories."

983. Berman, Jeffrey. "Conrad's Lord Jim and the Enigma of Sublimation." *American Imago*, 33 (1976), 380-402.

Lord Jim explores the following problematic questions: 1. gratification versus restraint; 2. body versus mind; 3. love versus work.

984. ─────. "Writing as Rescue: Conrad's Escape from the 'Heart of Darkness'." *Literature and Psychology*, 25, 2 (1975), 65-78.

Applies the insights of Alvarez's study of suicide and artists, *The Savage God*, to the life and work of Conrad, who attempted suicide at the age of twenty.

985. Brown, P.L. "'The Secret Sharer' and the Existential Hero." *Conradiana*, 3 (1971-72), 22-30.

The traditional psychological interpretations of "The Secret Sharer" view the narrator's sympathy with Leggatt in terms of id psychology: Leggatt personifies the drives of the narrator's id. However, a more expanded interpretation will view Leggatt as "part of the narrator's subjective self" which "wants the kind of independence, courage, and self-reliance" the narrator finds in Leggatt.

986. Butler, Richard E. "Jungian and Oriental Symbolism in Joseph Conrad's *Victory*." *Conradiana*, 3 (1971-72), 36-54.

Compares the Jungian archetypes of "anima" and "shadow" to two characters in *Victory*, Lena and Jones. Conrad "was actually plumbing the depths of what Jung calls the 'collective unconscious'."

987. Haltresht, Michael. "Disease Imagery in Conrad's The Secret Agent." Literature and Psychology, 21, 2 (1971), 101-105.

The inner tensions of the characters of this novel are not resolved in overt action but are directed against the self. "Anxiety, self-pity, resentment, and hopelessness are the emotions that seek expression: outwardly directed anger is very definitely the exception, not the norm."

988. _____. "The Dread of Space in Conrad's The Secret Agent." Literature and Psychology, 22, 2 (1972), 89-98.

Considers the physical milieu of The Secret Agent in order to discover the deeper meaning of the work.

989. Hamilton, James W. "The Significance of Depersonalization in the Life and Writings of Joseph Conrad." Psychoanalytic Quarterly, 44 (1975), 612-630.

Argues that "Conrad made use of depersonalization in order to cope with the childhood loss of his parents and to avoid, whenever possible, psychotic regression." Depersonalization refers to a dissociation of the function of immediate experiencing from the function of self-observations.

990. Herbert, Wray C. "Conrad's Psychic Landscape: The Mythic Element in 'Karain'." Conradiana, 8 (1976), 225-232.

Views Conrad's story as a "schematic" of the human mind, and discusses Conrad's "darkness," or the unconscious, as revealed in Jungian "primordial images." "The narrator's story, intended as an objective retelling of the facts, is, like a dream, intruded upon by myth, and the words are forced to couch their meaning."

991. McIntyre, Allan. "Psychology and Symbol: Correspondences Between Heart of Darkness and Death in Venice." Hartford Studies in Literature, 7 (1975), 216-235.

"We may describe the authors' handling of psychology in these works as a progressive revelation of moral landscape, of configurations of human character."

992. Saveson, John E. "Contemporary Psychology in The Nigger of the Narcissus." Studies in Short Fiction, 7 (1970), 219-231.

A study in light of the Utilitarian psychologists, especially Théodule Ribot, whom Conrad had probably read. "Donkin's progress into malevolence, . . . like Wait's progress toward denial of the will to live, is governed by certain psychological principles found in Ribot."

993. _____. "Marlow's Psychological Vocabulary in Lord Jim." Texas Studies in Language and Literature, 12 (1970), 457-470.

Argues that a close study of Marlow's language in Lord Jim reveals that Conrad's psychological vocabulary was both competent and contemporary. "Contemporary" here means the psychology of James Sully.

994. Sperber, Michael A. "Sensory Deprivation in Autoscopic Illusion, and Joseph Conrad's The Secret Sharer." Psychiatric Quarterly, 43 (1969), 711-718.

"Focusing on Conrad's story, the present study will discuss certain of the psychic factors which may be responsible for autoscopic illusion."

Cortazar, Julio

995. Castillo, Ana Hernandez Del. Keats, Poe, and the Shaping of Cortazar's Mythopoesis. Amsterdam: John Benjamins B.V., 1981.

Cortazar has been influenced by works which "have one trait in common: they all deal with myth and ritual as symptomatic of mental processes and revelatory of the structure of the psyche."

Crane, Hart

996. Irwin, John. "Figurations of the Writer's Death: Freud and Hart Crane." In Smith, J.H., ed., The Literary Freud (Psychiatry and the Humanities, vol. 4). New Haven: Yale University Press, 1980, 217-260.

A discussion, through Freud and Crane, of "the way in which a writer deals with the inscribed image of his own death--both the certain death of his physical body and the possible death of the body of his work." Concludes that "for both Freud and Crane, the ability to come to terms with the fact of their physical deaths involves the confrontation with the written figuration of that death."

997. Zeck, Gregory R. "Hart Crane's 'The Wine Menagerie': The Logic of Metaphor." American Imago, 36 (1979), 197-214.

Discusses Crane's search for identity and how his aesthetic theory ("the logic of metaphor") helped him find that identity in "The Wine Menagerie."

Creeley, Robert

998. Hammond, John G. "Solipsism and the Sexual Imagination in Robert Creeley's Fiction." Criticism, 16 (1975), 59-69.

Creeley's fiction demonstrates both the supreme importance of love and its failure. Failure is usually caused by the male's delusions about sex which lead to solipsism and the impossibility of dealing with reality and meaningful sexual interaction. These ideas are most fully illustrated in The Island.

Cummings, E.E.

999. Forrest, David V. "E.E. Cummings and Thoughts That Lie Too Deep for Tears: Of Defenses in Poetry." Psychiatry, 43 (1980), 13-42.

Distinguishes between the "poetry of mastery and the poetry of symptoms, or . . . between active (solving) versus passive (yielding) poetic defense." Cummings is an example of the former, Anne Sexton, the latter. Uses Cummings' poetry to demonstrate various mature and neurotic "defenses," such as, for instance, "denial," "orgasm," "madness," and "muteness."

1000. Haule, J. "E.E. Cummings as Comic Poet: The Economy of the Expenditure of Freud." Literature and Psychology, 25 (1975), 175-180.

An examination of Cummings' poem 128 in the Collected Poems in terms of Freud's Wit and Its Relation to the Unconscious. The poem establishes Cummings as a comic poet according to Freud's definition.

Davies, Robertson

1001. Keith, W.J. "The Manticore: Psychology and Fictional Technique." Studies in Canadian Literature, 3 (1978), 133-136.

A comment on Patricia Monk's "Psychology and Myth in The Manticore" (SCL 2, 1977; see item 1003). Suggests that The Manticore should be examined from a "literary-critical" viewpoint, rather than a psychological viewpoint: "Davies claims the privilege open to the artist but not to the psychologist of controlling the Unconscious."

1002. Merivale, Patricia. "The (Auto)-Biographical Compulsions of Dunstan Ramsay." In Laurence, Robert and Macey, Samuel, eds., Studies in Robertson Davies' Deptford Trilogy. Victoria, B.C.: University of Victoria, 1980, 57-75.

Points out correspondences between Fifth Business and Jung's autobiography, Memories, Dreams, and Reflections.

1003. Monk, Patricia. "Psychology and Myth in The Manticore." Studies in Canadian Literature, 2 (1977), 69-81.

Discusses Davies' ambivalence about Jungian concepts. Davies' attitude toward Jung's psychology is skeptical but at the same time quite Jungian in its ambivalence.

1004. Radford, F.L. "The Great Mother and the Boy: Jung, Davies, and Fifth Business." In Laurence, Robert and Macey, Samuel, eds., Studies in Robertson Davies' Deptford Trilogy. Victoria, B.C.: University of Victoria, 1980, 66-81.

Fifth Business "can be seen as educating the reader for the Jungian bias of the Deptford trilogy as a whole."

1005. Roper, Gordon. "Robertson Davies' *Fifth Business* and 'That Old Fantastical Duke of Dark Corners, C.G. Jung'." *Journal of Canadian Fiction*, 1 (1972), 33-39.

> A reading of the myth of individuation "which seems to structure *Fifth Business*--a structure enriched by many archetypal images, ideas and situations, and enhanced by interwoven signs."

Dickey, James

1006. Hamilton, James W. "James Dickey's *Deliverance*: Mid-Life and the Creative Process." *American Imago*, 38 (1981), 389-405.

> "James Dickey's novel *Deliverance* (1970) offers a unique opportunity to appreciate the significance of Jacques' and Levinson's contributions on the vicissitudes of mid-life as the main characters are in that phase of their lives as was Dickey himself when he wrote the book."

1007. Schechter, Harold. "The Eye and the Nerve: A Psychological Reading of James Dickey's *Deliverance*." In Filler, L., ed., *Seasoned Authors for a New Season: The Search for Standards in Popular Writing*. Bowling Green, Ohio: Bowling Green University Popular Press, 1980, 4-19.

> Dickey's novel is an example of what Carl Jung called "visionary literature." Its "mythic substructure" is the archetypal quest of the hero, the symbolic journey into psychic depths. In this, it is also in the American tradition of "dark romance."

Didion, Joan

1008. Geherin, D.J. "Nothingness and Beyond: Joan Didion's *Play It As It Lays*." *Critique: Studies in Modern Fiction*, 16 (1974), 64-78.

> The protagonist of this novel, Maria, suffers from what R.D. Laing calls "ontological insecurity," a lack of firm identity. Maria is not simply mentally disturbed but exhibits a metaphysical sickness, "a manifestation of her difficulty in adjusting to her newly discovered consciousness of absurdity."

Doctorow, E.L.

1009. Stark, John. "Alienation and Analysis in Doctorow's *The Book of Daniel*." *Critique: Studies in Modern Fiction*, 16 (1975), 101-110.

> Daniel is able to deal with his alienation and the deaths of his parents and sister by creating meaningful images, just as Doctorow, himself, has done in the writing of the novel. The book also discusses, more generally, the alienation of leftists, Jews, and all of humanity.

Donoso, José

1010. Callan, Richard J. "Animals as Mana Figures in José Donoso's 'Paseo' and 'Santelices'." *Essays in Literature*, 2 (1975), 115-123.

> Uses Jungian psychology in a study of the two stories, showing that "both protagonists experience an instinctual drive toward fulfillment." In "Paseo," Matilde submits to instinct and "abandons her former one-sided way of life." In "Santelices," Santelices "surrenders to the fascination of the unconscious images" and is overwhelmed and destroyed.

Doolittle, Hilda

1011. Friedman, Susan. *Psyche Reborn: The Emergence of H.D.* Bloomington: Indiana University Press, 1981.

> "*Psyche Reborn* argues that H.D.'s experience as an analysand with Sigmund Freud . . . nourished . . . a new kind of poetry and prose during the forties and fifties." Her interaction with psychoanalysis also becomes a particular instance "of a larger debate in modern thought between scientific and artistic modes of creating meaning."

1012. Romig, Evelyn M. "An Achievement of H.D. and Theodore Roethke: Psychoanalysis and the Poetics of Teaching." *Literature and Psychology*, 28 (1978), 105-111.

> Studies the teaching and the work of H.D. and Roethke, noting the connections between psychoanalysis, student-teacher relationships, and the creation of art. "Both the drama of psychoanalytic transference and the intensity of poetry are to be found in the ideal relationship of student and teacher."

Dreiser, Theodore

1013. Forrey, Robert. "Theodore Dreiser: Oedipus Redivivus." *Modern Fiction Studies*, 23 (1977), 341-354.

> A structuralist study. The basic, underlying structure of Dreiser's work and life was Oedipal. "Perhaps the most important feature of Dreiser's Oedipal development was that instead of passing *through* the anal, oral, and phallic stages . . . , Dreiser remained essentially oral in his psycho-sexual orientation."

1014. Hovey, Richard B., and Ralph, Ruth S. "Dreiser's *The 'Genius'*: Motivation and Structure." *Hartford Studies in Literature*, 2 (1970, 169-183.

> A Freudian study of the "psychosexual conflicts" of Eugene Witla. Witla exhibits the Don Juan syndrome and "pursues the pleasure principle; at the same time he regularly tries to gain acceptance by a matriarchal superego."

1015. Rosenberg, Seymour, and Jones, Russell. "A Method for Investigating and Representing a Person's Implicit Theory of Personality: Theodore Dreiser's View of People." Journal of Personality and Social Psychology, 22 (1972), 372-386.

> Drawing upon Dreiser's A Gallery of Women, devises a scale of "trait occurrence" for personality measurement. It is noted that while Dreiser was highly judgmental in his personal life, in Gallery he seems less so when he describes his characters.

1016. Seltzer, Leon F. "Sister Carrie and the Hidden Longing for Love: Sublimation or Subterfuge." Twentieth-Century Literature, 22 (1976), 192-209.

> A discussion of the inability to love in the characters in Sister Carrie and this inability's relationship to Dreiser's own life. "Carrie's longing is shown by Dreiser (though never clearly understood by him) to be a longing for love and emotional relatedness."

Dürrenmatt, Friedrich

1017. Wilson, Roger Edward. "The Devouring Mother: Analysis of Dürrenmatt's Der Besuch der Alten Dame." The Germanic Review, 52, 4 (1977), 274-288.

> Sees the Devouring Mother as the thematic nucleus of this play and argues that "one's grasp of the formal and thematic features of the work is enhanced when they are seen as having been arranged in conformity with . . . mythic patterns."

Eliot, T.S.
(See also item 916.)

1018. Chouinard, Timothy. "Eliot's Oeuvre, Bradley's 'Finite Centres,' and Jung's Anima Concept." Journal of Analytical Psychology, 16 (1971), 48-68.

> The early influence of F.H. Bradley on T.S. Eliot is seen in "Eliot's intuition of the relations between communication with the absolute and with the feminine other." A discussion of the Jungian anima imagery in Eliot's work demonstrates that he developed as a writer in a way parallel to Jung's four stages of anima development in the process of individuation.

1019. Freedman, William. "T.S. Eliot's 'Gerontion' and the Primal Scene." American Imago, 36 (1979), 373-386.

> The sexual imagery of "Gerontion" suggests "a primal fantasy or scene weaving its way beneath the surface texture and meaning of the poem." Note is also made of the relevance of this to Eliot's religious development.

1020. Johnson, John. "'Prufrock' as Mimetic Portrait: A Psychological Reading." *Gypsy Scholar*, 3 (1976), 96-110.

>Prufrock suffers from "what Ernest G. Schechtel has called the impulse toward embeddedness" which makes him "remain within the limits of a world which he knows and in which he feels secure." He also suffers from self-abasement and anxiety as described by Karen Horney. The theories of these two psychologists are helpful in showing Prufrock to be "mimetically real and highly complex."

1021. Jones, Joyce. *Jungian Psychology in Literary Analysis: A Demonstration Using T.S. Eliot's Poetry*. Washington, D.C.: University Press of America, 1979.

>Asserts, after an exposition of Jungian psychology and after a consideration of Eliot's poetry in the light of Jungian psychology, that the ultimate proof of Eliot's skill is that his poetry is not submerged by a Jungian analysis.

1022. Rusch, Frederik L. "Approaching Literature Through the Social Psychology of Erich Fromm. In Natoli, J.P., ed., *Psychological Perspectives on Literature*. New Haven: Archon, 1983.

>An analysis of the writing of T.S. Eliot, F. Scott Fitzgerald, and Arthur Miller, with emphasis on "The Love Song of J. Alfred Prufrock," *The Great Gatsby*, and *Death of a Salesman*. The characters in these works are personally doomed because they are no longer nurtured by their society and culture.

1023. Trosman, Harry. "T.S. Eliot and *The Waste Land*: Psychopathological Antecedents and Transformations." *Archives of General Psychiatry*, 30 (1974), 709-717.

>*The Waste Land* is a product of Eliot's psychological crises experienced previous to its composition. Thus the portrayal of social malaise in the poem, while typical of the modern era, is partially due to Eliot's personal problems. Contains biographical material on the importance of Eliot's psychiatrist and of Ezra Pound, Eliot's "alterego."

1024. Waldoff, Leon. "Prufrock's Defenses and Our Response." *American Imago*, 26 (1969), 182-193.

>Our response to the poem "is controlled by the defenses in" it. Traces the defenses which "enable Prufrock to transform his hopes and fears of love into a narcissistic, introspective, sometimes painful act of self-understanding and self-love." The reader "introjects" Prufrock's hopes and fears.

1025. Whitside, George. "A Freudian Dream Analysis of 'Sweeney Among the Nightingale's'." *Yeats Eliot Review*, 5 (1978), 14-17.

>In "Sweeney," Eliot has created a nightmare. It is Sweeney's dream, and it reveals his "sexual desire . . . and the female object of that desire . . . plus the dreamer's fear of being castrated . . . as punishment for that desire."

1026. _____. "T.S. Eliot's 'Dans Le Restaurant'." American Imago, 33 (1976), 155-173.

"Dans Le Restaurant" is studied as an example of a poem with a hidden personal meaning. The poem is actually two poems, one about a "sexual game" Eliot played with a girl when he was a child, the other about the death of a man who was his good friend. Such hiding of the personal element is also typical of Eliot's other poems.

Ellison, Ralph

1027. Abrams, Robert E. "The Ambiguities of Dreaming in Ellison's Invisible Man." American Literature, 49 (1978), 592-603.

In Invisible Man, Ellison demonstrates that, as he writes in Shadow and Act, the artist must probe the "inner world where reason and madness mingle with hope and memory and endlessly give birth to nightmare and dream." The upshot of such probing produces a fuller picture of human consciousness by examining and portraying the ambiguities of the "dream-plots and hallucinated images" of Ellison's characters. Although Ellison has been influenced by Freud, "Invisible Man collapses the Freudian distinction between manifest dream (prevaricating and deceptive) and the latent dream content (putatively definable)."

1028. Kist, E.M. "A Laingian Analysis of Blackness in Ralph Ellison's Invisible Man." Studies in Black Literature, 7 (1976), 19-23.

Ellison's concept of invisibility is like Laing's idea of "ontological insecurity." Discusses the "similarity between the apparently aberrant type, the schizoid personality, and Ellison's Everyman figure," of the narrator in the novel.

Faulkner, William

1029. Adamowski, T.H. "Addie Bundren's Solitude: The Self and Others." Review of Existential Psychology and Psychiatry, 15 (1977), 1-18.

An examination of the Addie Bundren section of As I Lay Dying, demonstrating that the novel is one "of paradox, of common project and individual motives, of grotesque comedy and excruciating pain." Addie "sees human existence defined by basic isolation" and projects a "solitude of consciousness."

1030. _____. "Bayard Sartoris: Mourning and Melancholia." Literature and Psychology, 23 (1973), 149-158.

Uses Freud's ideas on the nature of melancholia to analyze Bayard's behavior in Sartoris.

1031. _____. "'Meet Mrs. Bundren': As I Lay Dying--Gentility, Tact, and Psychoanalysis." University of Toronto Quarterly, 49 (1980), 205-227.

Discusses "hidden" orality and oedipal themes in Faulkner's novel. "But such themes . . . are failed camouflage, and beneath this screen we find not a dyad of mother and child but that menage a trois constituted by the presence of a father who is no buffoon."

1032. Bleikasten, André. "Fathers in Faulkner." In Davis, R.C., ed., *The Fictional Father: Lacanian Readings of the Text*. Amherst: University of Massachusetts Press, 1981, 115-146.

Fatherhood "appears throughout Faulkner's work as a complex function, both private and public, a symbolic agency operating on various scales and levels and within various patterns, and to discuss it only in terms of blood kinship and family structure would be to miss much of its deeper significance."

1033. Chabot, C. Barry. "Faulkner's Rescued Patrimony." *Review of Existential Psychology and Psychiatry*, 13 (1974), 274-286.

In Faulkner's writing, the passage of time is destructive to the characters, but the destruction can be mitigated by a strong feeling for ancestry and a sense of place. Personally, Faulkner also felt the pain of time passing. However, his writing enabled him to overcome this problem.

1034. Cowan, James C. "Dream-Work in the Quentin Section of *The Sound and the Fury*." *Literature and Psychology*, 24 (1974), 91-98.

Through fragmented day-dreams, sensory impressions, and free association, Faulkner invents a literary "dream-work" to portray the Oedipus complex and death wish of Quentin Compson. The surface incoherence of the Quentin section is made clear by the logic of the dream.

1035. Davis, Robert Con. "The Symbolic Father in Yoknapatawpha County." *The Journal of Narrative Technique*, 10 (1980), 39-55.

"*Absalom!*, through Rosa's narrative function, can lead the way to an understanding of the symbolic father's structure and of the 'other' side of his authority."

1036. Faber, M.D. "Faulkner's *The Sound and the Fury*: Object Relations and Narrative Structure." *American Imago*, 34 (1977), 327-350.

The male children in the Compson family are bound to images of mother, often manifested in Caddy as substitute mother. The focus here is on Quentin, who, like many heroes of Western literature, reveals "reactivation of early wounding bound up with maternal ambivalence, maternal mystery, maternal withdrawal, with the mother who is there and not there." Discussion deals with Quentin's "incestuous and pregenital fixation," experience of "betrayal and loss," and "suicidal resolution of intolerable conflict."

1037. Haselswerdt, Marjorie. "I'd Rather Be Ratliff: A Maslovian Study of Faulkner's Snopes." *The Literary Review*, 24 (1981), 308-327.

Considers Ratliff "in light of psychologist Abraham Maslov's theories regarding self-actualization in mentally healthy human beings."

1038. Holland, Norman N. "Fantasy and Defense in Faulkner's 'A Rose for Emily'." <u>Hartford Studies in Literature</u>, 4 (1972), 1-35.

"A Rose for Emily" demonstrates the "psychological process of transformation and defense," transforming "fantasy material from successive development levels of the psyche." The reader joins in the transformation of "the primitive into the intellectual and the esthetic."

1039. Irwin, John. "The Dead Father in Faulkner." In Davis, R.C., ed., <u>The Fictional Father</u>. Amherst: University of Massachusetts Press, 1981, 147-168.

Argues that the struggle between father and son "inevitably turns into a dispute about the nature of time."

1040. _____. <u>Doubling and Incest/Repetition and Revenge: A Speculative Reading of Faulkner</u>. Baltimore: The Johns Hopkins Press, 1975.

Refers to the work of Freud and Rank to show "the structural links between the repetition compulsion, the regressive character of the instincts, and the morbid anxiety evoked by the return of the repressed through the involuntary repetition involved in doubling."

1041. Jenkins, Lee. <u>Faulkner and Black-White Relations: A Psychoanalytic Approach</u>. New York: Columbia University Press, 1981.

A study of the "intuitive grasp" of the psychological conflict in Faulkner's work. "The mind divided against itself in all its anguish is Faulkner's great recurring theme." In race relations, Faulkner understood the necessity of "love and compassion and humane dealings with our fellows," and while in his writing, he had not "become sufficiently liberated to fulfill such a prescription, . . . he recognized the necessity of moving in that direction." Discusses <u>Light in August</u>, <u>The Unvanquished</u>, <u>The Sound and the Fury</u>, <u>Absalom, Absalom!</u>, <u>Go Down, Moses</u>, and <u>Intruder in the Dust</u>.

1042. Jenkins, Lee Clinton. "Faulkner, the Mythic Mind, and the Blacks." <u>Literature and Psychology</u>, 27 (1977), 74-91.

A discussion of mythic aspects of Faulkner's work, in terms of doubling and narcissism in white and black psyches. Faulkner's style is "mythic" in that it "embodies the psychohistorical determinants of a collective sense of identity and destiny." A major theme in Faulkner is "the mythic apparition of the black man as the one who was cured, the unredeemable Other in whose presence was personified the stain on life."

1043. Kloss, Robert. "Faulkner's <u>As I Lay Dying</u>." <u>American Imago</u>, 38 (1981), 429-444.

Argues that incest is the cause of tensions lying within Cash, Darl and Jewel.

1044. Norris, Nancy. "<u>The Hamlet</u>, <u>The Town</u> and <u>The Mansion</u>: A Psychological Reading of the Snopes Trilogy." <u>Mosaic</u>, 7 (1973), 213-235.

176 Psychocriticism

    The story of Flem Snopes is an "Orestean tale of intense wishes, murderous aggressive feelings, and resultant anxieties about disintegration."

1045. Peavy, Charles D. "'If I'd Just Had a Mother': Faulkner's Quentin Compson." *Literature and Psychology*, 23, 3 (1973), 114-121.

    A discussion of the neurotic character of Quentin Compson in *The Sound and the Fury*. Quentin cannot love because of his parents' tremendous problems with self-pity, narcissicism, and cynicism. Quentin's sister, Caddy, takes the role of the mother.

1046. _____. "Jason Compson's Paranoid Pseudocommunity." *Hartford Studies in English*, 2 (1970), 151-156.

    A study of *The Sound and the Fury*, using Norman Cameron's concept of the "paranoid pseudocommunity." Jason exhibits "most of the symptoms of a typical paranoid state" along with "sadistic and masochistic tendencies." He creates a "pseudocommunity" onto which he can "direct his hostile aggression . . . without feeling guilty."

1047. Poresky, Louise A. "Joe Christmas: His Tragedy as Victim." *Hartford Studies in Literature*, 8 (1976), 209-222.

    A study of Joe Christmas in *Light in August*, based on Erich Fromm's idea that "man acts and feels according to his character; that his character determines his behavior and is, as Heraclitus said, 'man's fate'." Joe moves from being a victim to being a victimizer.

1048. Rose, Gilbert J. "The Orchestration of Time in William Faulkner's *Light in August*." *A Psychoanalytic Approach to Form*. *Psychological Issues*, Monograph 49, IUP, 1979, Ch. 11, 168-192.

    Faulkner's style and use of time and insistence on recurrent time resemble the mental processes of human beings. The rhythms of his style resemble the rhythms of the mind, and "timelessness is . . . conveyed by numerous reworkings of the primal scene in the latent content of the novel."

1049. _____. "William Faulkner's *Light in August*: The Orchestration of Time in the Psychology of Artistic Style." In *The Psychoanalytic Study of Society*, vol. 8. New Haven: Yale University Press, 1979, 251-276.

    A study of the conflict between time as representing progress and time as timelessness and recurrence as an important aspect of Faulkner's aesthetic. "Faulkner's style, like human mental processes, resembles recurrent time. . . . Timelessness is also conveyed by numerous reworkings of the 'primal scene' in the latent content of the novel."

1050. Rosenzweig, Paul J. "Faulkner's Motif of Food in *Light in August*." *American Imago*, 37 (1980), 93-112.

    Food represents a central part of Joe Christmas' three needs of food, sex, and women. Moreover, a psychological study of various characters' attitudes toward food enables the reader to understand better those characters and to get a more complete picture of the structure of the novel.

1051. Rossky, William. "The Pattern of Nightmare in *Sanctuary*: or Miss Reba's Dogs." *Modern Fiction Studies*, 15 (1969), 503-515.

Faulkner goes beyond mere nightmare of psychosexual origin by portraying "the impotent terror before the nightmare of existence." The nightmare imagery in the novel depicts fear, "clotting stasis," and "cringing impotence."

1052. Seltzer, Leon F. "Narrative Fiction vs. Psychopathology: The Problem of Darl in *As I Lay Dying*." *Literature and Psychology*, 25, 2 (1975), 49-64.

An analysis of Darl's character, according to the theories of R.D. Laing on schizophrenia. Darl's burning of barns is a product of hysteria.

1053. Slater, Judith. "Quentin's Tunnel Vision: Modes of Perception and Their Stylistic Realization in *The Sound and the Fury*." *Literature and Psychology*, 27 (1977), 4-15.

"Quentin's mental constructs rest to a considerable extent on perceptual distortions which seem to be attempts to reduce the incongruity between experience and his sense of ego integrity." Draws upon David Shapiro's theories on general response modes.

1054. Tefs, Wayne A. "Norman N. Holland and 'A Rose for Emily'--Some Questions Concerning Psychoanalytic Criticism." *Sphinx*, 2 (1974), 50-57.

A reaction to Holland's "Fantasy and Defense in Faulkner's 'A Rose for Emily'" (item 1038), suggesting that Holland had "anesthetized" the story. "If Holland is dealing with response dynamics, then, he should begin with the most affective passages in the story, . . . the final paragraphs," which Holland ignores. Holland's article "raises the question whether it is possible to make meaningful psychoanalytic statements about a literary character." Also contains "A Demurrer from Ralph Smith" and Tef's reply to it.

1055. Turner, Dixie M. *A Jungian Psychoanalytic Interpretation of William Faulkner's As I Lay Dying*. Washington: University Press of America, 1981.

"The writer will show that the Bundren family in Faulkner's *As I Lay Dying*, represents Jungian archetypes of unconscious racial memory."

1056. Whitely, Deborah. "Phenomenological Psychology and the Interior Monologue: Interpreting Whitfield's Passage." *The CEA Critic*, 44 (1982), 33-36.

Uses the phenomenological method to analyze the Reverend Whitfield passage in *As I Lay Dying*. "The process of his thoughts as he evaluates his experience and integrates it with self-contempt accurately reveals his personality as no outside observer could have done."

Fitzgerald, F. Scott
(See also item 1022).

1057. Berman, Jeffrey. "Tender Is the Night: Fitzgerald's A Psychology for Psychiatrists." Literature and Psychology, 29 (1979), 34-48.

Focuses on "Fitzgerald's use of the transference-love relationship between Dr. Dick Diver and Nicole Warren," with a discussion of Diver's romantic involvement with the schizophrenic Nicole, and her recovery. Also examines the novel in light of Fitzgerald's life and relationship with his wife.

1058. Hoffman, Madelyn. "This Side of Paradise: A Study in Pathological Narcissism." Literature and Psychology, 28 (1978), 178-185.

Amory Blaine is "pathologically narcissistic," and his "ultimate equation of beauty with evil represents an awareness . . . that the narcissistic personality's weakness for charisma in others represents a quest for re-union with the original narcissistic charismatic parent." His narcissistic personality pathology is reinforced by a social pathology.

1059. Johannsen, Pauline Renee, and Nash, Lee. "Alienation in The Great Gatsby: A Socio-Psychological Perspective on the 1920's." Rocky Mountain Social Science Journal, 10 (1973), 85-103.

A content analysis of Fitzgerald's novel, demonstrating similarities in the Lost Generation to the 1960's. Cites passages from Gatsby illustrative of various aspects of alienation.

1060. Kolbenschlag, Madonna C. "Madness and Sexual Mythology in Scott Fitzgerald." International Journal of Women's Studies, 1 (1978), 263-271.

A study of the heroines in Fitzgerald's novels, with emphasis on Tender is the Night. Notes "the Freudian paradigms which underlie the fictional structures, . . . and third-force psychologists are invoked to 'demythologize' the meaning of these structures." Fitzgerald's "characters reflect his own ambivalent conceptions of masculinity and femininity."

1061. Murphy, George D. "The Unconscious Dimension of Tender Is the Night." Studies in the Novel, 5 (1973), 314-322.

A discussion of Dick Diver's psyche in terms of Oedipal hostility, incest, failure of super-ego, and perverse sexuality. "The role of . . . psychological dysfunction in Diver's psyche accounts for the novel's formal imperfection and foreshadows Fitzgerald's own breakdown."

1062. Paulson, A.B. "The Great Gatsby: Oral Aggression and Splitting." American Imago, 35 (1978), 311-330.

A psychoanalytic study focusing on the symbolic significance of the "fresh, green breast" image at the end of the novel. The image suggests the once virgin land of America, but also it represents "a cluster of androgynous images which all promise reassurance in the face of vexing fears about gender and sexual identity." It also suggests "oral trust."

1063. Robson, Vincent. "The Psychological Conflict and the Distortion of Time: A Study of Diver's Disintegration in Tender Is the Night." Language and Literature, 1, 2 (1972), 55-64.

Describes Dick Diver's psychosocial conflict as "the dissension between an individual and his present social environment." Diver cannot adjust his ideas to the harsh, real environment in which he finds himself.

1064. Rusch, Frederik L. "Marble Men and Maidens, The Necrophilous People of F. Scott Fitzgerald: A Psychoanalytic Approach in Terms of Erich Fromm." Journal of Evolutionary Psychology, 3 (1982), 28-40.

A discussion of the death of the American Dream. In both Fitzgerald and Fromm, the burden of modern freedom is seen as, paradoxically, leading to an escape into necrophilia and the turning of human beings into things. The ultimate emotional deterioration is the turning of love into a commodity. Fitzgerald's The Crack-Up, This Side of Paradise, "The Ice Palace," and, especially, The Great Gatsby are discussed.

1065. Schenk, Jerome M. "Sleep Paralysis in F. Scott Fitzgerald's The Beautiful and the Damned." New York State Journal of Medicine, 71 (1971), 378-379.

Fitzgerald gave "a precise description of sleep paralysis, without use of the term" in his description of Gloria, who suffers from a "half-awake, half-asleep feeling; the awareness of actual surroundings; inability to move; inability to cry out; the sense of anxiety; the distorted, apparent prolongation of time; the feeling of weight."

Ford, Ford Madox

1066. Hurt, James. "The Primal Scene As Narrative Model in Ford's The Good Soldier." Journal of Narrative Technique, 8 (1978), 200-210.

Argues that the key to Dowell's personality is "that he unconsciously holds an infantile theory of sex and that this 'theory' is the one Freud identified with the primal scene fantasy, that of seeing one's parents copulate."

1067. Johnson, E. Bond. "Self-Conscious Use of Narrative Point of View: Controlling Intelligence and Narrating Consciousness in The Good Soldier and Doctor Faustus." In Strelka, J.P., ed., Literary Criticism and Psychology. University Park: Pennsylvania State University Press, 1976, 137-149.

"The controlling intelligence acts to establish a plateau of awareness to which the reader aspires in his experience of the work. 'Narrating consciousness' signifies the mind through which the fiction is recounted to the reader."

180   Psychocriticism

Forster, E.M.

1068. Centola, Steven. "Individuation in E.M. Forster's Maurice." Journal of Analytical Psychology, 26 (1981), 49-63.

" . . . it is possible that Forster's analysis of the ordeals which a homosexual such as Maurice encounters during his quest for wholeness reveals something about his own movement toward individuation."

Fowles, John

1069. Rose, Gilbert J. "The French Lieutenant's Woman: The Unconscious Significance of a Novel to Its Author." American Imago, 29 (1972), 165-176.

"The artist . . . through a transient unconscious identification with the primal mother may not only feel replenished--he may receive the impetus for creative work."

Freud, Sigmund
(See also items 726, 967, 996.)

1070. Brooks, Peter. "Freud's Masterplot." Yale French Studies, 55-56 (1977), 280-300.

Freud's Beyond the Pleasure Principle is viewed as "a model for narrative plot." It is "an essay about the dynamic interrelationship of ends and beginnings, and the kind of processes that constitute a middle."

1071. Davis, Robert Gorham. "A Note on 'The Use of Force' and Freud's 'The Dream of Irma's Injection'." William Carlos Williams Newsletter, 2 (1976), 9-10.

Notes parallels between the two narratives, suggesting that Williams was thinking of Freud's narrative when he wrote "The Use of Force."

1072. Derrida, Jacques. "Coming into One's Own." In Hartman, G.H., ed., Psychoanalysis and the Question of the Text. Baltimore: Johns Hopkins University Press, 1976, 114-148.

A typical allusive, free-associative Derridean commentary on a text, this time of Freud's Beyond the Pleasure Principle. This "unreading" ensnares Freud in a "mirror-like relationsihp with the child he is observing."

1073. _____. "Freud and the Scene of Writing." In Writing and Difference. Chicago: University of Chicago Press, 1978, 196-231.

"Our aim is limited: to locate in Freud's text several points of reference and to isolate, on the threshold of a systematic examination, what in psychoanalysis can be contained but with difficulty by the logocentric enclosure, as it limits not only the history of philosophy but the orientation of the 'human sciences,' notably of a certain linguistics."

1074. Hyman, Stanley Edgar. "Images of Sigmund Freud," (1962). In The Critic's Credentials: Essays and Reviews. New York: Atheneum, 1978, 279-283.

A review of recent (1962) books on Freud. Contains a short review of Henry Denker's play about Freud, A Far Country, "a vulgar and meretricious travesty." In the play, Freud is depicted as a "soap-opera hero."

1075. Kanter, V.B. "Freud's Reading of Shakespeare." Bulletin of the British Psychological Society, 22 (1969), 225-226.

A review of Freud's great interest and appreciation of Shakespeare's work, noting his personal collection of the plays and his attendance at performances of many of them. "Freud not only enriched our understanding of Shakespeare but it seems likely that he derived from his plays some of the hypotheses which he tested in his psychoanalytic researches." Cites Freud's address in the Goethe House (1930) as "the best approach towards understanding his attitude to Shakespeare."

1076. Kubal, David. "Freud, Orwell, and the Bourgeois Interior." Yale Review, 67 (1978), 389-403.

Both Freud and Orwell, believing themselves perched at the end of Western civilization, yet upheld reason and the family (the Bourgeois Interior). " . . . the self grows to its fullest freedom in intimate, erotic touch with others."

1077. Rey, Jean-Michel. "Freud's Writing on Writing." Yale French Studies, 55-56 (1977), 301-328.

A review of Freud's theories about literature, showing, among other things, his acknowledgement that fiction, drama, and poetry often outflanked and anticipated his own ideas.

1078. Spector, Jack J. The Aesthetics of Freud: A Study in Psychoanalysis and Art. New York: Praeger, 1972.

An examination of Freud's interest in artists and art, as a way of coming to a greater understanding of his personality. Studies Freud's taste, aesthetic theories, and influence on art and literature. Emphasis on Freud's Interpretation of Dreams.

1079. Vranich, Stanko B. "Sigmund Freud and the 'Case History of Berganza': Freud's Psychoanalytic Beginnings." Psychoanalytic Review, 63 (1967), 73-82.

Freud's early interest in psychoanalysis is demonstrated by the fact that he liked to think of himself as Cipión, a character in Cervantes' The Colloquy of the Dogs, when he was a teen-ager. Cipión likes to help others by listening to their problems.

Frost, Robert
(See also item 121.)

1080. Chabot, C. Barry. "The 'Melancholy Dualism' of Robert Frost." *Review of Existential Psychology and Psychiatry*, 13 (1974), 42-56.

   Through his biography and poetry, traces Frost's attempts "to differentiate clearly between self and not-self" and his struggle for self-assurance in an existence he portrayed as often "hopelessly melancholic."

1081. Henderson, Archibald. "Robert Frost's '"Out, Out"--'." *American Imago*, 34 (1977), 12-27.

   A psychoanalytical discussion of Frost's poem, demonstrating the psycho-sexual imagery suggested by the boy's encounter with the buzz saw. Symbolically, the poem deals with such things as guilt, masturbation, the primal scene, and the reality principle.

1082. Jayne, Edward. "Up Against the 'Mending Wall': The Psychoanalysis of a Poem by Frost." *College English*, 34 (1973), 934-951.

   Unconscious feelings of homosexuality are seen in the metaphors, puns, and images in "Mending Wall." This illustrates how literary conventions are used "to manage homosexuality."

1083. Kann, David. "Deadly Serious Play: Robert Frost's 'Design'." *University of Hartford Studies in Literature*, 14 (1982), 23-32.

   Applies Holland's "core fantasy" approach to this poem and concludes that "as with the child in the creation of his game, Frost uses formal devices to restructure and thereby master a frightening event."

1084. Marcus, Mordecai. "Psychoanalytic Approaches to 'Mending Wall'." In Harris, K.G., ed., *Robert Frost: Studies of the Poetry*. Boston: G.K. Hall, 1979, 179-190.

   In an effort to be less reductionist than Norman Holland's reading, applies Erik H. Erikson's "theory of eight developmental stages of human life" to "Mending Wall." Contains also "a brief psychosexual fantasy interpretation and an Eriksonian developmental reading" of Frost's "After Apple-Picking" and "The Onset."

1085. _____. "The Whole Pattern of Robert Frost's 'Two Witches': Contrasting Psycho-sexual Modes." *Literature and Psychology*, 26 (1976), 69-78.

   An analysis of "The Witch of Coos" and "The Pauper Witch of Grafton." The former is "a study of sexual failure between one kind of witch and her husband;" the latter is "a study of sexual triumph between a different kind of witch and her husband." Furthermore, "the two poems taken together make an ironic comment on society's capacity for bumbling judgments about interrelations between sex, society, and morality."

Fuentes, Carlos

1086. Callan, Richard J. "The Function of Myth and Analytical Psychology in Zona Sagrada." Kentucky Romance Quarterly, 21 (1974), 261-274.

   In Zona Sagrada, Carlos Fuentes "has used depth psychology as a technical device to depict the disturbed protagonist, Guillermo."

1087. _____. "The Jungian Basis of Carlos Fuentes' Aura." Kentucky Romance Quarterly, 18 (1971), 65-75.

   Felipe Montero, the protagonist of this novella, engages in the heroic stage of psychic development "wherein he is to separate Aura, his Anima, from Consuelo, the Great Mother." The realm of the novel is therefore the collective unconscious.

1088. Gyurko, Lanin A. "Self, Double, and Mask in Fuentes' La Muerte de Artemio Cruz." Texas Studies in Literature and Language, 16 (1974), 363-384.

   A study of Fuentes' use of mirror images as representing alter-egos and "the discrepancy between the idealistic self-image and the opportunistic self of reality." His doubles are at once "compensatory and antagonistic."

Garcia Lorca, Federico

1089. Allen, Rupert. The Symbolic World of Federico Garcia Lorca. Albuquerque: University of Mexico Press, 1972.

   "This is a book about Lorca, but it is not a book about a foreign poet so much as it is about the world of symbols which all of us inhabit and the transformation of that world into poetry."

1090. Feal-Deibe, Carlos. "Lorca's Two Farces: Don Perlimplin and Don Cristobal." American Imago, 27 (1970), 358-377.

   Examines both plays in regard to an Oedipal conflict.

Genet, Jean

1091. Ragland-Sullivan, Ellie. "Jacques Lacan, Literary Theory, and The Maids of Jean Genet." In Natoli, J.P., ed., Psychological Perspectives on Literature. New Haven: Archon, 1983.

   Discusses Lacan's major concepts, his value for literary studies and applies Lacanian theory to The Maids.

1092. _____. "The Psychology of Narcissism in Jean Genet's The Maids." Gradiva: International Contemporary Journal, 2 (1979), 19-40.

   "I contend that in The Maids Genet unwittingly dramatized the psychology of narcissism. . . . " Uses the "Lacanian view of narcissism to elucidate the deep dramatic structure of The Maids."

Gide, André

1093. Gulbertson, Diana, and Valley, John. "Personality Theory in Gide: The Plume of the Eagle." Hartford Studies in Literature, 8 (1976), 98-115.

Gide's personality theory involves a conflict between the integral, healthy human and an oppressive stagnant society. His concern is the "possibilities and consequences of a psychology of individualism and revolt."

1094. Kloss, Robert. "The Gratuitous Act: Gide's Lafcadio Reconsidered." Psychoanalytic Review, 64, 1 (1977), 111-134.

Argues that there is an unconscious motive for Lafcadio's act of murder-parricide. Fleurissoire becomes an image of the father.

Goytisolo, Juan

1095. Giles, Mary E. "Juan Goytisolo's Juego de Manos: An Archetypal Interpretation." Hispania, 56 (1973), 1021-1029.

Focuses on the scapegoat motif wherein "the scapegoat redeems his people by consciously and willingly assuming their collective guilt and allowing himself to be sacrificed in atonement for their sins."

Grass, Günter

1096. Mahlendorf, Ursula. "Sculpture and Mother Figures in Günter Grass' Tin Drum." Psychoanalytic Review, 66 (1979), 227-243.

Presents a psychological interpretation of sculpture in the Tin Drum. "The Sculptures function as matrixes upon which the hero and other male characters project their conscious and unconscious attitudes, feelings, wishes, fears, needs, and desires concerning women."

Green, Hannah

1097. Diamond, Ruth. "The Archetype of Death and Renewal in I Never Promised You a Rose Garden." Perspectives in Psychiatric Care, 8 (1975), 21-24.

A Jungian discussion of Green's novel. The heroine's development from insanity to health is compared to the archetypal journey to the lower world as seen in shamanistic ritual and mythical tales of death and rebirth.

1098. Lichtenberg, Philip, and Norton, Dolores, G. "Honesty, Trust, Equality in the Treatment of Schizophrenia: An Analysis of I Never Promised You a Rose Garden." Pennsylvania Psychiatric Quarterly, 10, 1 (1970), 33-40.

> A content analysis of Green's novel, which can be seen as a "source of data for evaluation" of the treatment of schizophrenia. The analysis found that "the positive aspects of honesty, trust and personal equality were related to improved functioning in the adolescent, schizophrenic girl depicted and that the negative aspects were related to deterioration in functioning."

1099. Wolfe, Kary K., and Wolfe, Gary K. "Metaphors of Madness: Popular Psychological Narratives." Journal of Popular Culture, 9 (1976), 895-907.

> Analyzes I Never Promised You a Rose Garden as a representation of popular narrative portraying psychological themes.

Greene, Graham

1100. Cassis, A.F. "The Dream as Literary Device in Graham Greene's Novels." Literature and Psychology, 24, 3 (1974), 99-108.

> Greene "makes considerable use of the dream as a literary device in all his major novels to introduce the reader to the level of the unconscious in his characters, to familiarize him, through a dramatic presentation, with the most secret, personal and conflicting impulses, and also to reveal the truth and absolute reality of a character."

Grey, Zane

1101. Steele, Robert S., and Swinney, Susan V. "Zane Grey, Carl Jung and the Journey of the Hero." Journal of Analytical Psychology, 23 (1978), 63-89.

> Grey's Wanderer of the Wasteland is seen as a product of his collective unconscious, demonstrating Jung's process of individuation.

Grove, Frederick Philip

1102. Bailey, Nancy. "F.P.G. and the Empty House." Journal of Canadian Fiction, 31-32 (1981), 177-193.

> Frederick Philip Grove's Over Prairie Trails, 1922, contains characters who correspond closely to the Jungian map of the psyche.

Hawkes, John

1103. Kraus, Elisabeth. "Psychic Sores in Search of Compassion: Hawkes' *Death, Sleep and the Traveler*." *Critique: Studies in Modern Fiction*, 17 (1976), 39-52.

The theme of Hawkes' novel is "the conflict between the rational, judgmental ego and the irrational, imaginative id of our culture-repressed unconscious."

1104. Stubbs, John C. "John Hawkes and the Dream-Work of *The Lime-Twig* and *Second Skin*." *Literature and Psychology*, 21, 3 (1971), 149-160.

Both novels are structured for psychological coherence and "consist primarily of dreamlike scenes or visualizations which are repeated in their varied forms until Hawkes' view of man's psychic world is completed."

Hayden, Robert

1105. Lewis, Richard O. "A Literary-Psychoanalytic Interpretation of Robert Hayden's 'Market'." *Negro American Literary Forum*, 9 (1975), 21-24.

"Market" illustrates the author's fears about losing his identity, as shown by various fantasies with oral, anal, and phallic content.

Hemingway, Ernest

1106. Adair, William. "*A Farewell to Arms*: A Dream Book." *Journal of Narrative Techniques*, 5 (1975), 40-56.

Taking his cue from Malcolm Cowley's remark that Hemingway's fiction has a "waking-dreamlike quality," Adair points out numerous dream images in *A Farewell to Arms*. Specifically, the novel portrays Fredric's redreaming of the trauma of his wounding, which can only be excised by the death of Catherine, his "other self." The redreaming of the trauma takes place in the fall and spring sections of the book while the summer and winter sections suggest escapes from the nightmare of the trauma through dreams that are erotic.

1107. Johnston, Kenneth G. "Hemingway's 'Out of Season' and the Psychology of Errors." *Literature and Psychology*, 21 (1971), 41-46.

The couple's quarrel with each other is brought to the surface by the wife's confusion of the words "doctor" and "daughter." This is a "Freudian slip" which "leads us to the very moral center" of the story.

1108. Leigh, David J. "*In Our Time*: The Interchapters as Structural Guides to a Psychological Pattern." *Studies in Short Fiction*, 12 (1975), 1-8.

The relationship between the interchapters and the stories reveals "patterns of existential neurosis." Nick Adams "is the existential neurotic seeking his peace separated from the violence of the present order in our time."

1109. Lowry, E.D. "Chaos and Cosmos in *In Our Time*." *Literature and Psychology*, 26 (1976), 108-117.

> A psycho-mythological interpretation of Hemingway's book. *In Our Time* depicts "the rhythmic interplay of life and death, destruction and renewal, chaos and cosmos." This reflects Hemingway's "own symbolic death and rebirth on the Italian front in 1918."

1110. Muller, Gilbert H. "*In Our Time*: Hemingway and the Discontents of Civilization." *Renascence*, 29 (1977), 185-192.

> An analysis using the ideas of Arthur Janov. "The metaphor of the scream" is a unifying device in *In Our Time*. "The accumulated pains, the repressed screams, the pandemic nausea: all work outward from the personal toward a vision of civilization in a process of disintegration." Hemingway's characters "never scream out at the fragmentation of existence; like their creator, they never complete this necessary voyage." Instead, they become stoics, a self-destructive stance.

1111. Tavernier-Courbin, Jacqueline. "Striving for Power: Hemingway's Neurosis." *Journal of General Education*, 30 (1978), 137-153.

> A discussion of Hemingway's life and writing in terms of his "neurotic competitiveness" and how he became "other-directed" and pursued his own self-image. His public personality was "characteristic of what Karen Horney describes as the neurotic quest for power."

1112. Watt, Donald. "Hemingway's How to Be." *Review of Existential Psychology and Psychiatry*, 15 (1977), 210-226.

> An existential interpretation of *The Old Man and the Sea* and *The Sun Also Rises*, with a comparison to the work of Sartre and Camus.

1113. Yalom, Irvin D., and Yalom, Marilyn. "Ernest Hemingway: A Psychiatric View." *Archives of General Psychiatry*, 24 (1971), 485-494.

> "Hemingway struggled all his life with severe characterological problems and, in a severe paranoid depression, committed suicide." An analysis of Hemingway's life and writing reveals the "major psychodynamic conflicts" which led to his suicide. Essay also draws upon the memories of a close friend of Hemingway.

Herbert, Frank

1114. McNelly, Willis E. "Archetypal Patterns in Science Fiction." *CEA Critic*, 35 (1973), 15-19.

> Focuses on Jungian archetypal patterns in Frank Herbert's *Dune* and Ursula K. LeGuin's *The Left Hand of Darkness*.

Hersey, John

1115. Haltresht, Michael. "Dreams as a Characterization Device in Hersey's White Lotus." Notes on Contemporary Literature, 1 (1971), 4-5.

>Hersey's characters' dreams reveal their inner conflict as members of oppressed minority groups. This conflict is one of anger versus fear, leading to anger "redirected against the self" and "psychosomatic illness."

Hesse, Herman

1116. Anshin, Roman. "Creativity, Mid-Life Crisis, and Herman Hesse." Journal of the American Academy of Psychoanalysis, 4 (1976), 215-226.

>Hesse is an example of a person who successfully resolved his mid-life crisis, as seen by his later life and writing. Thus a study of Hesse and his work would be useful for analysts dealing with the mid-life problem.

1117. Brink, A.W. "Herman Hesse and the Oedipal Quest." Literature and Psychology, 24, 2 (1974), 66-79.

>Rather than writing literature of escape, Hesse tried to show the value of making the unconscious conscious. Hesse's major works show the importance of literature in bringing the neurotic's unconscious to light. This is an important purpose of psychoanalysis, and literature is a pleasant way of doing it.

1118. Mileck, Joseph. "Freud and Jung, Psychoanalysis and Literature, Art and Disease." Seminar, 14 (1978), 105-116.

>Through discussion of Herman Hesse's encounters with psychoanalysis and his relations with Freud, whom he admired without qualification, and Jung, whom he was critical of but deferred to.

Himes, Chester

1119. Reckley, Ralph. "The Oedipal Complex and Intraracial Conflict in Chester Himes' The Third Generation." College Language Association Journal, 21 (1977), 275-281.

>A study of Charles, the third son, and his mother and father in The Third Generation. "It is the Oedipus Complex that destroys the son and breaks up the family." Lillian hates and emasculates her husband, sublimates her attraction to her father, and "destroys her son by developing guilt in him because of his incestuous love for her."

1120. _____. "The Use of the Doppelganger or Double in Chester Himes' Lonely Crusade." College Language Association Journal, 20 (1977), 448-458.

A study of Lee Gordon, Lester McKinley, and Luther McGregor to show how Himes uses doubles to demonstrate emasculation in the black male in Lonely Crusade. "The doubling technique results in complexity of structure in the novel. Furthermore, it intensifies Himes' protest theme by giving us not one but three examples of the effects of racism on the Black male."

Hughes, Langston

1121. Miller, R. Baxter. "'No Crystal Stair': Unity, Archetype, and Symbol in Langston Hughes's Poems on Women." Negro American Literary Forum, 9 (1975), 109-114.

Archetypal images of women as devine mothers give unity to Hughes' poems about women. However, in his later verses, the archetypal imagery wanes, with a consequent waning of universal structure.

Huxley, Aldous
(See also item 346.)

1122. Meckier, Jerome. "Our Ford, Our Freud and the Behaviorist Conspiracy in Huxley's Brave New World." Thalia: Studies in Literary Humor, 1 (1978), 35-59.

In Brave New World, Henry Ford, John Watson, the behaviorist, and Freud are satirized for their "essentially mechanistic conception of human behavior."

1123. Muzina, Matej. "Reverberations of Jung's Psychological Types in the Novels of Aldous Huxley." Studia Romanica et Anglica Zagrabiensia, 33-36 (1972-1973), 305-334.

Discusses Huxley's interest in human typology and his early fascination with Jung's theories. Provides numerous examples of characters from Huxley's novels who fit Jungian types.

Inge, William

1124. Mitchell, Marilyn L. "William Inge." American Imago, 35 (1978), 297-310.

A survey of Inge's plays and novels in terms of his obsessive love for his mother and the hopelessness this obsession caused.

Ionesco, Eugene

1125. de Furia, Richard. "At the Intersection of Freud and Ionesco." Modern Language Notes, 87 (1972), 971-976.

"I hope to show a Freudian evolution in some joke-like passages from Ionesco."

Jackson, Shirley

1126. Hoffman, Steven K. "Individuation and Character Development in the Fiction of Shirley Jackson." Hartford Studies in Literature, 8 (1976), 190-208.

An application of Jung's ideas on maturation to Jackson's writing, to demonstrate her complexity, skill of character development, and universality.

Jensen, Wilhelm

1127. Hamilton, James W. "Jensen's Gradiva: A Further Interpretation." American Imago, 30 (1973), 380-411.

Adds to a psychoanalytic interpretation of Gradiva in the light of ego psychology.

Jong, Erica

1128. Stone, Carole. "Three Mother-Daughter Poems: The Struggle for Separation." Contemporary Psychoanalysis, 11 (1975), 227-239.

An analysis of Erica Jong's "Mother," Sylvia Plath's "The Disquieting Muses," and Anne Sexton's "Dreaming of Breasts." The poems suggest ambivalent feelings towards mothers as their children move towards independence. It is also observed that two of the poets killed themselves.

Joyce, James

1129. Anderson, Chester G. "Leopold Bloom as Dr. Sigmund Freud." Mosaic, 6 (1972), 23-43.

Notes intentional references to Freud's The Psychopathology of Everyday Life in the "Lestrygonians" episode of Ulysses.

1130. Beja, Morris. "Dividual Chaoses: Case Histories of Multiple Personality and Finnegans Wake." James Joyce Quarterly, 14 (1977), 241-250.

Attempts to associate several well-known cases of multiple personality to passages in the Wake.

1131. Brivic, Sheldon. Joyce Between Freud and Jung. Port Washington: Kennikat, 1980.

"In my effort to trace the nature and development of Joyce's mind as reflected in his work, I will first use Freudian insights to show how Joyce's mind was formed and to explore its unconscious aspect. Then I will show the relation between these influences and Joyce's conscious, mature ideas, which I'll explain partly in Jungian terms."

1132. _____. "Joyce in Progress: A Freudian View." James Joyce Quarterly, 13 (1976), 306-327.

A discussion of the variety and development in the Joyce oeuvre, using depth psychology to examine "the Joyce canon dynamically, seeing it as a continuous process in which issues are worked out and possibilities created as personality develops."

1133. Brivic, Sheldon R. "James Joyce: From Stephen to Bloom." In Crews, F., ed., Psychoanalysis and Literary Process. Cambridge, Mass.: Winthrop, 1970, 118-162.

A psychoanalytic inquiry into "why Joyce views experience in terms of exile or relations through separation." Discusses Stephen Dedalus' Oedipal conflicts and "the idea of union through separation, reconciliation through sundering."

1134. Dervin, Daniel. "Why Does Molly Menstruate? A New View of Psychoanalysis and Creativity." Literature and Psychology, 28 (1978), 125-136.

A study of creativity in the work of Joyce, emphasizing "that the task of object-restoration as well as self-reconstitution is the work of the ego in the process of normal development. . . . To conceptualize creativity within the area of separation-individuation is to shift one's focus from id to ego and from narcissistic self-display to a struggle toward working through."

1135. Gordon, William A. "Submission and Autonomy: Identity Patterns in Joyce's Portrait." Psychoanalytic Review, 61 (1974-75), 535-555.

In A Portrait of the Artist As A Young Man, Joyce demonstrates a keen understanding of how an artist transforms his personal experiences into art. The artist undergoes a change in his attitude towards his experience so that he becomes dominated by the idea of objectifying his experience as a work of art.

1136. Henke, Suzette A. "Joyce and Krafft-Ebing." James Joyce Quarterly, 17 (1979), 84-86.

"If Joyce was indeed familiar with Psychopathia Sexualis, it seems possible that he may have been satirizing the book's ideas in the 'Penelope' episode of Ulysses."

1137. _____. "Joyce's Bloom: Beyond Sexual Possessiveness." American Imago, 32 (1975), 329-334.

The "Ithaca" episode of Ulysses frees Bloom from his erotic desire for Molly because she offers him "mother's love," or agape. Bloom, therefore, can satisfy his oedipal desires as a husband/son.

1138. Kimball, Jean. "Freud, Leonardo, and Joyce: The Dimensions of A Childhood Memory." James Joyce Quarterly, 17 (1980), 165-182.

" . . . an examination of the links between Joyce's text and Freud's promises something different from another 'Freudian' reading." Freud's essay on Leonardo, which Joyce owned, is the basis of this new reading.

1139. _____. "James Joyce and Otto Rank: The Incest Motif in Ulysses." James Joyce Quarterly, 13 (1976), 366-382.

"I should like in this essay to consider the implications of some correspondences between apparently distinctive features of the Hamlet theory which Joyce filters through Stephen Dedalus in Ulysses and Rank's analysis of Hamlet as an 'incest drama' in . . . (The Incest Motif in Poetry and Saga: The Fundamentals of a Psychology of Poetic Creation)."

1140. Kloss, Robert J. "The Function of Forgetting in Joyce's 'Clay'." Hartford Studies in Literature, 6 (1974), 167-179.

The forgetting of the plumcake, the stanza, the corkscrew and nutcracker (four things similar to one another as "openers") "is related to Maria's frustrated sexuality."

1141. Mannoni, Octave. "Fiction III: Introduction (Literature and Psychoanalysis)." Sub-stance, 30 (1981), 3-15.

A fictional conversation between Joyce and an analyst. Joyce here exclaims "You, the analyst, your work cannot be to explain writers but to explain what psychoanalysis owes to the work of writers."

1142. McKnight, Jeanne. "Unlocking the Word-Hoard: Madness, Identity and Creativity in James Joyce." James Joyce Quarterly, 14 (1977), 420-433.

An analysis of Joyce's language, revealing that "Stephen Dedalus is haunted by needs and fears that have something to do with his relationship with his mother, a relationship that is . . . implied in Stephen's behavior, his language, and the language of Joyce's own narrative." Stephen suffers from an "oral-narcissistic dilemma."

1143. Newman, Robert D. "The Shadow of Stephen Dedalus." Journal of Evolutionary Psychology, 2 (1981), 112-124.

A Jungian study of Ulysses. "Stephen's bondage to his shadow projections has turned his life into the ghost story which he refuses to tell his students in 'Nestor'."

1144. Norris, Margot C. "The Language of Dream in Finnegans Wake." Literature and Psychology, 24, 1 (1974), 4-11.

"If we assume that the dreamer can be found there where conflicts and tensions appear in the language of Finnegans Wake, we have made a giant step toward locating his function, as well as rendered nugatory the question of his identity."

1145. O'Brien, Darcy. "A Critique of Psychoanalytic Criticism, or What Joyce Did and Did Not Do." James Joyce Quarterly, 13 (1976), 275-292.

As materialists, Americans are good Freudians, "pleased to learn from Freud that there is nothing apart from the physical, that the self is a thing and that the seat of the affections lies in the seat." But Joyce's work demands that we recognize values different from our own.

1146. _____. "Some Psychological Determinants of Joyce's View of Love and Sex." In Senn, F., ed., New Light on Joyce from the Dublin Symposium. Bloomington: Indiana University Press, 1972, 15-27.

Argues that Joyce suffered from a "Hibernian version of Portnoy's complaint"--a Western complaint in which men are unable to combine tenderness and sexuality. The Freudian view is that this complaint is due to a failure to overcome the incestuous fixations of early childhood.

1147. Rabaté, Jean-Michel. "A Clown's Inquest into Paternity: Fathers, Dead or Alive, in Ulysses and Finnegans Wake." In Davis, R.C., ed., The Fictional Father. Amherst: University of Massachusetts Press, 1981, 73-114.

Joyce's definition of a father in Finnegans Wake--"a personal problem, a locative enigma"--"helps us to replace the question of designation by an exploration in positioning; if . . . a father is defined by his absence, paternity and patriarch are set adrift in a world of substitutes, in which everybody is endlessly elsewhere."

1148. Shechner, Mark. "Freud on Joyce." James Joyce Quarterly, 9 (1971), 280-296.

A review of Edward Brandabur's A Scrupulous Meanness: A Study of Joyce's Early Work (1971), Edmund Epstein's The Ordeal of Stephen Dedalus: The Conflict of Generations in James Joyce's A Portrait of the Artist As a Young Man (1971), and Sheldon Brivic's "James Joyce: From Stephen to Bloom," in F. Crews, ed. Psychoanalysis and Literary Process (1970).

1149. _____. "Joyce and Psychoanalysis: Two Additional Perspectives." James Joyce Quarterly, 14 (1977), 416-419.

An overview of recent psychologically oriented articles on Joyce, including Jeanne McKnight's "Unlocking the Word-Hoard: Madness, Identity and Creativity in James Joyce" (JJQ 14, 1977); Sheldon Brivic's "Joyce in Progress: A Freudian View" (JJQ 13, 1976); and James Klein's "Out of Mere Words" (JJQ 13, 1976).

1150. _____. Joyce in Nighttown: A Psychoanalytic Inquiry into Ulysses. Berkeley: University of California Press, 1974.

"A study of Joyce's own self-encounters and a theory of Ulysses, both as the record of those encounters and as an instrument for handling them. Art . . . is a strategy for meeting the faces that we meet within ourselves, . . . and it is a lesson Joyce knew by heart."

1151. Tarbox, Raymond. "Auditory Experience in Joyce's Portrait." American Imago, 27 (1970), 301-328.

A psychological study of Stephen Dedalus as a "sound-sensitive hero." Such a hero often associates "bad sound" with loss and betrayal, and strives to "transform bad noise into good" in order to improve his self-esteem.

1152. Tomasi, Barbara R. "The Fraternal Theme in Joyce's Ulysses." American Imago, 30 (1973), 177-191.

The atmosphere of fraternal rivalry permeates Ulysses.

1153. Walcott, William. "Notes by a Jungian Analyst on the Dreams in Ulysses." James Joyce Quarterly, 9 (1971), 37-48.

"I contend that an intensive analysis of the Haroun al Raschid dream, the major link in the chain of foreshadowing coincidences forged by Joyce, brings one to a psychological explanation that ties them all together as well as illuminating the meaning for Stephen of his meeting with Bloom." Joyce anticipated Jung's theory of Synchronicity, i.e., meaningful coincidences.

Kafka, Franz
(See also items 100, 298, 636.)

1154. Brand, Harry. "Kafka's Creative Crisis." Journal of the American Academy of Psychoanalysis, 4 (1976), 249-260.

Despite and because of his extreme hysteria, paranoia, and problems with his parents, Kafka was able to write effectively and become a major voice of the twentieth century.

1155. Dodd, William J. "Kafka and Freud: A Note on In der Strafkolonie." Monatshefte, 70 (1978), 129-137.

There is an ironic allusion to Freud's scheme of consciousness in Kafka's description of the execution apparatus in In The Penal Colony.

1156. Friedrich, Reinhart. "The Dream-Transference in Kafka's Ein Landarzt." Papers on Language and Literature, 9 (1973), 28-34.

Argues that the story is based on a dream pattern and should not be interpreted as traditional realism vulnerable to "the customary tools of character and plot analysis."

1157. Jofen, Jean. "Metamorphosis." American Imago, 35 (1978), 347-356.

Interprets Metamorphosis on three levels: Kafka's familial and social concerns, his fear of illness, and his love/hatred for his parents.

1158. Lesser, Simon O. "The Source of Guilt and the Sense of Guilt: Kafka's The Trial." (1962) In Sprich, R., and Noland, R., eds., The Whispered Meanings: Selected Essays of Simon O. Lesser. Amherst: University of Massachusetts Press, 1977, 68-85.

The reader identifies with the vaguely drawn Joseph K and shares with him his attempt to resolve an abiding sense of guilt. K's super-ego is dominant and he submits to it while his ego sense of reality is as weak as Prince Myshkin's.

1159. Levine, Robert T. "The Familiar Friend: A Freudian Approach to Kafka's 'The Judgment' ('Das Urteil')." Literature and Psychology, 27, 4 (1977), 164-173.

Argues that "The Judgment" can be approached as a dream and that it exhibits dream mechanisms such as disguise, displacement, reversal, and secondary revision.

1160. Mahony, Patrick. "A Hunger Artist: Content and Form." American Imago, 35 (1978), 357-374.

The literary work coheres as a Symbolic Gestalt because "both form and content attain a higher complex integration than is present in dream work, joke work, or in the free association of clinical discourse."

1161. McLean, Sammy. "Doubling and Sexual Identity in Stories by Franz Kafka." Hartford Studies in Literature, 12 (1980), 1-17.

Traces Kafka's developing uses of doubling. Doubling "is a basic means for the expression of the psychological aspect of Kafka's thematic matter which deals with problems of human sexual identity." Discusses "The Judgment," "The Metamorphosis," "A Country Doctor," and "Josephine the Singer, or the Mouse Folk."

1162. Murrill, V., and Marks, W.S., III. "Kafka's 'The Judgment' and The Interpretaion of Dreams." Germanic Review, 48 (1973), 212-228.

Notes similarities of narrative and plot in "The Judgment" to narratives in Freud's The Interpretation of Dreams. Kafka used his story for self-understanding, as a psychoanalyst uses dreams.

1163. Neumann, Erich. "Kafka's The Trial: An Interpretation Through Depth Psychology." In Creative Man: Five Essays. Princeton: Princeton University Press, 1980, 3-112.

This lengthy discussion by Jung's prominent disciple, Erich Neumann, presents the analytical psychologist's view of Joseph K's estrangement from the "knowing foundation of his nature"--his unconscious mind. Neumann suggests that Joseph K is brought to trial because he intuitively suspects he is "guilty" of leading a life constricted by his conscious mind.

1164. Neumarkt, Paul. "Kafka's A Hunger Artist: The Ego in Isolation." American Imago, 27 (1970), 109-121.

A study of the dangers of ego isolation, concentrating on "nostalgic regression," "latent homosexuality," "the psychotic darkness of chaos," and "Liebestod . . . flirtation with the finality of death."

1165. Norris, Margot. "Sadism and Masochism in Two Kafka Stories: 'In der Strafkolonie' und 'Ein Hungerkunstler.'" MLN, 93 (1978), 430-447.

Argues that if "suffering is seen as a means whose end is not the Law or the Ideal, but pleasure, then Law and Ideal become mere pretexts, fraudulent rationales in a pornological fantasy."

1166. Politzer, Heinz. "The Alienated Self: A Key to Franz Kafka's Castle?" Michigan Quarterly Review, 14 (1975), 398-414.

Argues that the real plot of The Castle is K's aimless wandering in a void, signifying his estrangement, his loss of identity.

1167. Sizemore, Charles. "Anxiety in Kafka: A Function of Cognitive Dissonance." Journal of Modern Literature, 6 (1977), 380-387.

Utilizes Leon Festinger's theory of cognitive dissonance (cognitive elements exist as internally consistent and any break in that consistency creates dissonance) to explain why the dual "realities" (Kafka's and the reader's) in Kafka's works are disturbing to the reader.

1168. Stockholder, Katherine. "A Country Doctor: The Narrator as Dreamer." American Imago, 35 (1978), 331-346.

Looks to the language and imagery of this work as a substitute for the free associations provided by a real dreamer. A literary work negotiates between the unconscious and consciousness and that negotiation which does not exist in dream, must be acknowledged in psychoanalytic criticism.

1169. Street, James. "Kafka through Freud: Totems and Taboos in In der Strafkolonie." Modern Austrian Literature, 6 (1973), 93-106.

"The striking manner in which the two works flirt with similar themes of social and religious criticism offers some hope that an analysis of Kafka's arcane tale in terms of the theories offered by Freud in Totem and Taboo might provide another set of clues rendering In der Strafkolonie more comprehensible."

1170. Sussman, Henry. "The Court as Text: Inversion, Supplanting, and Derangement in Kafka's Der Prozess." PMLA, 92 (1977), 41-55.

Focuses on the whipping scene in The Trial, a moment when "the delineations separating accused, accuser, and the arm of the law fall away."

Kazantzakis, Nikos

1171. Hartocollis, P. "Mysticism and Violence: The Case of Nikos Kazantzakis." International Journal of Psycho-Analysis, 55 (1974), 205-213.

Argues that the mystic's struggle is against his own internal violence and that Kazantzakis's life and work support such a contention.

Kesey, Ken

1172. Benert, Annette L. "The Forces of Fear: Kesey's Anatomy of Insanity." Lex et Scientia: International Journal of Law and Science, 13, 1-2 (1977), 22-26.

   A study of Bromden's psyche through his Jungian projections in One Flew Over the Cuckoo's Nest. "What Bromden must primarily come to terms with is his own fear, . . . fear of unused psychic possibilities." His task is to free himself from that fear and his destructive fantasies in order to find his true nature.

1173. Forrey, Robert. "Ken Kesey's Psychopathic Savior: A Rejoinder." Modern Fiction Studies, 21 (1975), 222-230.

   One Flew Over the Cuckoo's Nest depicts a group of men whose paranoic and megalomaniacal feelings may come from, as Freud suggested, repressed homosexual longings. These feelings are sublimated in games, violence, and psychopathological pranks. McMurphy is a masculine, Christlike savior to these men.

1174. Sullivan, Ruth. "Big Mama, Big Papa, and Little Sons in Ken Kesey's One Flew Over the Cuckoos' Nest." Literature and Psychology, 25, 1 (1975), 34-44.

   A discussion of oedipal themes in Kesey's novel. The patients, as sons, want love from Big Nurse, as a mother figure. It is up to McMurphy, as father figure, to help them.

1175. Wills, Arthur. "The Doctor and the Flounder: Psychoanalysis and One Flew Over the Cuckoo's Nest." Studies in the Humanities, 5 (1976), 19-25.

   An examination of the fishing trip scene in Kesey's novel. The trip "evokes corrective laughter . . . and it draws upon psychology, perhaps unconsciously, to define a national aberration that passes for normality."

Kosinski, Jerzy

1176. Hanson, John. "The Child Archetype and Modern Primitivism: Kosinski's The Painted Bird." University of Hartford Studies in Literature, 14 (1982), 85-95.

   The Painted Bird depicts a Jungian child archetype who is a symbol "of both estranged realms, the inner and the outer."

1177. Lale, Meta, and Williams, John S. "The Narrator of The Painted Bird: A Case Study." Renascence, 24 (1972), 198-206.

   "The analysis that follows . . . is our description of the defense mechanisms developed by Kosinski's narrator in order to survive meaningfully under the most horrendous conditions of stress imaginable."

1178. Mortimer, Gail L. "'Fear Death By Water': The Boundaries of the Self in Jerzy Kosinski's The Painted Bird." Psychoanalytic Review, 63 (1976-1977), 511-528.

> A Laingian interpretation of Kosinski's novel. "The specific schizoid fears of engulfment, implosion, and petrification (Laing's terms) are pervasively reflected in Kosinski's novel. . . . The Child's increasing withdrawal ends within a symbolic dissolution into schizophrenia, the blizzard which cuts him off finally from others."

1179. Sewell, Ernestine. "The Jungian Process of Individuation as Structure in The Painted Bird." South Central Bulletin, 38 (1978), 160-163.

> The young protagonist of this novel is moving toward the Jungian "self" amidst the horrors of war.

Lampedusa, Guiseppe di

1180. Kuhns, Richard F. "Modernity and Death: The Leopard by Guiseppe di Lampedusa." Contemporary Psychoanalysis, 5 (1969), 95-128.

> The Leopard is a novel that demonstrates Freud's idea that in literature "we still find people who know how to die." It presents a "tragedy of endurance" rather than a "tragedy of reversal and recognition." It is a novel about dying, presenting a hero who accepts "the changes of modernity" while "perpetuating in his private concerns the traditional attitudes of the past towards death." Reference is made to parallels between the theme of the novel and Freud's "The Theme of the Three Caskets." A discussion of Kuhns' article, by Miltiades L. Zaphiropoulous, Charles Clay Dahlberg, and Frank A. Hale, follows the article.

Laurence, Margaret

1181. Davidson, Cathy N. "Geography as Psychology in the Manitoba Fiction of Margaret Laurence." Kate Chopin Newsletter, 2, 2 (1976), 5-10.

> In Laurence's work, landscape and locale become "as much a state of mind as a place on the map. But by recognizing the complex interrelationship of geography to psychology, Laurence's characters survive and a few even manage to achieve art."

Lawrence, D.H.
(See also items 426, 715, 764.)

1182. Adamowski, T.H. "Character and Consciousness: D.H. Lawrence, Wilhelm Reich, and Jean-Paul Sartre." University of Toronto Quarterly, 43 (1974), 311-334.

> "What I should like to do here is to consider certain aspects of the

thinking of Sartre and Lawrence on character by reference to the work of the first 'Freudian radical,' Wilhelm Reich."

1183. _____. "The Father of All Things: The Oral and the Oedipal in Sons and Lovers." Mosaic, 14 (1981), 69-88.

Calls for a future effort to establish the hypothesis that a "negative oedipal phase" informs Sons and Lovers.

1184. _____. "Intimacy at a Distance: Sexuality and Orality in Sons and Lovers." Mosaic, 13 (1980), 71-89.

"What I want to examine here is the basic source of Lawrence's insistence on separateness, his concern with the barrier to fusion which the body predicates, and also his emphasis upon the transcendence of otherness that occurs in sexual experience."

1185. _____. "Self/Body/Other: Orality and Ontology in Lawrence." D.H. Lawrence Review, 13 (1980), 193-208.

Employs Lawrence's metaphors of Spirit and Flesh to describe existential themes of existence as well as the "pre-oedipal" stage in Lawrence's work.

1186. Davies, Rosemary. "The Mother as Destroyer: Psychic Division in the Writings of D.H. Lawrence." D.H. Lawrence Review, 13 (1980), 220-238.

Draws upon Erich Fromm's The Anatomy of Human Destructiveness in order to resolve certain dilemmas in Lawrence's attitudes towards his mother, women in general, and the conflict of love and power as displayed in his work.

1187. Dervin, Daniel. "Play, Creativity and Matricide: The Implications of Lawrence's 'Smashed Doll' Episode." Mosaic, 14 (1981), 81-94.

Focuses on D.W. Winnicott and the object-relations school view of play. Play is the "stage in the artist's personal growth when his emotions and drives manifest themselves . . . or . . . first become available to him for creative disposal." Applies the third phase of play to Sons and Lovers.

1188. Dervin, Daniel A. "D.H. Lawrence and Freud." American Imago, 36 (1979), 95-117.

A thorough-going discussion of the similarities and dissimilarities of Lawrence and Freud.

1189. Efron, Arthur. "The Mind-Body Problem in Lawrence, Pepper and Reich." Journal of Mind and Behavior, 1 (1980), 247-270.

Presents the philosophical dimensions of the mind-body linkage involved in Reich's theory.

1190. Hirsch, Gordon D. "The Laurentian Double: Images of D.H. Lawrence in the Stories." D.H. Lawrence Review, 10, 3 (1977), 270-276.

Neither the weak male nor the virile male (the Laurentian Double) possesses a secure identity, one which enables him to relate to women.

1191. Hoerner, Dennis. "Connie Chatterley: A Case of Spontaneous Therapy." Energy and Character: The Journal of Bioenergetic Research, 12 (1981), 48-55.

A Reichian interpretation of Lady Chatterley's Lover.

1192. _____. "D.H. Lawrence's 'Carbon' and Wilhelm Reich's 'Core' in The Rainbow." Journal of Orgonomy, 12 (1978), 92-99.

An interpretation of the sheave-gathering scene in which Will Brangwen and Anna Brangwen engage in abortive sexual ritual.

1193. Kleinbard, David J. "Laing, Lawrence, and the Maternal Cannibal." Psychoanalytic Review, 58, 1 (1971), 5-13.

Discusses Paul Morel of Sons and Lovers in terms of R.D. Laing's notion of "ontological insecurity"--loss of a firm sense of one's own and other people's reality and identity.

1194. Panken Shirley. "Some Psychodynamics in Sons and Lovers: A New Look at the Oedipal Theme." Psychoanalytic Review, 61 (1974-1975), 571-589.

Argues that the entire family matrix must be considered in a psychoanalytical discussion of Sons and Lovers. "Oedipal patterns do not remain immutable but are affected by and interact with the total life cycle."

1195. Ragussis, Michael. "The Subterfuge of Art: Lawrence, Freud, and 'Verbal Consciousness'." In The Subterfuge of Art. Baltimore: Johns Hopkins University Press, 1978, 1-5.

The artist contests the subterfuge of all art (Lawrence's view) by utilizing the Freudian "verbal consciousness," a self-reflective, self-critical use of language.

1196. Ruderman, Judith. "Lawrence's 'The Fox' and Verga's 'The She-Wolf': Variations on the Theme of Devouring Mother." MLN, 94 (1979), 153-165.

Argues that Lawrence, inspired by the short stories of Giovanni Verga, went to extremes in The Fox "in order to fight the battle against the 'devouring mother'."

1197. Schwartz, Murray M. "D.H. Lawrence and Psychoanalysis: An Introduction." D.H. Lawrence Review, 10 (1977), 215-222.

Introduces psychoanalysts whose work relates to Lawrence's. Serves as an introduction to this special issue, "Psychoanalytic Criticism of the Short Stories."

1198. Tenenbaum, Elizabeth. The Problematic Self: Approaches to Identity in Stendahl, D.H. Lawrence, and Malraux. Cambridge: Harvard University Press, 1972.

Views of Lawrence are considered within a context similar to Abraham Maslow's Toward A Psychology of Being.

1199. Thornham, Susan. "Lawrence and Freud." Durham University Journal, 70 (1977), 73-82.

Discusses Freud's view that the life-force is primitive and dangerous, and Lawrence's contrary belief that the life-force is wholly positive.

1200. Trail, George. "The Psychological Dynamics of D.H. Lawrence's 'Snake'." American Imago, 36 (1979), 345-356.

"I propose that 'Snake' begins as a deliberate, even careful repudiation of Freudian theory, particularly as it concerns the Oedipus Complex, and then breaks down under the pressures of a severe confrontation with castration anxieties."

1201. Tristram, Philippa. "Eros and Death (Lawrence, Freud and Women)." In Smith, Anne, ed., Lawrence and Women. London: Vision, 1978, 136-155.

Uses Freud as a gloss to The Rainbow, Women In Love, and Aaron's Rod. "Where Freud sought to know, Lawrence sought to be."

Lehmann, Rosamond

1202. Kaplan, Sydney Janet. "Rosamond Lehmann's The Ballad and the Source: A Confrontation with 'The Great Mother'." Twentieth Century Literature, 27 (1981), 127-145.

Lehmann interweaves the Demeter myth "into a subtle pattern in which archetypal images related to the basic core of that myth--the presence of 'The Great Mother'--enhance and effect the story's emotional resonance."

Leonov, Leonid

1203. Plank, D.L. "Unconscious Motifs in Leonid Leonov's The Badgers." Slavonic and East European Journal, 16 (1972), 19-35.

A study of the unconscious symbolism and latent content in Leonov's novel, a naive "post-Freudian allegory."

Leroux, Etienne

1204. Berner, R.L. "Etienne LeRoux: A Jungian Introduction." Books Abroad, 49 (1975), 225-262.

"The following discussion . . . is intended as an introduction to LeRoux's art in the form of an admittedly tentative reading of 18/44 in terms of its Jungian content."

Lessing, Doris
(See also item 559).

1205. Berets, Ralph. "A Jungian Interpretation of the Dream Sequence in Doris Lessing's The Summer Before the Dark." Modern Fiction Studies, 26 (1980), 117-130.

    Argues that in this novel Lessing criticizes the Freudian prejudice regarding women and "attempts to define new territory that establishes the female as an integrated whole and one worthy of major focus in a male dominated world." Uses Jungian psychology, especially individuation, as a gloss.

1206. Kaplan, Sydney Janet. "The Limits of Consciousness in the Novels of Doris Lessing." In Pratt, A., and Dembo, L.S., eds., Doris Lessing: Critical Studies. Madison: University of Wisconsin Press, 1974, 119-132.

    Notes Lessing's attempts at depicting a kind of Jungian "collective unconscious" with an "ocean of images" within her characters, rather than an individual "stream of consciousness." The very form of the novel places certain limites on these attempts.

1207. Lefcowitz, Barbara F. "Dream and Action in Lessing's The Summer Before the Dark." Critique: Studies in Modern Fiction, 17 (1975), 107-120.

    Kate Brown's dreams represent her desire for autonomy. Yet, consciously she cannot free herself from her previous family home life. This conflict between the unconscious and the conscious prohibits her from actually escaping from her old, stereotypical female role.

1208. Markow, Alice B. "The Pathology of Feminine Failure in the Fiction of Doris Lessing." Critique: Studies in Modern Fiction, 16 (1974), 88-100.

    A study of sick male-female relationships and the "neurotic-psychotic" personalities of Lessing's female characters. Both Lessing's traditional women and her liberated women are trapped in the transition from old to new life styles. Lessing is ambivalent about the roles of women.

1209. Pickering, Jean. "Marxism and Madness: The Two Faces of Doris Lessing's Myth." Modern Fiction Studies, 26 (1980), 17-30.

    A discussion of the visionary, psychological and political implications of Lessing's work. Her "politics on the left" and "politics of madness," are connected in "a vision of Jerusalem, the archetypal city." This connection can be seen most strongly "in the evolving consciousness of Martha Quest," whose own quest is individuation.

1210. Rose, Ellen Cronan. "The Eriksonian Bildungsroman: An Approach Through Doris Lessing." Hartford Studies in Literature, 7 (1975), 1-17.

    Lessing's Children of Violence, an example of a modern Bildungsroman, is best analyzed through Erik Erikson's ego-psychology because Erikson concentrates on the interaction of the psyche with its environment. This is more useful than psychoanalytic criticism. *Wilhelm Meister* and Erikson's biography of Luther are also discussed with this in mind.

1211. Rubenstein, Roberta. "Briefing on Inner Space: Doris Lessing and R.D. Laing." *Psychoanalytic Review*, 63 (1976), 83-93.

> An examination of Lessing's *Briefing for a Descent into Hell* through ideas of R.D. Laing. Watkins, the protagonist of *Briefing*, has a psychic journey parallel to a patient of Laing in *The Politics of Experience*. Lessing, "like Laing, . . . suggests that . . . schizophrenia may be less in Watkins than in the world from which he withdrew. But unlike Laing, she doubts that madness is a necessary route to sanity."

1212. _____. "Doris Lessing's *The Golden Notebook*: The Meaning of Its Shape." *American Imago*, 32 (1975), 40-58.

> Anna comes to psychic integrity through a process of chaos moving to wholeness, as seen, in the final sections of the book, by Saul Green, Anna's alter ego. The form of *The Golden Notebook* leads the reader to understand the whole in relationship to its parts, and thus it reflects Anna's psychic development.

1213. Sternberg-Perrakis, Phyllis. "Doris Lessing's *The Golden Notebook*: Separation and Symbiosis." *American Imago*, 38 (1981), 407-428.

> "The emotional configuration that underlies the novel's formal and thematic complexity involves the fear of loss of a loved one and the attempts to deny or restore that loss."

1214. Vlastos, Marion. "Doris Lessing and R.D. Laing: Psychopolitics and Prophecy." *PMLA*, 91 (1976), 245-258.

> Traces similarities of Laing's thought and Lessing's major novels. Both writers view the insane person as a victim of society who understands the ills of that society. Lessing's *The Four-Gated City*, *The Golden Notebook*, and *Briefing for a Descent into Hell* are discussed.

Levertov, Denise

1215. Holland, Norman N. "Poem Opening: An Invitation to Transactive Criticism." *College English*, 40 (1978), 2-16.

> A presentation of ten "transactions" of Denise Levertov's poem "To The Snake."

Lewis, C.S.

1216. Carnell, Corbin. "Ransom in C.S. Lewis' *Perelandra* as Hero in Transformation: Notes toward a Jungian Reading of the Novel." *Studies in the Literary Imagination*, 14 (1981), 67-71.

Ransom "goes through a process of individuation which includes initiation, trials, suffering, and other aspects of the psychoanalytic 'monomyth'." And Jung displays some affinities to Lewis' brand of Christianity.

Lewis, Sinclair

1217. Carothers, James B. "Midwestern Civilization and Its Discontents: Lewis's Carol Kennicott and Roth's Lucy Nelson." *Midwestern Miscellany*, 9 (1981), 21-30.

> Roth's *When She Was Good* may have been modeled on Lewis' *Main Street*. However, "substantial differences between the two novels and their central characters may be taken to illustrate the radical transition from a pre-Freudian to a post-Freudian psychology of fiction that began about the time *Main Street* was published."

Lind, Jakov

1218. Karpowitz, Stephen. "Conscience and Cannibals: An Essay on Two Exemplary Tales--*Soul of Wood* and *The Pawnbroker*." *Psychoanalytic Review*, 64 (1977), 41-62.

> Examines Jakov Lind's "Soul of Wood" and Edward Wallant's *The Pawnbroker* in terms of "the development of types of superegos representative of anti-Semites and Jews, of fictional characters and historical ones."

Lockridge, Ross, Jr.

1219. Clarke, Delia. "*Raintree County*: Psychological Symbolism, Archetype, and Myth." *Thoth*, 11 (1970), 31-39.

> *Raintree County* universalizes the American experience through myth and ritual. Shawnessy "is one man and all men; his life is a recreation of the ancient and primordial life of the human race." He has two personalities, representing "the Freudian separation of id and ego." J.W. Stiles represents Jung's "shadow archetype."

London, Jack

1220. Cooper, James Glennon. "The Womb of Time: Archetypal patterns in the Novels of Jack London." *Jack London Newsletter*, 9 (1976), 16-28.

> A demonstration of how the heroes in London's stories conform to the heroic patterns described by Joseph Campbell, Otto Rank, and Lord Raglan. The typical London hero's crime is seen in "his attitude that wealth is his due."

1221. Forrey, Robert. "Male and Female in London's *The Sea Wolf*." *Literature and Psychology*, 24 (1974), 135-143.

> The conflict between Humphrey Van Weyden and "Wolf" Larsen may be an unconscious representation of London's conflict between his rough and adventurous outer self with his inner self. Van Weyden's possible homosexuality remains latent as he decides, in the cruel world of sailors, "to toughen up rather than come out."

1222. _____. "Three Modes of Sexuality in London's *The Little Lady of the Big House*." *Literature and Psychology*, 26 (1976), 52-60.

> *Little Lady of the Big House* reflects London's interest in the psychological novel, and it unconsciously deals with heterosexuality, bisexuality, and homosexuality. The novel moves toward the exposure of "the myth of the heterosexual superman."

1223. Jørgenson, Jens Peter. "Jack London's 'The Red One'; A Freudian Approach." *Jack London Newsletter*, 8 (1975), 101-103.

> "Bassett's uncontrollable libido expresses itself as curiously, sublimitated sexual behavior," and he is destroyed by it. Bassett is compared to Conrad's Kurtz in *Heart of Darkness*.

1224. Mann, John S. "The Theme of the Double in *The Call of the Wild*." *Markham Review*, 8 (1978), 1-5.

> A study of the dog Buck and "the theme of the double in the consciousness of a dog--the working out of individual action amidst the conflict and final transformation of the divided self." At the end of *The Call of the Wild*, "Buck enters the realm of myth . . . and becomes a kind of Ur-dog."

1225. McClintock, James I. "Jack London's Use of Carl Jung's *Psychology of the Unconscious*." *American Literature*, 42 (1970), 336-347.

> A demonstration of how London incorporated Jung's language as well as his theories of the heroic journey, the facing of the dead, and rebirth, in his late stories, especially those in *On the Makaloa Mat*. It is noted that London had read *Psychology of the Unconscious*, but Jung's theories did not keep him from suicide.

Lowell, Robert

1226. McFadden, George. "'Life Studies': Robert Lowell's Comic Breakthrough." *PMLA*, 90 (1975), 96-106.

> A study of the fifteen "Life Studies" poems, which are unified by the use of Freud's myths of maturation and family. Lowell employs a Freudian comic mode, which gives him a rhetorical rather than a confessional stance. This tactic is similar to the one Pound used in *The Pisan Cantos*.

Lowry, Malcolm

1227. Boyd, Wendy. "Malcolm Lowry's *Under the Volcano*: La despedida." *American Imago*, 37 (1980), 49-64.

> Analyzes the identity theme in *Volcano* in order to understand Lowry's creative process and the reasons for his suicide.

Macdonald, Ross

1228. Kiell, Norman. "The Very Private Eye of Ross Macdonald," (parts I and II). *Literature and Psychology*, 27 (1977), 21-34; 67-73.

> "The metastasized eye" in Macdonald's fiction "leads to the hypotheses of an unresolved oedipal conflict, anxieties incurred by fantasies of the primal scene, and the . . . search for identity exemplified in the search for the father."

Maeterlinck, Maurice

1229. Knapp, Bettina. "Maeterlinck's *The Blind* or The Dying Complex." *Yale Theatre*, 5, 3 (1974), 79-86.

> Views Maeterlinck's play as a dramatization of "the dying complex" and "an attempt . . . to come to terms with the notion of death on a conscious level."

Mailer, Norman

1230. Begiebing, Robert J. "Norman Mailer's *Why Are We in Vietnam?*: The Ritual of Regeneration." *American Imago*, 37 (1980), 12-37.

> An allegorical reading of Mailer's novel. "*Why Are We in Vietnam?* is a record of the victory of the Satanic act and the defeat of expiation and rebirth."

1231. Evans, Timothy. "Boiling the Archetypal Pot: Norman Mailer's *American Dream*." *Southwest Review*, 60 (1975), 159-170.

> The center of *American Dream* "is an inverted Oedipal compulsion. Just as in Freud's scheme, the murder of the father and incest with the mother initiated a new social order based on taboos surrounding those transgressions, so here . . . Mailer's formulation requires equally actual but reversed transgressions."

1232. Gordon, Andrew. "The Modern Dream-Vision: Freud's *The Interpretation of Dreams* and Mailer's *An American Dream*." *Literature and Psychology*, 27 (1977), 100-105.

Mailer attempts "to release to the surface that '"daemonic" power' that lies within each of us." Nevertheless, "the force of the novel derives from precisely those things which Mailer refuses to admit."

1233. _____. "The Naked and the Dead: The Triumph of Impotence." Literature and Psychology, 19, 3 (1969), 3-14.

A study of Norman Mailer's anal-phallic writing. The Naked and the Dead contains characters with castration complexes and fear of being impotent. These problems along with latent homosexuality and anal repression suggest oedipal situations that have not been resolved.

1234. _____. "Why Are We in Vietnam?: Deep in the Bowels of Texas." Literature and Psychology, 24 (1974), 55-65.

A discussion of the "disembowelment diagrams" in Mailer's novel as a way of understanding it. "Vietnam is an excessively manic and anally sadistic novel, but much of its aggression is directed against the reader." D.J.'s language is a "lingual bowel movement."

1235. Silverstein, Howard. "Norman Mailer: The Family Romance and the Oedipal Family." American Imago, 34 (1977), 277-286.

A discussion of Mailer's major works. Notes oedipal and incestuous aspects within families portrayed in those works. Sees both heterosexual and homosexual struggles, and notes connections of those struggles to Mailer himself.

Malamud, Bernard

1236. Lefcowitz, Barbara F. "The Hybris of Neurosis: Malamud's Pictures of a Fidelman." Literature and Psychology, 20 (1970), 115-120.

"Malamud both depicts and parodies neurosis by juxtaposing two sets of values, the first composed of the private world of Fidelman as victim and obsessional neurotic, and the second of the socio-historical world of Fidelman as victimizer." Fidelman cannot perceive this split.

Mann, Thomas
(See also items 764, 991, 1067.)

1237. Davidson, Leah. "Mid-Life Crisis in Thomas Mann's Death in Venice." Journal of the American Academy of Psychoanalysis, 4 (1976), 203-214.

Mann's novel is a good picture of the typical problems of a middle-aged man who feels he has failed. It also parallels some of Mann's own problems, as a writer, with the onset of middle-age.

1238. Hannum, Hunter. "Mann's Joseph Novels: A Journey Toward Individuation." Psychological Perspectives, 6 (1975), 163-175.

Discusses Joseph and His Brothers in terms of Jungian psychology. Joseph's life takes on meaning when his awareness moves in a very Jungian direction. Joseph perceives "the relevance of his archaic heritage . . . in his search for a soul: his life takes on meaning and direction as it is seen in reference to . . . pre-existent patterns."

1239. Magliola, Robert. "The Magic Square: Polar Unity in Thomas Mann's Doctor Faustus." Hartford Studies in Literature, 6 (1974), 55-71.

"In this paper I shall attempt first a definition of the dialectic as the novel reveals it, and then an examination of how it applies to the themes involved."

1240. Murdaugh, Elaine. "Thomas Mann and the Bitch Goddess. Rejection and Reconstruction of the Primal Mother in Joseph and His Brothers." Revue des Langues Vivantes, 44 (1977), 395-407.

A study of the traditional light-dark (male-female) dichotomy in Mann's novel, showing that while Mann "initially agrees with and uses this mythical division of the sexes, he ultimately 'rescues' the female element from its stereotype of destructive irrationality."

1241. Slochower, Harry. "Thomas Mann's Death in Venice." American Imago, 26 (1969), 99-122.

Mann's rebellion takes the form of an esthetic homoeroticism which is preferable to a world preparing for war.

1242. Tarbox, Raymond. "Death in Venice: The Aesthetic Object as Dream Guide." American Imago, 26 (1969), 123-144.

Traces stages of the depressive, suicidal process in Aschenbach. Death in Venice is a representative of the "literature of depressive response."

1243. Zinkin, L. "Death in Venice--A Jungian View." Journal of Analytical Psychology, 22 (1977), 354-366.

Cites a correspondence between the author's patients and Mann's novella in order to illuminate "what one is trying to do as a Jungian analyst."

Maugham, Somerset

1244. Burt, Forrest D. "William Somerset Maugham: An Adlerian Interpretation." Journal of Individual Psychology, 26, 1 (1970), 64-82.

"The present paper is an attempt to shed light on the 'enigma' of Maugham by examining his life and especially his work from the viewpoint of Adler's Individual Psychology." The "enigma" is Maugham's contradictory personality characteristics.

1245. Weiss, F. "Of Human Bondage." American Journal of Psychoanalysis, 33 (1973), 68-76.

Relates Of Human Bondage to a theory of modern constructive psychoanalysis in which we are free to detach ourselves from compulsive drives.

Mauriac, François

1246. Farrell, Frederick, Jr., and Farrell, Edith F. "The Multiple Murders of Thérèse Desqueyroux." Hartford Studies in Literature, 2 (1970), 195-206.

Argues that Thérèse poisoned Bernard "when her frustration reached the point where fantasy would not relieve it."

1247. Flower, J. "Towards a Psychobiographical Study of Mauriac--The Case of Genitrix. In North, R.J., ed., Literature and Society. Birmingham: University of Birmingham, 1980, 166-176.

Suggests that in Genitrix, we have "a subconscious expression of Mauriac's love for his mother which was at once both pure, and, as in the case with many children, deeply sexual, if only subconsciously so."

McCullers, Carson

1248. Dalsimer, Katherine. "From Preadolescent Tomboy to Early Adolescent Girl: An Analysis of Carson McCullers' The Member of the Wedding." In The Psychoanalytic Study of the Child, vol. 34. New Haven: Yale University Press, 1979, 445-461.

A study of Frankie Addams' process of development. In her early adolescence, Frankie is in "the second individuation process," highlighted by "the renunciation of familiar and incestuous objects" and "estrangement from the familiarity" of her body. Frankie fights her growth by cultivating a tomboy image. At the end of the novel, however, she accepts her growth towards womanhood, giving up Frankie for her real name, Frances.

1249. Snider, Clifton. "Jungian Theory, Its Literary Application, and a Discussion of The Member of the Wedding." In Natoli, J.P., ed., Psychological Perspectives on Literature: Freudian Dissidents and New-Freudians. New Haven: Archon, 1983.

A succinct summary of Jungian psychology's usefulness to literature, describing pertinent Jungian theory and practice. Argues that The Member of the Wedding is "a myth for our time, for today; as in the forties, humanity is in need of wholeness and growth, just as Frankie is in need of psychic wholeness and growth."

Miller, Arthur
(See also item 1022.)

1250. Evans, Richard I. Psychology and Arthur Miller. New York: Dutton, 1969.

An interview with Arthur Miller on such subjects as "The Writer as Creator," "The Writer and Psychology," and "The Writer and Society." Among other things, Miller discusses how he creates his characters, his attitudes towards motivation, how he expects his audience to react, and his own attitudes towards various concepts in psychology.

1251. Feldman, Robert L. "Tragedy and the Common Man: Existential Analysis and Arthur Miller." *Family Therapy*, 7, 1 (1980), 1-71.

A discussion, using essays and interviews of Miller and the existential psychotherapy of Rollo May and Viktor Frankl, of how Miller portrays the behavior of people who are trapped in a life crisis. Examines *All My Sons*, *The Crucible*, and *Death of A Salesman*.

1252. Jacobson, Irving. "The Child As Guilty Witness." *Literature and Psychology*, 24 (1974), 12-23.

Arthur Miller's "I Don't Need You Any More" contains the three ideas of "home" typical in Miller: childhood sense of harmony; the parallel feeling when the individual is part of society; the guilt and fear engendered by being in a family. In his family life, Martin suffers from isolation and guilt, caught between the two worlds of his mother and father.

1253. Rothenberg, Albert, and Shapiro, Eugene D. "The Defense of Psychoanalysis in Literature: *Long Day's Journey into Night* and *A View from the Bridge*." *Comparative Drama*, 7 (1973), 51-67.

A psychoanalytic study of *Long Day's Journey*, using "all but one of the classical defenses," especially "denial, projection, and rationalization," as manifested in the characters. *A View from the Bridge* illustrates fewer types of defense. This type of discussion aims to rescue psychoanalytic criticism from the "banal and reductionistic" form it often takes.

1254. Seidenberg, Robert. "Catcher Gone Awry." *International Journal of Psycho-Analysis*, 51 (1970), 331-339.

An interpretation of Arthur Miller's *After the Fall*. Notes that there are two types of characters: 1) the "catcher" who seeks to rescue others, and 2) the person who is indifferent to others. Both types are selfish, and marriage to either can lead to disaster.

Miller, Henry

1255. Jackson, Paul R. "Henry Miller's Literary Pregnancies." *Literature and Psychology*, 19 (1969), 35-49.

Miller transforms "personal doubt and middle-class uncertainty into a grand myth of personal regeneration."

Milne, A.A.

1256. Cocks, Geoffrey. "A.A. Milne: Sources of his Creativity." American Imago, 34 (1977), 313-326.

> Demonstrates that the source of Milne's creativity was in his fixation on his childhood stemming from his "early unconscious perceptions of his world."

Mishima, Yukio

1257. Arlow, Jacob A. "Pyromania and the Primal Scene: A Psychoanalytic Comment on the Work of Yukio Mishima." Psychoanalytic Quarterly, 47 (1978), 24-51.

> Mishima's writing is filled with fantasies and scenes of fire. Fire is used to avenge those who were seen in the act of sexual intercourse. Clinical evidence also suggests connections between pyromania and the primal scene. Psychoanalytic study of Mishima's writing may help explain his life and suicide.

Mitchell, Margaret

1258. Wells, Charles E. "The Hysterical Personality and the Feminine Character: A Study of Scarlett O'Hara." Comprehensive Psychiatry, 17 (1976), 353-359.

> The heroine of Gone With the Wind, while exhibiting outward traits of hysteria, does not convey the characteristics of the "hysterical personality" in the basic structure of her character.

Mojtabai, A.G.

1259. Olson, Carol Booth. "Mirrors and Madness: A.G. Mojtabai's Mundome." Critique: Studies in Modern Fiction, 20 (1978), 71-82.

> Viewing Richard and Meg as "psychological components of a multiple personality" clarifies some of the ambiguities in the novel. Furthermore, the "numerous references to the theme of the double" reinforce "the inextricable relationship of Richard and Meg."

Moraes, Dom

1260. Mollinger, Robert N. "Psychic Images and Poetic Technique in Dom Moraes' Poetry." World Literature Written in English, 14 (1975), 322-328.

> A discussion of Moraes' poetry in which, in Jungian terms, "his psyche has transformed 'material objects into psychic images'."

Moravia, Alberto

1261. Culbertson, Diana, and Valley, John. "Alberto Moravia's Melancholy Murderer: The Conformist as Personality Type." Literature and Psychology, 25, 2 (1975), 79-85.

> Uses Maslow's "The Authoritarian Character Structure" (1943) as a description of the character Marcello Clerici in Moravia's The Conformist.

Musil, Robert

1262. Sjögren, Christine Oertel. "An Inquiry into the Psychological Condition of the Narrator in Musil's 'Tonka'." Monatshefte, 64 (1972), 153-161.

> The protagonist of "Tonka" is "psychologically unsound," and his psychosis, caused by a childhood trauma, distorts his understanding of reality. However, although the protagonist exhibits "classical symptoms of schizophrenia" it is an oversimplification of the story to discuss it only in the "clinical light of Freudian psychology."

Nabokov, Vladimir

1263. Roth, Phyllis A. "The Psychology of the Double in Nabokov's Pale Fire." Essays in Literature, 2 (1975), 209-229.

> Nabokov's use of the psychoanalytic theory of the double is basic to an understanding of Pale Fire. Kinbote's claims that he is Charles of Charles of Zembla and his various other fabrications are indications of his ambivalence about himself.

Nin, Anais

1264. Spencer, Sharon. "The Dream of Twinship in the Writings of Anais Nin." Journal of the Otto Rank Association, 9, 2 (1974-75), 81-90.

> Nin was a patient and friend of Rank. Notes parallels in Rank and Nin, especially in the concept of "dreams of doubles." Narcissism and the nature of the woman artist are also discussed.

Oates, Joyce Carol

1265. Burwell, R.M. "Process of Individuation as Narrative Structure: Joyce Carol Oates' Do With Me What You Will." Critique: Studies in Modern Fiction, 17 (1975), 93-106.

Elena Howe's suppression of the parts of herself which Jung connected to the Shadow archetype leads to mental deterioration and near suicide until she recognizes the Shadow. The narrative proposes the necessity of creating one's ideas of self without social props.

1266. Goodman, Charlotte. "Women and Madness in the Fiction of Joyce Carol Oates." Women and Literature, 5, 2 (1977), 17-28.

Oates' female characters are powerless and depressed in a hostile world. Some retreat into madness, "which confers upon them the blessings of safety and peace."

1267. Pinsker, Sanford. "Joyce Carol Oates's Wonderland: A Hungering for Personality." Critique: Studies in Modern Fiction, 20 (1978), 59-70.

A discussion of Jesse's personality and crisis of identity. "Wonderland tests out Jesse's faith in an uncluttered, linear mode of achieving personality. . . . The novel impresses a model of the mind upon the larger patterns of Jesse's quest, one in which convoluting structures implode against themselves."

O'Connor, Flannery

1268. Barcus, Nancy B. "Psychological Determinism and Freedom in Flannery O'Connor." Cithara, 12 (1972), 26-33.

A study of The Violent Bear it Away. Despite a "psychological apparatus" which parallels Freud's A General Introduction to Psychoanalysis and "deliberate use of psychological determinism in her characterization," O'Connor rejects psychological determinism "as a final explanation of the nature of reality."

1269. LeClair, Thomas. "Flanner O'Connor's Wise Blood: the Oedipal Theme." Mississippi Quarterly, 29 (1976), 197-205.

Haze Motes' blinding himself "is a consistent resolution of the Oedipal theme" in Wise Blood. Discusses how Motes deals with and overcomes his "Oedipal attachment."

1270. Murphy, George D., and Cherry, Caroline L. "Flannery O'Connor and the Integration of Personality." Flannery O'Connor Bulletin, 7 (1978), 85-100.

Demonstrates that many of O'Connor's short stories "reveal a kind of psycho-drama of the dynamics of personality: a chronically unresolved conflict between the conscious and the unconscious elements of the mind."

O'Hara, Frank

1271. Skoller, Eleanor. "Franked Letters: Crossing the Bar." Visible Language, 14 (1980), 306-319.

"The discontinuity of consciousness in Freud's theory of memory which may lie 'at the bottom of the origin of the concept of time' is manifest in Frank O'Hara's New York poems, especially his walking lunch hour poems."

O'Neill, Eugene
(See also item 1253.)

1272. Feldman, Robert. "The Longing for Death in O'Neill's Strange Interlude and Mourning Becomes Electra." Literature and Psychology, 31 (1981), 39-48.

Compares Freud's theories of death to the death theme in these plays and points out the distinctions between psychoanalysis and playwrighting.

1273. Halling, Steen. "Eugene O'Neill's Understanding Forgiveness." Duquesne Studies in Phenomenological Psychology, 3 (1979), 193-206.

Applies phenomenological psychology to O'Neill's Long Day's Journey Into Night and A Moon for the Misbegotten in order to describe forgiveness, despair, blame, "the experience of time, revenge and other significant themes."

1274. Hamilton, James W. "Early Trauma, Dreaming and Creativity: The Works of Eugene O'Neill." International Review of Psycho-Analysis, 3 (1976), 341-364.

Relates O'Neill's trauma of his childhood, problematical relationship with his depressed and addicted mother to the nature of his creative output. His creativeness was a means of controlling his "oral-sadistic" anger.

1275. Lichtenberg, Joseph D., and Lichtenberg, Charlotte. "Eugene O'Neill and Falling in Love." Psychoanalytic Quarterly, 41 (1972), 63-89.

A psychoanalytic study, drawing upon O'Neill's life and plays. Concludes that O'Neill's personal development never went beyond late adolescent or early adult love, and thus his arrested psychosexual development inhibited his having adult love relationships.

1276. Porter, Thomas E. "Puritan Ego and Freudian Unconscious." In Myth and Modern American Drama. Detroit: Wayne State University Press, 1969, 26-52.

A study of Eugene O'Neill's Mourning Becomes Electra and its use of "popular" Freudianism. Discusses Freudian aspects of Puritan repressiveness and notes that in O'Neill's play Freudian theories of character are "a version of reality that 'explains' the crimes of the Mannons as the Puritan heritage 'explains' their feelings of guilt."

1277. Rothenberg, Albert. "The Iceman Changeth: Toward an Empircal Approach to Creativity." Journal of the American Psychoanalytic Association, 17 (1969), 549-607.

A study of O'Neill's life and manuscript revisions of The Iceman Cometh is used to gather insight into the creative process. The process is one of deleting and choosing material for the purpose of moving from the specifically personal to the more generally social.

Onetti, Juan Carlos
(See also item 960.)

1278. Deredita, John. "Dream and Spatial Form." Review, 16 (1975), 19-23.

A discussion of Juan Carlos Onetti's A Brief Life. Although A Brief Life appears to present a linear narration, "the defining gesture" of the novel "exhaustively tests the power of fantasy and ficitonal imagination as a counter to the flow of time, which is intolerable for the Onettian Subjectivity." Reference is made to Freud's idea that "fantasy at one and the same time hovers between three periods of time."

Orwell, George
(See also items 346, 1076.)

1279. Carter, Thomas N. "Group Psychological Phenomena of a Political System as Satirized in Animal Farm: An Application of the Theories of W.R. Bion." Human Relations, 27 (1974), 525-546.

"The attempt in this paper has been to show that Bion's theoretical concepts of group psychology . . . can be applied . . . " to an understanding of Orwell's Animal Farm.

1280. Dooley, D.J. "Freudian Critics." Triumph, 9, 2 (1974), 34-39.

Analyzes two articles on George Orwell (one by Marcus Smith, one by Gerald Fiderer) to demonstrate the distortiveness and general invalidity of Freudian literary criticism.

1281. Fiderer, Gerald. "Masochism as Literary Strategy: Orwell's Psychological Novels." Literature and Psychology, 20, 1 (1970), 3-21.

Argues that the "psychological authenticity of Orwell's characters derives from the union of sadism, provocation, and masochism."

1282. Knapp, John. "The Double Life of George Bowling." Review of Existential Psychology and Psychiatry 14 (1976), 109-125.

"This essay will show that Coming Up For Air develops the theme of the doppleganger, or double, in order to illustrate the self-fragmentation of the common man taking place during the period between the two world wars."

1283. Roazen, Paul. "Orwell, Freud, and 1984." Virginia Quarterly Review, 54 (1978), 675-695.

Although Freud and Orwell had no interest in each other's work, 1984 displays many correspondences between the two: view of unconscious fantasies, of memory, of women, and language.

1284. Smith, M. "Wall of Blackness: A Psychological Approach to 1984." Modern Fiction Studies, 14 (Winter 1968-1969), 423-433.

Argues that Winston Smith "is clearly and carefully developed along familiar Oedipal lines and an accurate understanding of 1984 must take this into account. . . . "

Osborne, John

1285. Faber, M.D. "The Character of Jimmy Porter: An Approach to Look Back in Anger." Modern Drama, 13 (1970), 67-77.

A study of the play's metaphorical structure and its connection to Porter's psychology. Porter "is an orally fixated neurotic who projects his own psychological shortcomings onto the external environment." His neurotic personality is filled with self-deception.

Oyono, Ferdinand

1286. Nnolim, C.E. "Jungian Archetypes and the Main Characters in Oyono's Une Vie de Boy." African Literature Today, 7 (1975), 117-122.

Une Vie de Boy is deeply embedded in Jungian psychology and the Judaeo-Christian mythopoeia.

Pasternak, Boris

1287. Dreistadt, Roy. "A Unifying Psychological Analysis of the Principal Characters in the Novel Dr. Zhivago by Boris Pasternak." Psychology, 9, 3 (1972), 22-35.

An analysis of the four main characters in Dr. Zhivago, in an attempt to unify the theories of Freud, Adler, Jung, and Maslow.

Paz, Octavio

1288. Callan, Richard J. "Some Parallels between Octavio Paz and Carl Jung." Hispania, 60 (1977), 916-926.

Argues that the "insights and range of La Berinto are confirmed and amplified by being placed alongside of the discoveries of depth psychology."

Percy, Walker

1289. Natoli, Joseph. "The Lebenswelt of Lancelot Lamar." *Journal of Phenomenological Psychology*, 12 (1981), 63-74.

    Applies and expands J.H. van den Berg's use of pathography in order to describe Lancelot Lamar's "human life-world." This is a praxis essay based on the author's theoretical essay, "Fiction as Pathography."

1290. Quagliano, Anthony. "Existential Modes in *The Moviegoer*." *Research Studies*, 45 (1977), 214-223.

    An examination of the novel in terms of Percy's own writing on psychology and philosophy. In *The Moviegoer*, "three existential modes, . . . alienation, rotation, and repetition," are described through Binx Bolling. "The mode of alienation is the primary one; the other two modes are potential escapes from alienation once it is perceived." Percy, like Kafka, in "pointing at and naming alienation has already reversed it, healing the very wound it represents."

Pinero, Arthur

1291. Veszy-Wagner, L. "Pinero's Farce *The Magistrate* as an Anxiety Dream." *American Imago*, 32 (1975), 200-214.

    "The farce, especially 'The Magistrate,' is the anxiety dream of a good man of middle age, returning in a palatable, symbolic, more sublimated, but nonetheless schizoid framework."

Pinter, Harold
(See also item 924.)

1292. Gabbard, Lucina P. *The Dream Structure of Pinter's Plays: A Psychoanalytic Approach*. Cranbury, N.J.: Associated University Presses, 1976.

    Proposes to deal with the latent level of Pinter's plays while leaving "the play's poetic ambiguity intact."

1293. Lesser, Simon O. "Reflections on Pinter's *The Birthday Party*." (1972) In Sprich, R., and Noland, R., eds., *The Whispered Meanings: Selected Essays of Simon O. Lesser*. Amherst: University of Massachusetts Press, 1977, 203-211.

    The play focuses on "subjective concerns, many of which go back to infancy."

1294. Powlick, Leonard. "A Phenomenological Approach to Harold Pinter's *A Slight Ache*." *The Quarterly Journal of Speech*, 60 (Fall 1974), 25-32.

Applies the Heideggerian notion of "Dasein"--Being-in-the-world--in order to demonstrate that the "menace" in Pinter's early plays is not external but internal.

1295. Roland, Alan. "Pinter's <u>Homecoming</u>: Images in Dramatic Action." <u>Psychoanalytic Review</u>, 61 (1974), 415-427.

Ruth's behavior reflects the images that the five men had of the dead mother. Thus "Pinter is able to explore the psychic roots of violence within the family."

<u>Pirandello, Luigi</u>
(See also item 228.)

1296. Decina, Paolo. "<u>Henry IV</u> by Luigi Pirandello--A Psychiatric Comment." <u>Journal of the American Academy of Psychoanalysis</u>, 6 (1978), 79-87.

An analysis of delusion and psychopathology and the growth of schizophrenia in <u>Henry IV</u>. Suggests that therapists must not go along with a patient's delusions, but, rather, they should represent reality.

1297. Rolfs, Daniel. "Pirandello's Theme of Madness." <u>Forum Italicum</u>, 10 (1976), 377-397.

Madness is "a rich yet largely unexplored theme" in much of Pirandello's work, and it "relates to the core of his distinctive philosophy." His wife's insanity is clearly related to his "major preoccupations . . . such as relativism, solipsism, and multiple personality." There are three levels of "madness as a literary theme" in Pirandello's work: madness "as a figure of speech, as a social myth, and as an actual state of mind."

<u>Plath, Sylvia</u>
(See also item 1128.)

1298. Blessing, Richard Allen. "The Shape of the Psyche: Vision and Technique in the Late Poems of Sylvia Plath." In Lane, G., ed., <u>Sylvia Plath: New Views on the Poetry</u>. Baltimore: Johns Hopkins University Press, 1979, 57-73.

Suggests that "the energies of Plath's poems flowed along channels gouged by her own sexual myth, that dominance and submission are as important in her poetry as are imagination and reality." Her poems were a vehicle "for releasing the energy of her psyche from the mortal wrapping against which she had struggled until the end."

1299. Broe, Mary Lynn. "A Subtle Psychic Bond: The Mother Figure in Sylvia Plath's Poetry." In Davidson, C.N., and Broner, E.M., eds., <u>The Lost Tradition: Mothers and Daughters in Literature</u>. New York: Ungar, 1980, 217-230.

A psychological study of the relationship between Sylvia Plath and her mother, Aurelia, drawing upon Plath's letters and poetry. A "passionate bond between mother and child, however thwarted or realized by Aurelia and Sylvia's relationship" is revealed.

1300. Kloss, Robert. "Further Reflections on Plath's 'Mirror'." University of Hartford Studies in Literature, 14 (1982), 11-22.

"Mirror" displays "Plath's design to faithfully reflect the individuation process, the infant's attempt to establish its own ego boundaries apart from those of the mother and the occasional confusion and fusion of the two."

1301. Lameyer, Gordon. "The Double in Sylvia Plath's The Bell Jar." In Butscher, E., ed., Sylvia Plath: The Woman and the Work. New York: Dodd, Mead, 1977, 143-165.

Notes Plath's interest in the psychological double in the work of Dostoevsky and Otto Rank. In The Bell Jar, "some of the 'doubles' are positive and innocent, while others represent antipathies or the repressed libidinal urges of the heroine." Furthermore, Plath's "narcissism, developing from the loss of love, . . . caused her to project upon innocent and evil doubles her conflicting polarized selves."

1302. Salamon, Lynda B. "'Double, Double': Perception in the Poetry of Sylvia Plath." Spirit: A Magazine of Poetry, 37 (1970), 34-39.

Plath views the world in a schizophrenic manner: "Always she is aware of the doubleness of things." Such a viewpoint leads to pain, "fear," and "despair" because it suggests that the world is not what it seems.

1303. Schwartz, Murray M., and Bollas, Christopher. "Absence at the Center: Sylvia Plath and Suicide." Criticism, 19 (1976), 147-172.

Plath's art is "an expression of personal style," and her suicide is "a convergence of actions, inner and outer." Plath's inability to love was a major aspect of her life, caused by her "failure to integrate her inner world sufficiently to make a coherent sense of personal identity possible." Her suicide is explained through a discussion of her relationships with her father and mother, her failures in development, and her experience of her inner and outer worlds, all seen through her writing.

1304. Weisblatt, Sanford. "The Creativity of Sylvia Plath's Ariel Period: Toward Origins and Meanings." In The Annual of Psychoanalysis, vol. 5. New York: IUP, 1977, 379-404.

An analysis of Plath's creativity through a study of her poems and life. Discusses early traumas in Plath's life, the impact of the birth of her son, and her marital break-up. Plath failed in her "attempt at mastery of the regressively resonated traumatic state."

Proust, Marcel

1305. Bychowski, Gustav. "Marcel Proust as Poet of Psychoanalysis." *American Imago*, 30 (1973), 26-32.

> Comments on Proust's great ability to penetrate into the minds of others, suggesting a fine knowledge of himself and the important achievement of empathy, leading to beautiful art.

1306. Gandelman, Claude. "Proust's Draft Copy-Books: Sketches of his Dreams." *American Imago*, 34 (1977), 297-312.

> A study of Proust's dream doodles in the margins of the manuscript drafts of his writing. The doodles reflect Proust's obsessions and act as sublimation. Furthermore, they "show that Proust was, like everybody else, a 'sexual' creature, and not only a 'technician' of Literature. They do not leave any doubt as to his homosexuality." Contains photo-copies of some of the doodles.

1307. Girard, René. "Narcissism: The Freudian Myth Demystified by Proust." In Roland, A., ed., *Psychoanalysis, Creativity, and Literature: A French-American Inquiry*. New York: Columbia University Press, 1976, 293-311.

> "A Proustian reading of Freud," using *Remembrance of Things Past* as the basis for a critique of Freud's *On Narcissism*. Proust sees through Freud's defense mechanisms. "Narcissism is one of the most questionable points in psychoanalysis" when seen in light of an "encounter between *Narcissism* and *Remembrance of Things Past*."

1308. O'Brien, Justin. "Proust Confirmed by Neuro Surgery." *PMLA*, 85 (1970), 295-297.

> Shows how Proust's writing anticipated the discoveries of neruosurgeon Wilder Penfield, who believed that "there is a permanent record of the stream of consciousness within the brain," which he compared to "the sequence on a wire recorder or to a continuous film-strip with sound track."

1309. Splitter, Randolph. "The 'Economic' Problem in Proust and Freud." *Hartford Studies in Literature*, 11 (1979), 123-139.

> A discussion of the symbolic and psychological connections between money and excrement in the work of Freud and Proust.

1310. _____. *Proust's 'Recherche': A Psychoanalytical Interpretation*. London and Boston: Routledge and Kegan Paul, 1981.

> A psychoanalytical reading based to some extent on post-structuralist criticism.

1311. Swartz, Paul. "Marcel Proust and the Problem of Time and Self." *Psychological Reports*, 43 (1978), 291-297.

> An exposition of Proust's notion that the true self illuminates time and becomes sensitive to the essence of things via memory.

1312. _____. "A Rose for Behaviorism." Psychological Reports, 27 (1970), 364.

"Proust holds not one but many roses for psychology, and in this he but epitomizes the situation of countless other artists."

Purdy, James

1313. Baldanza, Frank. "James Purdy's Half-Orphans." Centennial Review, 18 (1974), 225-272.

A major theme in Purdy is a basic rootlessness in his characters. His children are reared by only one parent or by grandparents. Thus his characters illustrate a "fetishistic attachment to objects or symbols" representing the missing parent. Purdy's novel Jeremy's Version provides a major rendering of this theme.

1314. _____. "The Paradoxes of Patronage in Purdy." American Literature, 46 (1974), 347-356.

The relationships described in Purdy's novels and stories "are pervaded by the assumption of patron-protege roles." The older patrons often develop actual or suggested sado-masochistic relationships with their younger proteges.

Pynchon, Thomas

1315. Davidson, Cathy N. "Oedipa as Androgyne in Thomas Pynchon's The Crying of Lot 49." Contemporary Literature, 18 (1977), 38-50.

Discusses the psychological growth of Oedipa. "Oedipa achieves heroism by becoming . . . a woman of her own identity, a person more fully human, and an andorgyne."

1316. Simmon, Scott. "Gravity's Rainbow Described." Critique: Studies in Modern Fiction, 16, 2 (1974), 54-67.

Uses Freudian ideas about disgust for the body, and sex and aggression, to clarify aspects of Pynchon's novel. Pynchon's "characters seem unreal because, paradoxically, they are used to explore psychological realities not usually probed. Pynchon explores history as a representation of collective neurosis."

1317. Wolfley, Lawrence C. "Repression's Rainbow: The Presence of Norman O. Brown in Pynchon's Big Novel." PMLA, 92 (1977), 873-889.

"Brown's neo-Freudian view of repression as the source of man's uniqueness in nature is mirrored in virtually every thematic aspect of Gravity's Rainbow." Both Brown and Pynchon see history as "the slow return of the repressed." Gravity can be viewed as a metaphor for repression.

Rand, Ayn

1318. Deane, Paul. "Ayn Rand's Neurotic Personalities of Our Times." Revue des Langues Vivantes, 36 (1970), 125-129.

A discussion of The Fountainhead, noting parallels between personality types described by Karen Horney in The Neurotic Personality of Our Time and the characterizations in Rand's novel.

Rhys, Jean

1319. Abel, Elizabeth. "Women and Schizophrenia: The Fiction of Jean Rhys." Contemporary Literature, 20 (1979), 155-177.

A study, drawing upon the theories of R.D. Laing, of Rhys' heroines. These women are very passive, and they manifest "several specific symptoms of schizophrenia: impoverished affect, apathy, obsessive thought and behavior coupled with the inability to take real initiative, a sense of the unreality of both the world and self, and a feeling of detachment from the body." They are isolated and see the world as hostile.

Rilke, Rainer Maria

1320. Simenauer, Erich. "R.M. Rilke's Dreams and His Conception of Dreams." In Baron, F., et. al., eds., Rilke: The Alchemy of Alienation. Lawrence, Kansas: Regents Press, 1980, 243-262.

Notes that Rilke was a prodigious dreamer and that "his conception of the dream is like an echo of diverse ideas about dreams from different epochs up until modern notions and the psychoanalytical theory of dreams." Discusses Rilke's actual dreaming and his literary dreams and dream imagery in a psychological framework, to give insight into his writing.

Rivera, José Eustasio

1321. Callan, Richard J. "The Archetype of Psychic Renewal in La Vorágine." Hispanica, 54 (1971), 470-476.

The protagonist of José Rivera's novel La Voragine is here viewed as a man whose self-renewal is "stalled on the threshold of the process known as 'the crystallization of the anima from the mother archetype'."

Robbe-Grillet, Alain

1322. Porter, Dennis. "Sartre, Robbe-Grillet and the Psychotic Hero." Modern Fiction Studies, 16 (1970), 13-26.

Analyzes Roquentin from La Nausée and the Robbe-Grillet hero in order to define twentieth-century France's existentialist challenge to a Freudian, bourgeois psychology of the normal and the abnormal.

1323. Storey, Robert. "Oedipus in the Labyrinth: A Psychoanalytic Reading of Robbe-Grillet's In The Labyrinth." Literature and Psychology, 28 (1978), 4-16.

The protagonist's suffering and guilt are due to oedipal romance.

Robinson, Edwin Arlington

1324. Kavka, Jerome. "Richard Cory's Suicide: A Psychoanalyt's View." Colby Library Quarterly, 11 (1975), 150-159.

Cory is a narcissist who cannot adapt to an adult environment because he has not outgrown infant megalomania.

1325. _____. "The Suicide of Richard Cory: An Explication of the Poem by Edwin Arlington Robinson." In The Annual of Psychoanalysis, Vol. 4. New York: IUP, 1976, 479-500.

Discusses Cory's narcissism and speculates on the biographical relationship of Cory to Robinson. "If the group (supporting environment) can be seen as being the representation of the failure of a supporting maternal matrix--and here we turn to Robinson's own personal history--then Cory's personality and tragic demise become meaningful as the failure of self-cohesion in a narcissistically traumatized individual."

1326. Wolf, H.R. "E.A. Robinson and the Integration of the Self." In Mazzaro, J., ed., Modern American Poetry: Essays in Criticism. New York: McKay, 1970, 40-59.

Writing "at a time of idealistic uncertainty and relative psychological unknowingness, at the crossroads of late Victorian positivism and psychoanalytic origins," Robinson created "psychological romance." Many of his poems depict "agonizing struggles with contingency and the shape of self."

Roethke, Theodore
(See also item 1012.)

1327. Corrigan, Matthew. "A Phenomenological Glance at a Few Lines of Roethke." Modern Poetry Studies, 2 (1971), 165-174.

A discussion of Roethke's levels of consciousness revealed in "The Lost Son." The stanzas discussed, "in their very general nature, could not have been written in any other age." The poem, "a collage of phenomena," is a "setting off of inner space" revealing the "mind prints" of its author.

1328. La Bell Jenijoy. "Theodore Roethke's 'The Lost Son': From Archetypes to Literary History." Modern Language Quarterly, 37 (1976), 179-195.

A discussion of Roethke's uses of Jungian psychology as taken from his reading of Maud Bodkin's Archetypal Patterns in Poetry. "For Roethke, Jung and Bodkin were less significant as explorers of the human mind than as discoverers of a means for organizing the past so that it stimulates creation in the present."

Roth, Philip
(See also items 541, 1217.)

1329. Bettelheim, Bruno. "Portnoy Psychoanalyzed: Therapy Notes Found in the Files of Dr. O. Spielvogel, a New York Psychoanalyst." Midstream, 16, 6 (1969), 3-10.

Presents the fictional Dr. Spielvogel's notes on six psychoanalytic sessions with the hero of Roth's Portnoy's Complaint, noting Portnoy's narcissism, oral fixations, sexual obsession, and self-hatred.

1330. Gordon, Lois G. "Portnoy's Complaint: Coming of Age in Jersey City." Literature and Psychology, 19 (1969), 57-60.

Portnoy is filled with "rage, guilt, self-abasement, narcissism, polymorphous perversity and pure pain." His adult behavior disguises "nightmares of his early childhood which he has been re-living daily."

1331. Rice, Julian C. "Philip Roth's The Breast: Cutting the Freudian Cord." Studies in Contemporary Satire, 3 (1976), 9-16.

"The Breast is a satire on the culturally reductive and artistically inhibiting aspects of Freudian psychology." Furthermore, "although the Freudian Eden has been lost, the rejection of popular Freudianism makes it possible for man to create a less secure but more fulfilling concept of himself."

Saint-Exupery, Antoine de

1332. Meyer, Bernard. "The Little Prince: Speculations on the Disappearance of Antoine de Saint-Exupery." Journal of the American Psychoanalytic Association, 22, 1 (1974), 142-159.

"Evidence is presented in the support of the hypothesis that the mysterious disappearance of this celebrated airman-poet was the ultimate expression of a leitmotif that is recurrently discernible throughout his life and writings."

Salinger, J.D.

1333. Bryan, James E. "The Psychological Structure of The Catcher in the Rye." PMLA, 89 (1974), 1065-1074.

A psychoanalytical study of the structure of Holden Caulfield's behavior as both sexually aggressive and withdrawing.

1334. Bufithis, Philp H. "J.D. Salinger and the Psychiatrist." West Virginia University Bulletin: Philological Papers, 21 (1974), 67-77.

In his heroes, Salinger emphasizes the importance of the artist rather than the psychiatrist as a means of understanding ourselves. Thus Buddy Glass attains identity by being an artist. "Art is the transference of neurosis from self (subjectivity) into artifact (objectivity)."

1335. Huber, R.J. "Adlerian Theory and Its Application to The Catcher in the Rye--Holden Caulfield." In Natoli, J.P., ed., Psychological Perspectives on Literature. New Haven: Archon, 1983.

A summary of Adlerian theory and its usefulness to a study of literature and a discussion of Holden as maladjusted according to Adlerian terms.

1336. Huber, R. John, and Ledbetter, Gail. "Holden Caulfield, Self-Appointed Catcher in the Rye: Some Additional Thoughts." Journal of Individual Psychology, 33 (1977), 250-256.

An Adlerian reading of Salinger's novel. The hostile Holden fits Adler's picture of the maladjusted individual with feelings of inferiority, his self-isolation, and his idea that he is among enemies in an alien land. His compensation for this is his wishing for impossibilities and his declarations that he is very masculine. Augments Joanne Irving's discussion (item 1337).

1337. Irving, Joanne. "The Catcher in the Rye: An Adlerian Interpretation." Journal of Individual Psychology, 32 (1976), 81-92.

Holden Caulfield has poor self-confidence because he is a second child. To counteract this he claims to be superior, and rebels. He is self-centered, with "impaired social interest." In the Adlerian view, "Holden does not get sick, but rather he suffers from profound discouragement about growing up."

Sartre, Jean Paul
(See also item 1322.)

1338. Doubrovsky, Serge. "'The Nine of Hearts': Fragment of a Psychoreading of La Nausée." In Roland, A., ed., Psychoanalysis, Creativity, and Literature. New York: Columbia University Press, 1978, 312-322.

Argues that "psychocriticism begins right where other forms of criticism stop: at the production, in the text, of an insignificant detail which cannot be accounted for by either the Sartrian metatext or by another metadiscourse." Perceives bisexuality in La Nausée.

1339. Tarbox, Raymond. "Exhaustion Psychology and Sartre's The Age of Reason." American Imago, 30 (1973), 80-96.

"The aim of adult scream behavior is to overcome feelings of exhaustion or helplessness and fears of imminent ego collapse--psychic catastrophes which, in part, are the outcome of prolonged periods of waiting to 'connect' with a delaying or inconsistent maternal figure."

1340. Wolf, Ernest. "The Disconnected Self." In Roland, A., ed., Psychoanalysis, Creativity, and Literature. New York: Columbia University Press, 1978, 103-115.

Discusses the newer concepts of psychoanalysis regarding self-object transferences and applies them to La Nausée, and Mrs. Dalloway.

1341. Woodle, Gary. "'Erostrate': Sartre's Paranoid." Review of Existential Psychology and Psychiatry, 13 (1974), 30-41.

A psychoanalytic interpretation of Hilbert "doesn't exhaust the meaning of his act any more than a reduction to complexes exhausts, in Sartre's view, human reality."

Schnitzler, Arthur

1342. Bareikis, Robert. "Arthur Schnitzler's Fraulein Else: A Freudian Novella?" Literature and Psychology, 19, 1 (1969), 19-34.

Argues that Fraulein Else is a showcase of Schnitzler's pioneering efforts in the emerging field of depth psychology.

1343. Katan, M. Schnitzler's 'Das Schicksal des Freherrn von Leisenbohg'." Journal of the American Psychoanalytic Association, 17 (1969), 904-926.

The story, published in 1903, shows Schnitzler's excellent psychological insights, especially dealing with the taboo of virginity. It is with good reason that Freud later found the story interesting.

1344. Mahlendorf, Ursula. "Arthur Schnitzler's The Last Letter of a Litterateur: The Artist as Destroyer." American Imago, 34 (1977), 238-276.

In The Last Letter of a Litterateur, Schnitzler " . . . reveals the developmental psychic roots of dilemmas that confront the impotent artist . . . , uncovers the conscious and unconscious meanings of this artist's quest, and explores the different functions of artistic work in the artist's life."

1345. Russell, Peter. "Schnitzler's Blumen: The Treatment of a Neurosis." Forum for Modern Language Studies, 13 (1977), 289-302.

Notes how close Schnitzler's thinking was to Freud's. Blumen, "as well as sharing the assumptions and using the technique of a psychoanalytic treatment, . . . also in a sense reproduces the course of such a treatment, . . . a successful course of psychoanalysis."

1346. Sherman, Murray H. "Reik, Schnitzler, Freud, and "The Murderer": The Limits of Insight in Psychoanalysis." Modern Austrian Literature, 10, 3-4 (1977), 195-216.

Reviews the personal relationships of Theodor Reik, Arthur Schnitzler, and Sigmund Freud and the importance of the role of The Murderer in Schnitzler's writing. Contains a psychoanalytic reading of Schnitzler's novel: "the plot epitomizes the split between the tender and aggressive aspects of sex."

Scott, Paul

1347. Weinbaum, Francine. "Psychological Defenses and Thwarted Union in The Raj Quartet." Literature and Psychology, 31 (1981), 75-87.

Discusses Scott's "unconscious association of India with the human body, England with the Soul, as part of a description of the thwarted union of individuals, a state some psychoanalytic thinkers regard as characteristic of civilized man."

Selby, Hubert

1348. Wertime, Richard A. "Psychic Vengeance in Last Exit to Brooklyn." Literature and Psychology, 24 (1974), 153-166.

Selby--and thus the reader--is ambivalent about the violent justice in his novel. "Our ambivalence results from Selby's handling of a group called 'psychic avengers,' which consists of juvenile thugs."

Shaffer, Anthony and Peter

1349. Glenn, Jules. "Anthony and Peter Shaffer's Plays: The Influence of Twinship on Creativity." American Imago, 31 (1974), 270-292.

Demonstrates that many of the characters in the Shaffers' plays have personalities that are typical of twins even though they are not twins. Equus, White Lies, The Public Eye, and The White Liars are studied.

1350. _____. "Twins in Disguise: I. A Psychoanalytic Essay on Sleuth and The Royal Hunt of the Sun." Psychoanalytic Quarterly, 43 (1974), 288-302.

In both plays, the protagonists "manifest the personality characteristics and interactions of twins even though they are not represented as such."

1351. _____. "Twins in Disguise: II. Content, Form and Style in Plays by Anthony and Peter Shaffer." International Review of Psycho-Analysis, 1 (1974), 373-381.

Looks beyond obvious factors of twinning in how the personalities of authors influence creativeness. The fact that an author is a twin does not explain all facets of his or her creativeness.

Shaffer, Peter

1352. Burland, J. Alexis. "Discussion of Papers on Equus." *International Journal of Psychoanalytic Psychotherapy*, 5 (1976), 501-505.

   A review of four essays on Equus in IJPP 5, 1976. Discusses the "difficulties inherent in the psychoanalytic interpretation of literature, the issue of 'passion,' and the nature of the creative process."

1353. Gifford, Sanford. "'Pop' Psychoanalysis, Kitsch, and the 'As If' Theater: Further Notes on Peter Shaffer's Equus." *International Journal of Psychoanalytic Psychotherapy*, 5 (1976), 466-471.

   It is futile to subject Equus "to a traditional psychoanalytic investigation, as a product of the playwright's unconscious, when the play represents a skillful, highly conscious use of analytic cliches to manipulate the audience." Furthermore, the play is not a real tragedy because it coerces the audience "by exaggerated, unconvincing theatrical devices" so that it does not empathize with the characters.

1354. Glenn, Jules. "Alan Strang as an Adolescent: A Discussion of Peter Shaffer's Equus." *International Journal of Psychoanalytic Psychotherapy*, 5 (1976), 473-487.

   "Alan Strang . . . has undergone a retreat from Oedipal wishes to narcissism. . . . His fragile attempts at achieving a sound sense of identity are undermined when his seeking of a nonincestuous object produces panic and impotence."

1355. Lee, Ronald J. "Jungian Approaches to Theater: Shaffer's Equus." *Psychological Perspectives*, 8 (1977), 10-21.

   " . . . an exercise in practical or applied Jungian aesthetics, and the specific point of focus is the issue of how a theatricality is achieved which is appropriate to the fundamentally Jungian subject matter of this story."

1356. Rice, Julian C. "Equus and the Jungian True Symbol." *International Journal of Symbology*, 7, 2 (1976), 60-65.

   Equus "communicates the numinous symbolic experience, which Jung found necessary for individuation." Furthermore, "while society at large attempts to literalize all experience into a sign system, so as to make 'crucifixion,' or objectification, permanent, religion and art communicate through symbols, which ritually incarnate in order to liberate, rather than confine, experience."

1357. Slutzky, Jacob E. "Equus and the Psychopathology of Passion." *International Journal of Psychoanalytic Psychotherapy*, 5 (1976), 489-500.

   Discusses the "psychopathological expressions of passion" in the main characters in Equus. Alan manifests "psychotic identification with Equus and his blinding of the horses." Dysart has a "greatly inhibited sense of passion." Both are analyzed "in terms of level of object relations, ego functions, and unconscious fantasy."

1358. Stamm, Julian L. "Peter Shaffer's Equus--A Psychoanalytic Exploration." International Journal of Psychoanalytic Psychotherapy, 5 (1976), 449-461.

Analyzes Alan and his therapist, Dysart, in terms of the pre-oedipal and oedipal situations. The play "represents an eloquent mythopoetic expression and combination of id and ego (autonomous ego functions)."

Shaw, George Bernard

1359. Albert, Sidney P. "Reflections on Shaw and Psychoanalysis." Modern Drama, 14 (1971), 169-195.

Adds to Arthur Nethercot's article "Bernard Shaw and Psychoanalysis," Modern Drama, 11 (1969), pointing out his disagreements with that article and concluding that we are yet far from knowing the whole story of Shaw's views on psychoanalysis.

1360. Dervin, Daniel. Bernard Shaw: A Psychological Study. Lewisburg, Pa.: Bucknell University Press, 1975.

Discusses Shaw's energies, particularly his creativity, in terms of the 'Libido' school of psychology.

1361. Gordon, David J. "Literature and Repression: The Case of Shavian Drama." In Smith, J.H., ed., The Literary Freud. New Haven: Yale University Press, 1980, 181-203.

Discusses two kinds of cross-implications (antithetical and counter-intended) in Shavian drama. When conflicting attitudes are contained, the concept of repression need not be involved. When they are unbalanced, the concept of repression seems clearly visible.

1362. Holland, Norman N. "Human Identity." Critical Inquiry, 4 (1978), 451-469.

Argues that the principle of identity ("the organism's drive to maintain its own continuity of being") is the real legacy of psychoanalysis and that it enables us to "speak rigorously about individuals." Discusses G.B. Shaw's identity theme, encompassing "his style of friendship, his politics, his way of writing plays, his love affairs, and his dietary habits. . . . "

1363. Silver, Arnold. Bernard Shaw: The Darker Side. Standord: Stanford University Press, 1982.

Psychoanalytic analysis of The Simpleton of the Unexpected Isle, An Unsocial Socialist, Candida, Man and Superman and Pygmalion. Detects a sado-masochistic sexuality, incestuous impulses and elitism in Shaw.

1364. Wasserman, Marlie Parker. "Vivie Warren: A Psychological Study." In Weintraub, Rodelle, ed., Fabian Feminist: Bernard Shaw and Women. University Park: Pennsylvania State University Press, 1977, 168-173.

Discusses the depth of psychological insight Shaw brought to his character, Vivie Warren. "His portrayal is a psychological one, probing Vivie as a living woman, not just typing Vivie as a liberated woman."

Shintaro, Ishiwara

1365. Wagatsuma, Hiroshi. "Ishiwara Shintaro's Early Novels and Japanese Male Psychology." *Journal of Nervous and Mental Disease*, 157 (1973), 358-369.

Reviews the literature on the psychology of the Japanese male and compares it to a psychoanalytic interpretation of Shintaro's *Season of the Sun*. Ishiwara depicts "the 'Oedipus Complex' in persons whose character structure is primarily 'phallic'."

Singer, Isaac Bashevis

1366. Wolf, Howard. "Singer's Children's Stories and *In My Father's Court*: Universalism and the Rankian Hero." In Allentuck, M., ed., *The Achievement of Isaac Bashevis Singer*. Carbondale: Southern Illinois University Press, 1969, 145-158.

Argues that Singer's presentation of the young hero in the story *Mazel and Schlimazel* supports and enhances Otto Rank's psycho-sexual view of the hero as presented in *The Myth of the Birth of the Hero*.

Skinner, B.F.

1367. Kirchner, John H. "Psychology of the Scientist: XXIV. Consider This: A Psycholiterary Study of *Walden Two*." *Psychological Reports*, 26 (1970), 403-412.

An examination of Skinner's humanism and personality as manifested in *Walden Two*. The characters Frazier and Burris are projections of two parts of Skinner's personality. Skinner's writing and life are drawn upon.

Solzhenitsyn, Alexander

1368. Abram, Harry S. "The Psychology of Terminal Illness as Portrayed in Solzhenitsyn's *The Cancer Ward*." *Archives of Internal Medicine*, 124 (1969), 758-760.

A discussion of Solzhenitsyn's insights into the nature of psychotherapeutic care for dying people. He accurately portrays typical psychological aspects of dying patients, such as "denial," "dehumanization," "fear of mutilation and loss of sexuality," along with comment on patients' rights.

St. Omer, Garth

1369. Thieme, John. "Double Identity in the Novels of Garth St. Omer." Ariel: Review International of English Literature, 8, 3 (1977), 81-97.

St. Omer's characters suffer from "psychic division." In St. Omer's world, this division "is the normal state of the human personality. Understood, it can be controlled; failure to understand results in tragedy." Discusses A Room on the Hill, Shades of Grey, Nor Any Country, and J____, Black Bam and the Masqueraders.

Stafford, Jean

1370. Mann, Jeanette W. "Toward New Archetypal Forms: Boston Adventure." Studies in the Novel, 8 (1976), 291-303.

The fact that the hero of this novel is a woman has made it difficult to apply the myth of the hero, a basic archetypal pattern of human experience, to this work. The author argues that the best approach "would seem to be to accept the novel as true and to analyse the psycho-mythological patterns against the perceptions of one young woman on a journey toward consciousness, with the intention not of disproving psychological theory but of developing critical approaches appropriate to the study of women writers."

Steinbeck, John

1371. May, Charles E. "Myth and Mystery in Steinbeck's 'The Snake': A Jungian View." Criticism, 15 (1973), 322-355.

The woman in "The Snake" is "an archetypal symbol of the anima" in the unconscious of the doctor. She challenges the doctor's "detached and scientific mode of being and knowing" by insisting he "be devoured by the vagina dentata." However, the doctor refuses "to participate in this symbolic death necessary for a new life."

1372. _____. "Myth and Mystery in Steinbeck's 'The Snake': A Jungian View." In Tennenhouse, L., ed., The Practice of Psychoanalytic Criticism. Detroit: Wayne State University Press, 1976, 237-251.

See item 1371.

1373. Stone, Donal. "Steinbeck, Jung, and The Winter of our Discontent." Steinbeck Quarterly, 11 (1978), 87-96.

Illustrates the working out of the Jungian "individuation archetype" in The Winter of Our Discontent, demonstrating how much "in tune with man's collective unconscious" Steinbeck was.

1374. Yano, Shigeharu. "Psychological Interpretations of Steinbeck's Women in The Long Valley. In Hayashi, T., Hashiguchi, Y. and Peterson,

R.F., <u>John Steinbeck: East and West</u>. Muncie, Indiana: Ball State University Press, 1978, 54-60.

> Uses Jung's method of classifying people as introverts or extroverts to classify the women in Steinbeck's book, finding "that the image Steinbeck's women . . . project is more Eastern than Western," more introverted than extroverted. Also draws upon Karen Horney's <u>Feminine Psychology</u> and her idea that for a woman, "in her unconsciousness all her conflicting desires are expected to be gratified." Concludes with a twelvefold categorization of the women in Steinbeck's book.

Stevens, Wallace

1375. Hines, Thomas J. <u>The Later Poetry of Wallace Stevens: Phenomenological Parallels with Husserl and Heidigger</u>. Lewisburg, Pa.: Bucknell University Press, 1976.

> An examination of "Being and time" in Stevens' poetry written after the publication of <u>Harmonium</u>. Discusses the problems of epistemology and ontology in Stevens' work.

1376. Lehman, David. "Three Meditations on Wallace Stevens." <u>Shenandoah</u>, 32 (1981), 85-101.

> Includes a discussion of "Stevens's quarrel with Freud." Points out that "the uneasy relations between reality and the imagination call forth paradoxical responses from both authors."

1377. McCann, Janet. "'Prologues to What Is Possible': Wallace Stevens and Jung." <u>Ball State University Forum</u>, 17 (1976), 46-50.

> Stevens often used Jung's terminology, and "as Stevens' work is in a sense a metapoetry in which other poets, artists, philosophers are used as symbols, Stevens may have used Jungian figures and ideas deliberately." Discusses Stevens' views of the poetic process as "a journey through appearances (as ifs) toward a hypothetical center of reality."

1378. Mollinger, Robert N. "The Hero as Poetic Image." <u>Psychological Perspectives</u>, 5 (1974), 60-66.

> Using the theory of the Jungian archetype, analyzes the hero as world redeemer in the work of Wallace Stevens.

1379. Sexon, Michael. "Wallace Stevens' Theatre of Clouds: Imaginal Reality and the Idea of the Postmodern." <u>University of Hartford Studies in Literature</u>, 14 (1982), 33-40.

> Stevens, as a representative postmodern poet, goes beyond Jungian Individuation and classifies it also as a fiction. Steven's postmodernism lies in his view that "we have no life except in fiction" and his view that "reality (psyche) has no bottom."

Still, James

1380. Gunter, G.O. "The Archetypal Trickster Figure in James Still's River of Earth." Appalachian Heritage, 7 (1979), 52-55.

The uncle in Still's novel River of Earth "is a true Trickster, such as has been described and analyzed by Paul Radin, Carl Jung, and others."

Storey, David

1381. Kalson, Albert E. "Insanity and the Rational Man in the Plays of David Storey." Modern Drama, 19 (1976), 111-128.

Storey's use of madness is a reflection of his "attempt to reconcile himself to a bewildering universe where the line between sanity and insanity is often invisible." Losing one's mind may be a way to self-understanding, and in the modern world what is called madness may be "part loneliness, part guilt, part fear--the quiet desperation which constantly threaten's man's reason."

Styron, William

1382. Huffman, James. "A Psychological Redefinition of William Styron's Confessions of Nat Turner." The Literary Review, 24 (1981), 279-307.

"Karen Horney's theory of anxiety neurosis reveals Styron's intuitive grasp of human psychology in the novel more fully than Freud."

Svevo, Italo

1383. Lauretis, Teresa de. "Discourse and the Conquest of Desire in Svevo's Fiction." Modern Fiction Studies, 18 (Spring 1972), 91-109.

"In this essay, I intend to show how Svevo's unity of vision, which makes of his novels a Dantesque pilgrimage through the three kingdoms of the psyche, focuses itself on human desire and the conquest of it through symbolic discourse."

1384. _____. "Dreams as Metalanguage in Svevo's Confessions of Zeno." Language and Style, 4 (1971), 208-220.

Analyzes dreams in Svevo's novel in order to prove Freud's influence and that Confessions is a revolutionary novel in terms of form.

1385. Molony, Brian. "Psychoanalysis and Irony in La Conscienza di Zeno." Modern Language Review, 67 (1972), 309-318.

A discussion of Svevo's La Conscienza and his attitudes towards psy-

choanalysis. Svevo's work is an early example of deliberate use of
Freud's theories and therapy in literature.

Thomas, Dylan

1386. Jackaman, Rob. "Man and Mandala: Symbol as Structure in a Poem by Dylan Thomas." *Ariel: Review of International English Literature*, 7 (1976), 22-33.

> Argues that Thomas' poem "The Boys of Summer" has a structure which forms a mandala. Thus, this poem is "a splendid resolution of vital energies, a positively archetypal affirmation."

1387. Sautter, Diana. "Dylan Thomas and Archetypal Domination." *American Imago*, 31 (1974), 335-359.

> Argues that an archetypal reading mediates between excessive Freudian rationalization as well as mystical infatuation.

Tolkien, J.R.R.
(See also item 505.)

1388. Matthews, Dorothy. "The Psychological Journey of Bilbo Baggins." In Lobdell, J., ed., *A Tolkien Compass*. La Salle, Ill.: Open Court, 1975, 29-42.

> Bilbo is on a trip for psychic wholeness in terms of Jung. His journey is seen as "a metaphor for the individuation process, his quest as a search for maturity and wholeness, and his adventures as symbolically detailed rites of maturation."

Traven, B.

1389. Gutierrez, Donald. "B. Traven's Death-Ship Commune." *Texas Quarterly*, 20, 4 (1977), 59-78.

> Presents the view that B. Traven's novel *The Death Ship* foreshadows Hannah Arendt's *The Origins of Totalitarianism* in regard to the individual's struggle to preserve life and liberty in the face of a modern, dehumanized society.

Trilling, Lionel

1390. Krupnick, Mark. "Lionel Trilling, Freud, and the Fifties." *Humanities in Society*, 3 (1980), 265-281.

> "If Freud had not existed, Trilling would have had to invent him." Trilling did indeed adapt Freud to his own ends, converting Freud's

two principles to a celebration of "moral realism." Trilling defended Freudian orthodoxy against Fromm, Marcuse, Brown and Laing.

Unamuno, Miguel de

1391. Palmer, Donald D. "Unamuno, Freud and the Case of Alonso Quijano." Hispania, 54 (1971), 243-249.

> Views Unamuno's Vida de Don Quijote y Sancho as a psychoanalytic study of Don Quixote. Unamuno's work reveals parallels to Freud's ideas on sublimation. Both Unamuno and Freud were influenced by nineteenth century German philosophy.

Updike, John

1392. Detweiler, Robert. "Updike's A Month of Sundays and the Language of the Unconscious." American Academy of Religion Journal, 47 (1979), 609-625.

> A study in terms of Jacques Lacan's structuralist psychoanalysis. "Four pairs of oppositional terms can be borrowed from Lacan and applied to A Month of Sundays: language and the unconscious, self and other, the Imaginary and the Symbolic, and the penis and the phallus." Marshfield's sermons reveal "linguistic displacement and condensation" and his "problems with sex and religion handled therapeutically through language."

1393. Hunt, George W. "Updike's Omega-Shaped Shelter: Structure and Psyche in A Month of Sundays." Critique: Studies in Modern Fiction, 19 (1978), 47-60.

> Thomas Marshfield's motel diary "records a man's psychic movement from his concerns with his Ego . . . to his encounter with the unconscious symbol of his Self." Furthermore, Marshfield's description of his motel as in the shape of an omega suggests a Jungian concept of a circular omega as "the perfect ideograph for the unconscious Self toward which the conscious Ego aspires."

Valéry, Paul

1394. Lewis, Dorothy O., and Lewis, Melvin. "The Psychoanalytic Model of a Dream Used as Poetic Form: Valéry and Freud." Psychoanalytic Review, 63 (1976), 459-469.

> "We will examine Paul Valéry's apparently independent use of the identical mechanisms conceptualized in the psychoanalytic theory of dreams to construct the poem 'La Jeune Parque' ('The Youngest Fate')."

Warren, Robert Penn

1395. Herring, Henry. "Madness in At Heaven's Gate: A Metaphor of the Self in Robert Penn Warren's Fiction." Four Quartets, (1972), 143-156.

   Employs the ideas of Bateson, Laing and others as a psychological model for interpretation.

Waters, Frank

1396. Hoy, Christopher. "The Archetypal Transformation of Martiniano in The Man Who Killed the Deer." South Dakota Review, 13 (1976), 53-56.

   A study in terms of C.G. Jung and Erich Neumann. Traces Martiniano's transformation from "a patriarchal, ego-centric alien" to a person at one with this tribe: from alienation from "The Great Mother" to acceptance and discovery of his mandala.

Welty, Eudora

1397. Arnold, St. George Tucker, Jr. "The Raincloud and the Garden: Psychic Regression as Tragedy in Welty's 'A Curtain of Green'." South Atlantic Bulletin, 44 (1979), 53-60.

   A study of Welty's story in terms of Carl Jung and Erich Neumann. The story 'demonstrates the power of an intense psychic shock to propel a mature psyche into tragic regression to a primary state of conscious development." Mrs. Larkin travels "the Night Journey to the sources of her psychic being" but does not return. Thus, "her remaining conscious existence will be death-in-life."

1398. Herrscher, Walter. "Is Sister Really Insane? Another Look at 'Why I Live at the P.O.'." Notes on Contemporary Literature, 5 (1975), 5-7.

   Sister is not insane. She is "solid and practical," living in a neurotic family.

1399. May, Charles E. "Why Sister Lives at the P.O." Southern Humanities Review, 12 (1978), 243-249.

   A reading of "Why I Live at the P.O.", using R.D. Laing's ideas on schizophrenia to show "the nature and result of Sister's self justification: she tries to preserve the self by withdrawing into a central citadel and writing off everything else except the self." The "drama of the story is the reader's discovery of the logical and phenomenological circle in which Sister is trapped."

West, Nathanael

1400. Clarke, Bruce. "Miss Lonelyhearts and the Detached Consciousness." Paunch, 42-43 (1975), 21-39.

> Miss Lonelyhearts becomes emotionally dead in the course of the novel. As he becomes involved in the sufferings of others, he denies his own emotional needs. His mind and body become split. Betty tries to help him become whole again, without success because he is so emotionally crippled.

1401. DiStasi, Lawrence W. "Aggression in Miss Lonelyhearts: Nowhere to Throw the Stone." In Madden, D., ed., Nathanael West: The Cheaters and the Cheated. DeLand, Fla.: Everett/Edwards, 1973, 83-101.

> A study of West's novel as a depiction of the prophecy of Freud in Civilization and Its Discontents "that the steadily increasing repressions, particularly of aggression, which complex civilization required, were reaching combustible levels."

1402. Geha, Richard, Jr. "Miss Lonelyhearts: A Dual Mission of Mercy." Hartford Studies in Literature, 3 (1971), 116-131.

> A psychological study showing "that Miss Lonelyhearts unconsciously attempts to undo the inadequately repressed childhood memory of mutilation to the woman's body, her 'castration'." Thus he entertains the fantasy of rescuing women by identifying with them. "But if he becomes a woman, he is then that woman with a penis--the pre-oedipal androgyne, the queen-king of denial."

1403. Hickey, James W. "Freudian Criticism and Miss Lonelyhearts." In Madden, D., ed., Nathanael West: The Cheaters and the Cheated. DeLand, Fla.: Everett/Edwards, 1973, 111-150.

> Notes the ease of applicability of Freudian theory to Miss Lonelyhearts. The text is "treated as a written record of Miss Lonelyheart's consciousness." The book's themes are regarded as "symptoms of Miss Lonelyheart's disturbance."

1404. Tuch, Ronald. "The Dismantled Self in the Fiction of Nathanael West." Psychocultural Review, 1 (1977), 43-48.

> "Nathanael West's Miss Lonelyhearts realizes with the most detailed understanding the condition of schizophrenia as delineated by existential psychoanalysis and particularly by R.D. Laing."

Wharton, Edith

1405. Friedman, Henry J. "The Masochistic Character in the Work of Edith Wharton." Seminars in Psychiatry, 5 (1973), 313-329.

> Wharton's characters suffer from a "fate neurosis" and "fit Freud's description of moral masochism." They have unconscious guilt, which

is self-induced. They "are unable to express anger directly with important people in their lives." Discusses Ethan Frome, The Custom of the Country, The Reef, and The House of Mirth.

1406. Robinson, James A. "Psychological Determinism in The Age of Innocence." Markham Review, 5 (1975), 1-5.

Newland Archer's behavior is very much determined by his high society environment. This is brought out in his conflict between allegiance to his wife and his growing interest in Ellen Olenska. Ultimately, the conventions of his society determine his behavior, and he resists his romantic desire for freedom.

Williams, Charles

1407. Bolling, Douglass. "The Journey into Self: Charles Williams' The Place of the Lion." The Cresset, 37, 6 (1974), 14-18.

A discussion of Williams' use of Jungian insight to portray the "psychological and spiritual transformation of . . . Damaris Tighe, from a sterile and debilitating egoism and intellectualism to the threshold of maturity and wholeness."

Williams, J.W.

1408. Fleming, Robert E. "The Nightmare Level of The Man Who Cried I Am." Contemporary Literature, 14 (1973), 186-196.

In The Man Who Cried, Williams has gone beyond the protest novel that has dominated black writing since Richard Wright. Williams demonstrates the psychological problems produced in blacks by American society by depicting the "nightmare level" of their lives in terms of "sexual perversion, ritual cannibalism, and the impending death of the protagonist from rectal cancer."

Williams, William Carlos
(See also item 1071.)

1409. Hurry, D. "The Use of Freudian Dream Symbolism in William Carlos Williams' Paterson." Literature and Psychology, 31 (1981), 16-20.

"When The Interpretation of Dreams demonstrated to Williams that this was precisely how dreams worked, Paterson was given its major means of structuring and signification."

1410. Hurry, David. "William Carlos Williams' Paterson and Freud's Interpretation of Dreams." Literature and Psychology, 28 (1978), 170-177.

Paterson illustrates Williams' interest in Freud's work on dreams. He wished in Paterson to create a new order as prepresented by the analogy of "the imagination acting in a poem, and the subconscious acting in a dream."

1411. Green, Jesse D. "Williams' Kora in Hell: The Opening of the Poem as 'Field of Action'." Contemporary Literature, 13 (1972), 295-314.

In Kora in Hell: Improvisations, Williams anticipates Paterson in portraying personal growth by "experiencing the opposites" (the "field of action") as suggested by Jung. "Williams' 'descent' in Kora . . . lends itself to comparison in some detail with Jungian archetypes."

1412. Quinn, Bernetta. "Paterson: Landscape and Dream." Journal of Modern Literature, 1 (1970), 523-548.

Discusses Williams' dreamlike associational techniques and "the metamorphosis Freud and Jung find in dreams."

1413. Schwartz, Murray M. "'The Use of Force' and the Dilemma of Violence." Psychoanalytic Review, 59 (1972-1973), 617-625.

A psychoanalytic study of W.C. Williams' short story "to identify its core fantasies, to explore the relationship between manifest and unconsciously acted roles, and to suggest some explanations of its violence."

1414. Trouard, Dawn. "Perceiving Gestalt in 'The Clouds'." Contemporary Literature, 22 (1981), 205-217.

"Gestalt analysis of perception provides a model analogous to Williams' 'field of action' in operation." The structure of Gestalt not only grows out of Williams' work but accommodates "many critical attitudes toward the poet's work."

Wolfe, Thomas

1415. Steele, Richard. Thomas Wolfe: A Study in Psychoanalytic Literary Criticism. Philadelphia: Dorrance, 1976.

Part One is a psychoanalytical discussion of Wolfe's personality as reflected in Look Homeward, Angel. Deals with such themes as alienation, death, search for self, violence, racism, and narcissism. Part Two is a more general discussion of psychoanalysis, the writer and his work, and the nature of creativeness.

Woolf, Virginia
(See also items 559, 1340.)

1416. Corsa, Helen. "To The Lighthouse: Death, Mourning, and Transfiguration." Literature and Psychology, 21, 3 (1971), 115-132.

Relates Virginia Woolf's mourning for her own mother and father to the resolution she sketches for the main characters of To The Lighthouse.

1417. Kushen, Betty. "'Dreams of Golden Domes,' Manic Fusion in Virginia Woolf's *Orlando*." Literature and Psychology, 29 (1979), 25-33.

Views Orlando as a book "to relieve other books as well as to alleviate Virginia Woolf's temperament."

1418. _____. "The Psychogenic Imperative in the Works of Virginia Woolf." Literature and Psychology, 27, 2 (1977), 52-66.

Considers the influence of Virginia Woolf's own biography in the subject matter and form of her works.

1419. _____. "Virginia Woolf: Metaphor of the Inverted Birth." American Imago, 38 (1981), 279-304.

The metaphors of swallowing are seen "as a compensatory defense against separation, loss, deprivation and their consequence: oral rage."

1420. Love, Jean O. Worlds in Consciousness: Mythopoeic Thought in the Novels of Virginia Woolf. Berkeley: University of California Press, 1970.

"Since literatue is knowledge or cognition that has been expressed and has changed developmentally through the process of expression, literature may be studied by using the developmental hypothesis . . . as a theoretical model or device for systematic, orderly analysis and description."

1421. Poresky, Louise A. The Elusive Self: Psyche and Spirit in Virginia Woolf's Novels. Newark: University of Delaware Press, 1981.

"The heart of Virginia Woolf's work is her search for the Self," a Jungian Self which is the goal of the individuation process. Woolf's novels depict a struggle to break the barriers of the societal self and reach the Self, an accomplishment which cannot be sustained.

1422. Schlack, Beverly A. "A Freudian Look at Mrs. Dalloway." Literature and Psychology, 23, 2 (1973), 49-58.

Clarissa Dalloway is ultimately a poor model for Virginia Woolf who "could not maintain her own existence on Clarissan terms."

1423. Snider, Clifton. "The Single Self: A Jungian Interpretation of Virginia Woolf's *Orlando*." Modern Fiction Studies, 25 (1979), 263-268.

Orlando best exemplifies Woolf's idea of the androgynous, an idea she shared to some extent with Jung.

1424. Spilka, Mark. "On Lily Briscoe's Borrowed Grief: A Psycho-Literary Speculation." Criticism, 21 (1979), 1-33.

In To the Lighthouse, Lily's grief is a projection of Virginia Woolf's grief and anger on the death of her mother. "Lily at 44, divided between life and art, is like Virginia Woolf in her forties as she writes this novel, trying to convert her ungrieved grief into a lasting portrait of the lost beloved."

Wright, Richard

1425. Bolton, H. Philip. "The Role of Paranoia in Richard Wright's Native Son." Kansas Quarterly, 7 (1975), 111-124.

Bigger Thomas has delusions of grandeur derived from the racist image of the mythical black rapist/murderer. Using the ideas of Freud and Morton Schatzman, Bolton shows that in this somewhat autobiographical novel Bigger's problems are caused by the traditional "paranoidogenic" racial customs in the United States.

1426. Gounard, J.F., and Gounard, Beverly Roberts. "Richard Wright's Savage Holiday: Use or Abuse of Psychoanalysis?" College Language Association Journal, 22 (1979), 344-349.

Savage Holiday is Wright's "psychoanalytic study of a criminal mind," but the use of psychoanalytic concepts makes the novel stilted. However, said concepts are interesting tools "to carry one forward as the novel progresses."

Yeats, William Butler

1427. Allen, James. "The Road to Byzantium: Archetypal Criticism and Yeats." Journal of Aesthetics and Art Criticism, 32 (1973), 53-64.

Defends the use of archetypal criticism in a study of Yeats but prefers Philip Wheelwright's brand of such criticism to the prevalent but unsatisfactory Jungian and Frye brands.

1428. Brown, P.L.R. "Psychological Aspects of Some Yeatsian Concepts." Mosaic, 11, 1 (1977), 21-35.

Uses the psychology of Jung in order to illuminate the psychological dimension of Yeats's A Vision.

1429. Hollis, James R. "Convergent Patterns in Yeats and Jung." Psychological Perspectives, 4, 1 (1973), 60-68.

Argues that through Jung's work "we may learn something of the relationship of Yeats's personality to his creative process." Yeats and Jung have similar ideas regarding mask and persona, Spiritus Mundi, collective unconscious, anima-animus, symbol, archetype, mandala, quaternity, and individuation.

1430. Lesser, Simon O. "'Sailing to Byzantium': Another Voyage, Another Reading." In Sprich, R., and Noland, R., eds., The Whispered Meanings: Selected Essays of Simon O. Lesser. Amherst: University of Massachusetts Press, 1977, 128-148.

Challenges Elder Olsen's interpretation of this poem and discusses the latent rather than philosophical content.

1431. Olney, James. "'A Powerful Emblem': The Towers of Yeats and Jung." South Atlantic Quarterly, 72 (1973), 494-515.

> A comparison of the towers of Yeats and Jung can lead us to "a clearer understanding of the function of the symbol . . . as it transforms energy in Jungian psychology and as it creates meaning in Yeatsian poetry."

1432. Webster, Brenda. Yeats: A Psychoanalytic Study. Stanford, Ca.: Stanford University Press, 1973.

> Argues that in a life-long battle to "remake" himself, "to bring himself as man and artist into a satisfactory relationship both with his impulses and with a threatening reality," Yeats was haunted by childhood traumas, especially by an unsatisfactory relationship with a cold and despondent mother.

1433. _____. "Yeats' 'The Shadowy Waters': Oral Motifs and Identity in the Drafts." American Imago, 28 (1971), 3-16.

> Discusses Yeats's struggles in the 1890's against the abstract both in his work and in his personal relationships.

1434. Wheeler, Richard. "Yeats's 'Second Coming': What Rough Beast?" In Tennenhouse, L., ed., The Practice of Psychoanalytic Criticism. Detroit: Wayne State University Press, 1976, 152-170.

> Various readings of this poem--historical catastrophe, historical inevitability, or a recovery of radical innocence--are all based on a "core situation of infantile helplessness and separation overcome by a fantasy of omnipotent rage."

1435. Wilson, F.A.C. "Yeats' 'A Bronze Head': A Freudian Investigation." Literature and Psychology, 22, 1 (1972), 5-12.

> Yeats's goal in love "was someone who combines the characters of both sexes and . . . shared like other divided temperaments in the Freudian compromise between an impulse that seeks for a man and one that seeks for a woman."

Subject Index

The numbers following the items in this index refer to the numbered citations in the bibliography, not to page numbers.

Abandoned child, 767
Abrams, Meyer, 547
Action-language, 27, 237-239, 485
Actor, 964
Adam and Eve myth, 930
Adler, Alfred, 189
Adlerian psychology, 180, 334, 402, 406, 410, 519, 975, 1244, 1287, 1335-1337
Adolescence, 1, 358, 367, 1244, 1354
Adolescent fiction, 270
Adoption, 921, 923
Adult sexuality, 938
Aeschylus, 157, 220, 289-291
Aesthetics, 31, 164, 166, 997, 1078
Affective communication, 249
Affective stylistics, 67
Agape, 1137
Aggression,138, 338, 515, 1316, 1401
Aging, 52
Aiken, Conrad, 829, 914-918
Akedah, The, 294
Albee, Edward, 919-924
Alienation, 818, 1009, 1059, 1290, 1415
Allegory, 252
Allport, G.W., 684
Alter ego, 749, 765
Alvarez, Alfred, 984
Amazing Reader, 221
Ambivalence, 376

American dark romance, 1007
American Dream, 1064
American frontier, 243
American Gothic literature, 838
American literature, 153, 160, 178, 243, 265, 550, 555, 560, 564, 913
Anal-phallic writing, 1233
Anal sadism, 1234
Anality, 615, 842, 949
Andersen, Hans Christian, 568
Androgyne, 1315
Androgyny, 372
Anger, 153
Anima, 591, 740, 770, 819, 832, 986, 1018
Animalism, 934
Animals, 1010
Anti-Semites, 1218
Anti-Semitism, 555
Anxiety, 332, 543, 1167
Applied psychoanalysis, 678
Archetypal development, 324
Archetypal images, 916
Archetypal journey, 1097
Archetypal literary criticism, 105, 487, 890, 1427
Archetypal quest, 716, 1007
Archetypes, 32, 258, 511, 830, 930, 1114, 1121, 1219-1220, 1370, 1387, 1411
Architecture, 232
Anthropological literary criticism, 33

Subject Index

Aristotelian literary theory, 59
Aristotle, 52, 292
Arrabal, Fernando, 925
Arson, 2
Art, 232
Artaud, Antonin, 8, 98, 593
As if personality, 598
Associationist philosophers, 873
Associationist psychologists, 175
Atwood, Margaret, 559, 906
Auden, W.H., 375, 926-927
Audience-oriented criticism, 268
Auditory experience, 1151
Austen, Jane, 280, 551, 569-573
Authoritarian personality, 1261
Autism, 728
Autobiography, 48, 879, 908, 1002, 1250
Autoscopic illusion, 994
Awoonor, Kufi, 928
Bachelard, Gaston, 33, 88-89, 168
Bacon, Francis, 59
Balint, Michael, 44
Ballard, J.G., 929
Balzac, Honoré de, 86, 574-576
Baraka, Imamu Amiri, 930-932
Barnes, Djuna, 933-934
Barrie, James Matthew, 935-937
Barth, John, 55, 938-939
Barthelme, Donald, 541, 940
Basic trust, 898
Baudelaire, Charles, 577-578
Baudouin, Charles, 88
Beaumanoir, Philippe de, 323
Beaumarchais, Pierre Augustin Caron de, 309
"Beauty and the Beast," 293
Beauvoir, Simone de, 941
Behavioral psychology, 1122
Behaviorism, 557, 965
Beckett, Samuel, 157, 506, 942-946
Behn, Aphra, 498
Bellow, Saul, 905, 947-952
Bentley, Eric, 228
Beowulf, 280, 324
Bergman, Ingmar, 93
Bernanos, Georges, 953-954
Berryman, John, 955-956
Bi-active literary criticism, 127-129
Bible, The, 294-295, 574
Bibliography, 45, 56, 80, 85, 87, 142-143, 180, 196, 234, 270, 273, 286, 466
Bicameral mind, 276
Bierce, Ambrose, 579

Bildungsroman, 1210
Biography, 51, 460, 602, 605, 628-629, 631-633, 641, 654, 715, 763, 844, 864, 866, 869, 885, 891, 895, 897, 923, 967, 984, 989, 1011-1012, 1016, 1023, 1026, 1033, 1057, 1061, 1075, 1079-1080, 1111, 1113, 1118, 1124, 1150, 1154, 1157, 1171, 1225, 1235, 1237, 1257, 1264, 1274-1275, 1277, 1297, 1299, 1303-1304, 1320, 1325, 1332, 1344, 1346, 1367, 1415-1416, 1418, 1424, 1431-1433
Bion, Wilford, 1279
Birth, 610
Birth trauma, 878
Bisexuality, 1338
Bjørnson, Bjørnstjerne, 580
Black, Stephen A., 556, 889
Black males, 1120
Black writing, 1408
Blackmur, R.P., 79
Blais, Marie-Claire, 957
Blake, William, 188, 459, 499-509, 912
Bleich, David, 61, 74
Bloom, Harold, 958
Bly, Robert, 959
Boccaccio, Giovanni, 66, 326
Bodkin, Maud, 706, 1328
Body, 1316
Boisen, Anton, 504
Bombal, Maria Luisa, 960
Booth, Wayne, 148
Borchert, Wolfgang, 961
Borges, Jorge Luis, 55, 962-963
Bowel movement, 1234
Bradley, A.C., 463
Bradley, F.H., 1018
Brandabur, Edward, 1148
Breast, 541
Brecht, Bertold, 157, 230, 426, 964-965
Breton, André, 966-969
Brivac, Sheldon, 1148-1149
Broch, Hermann, 561, 571
Brodtkorp, Paul, Jr., 825
Brontë, Charlotte, 551, 559, 581-584
Brontë, Emily, 184, 190, 551, 585-590
Brown, Charles Brockden, 510-511
Brown, Norman O., 502, 1317, 1390
Browning, Robert, 375
Brutus, 94

Buffalo literary criticism, 149
Burgess, Anthony, 346
Burke, Edmund, 512
Burke, Kenneth, 79, 706
Burroughs, William S., 971
Burton, Robert, 207
Byron, George Gordon, 591
Cadoret, Remi, 910
Calderon (de la Barca), Pedro, 474
Cameron, Norman, 1046
Campbell, Joseph, 1220
Camus, Albert, 666, 781, 972-979, 1112
Canadian literature, 906
Cannibalism, 361
Capote, Truman, 184
Carnality, 919
Carpentier, Alejo, 960
Carroll, Lewis, 592-596
Castaneda, Carlos, 980
Castration, 543
Castration anxiety, 405
Castration complex, 1233
Catatonia, 782-783, 806
Catharsis, 59, 82, 250, 281
Celan, Paul, 981
Centlivre, Susanna, 498
Cervantes, Miguel de, 1079
Chaucer, Geoffrey, 325-333
Chekhov, Anton, 167, 597-598
Chesler, Phyllis, 575
Child archetype, 634, 1176
Childbirth, 425
Childhood, 549, 759, 1256, 1274
Childhood illness, 860
Childlessness, 277
Child-rearing, 133
Children, 9, 228, 294, 311, 313, 441, 560, 732, 736, 763, 887, 936, 976, 1252, 1299
Children's literature, 9, 266
Chopin, Kate, 599-600
Christian humanism, 461
Christianity, 1216
Christie, Richard, 456
Cleckley, Hervey, 463
Clemens, Samuel, 601-606
Cody, John, 556
Cognitive dissonance, 557, 1167
Cognitive psychology, 10, 106, 278, 672, 1245, 1420
Coleridge, Samuel Taylor, 17, 607-612, 708, 872
Collective unconscious, 732, 986, 1101, 1206
Comedy, 157, 261

Comic, the, 1000
Common man, 1251
Communion, 361
Confessional poetry, 1226
Conformist personality, 1261
Conrad, Joseph, 55, 135, 202, 982-994, 1223
Conscience, 601
Conscious, the, 474, 702
Consciousness, 259, 468, 775
Constant, Benjamin, 613
Core fantasy, 445, 590, 1083
Cortazar, Julio, 995
Countertransference, 163
Courage, 287
Cowley, Malcolm, 1106
Crane, Hart, 996-997
Crane, Stephen, 564, 614
Crashaw, Richard, 475
Creativity, 6, 18, 21-22, 24-25, 28-30, 46, 49, 51-52, 58, 60, 93, 98, 102-103, 143, 171-172, 182, 212, 218, 223, 232-235, 248, 254, 258, 261, 380, 430, 523, 579, 584, 591, 607, 624, 627, 687, 753, 769, 771, 810, 812, 818, 832, 848, 896, 945, 996, 1006, 1069, 1116, 1134-1135, 1142, 1150, 1154, 1250, 1256, 1264, 1274, 1277, 1304, 1349, 1351-1352, 1360, 1415
Creeley, Robert, 998
Crèvecoeur, Hector St. John de, 243
Crews, Frederick C., 72, 556, 701, 719
Cross-sexual identification, 165
Cuckoldry, 372
Cummings, E.E., 999-1000
Daimonic, the, 665
Dalton, Elizabeth, 179
Darwin, Charles, 615
Darwin, Erasmus, 894
Daughters, 104, 728, 1128
David, 94
Davies, Robertson, 1001-1005
Day, Douglas, 172
Day dreams, 880
Death, 300, 355, 588, 699, 717, 822, 899, 970, 996, 1097, 1109, 1180, 1229, 1272, 1415-1416, 1424
Death wish, 490, 1034
Defenses, 1024, 1253
Defoe, Daniel, 513-517
De la Mare, Walter, 23
Demeter myth, 1202
Denker, Henry, 1074

246   Subject Index

Depersonalization, 989
Depth psychology, 1342
De Quincey, Thomas, 616
Derrida, Jacques, 307, 567, 827
Desire, 1383
Destruction, 353
Detective fiction, 125
Devouring Mother, 1017, 1196
Diabolism, 702
Dickens, Charles, 190, 263, 544, 617-638
Dickey, James, 540, 1006-1007
Dickinson, Emily, 548, 551, 556, 639-642
Didacticism, 167
Didion, Joan, 188, 1008
Disease, 938
Disguises, 377, 722
Displacement, 555
Divided self, 715, 762
Doctorow, E.L., 1009
Dog imagery, 392
Don Juan story, 133
Don Juan syndrome, 1014
Donleavy, J.P., 184
Donne, John, 476
Donoso, José, 1010
Don Quixote, 6, 1391
Doodles, 1306
Doolittle, Hilda, 1011-1012
Döplin, Alfred, 561
Dostoevsky, Feodor, 55, 100, 206, 459, 554, 643-669, 680, 1158, 1301
Double, the, 55, 137, 197, 225, 327, 497, 529, 538, 565, 641, 650, 714, 746, 817, 819, 836-837, 963, 1088, 1120, 1161, 1190, 1224, 1259, 1263, 1282, 1301-1302, 1369
Double-bind analysis, 147
Doubling, 372, 931, 1040, 1042, 1264
Doubrovsky, Serge, 199
Doyle, Arthur Conan, 670
Dragon, 835
Drama, 157, 267
Dream imagery, 707, 953
Dreams, 92, 125, 211, 226-227, 252, 290, 326, 337, 344, 398, 545, 558, 592, 611, 616, 635, 657, 669, 677, 708, 720, 722, 769, 839, 880, 882, 902, 956, 959, 969, 981, 1025, 1027, 1034, 1100, 1104, 1106, 1115, 1144, 1153, 1159, 1162, 1168, 1205, 1207, 1232, 1291, 1306, 1320, 1384, 1394, 1409-1410, 1412

Dreams, erotic, 1106
Dreiser, Theodore, 564, 1013-1016
Dual consciousness, 964
Dufrenne, M., 247
Dürrenmatt, Friedrich, 1017
Dying, 1368
Edel, Leon, 748
Eden, 185
Edwards, Jonathan, 473, 792
Ego, 973, 1103
Ego isolation, 1164
Ego psychology, 364, 1127
Egogram, 737
Ego-splitting, 715
Ehrenzweig, Anton, 269, 942
Eichendorff, Joseph, 671-672
Eidetic imagery, 70
Eliot, George, 202, 673
Eliot, T.S., 86, 220, 249, 916, 1018-1026
Electra complex, 306
Electra myth, 288
Elizabethan humoral psychology, 470
Ellison, Ralph, 540, 1027-1028
Emasculation, 1120
Embeddedness, 1020
Emerson, Ralph Waldo, 153, 548, 674-676
Emotion, 272
Empathy, 1305
Empirical psychology, 155-156, 561
Endopsychic conflict, 436
Epic, 139
Epilepsy, 646
Episodic analysis, 244
Epistemology, 1375
Epstein, Edmund, 1148
Erikson, Erik, 350, 386, 453, 558, 736, 875
Eriksonian psychology, 72, 270, 318, 426, 908, 1084, 1210
Eros, 355
Erotic literature, 213
Eroticism, 362, 679, 710
Etymology, 527
Euripides, 220, 290, 296-299
Excrement, 1309
Excremental fantasies, 488
Exile, 1133
Existential neurosis, 1108
Existentialism, 196, 972
Existentialist psychology, 157, 199, 250, 424, 665, 700, 824, 907, 985, 1033, 1080, 1112, 1251, 1290, 1322
Extroversion, 1374

Fairy tales, 9, 47, 877
Family, 525, 630, 651, 1194, 1226, 1235
Fantasy, 102, 236, 476, 545, 557, 577, 861, 919-920, 1038, 1105, 1278
Father, 42-43, 63, 312, 366, 508, 560, 612, 623, 626, 631, 728, 735, 790, 793, 940, 1035, 1039, 1094, 1147, 1252
Father search, 1228
Father-daughter relationships, 460
Fatherhood, 682
Faulkner, William, 1029-1056
Fear, 754
Fecal symbols, 425
Female sexuality, 863
Feminism, 559
Feminist psychoanalytic literary criticism, 242
Festinger, Leon, 1167
Fiction, 151, 246, 261, 271, 563, 907, 909
Fiderer, Gerald, 1280
Field of action, 1411, 1414
Fielding, Henry, 518
Fish, Stanley, 59, 148, 179
Fitzgerald, F. Scott, 115, 554-555, 1022, 1057-1065
Flaubert, Gustave, 8, 41, 86, 167, 256, 677-681
Folktale, 337
Food, 1050
Ford, Ford Madox, 1066-1067
Ford, Henry, 1122
Forgetting, 1140
Forster, E.M., 1068
Fowels, John, 213, 1069
Frankl, Viktor, 684, 1251
Franklin, Benjamin, 473, 519
Fraser, Sylvia, 906
Fratricide, 372
Free will, 664, 792
French literary criticism, 33
French psychologists, 731
French writers, 144
Freud, Sigmund, 48, 82, 88, 100, 150, 362, 577, 626, 706, 884, 908, 966-967, 996, 1011, 1070-1079, 1122, 1232, 1343, 1346
Freudian aesthetics, 1078
Freudian literary criticism, 178, 218, 654, 701, 1280, 1403
Freudian psychology, 28, 65-66, 164, 217, 235, 243, 252, 317, 331, 344, 356, 364, 382, 401-402, 404, 414, 460, 472-473, 490-500, 502, 504, 512, 533, 536, 542, 562, 568, 578, 599, 636, 639, 642, 652, 665, 670, 683-684, 688, 696, 701, 748, 773, 782, 845, 848, 870, 902, 917, 934, 944, 955, 969, 1000, 1014, 1027, 1030, 1040, 1047, 1060, 1073, 1118, 1129, 1131-1132, 1138, 1141, 1145, 1155, 1159, 1162, 1169, 1188, 1195, 1199-1201, 1217, 1219, 1223, 1226, 1231, 1268, 1271-1272, 1276, 1278, 1283, 1287, 1307, 1309, 1316, 1322, 1331, 1345, 1376, 1384-1385, 1390-1391, 1394, 1401, 1412, 1422, 1425, 1435
Freudian slip, 1107
Fromm, Erich, 184, 960, 1186, 1390
Frommian psychology, 1022, 1064
Frost, Robert, 121, 1080-1085
Frye, Northrop, 50, 1427
Fuentes, Carlos, 1086-1088
Galdós, Benito Pérez, 682-684
Garcia Lorca, Federico, 1089-1090
Generosity, 455
Genesis, 100, 294
Genet, Jean, 1091-1092
Geneva literary criticism, 74, 149
Genius, 172
Gentility, 719
Geography, 1181
German romantic literature, 565
Gerontology, 435
Gerstenberg, Heinrich Wilhelm von, 520
Gestalt, 405
Gestaltist psychology, 73, 1414
Short story, 23
Gibson, William, 554
Gide, André, 1093-1094
Gilgamesh, 300
Gilman, Charlotte Perkins, 685
Girard, René, 197
Glass syndrome, 62
Goethe, Johann Wolfgang, 100, 521-523, 565, 872, 1210
Golden, Arthur, 884
Goncourt, Edmund (Hout) de, 686
Goncourt, Jules (Hout) de, 686
Good Mother, 369
Gothic novel, 124, 512
Goytisolo, Juan, 1095
Grass, Günter, 230, 1096
Gray, Thomas, 524
Great Mother, 528, 724, 1004, 1202

Greek, ancient authors, 286
Greek antiquity, 284
Greek myth, 190
Green, Hannah, 554, 910, 1097-1099
Greene, Graham, 1100
Greer, Germaine, 41
Grey, Zane, 1101
Grief, 484, 1424
Grillparzer, Franz, 687
Grimm, Jakob, 190, 688
Grimm, Wilhelm, 190, 688
Grotesque, the, 482-483
Grotesque literature, 134
Grove, Frederick Philip, 1102
Guilt, 100, 167, 310, 543, 601, 928, 979, 1081, 1252
Gutheil, Emil A., 92
Gynecocide, 190
H.D. See Doolittle, Hilda.
Hadfield, J.A., 92
Hair fetishism, 530
Hall, Calvin S., 92
Hamilton, Virginia, 266
Hardy, Thomas, 263, 689-696
Harte, Brett, 243
Hartmann, Heinz, 269
Hartmann von Aue, 334-335
Harvey, W.F., 23
Hate, 354, 430
Hawkes, John, 1103-1104
Hawthorne, Nathaniel, 39, 555, 567, 599, 697-724
Hayden, Robert, 1105
Heidegger, Martin, 972, 1294, 1375
Heine, Heinrich, 725
Heller, Erich, 145
Heller, Joseph, 913
Hemingway, Ernest, 81, 115, 555, 1106-1113
Heraclitus, 1047
Herbert, Frank, 1114
Herbert, George, 477
Herbert, William, 418
Hero, the, 75, 94, 1378
Heroines, 1060
Hersey, John, 1115
Hesse, Hermann, 1116-1118
Heterosexuality, 1235
Higginson, Thomas Wentworth, 642
Himes, Chester, 1119-1120
Hirsch, E.D., Jr., 263
Historical psychology, 219
Hoffman, Daniel G., 701
Hoffman, Frederick, 226
Hoffmann, E.T.A., 23, 565, 726-727

Holland, Norman N., 44, 59, 61, 72, 79, 148, 189, 193, 226, 262, 269, 279, 345, 590, 744, 748, 1054, 1084
Holmes, Oliver Wendell, 728
Homer, 42, 100, 301-304
Homosexuality, 388, 405, 434, 454, 711, 800, 802, 804, 1082, 1233, 1235, 1306
Horney, Karen, 189
Horneyan psychology, 26, 140, 201-204, 419-423, 531, 571-572, 582, 589, 619, 661-662, 673, 694, 752, 781, 950, 1020, 1111, 1318, 1374, 1382
Horror, 782, 833
Hostility, 184
Howells, William Dean, 564, 729-731
Hughes, Langston, 1121
Hugo, Victor, 86, 732
Hume, David, 873
Humor, 437, 782
Husserl, Edmund, 208, 780, 1375
Huxley, Aldous, 346, 1122-1123
Hypnagogic hallucination, 805
Hypnagogic state, 723
Hysteria, 795, 1052, 1258
Ibsen, Henrik, 220, 256, 733-742
Icarus complex, 978
Id, 505, 1103
Id psychology, 985
Idealism, 557
Identity theme, 109, 112-113, 124, 377, 453, 569, 997, 1227-1228, 1362
Illness, 461, 755
Imagery, 224, 353, 475, 977
Imagists, 70
Imagistic perception, 70
Impotency, 543, 802, 1354
Impotency fear, 1233
Incest, 457, 588, 591, 675, 1043, 1139, 1235
Individuation, 153, 608, 768, 803, 819, 886, 927, 1018, 1068, 1101, 1126, 1179, 1209, 1388, 1421
Infant megalomania, 1324
Infanticide, 356
Infantile autism, 809
Infantilism, 925
Inge, William, 1124
Initiation, 361
Insecurity, 947
Introversion, 314, 1374

Subject Index

Ionesco, Eugene, 220, 1125
Irigary, Luce, 575
Irrationality, 811
Irving, Joanne, 1336
Irving, Washington, 743-745
Iser, Wolfgang, 148
Jackson, Shirley, 1126
Jacobs, Theodore, 228
Jaensch, Erich Rudolf, 70
Jakobson, Roman, 887
James, Henry, Sr., 746
James, Henry, 8, 23, 65, 185, 190, 561, 564, 747-767
James, William, 526, 561, 747
Jamesian psychology, 729, 731, 948
Janet, Pierre, 966
Janov, Arthur, 1110
Janusian thinking, 232
Japanese men, 1365
Jargon, 68
Jaynes, Julian, 276
Jealousy, 449
Jeffers, Robinson, 2
Jensen, Wilhelm, 1127
Jews, 555, 1218
Johnson, Samuel, 525
Jones, Ernest, 414, 443, 706, 908
Jones, LeRoi. See Baraka, Imamu Amiri.
Jong, Erica, 1128
Jonson, Ben, 341
Joyce, James, 55, 1129-1153
Jung, Carl Gustave, 48, 88, 189, 501, 706, 1380, 1397, 1427, 1431
Jungian archetypes, 936
Jungian psychology, 4, 32, 36, 71, 103, 105, 130, 139, 144, 181, 211, 258-261, 273, 296, 306, 325, 339, 349, 374, 381, 390, 507, 528, 547-548, 558, 566, 586, 591, 604, 608, 634, 640, 665, 671, 676, 716, 723, 732, 740, 766, 791, 803, 814, 819, 870, 874, 877, 886, 893, 916-917, 919, 925-927, 933, 936, 959, 986, 990, 1002-1005, 1007, 1010, 1018, 1021, 1055, 1068, 1086-1087, 1101-1102, 1118, 1123, 1126, 1131, 1143, 1153, 1163, 1172, 1179, 1204-1205, 1216, 1219, 1225, 1238, 1243, 1249, 1260, 1265, 1286-1288, 1321, 1328, 1355-1356, 1371, 1373-1374, 1377-1379, 1388, 1393, 1396, 1407, 1411-1412, 1421, 1423, 1428-1429

Kafka, Franz, 100, 135, 172, 298, 636, 1154-1170, 1290
Kahlbaum, Karl, 806
Kaikhosrau, 94
Kazantzakis, Nikos, 1171
Keats, John, 485, 708, 768-775, 995
Kesey, Ken, 184, 913, 1172-1175
Kierkegaard, Søren, 642
Klein, G.S., 453
Klein, James, 1149
Klein, Melanie, 169, 269, 459, 772
Kleist, Heinrich von, 99, 101, 526, 776-779
Kligerman, Charles, 228
Knowles, John, 184
Kohut, Heinz, 145, 777
Kosinski, Jerzy, 1176-1179
Krafft-Ebing, Richard von, 1136
Kuhns, Richard F., 1180
Kyd, Thomas, 342
Lacan, Jacques, 189, 307, 827, 939, 954
Lacanian psychology, 28, 42-43, 131, 177, 214-217, 340, 375, 395, 415, 447, 567, 574, 576, 623, 790, 828, 856, 940, 1032, 1035, 1039, 1091-1092, 1392
Laing, R.D., 189, 207, 343, 453, 599, 638, 700, 823, 1008, 1193, 1214, 1390, 1395, 1404
Laingian psychology, 685, 738, 783, 824, 941, 947, 1028, 1052, 1178, 1211, 1319, 1399
Lampedusa, Guiseppi di, 1180
Land imagery, 146
Language, 592, 721, 1142
Latin literature, 286
Laughter, 217, 338
Laurence, Margaret, 906, 1181
Lawrence, D.H., 8, 81, 178, 426, 602, 715, 764, 1182-1201
Lebenswelt, 1289
LeGuin, Ursala K., 1114
Lehmann, Rosamond, 1202
L'Engle, Madeleine, 266
Leonardo da Vinci, 1138
Leonov, Leonid, 1203
Lerner, Arthur, 829
LeRoux, Etienne, 1204
Lesser, Simon O., 150, 570
Lessing, Doris, 559, 1205-1214
Levertov, Denise, 1215
Lévi-Strauss, Claude, 741
Lewis, C.S., 236, 1216

Subject Index

Lewis, Sinclair, 1217
Libido, 749, 1360
Lichtenstein, Heinz, 453, 569
Liebestod, 394
Life-force, 1199
Lind, Jakov, 1218
Linguistics, 205
Literary characters, 170
Literary critic, 277
Literary criticism, 207
Literary form, 19, 81, 345, 706, 759, 1048, 1384
Literary interpretation, 263
Literary studies, 69
Literature, 51
Lockridge, Ross, Jr., 1219
London, Jack, 555, 1220-1225
Loneliness, 173
Longfellow, Henry Wadsworth, 604
Lorca, Garcia. See Garcia Lorca, Federico.
Loss, 452
Lost Generation, 1059
Love, 354, 498, 707, 998, 1016, 1275
Lowell, James Russell, 555
Lowell, Robert, 1226
Lowes, John Livingston, 607
Lowry, Malcolm, 172, 1227
Lust, 454
Luther, Martin, 1210
Lycanthropy, 495, 588
Mach, Ernst, 561
Macdonald, Ross, 1228
Mackenzie, Henry, 526
Mad hero, 913
Madness, 46, 64, 94, 212, 248, 276, 298-299, 343, 348, 378, 403, 409, 467, 494, 506, 559, 658, 685, 807, 818, 911, 928, 968, 1099, 1209, 1211, 1214, 1266, 1297, 1381, 1395, 1398
Maeterlinck, Maurice, 1229
Mahler, Margaret, 453
Mailer, Norman, 41, 153, 185, 550, 905, 913, 1230-1235
Malamud, Bernard, 1236
Male, Roy, 701
Male-female relationships, 1208
Mallarmé, Stéphane, 86, 780
Malory, Thomas, 336
Malroux, André, 1198
Mandala, 768, 1386
Manic-depressive personality, 39
Mann, Thomas, 55, 172, 764, 991, 1067, 1237-1243
Marcuse, Herbert, 502, 884, 1390

Marlowe, Christopher, 343-344, 365
Marvell, Andrew, 478-479
Marxism, 131, 845, 1209
Masks, 955
Maslow, Abraham, 202-204, 684, 1037, 1198, 1261, 1287
Masochism, 534, 868-869, 1281, 1405
Mass psychology, 970
Masturbation, 914, 1081
Materialism, 175
Mathematics, 232, 445
Matricide, 76, 288, 653-654
Maturation, 337, 759, 1226, 1388
Maughm, Sommerset, 1244-1245
Maupassant, Guy de, 23, 579, 781
Mauriac, François, 1246-1247
Mauron, Charles, 88, 578
May, Rollo, 1251
McCarthy, Mary, 41
McCullers, Carson, 1248-1249
McKnight, Jeanne, 1149
Meaning in literature, 263
Medieval life, 334
Medieval literature, 322
Medieval personality, 321
Melancholia, 429, 691, 784, 1030
Melancholy, 330, 958, 1080
Melville, Herman, 11, 39, 81, 135, 153, 184, 206, 390, 550, 556, 567, 615, 658, 782-810
Mental breakdown, 1061
Mental disease, 779
Mental hospitals, 554
Meredith, George, 811
Merleau-Ponty, M., 275, 972
Mesmerism, 764
Metaphor, 223, 953
Metrics, 19
Michaux, d'Henri, 98
Middle age, 520, 875, 1006, 1116, 1237
Middleton, Thomas, 480-483
Miller, Arthur, 13, 230, 1022, 1250-1254
Miller, Edwin Haviland, 556
Miller, Henry, 1255
Miller, J. Hillis, 825
Milne, A.A., 1256
Milton, John, 39, 81, 219, 484-486
Minority groups, 1115
Mirror symbolism, 911
Misanthropy, 455
Mishima, Yukio, 115, 1257
Mitchell, Margaret, 1258
Modern literature, 903

Motjabai, A.G., 1259
Molière, Jean Baptiste Poquelin, 487
Money, 455, 1309
Money-lending, 425
Monk, Patricia, 1001
Monomania, 807
Monster, 579
Montaigne, Michel Eyquem, 219, 365
Monte Cristo tale, 549
Moraes, Dom, 1260
Moravia, Alberto, 1261
More, Thomas, 345-346
Mörike, Eduard, 812
Moritz, Karl-Philipp, 527
Morris, William, 813-814
Mother, 63, 228, 285, 311-313, 441, 508, 667, 767, 793, 850, 906, 926, 946, 976, 980, 1036, 1045, 1096, 1124, 1128, 1142, 1252, 1274
Mother figure, 1121, 1299
Motherhood, 682
Mozart, Wolfgang Amadeus, 812
Multiple personality, 1130, 1259
Munro, Alice, 906
Music, 232
Musil, Robert, 561, 1262
Mutilation, 1402
Mystery story, 91
Mysticism, 1171
Myth, 139, 382, 644, 677, 741, 865, 926, 933, 973, 990, 1042, 1109, 1219, 1224, 1226
Myth, Greek, 285, 901
Nabokov, Vladimir, 1263
Names, 86
Narcissism, 228, 300, 306, 310, 354, 380, 629, 679, 691, 756, 777, 884, 978, 1042, 1058, 1092, 1307, 1324-1325, 1329, 1354, 1415
Narcissus, 305
Narrative, 237-239, 1070, 1265
Naturalism, 557
Necrophelia, 1064
Negative capability, 771
Nemerov, Howard, 676
Neoclassicism, 557
Neo-organic psychiatry, 297
Nethercot, Arthur, 1359
Neumann, Erich, 1396-1397
Neurosis, 202, 407, 741, 1236
Neurosurgery, 1308
Neurotic, the, 1117
New Criticism, 647, 900
Nietzche, Friedrich Wilhelm, 98, 100, 172, 578

Night Journey, 1397
Nightmare, 1025, 1051
Nin, Anaïs, 1264
Nodier, Charles, 815
Noncreativity, 277
Norris, Frank, 564
North, Carol, 910
Not-self, 1080
Novalis, 528-529
Oates, Joyce Carol, 1265-1267
Object relations psychology, 24, 58, 169, 223, 453, 478, 493, 862, 1187
O'Brien, Fitz-James, 579
Obsession, 781
Occult, the, 547
O'Connor, Flannery, 1268-1270
Odets, Clifford, 22
Odysseus, 94
Oedipal conflict, 458, 496, 611, 643, 816, 851, 1284, 1323
Oedipus complex, 185, 285, 289, 312, 317, 362, 434, 442, 446, 491, 503, 518, 533, 555, 583, 639, 657, 710-711, 730, 750, 759, 813, 863, 919, 1013, 1031, 1034, 1061, 1090, 1117, 1119, 1133, 1137, 1174, 1183, 1194, 1200, 1228, 1231, 1233, 1235, 1269, 1358, 1365
Oedipus myth, 283, 287, 294, 317, 760, 778, 915
O'Hara, Frank, 1271
Olsen, Elder, 1430
O'Neill, Eugene, 93, 220, 1253, 1272-1277
Onetti, Juan Carlos, 960, 1278
Onomastics, 86
Ontological insecurity, 375, 1008, 1028, 1193
Ontological security, 375
Ontology, 1375
Onymy, 68
Oppression, 796
Oral aggression, 1062
Oral narcissism, 1142
Oral rage, 1419
Oral sadism, 842
Oral triad, 860
Orality, 369-370, 615, 949, 1013, 1031, 1183, 1185, 1285, 1329
Oral-sadistic anger, 1274
Orc, 505
Orestes myth, 288, 1044
Orlando, Francesco, 193
Orwell, George, 206, 346, 1076, 1279-1284

252 Subject Index

Osborne, John, 1285
Ovid, 305-306
Oyono, Ferdinand, 1286
Paranoia, 464, 867, 881, 1046, 1425
Paranoid, the, 1341
Paranoid consciousness, 709
Paranoid form, 132
Parental sexuality, 91
Parent-child relationships, 446, 1303
Parents, 104, 294, 370, 899, 1032, 1299, 1313
Passion, 585, 1352, 1357
Pasternak, Boris, 1287
Past time, 1328
Pater, Walter, 816
Patricide, 657
Pavlov, Ivan Petrovich, 965
Paz, Octavio, 1288
Penfield, Wilder, 1308
Pepper, Stephen, 1189
Perls, Fritz, 73
Personal identity, 219
Personality, 1015, 1267, 1270
Personality change, 739
Perversion, 535
Peter Pan myth, 937
Petrarch, 219
Phallic fallacy, 213
Phallic imagery, 789
Phenomenological literary criticism, 208, 912, 1327
Phenomenological psychology, 7, 188, 787, 1056, 1273, 1289
Phenomenologists, 279
Phenomenology, 3, 29-30, 35, 74, 90, 95, 126, 158-159, 168, 174, 196, 200, 236, 247, 271, 275, 424, 540, 747, 780, 825, 1294, 1375
Photophobia, 440
Piaget, Jean, 278
Picaresque, the, 488
Picasso, Pablo, 93
Pinero, Arthur, 1291
Pinter, Harold, 220, 924, 1292-1295
Pirandello, Luigi, 228, 1296-1297
Plath, Aurelia, 1299
Plath, Sylvia, 98, 115, 1128, 1298-1304
Plato, 190, 307-308
Plautus, 309
Play, 1187
Poe, Edgar Allan, 23, 115, 242, 547-548, 550, 599, 650, 817-838, 995

Poetic defenses, 66, 999
Poetic language, 224
Poetry, 272
Pope, Alexander, 530
Porphyria, 725
Post-Freudian allegory, 1203
Post-Freudian psychoanalysis, 163
Poulet, Georges, 174, 468
Pound, Ezra, 224, 1023, 1226
Present time, 1328
Priestly, Joseph, 792
Primal mother, 1240
Primal scene, 279, 583, 713, 750, 899, 915, 1019, 1048-1049, 1066, 1081, 1228, 1257
Primary process mentation, 416
Primordial images, 990
Projective delusional jealousy, 472
Proust, Marcel, 781, 1305-1312
Prudentius, 207
Pseudocommunity, 1046
Psychedelic drugs, 46
Psychiatric care, ancient Greek, 284
Psychiatry, 84, 118, 183, 192, 246, 248, 253, 304, 597, 941
Psychic development, 1212
Psychic vengeance, 1348
Psychoallegorical literary analysis, 798
Psychoanalysis, 164, 220, 674, 764, 903, 908, 1012, 1329, 1345
Psychoanalysts, 75, 742
Psychoanalytical literary criticism, 37-38, 40, 44-45, 53-54, 56, 65, 72, 85, 87-88, 92, 96-97, 99, 101, 114, 116-117, 121, 131, 135, 150, 154, 160-163, 176, 190, 222-223, 226-228, 241, 251, 254-255, 257, 262, 264-265, 274, 279-281, 286, 302-303, 309, 320, 333, 363, 394, 397, 404, 417, 430-431, 433, 466, 492, 495, 556, 558, 567-568, 593, 627, 637, 647, 679, 715, 719, 821, 840-841, 853, 954, 1048, 1054, 1105, 1150, 1175, 1197, 1253, 1338, 1340, 1346, 1352, 1358, 1365, 1413, 1415, 1426
Psychobiography, 33, 862
Psychobiological integration, 499
Psychodontia, 282
Psychodrama, 78
Psychohistory, 560
Psycholinguistic analysis, 86
Psychological conflict, 1063

Psychological determinism, 681, 1268, 1406
Psychological fiction, 546
Psychological literary criticism, 33-34, 50-51, 61, 73, 79-81, 141-142, 156, 186-187, 189, 194, 198, 202, 207, 209, 225, 234, 465, 552
Psychological novel, 1222
Psychological rhetoric, 873
Psychological romance, the, 710
Psychologist, 77
Psychology, 152
Psychology in literature, 1001
Psychopathology, 165, 182
Psychopaths, 463
Psychosexual development, 688
Psychosis, 683
Psychosomatic illness, 1115
Psychotherapy, 295
Purdy, James, 1313-1314
Puritanism, 473, 1276
Pushkin, Aleksandre Sergeyevich, 839-840
Pynchon, Thomas, 905, 1315-1317
Pyromania, 1257
Quevedo, Francisco de, 488
Rabelais, François, 347
Race relations, 931
Race relations, black-white, 1041
Racine, Jean, 8, 489-492
Racism, 1120, 1415, 1425
Radin, Paul, 1380
Raglan, Lord, 1220
Rallo, José, 682
Rand, Ayn, 1318
Rank, Otto, 605, 935, 1139, 1220, 1301
Rankian psychology, 103, 171, 461, 754, 1040, 1264, 1366
Reaction-formation, 17, 388
Reader-response literary criticism, 221
Reading, 12, 15, 35, 59, 113-114, 119, 122-123, 127, 152, 210, 231, 307, 387, 826
Realism, 20, 758, 776
Reality, 757
Reality perception, 210
Reality principle, 1081
Rebirth, 1098, 1109
Reception aesthetics, 149
Reed, T.J., 172
Regeneration, 1230, 1255
Regression, 925
Reich, Wilhelm, 189, 502, 891, 1182
Reichian literary criticism, 83

Reichian psychology, 57, 82-83, 206, 587, 654, 690, 692, 695, 891, 951-952, 1189, 1191-1192
Reid, Stephen, 455
Reid, Thomas, 873
Reik, Theodore, 1346
Reil, Johann Christian, 779
Religion, 1019
Religious allegory, 710
Renaissance literature, 340
Renan, Ernest, 375
Representational literary criticism, 245
Repressed sexuality, 919
Repression, 16, 18, 832, 1361
Responsibility, 308
Reverie, 3
Revolution, 557, 562
Rhetoric, 17, 191
Rhys, Jean, 1319
Ribot, Théodule, 992
Richards, I.A., 98
Richardson, Samuel, 531-534
Richler, Mordecai, 266
Rilke, Rainer Maria, 1320
Rimbaud, Arthur, 8, 841
Ritual, 361, 1219
Rivera, José Eustasio, 1321
Robbe-Grillet, Alain, 781, 1322-1323
Robinson, Edwin Arlington, 1324-1326
Roethke, Theodore, 1012, 1327-1328
Role-construct theory, 412-413
Rogers, Carl, 203-204, 684
Romance, the, 20, 337, 758
Romantic idealism, 818
Romantic poetry, 553
Romantic quest, 568, 749
Romantic radicalism, 698
Romanticism, 557, 566
Romanticism, American, 547-548
Romanticism, French, 558
Rorschach test, 5
Rose imagery, 222, 293
Rossetti, Christina Georgina, 842
Rossetti, Dante Gabriel, 843
Roth, Philip, 41, 541, 905, 913, 1217, 1329-1331
Ruskin, John, 844
Sade, marquis de, 535-536
Sadism, 427, 535, 1165
Sadomasochism, 294, 432, 657, 844, 920, 1046, 1314
Saint-Exupery, Antoine de, 1332
Salinger, J.D., 1333-1337

Sanity, 1398
Sarraute, Natalie, 943
Sartre, Jean Paul, 88-89, 220, 279, 941, 972, 1112, 1182, 1322, 1338-1341
Satanic act, 1230
Satire, 138
Savior, 1173
Scapegoat archetype, 1095
Scatology, 488
Schafer, Roy, 27, 189, 485
Schatzman, Morton, 1425
Schechtel, Ernest G., 1020
Schiller, Friedrich von, 537
Schizophrenia, 250, 375, 651, 686, 783, 794, 824, 864, 866, 910, 943, 947, 971, 1057, 1098, 1178, 1296, 1319, 1404
Schnitzler, Arthur, 1342-1346
Science, 232-233
Science fiction, 136, 764, 852, 1114
Scopophilia, 439-440
Scott, Paul, 1347
Scott, Walter, 848
Scream therapy, 1339
Seduction, 930
Selby, Hubert 1348
Self, 260, 464, 515, 529, 561, 703, 751, 758, 824, 888, 963, 1080, 1088, 1326, 1415, 1421
Self-consciousness, 365
Self-creation, 171
Self-destruction, 614
Self-hatred, 1329
Self-realization, 929
Self-renewal, 94
Self-repression, 799
Semantics, 527
Semiotics, 492
Senancour, Etienne, 846
Seneca, 443
Separation anxiety, 606
Separation-individuation, 93, 1134
Sex roles, 41, 559, 861, 879, 905, 1060, 1207
Sexton, Anne, 999, 1128
Sexual ambiguity, 800
Sexual allusions, 743
Sexual anxiety, 568
Sexual behavior, 498
Sexual disgust, 413
Sexual drives, 537
Sexual fantasy, 394
Sexual gratification, 433
Sexual identity, 1161

Sexual imagery, 914
Sexual incompatibility, 704
Sexual interaction, 998
Sexual literary analysis, 617
Sexual obsession, 1329
Sexual relationships, 924, 1085
Sexual repression, 2, 720, 859
Sexual symbols, 810
Sexual violence, 931
Sexuality, 223, 581, 603, 717, 802, 957, 1140, 1146, 1222, 1316
Shadow archetype, 139, 339, 986, 1265
Shaffer, Anthony, 1349-1351
Shaffer, Peter, 1349-1358
Shakespeare, William, 1, 55, 81, 106, 135, 157, 184, 188, 190, 193, 203, 206-208, 219-220, 298, 348-467, 706, 1075, 1139
Shamanistic ritual, 1097
Shame, 100
Shapiro, David, 1053
Sharpe, Ella Freeman, 414
Shaw, George Bernard, 81, 1359-1364
Shelley, Mary Wollstonecraft, 135, 551, 847-852
Shelley, Percy Bysshe, 66, 190, 853
Shengold, Leonard, 303
Shevchenko, Taras, 854
Shintaro, Ishiwara, 1365
Sidney, Philip, 66, 468
Simmel, Georg, 888
Sin, 717
Singer, Isaac Bashevis, 1366
Sir Gawain and the Green Knight, 337-338
Skinner, B.F., 1367
Slap, Joseph, 369
Slavery, 796
Sleep paralysis, 1065
Smith, Marcus, 1280
Smith, Ralph, 1054
Snodgrass, W.D., 667
Socialization, 133
Social psychology, 1022
Sociodontia, 282
Socrates, 308
Sodomy, 670
Solipsism, 900, 998
Solitude, 1029
Solon, 94
Solzhenitsyn, Alexander, 1368
Sons, 63, 312, 1142
Sophocles, 135, 290, 310-320
Sorceress, 306

Spenser, Edmund, 469-472
Spirituality, 919
Split ego, 842
Split self, 820
Splitting, 385, 1062
Sprague, Claire, 720
St. Omer, Garth, 1369
Stafford, Jean, 1370
Stedman, Edmund Clarence, 175
Steele, Richard, 538
Stekel, Wilhelm, 92
Steinbeck, John, 1371-1374
Stendhal, 8, 855-857, 1198
Sterne, Laurence, 539-540
Stevens, Wallace, 17, 221, 872, 1375-1379
Stevenson, Robert Louis, 55
Stewart, Dugald, 873
Stifter, Adalbert, 858
Still, James, 1380
Stoker, Bram, 859-863
Storey, David, 1381
Stream of consciousness, 729, 1206, 1308
Strindberg, August, 230, 864-866
Structuralism, 647, 1013
Structuralist literary criticism, 33
Structuralist psychoanalysis, 1392
Students, 1012
Styron, William, 1382
Subjective literary criticism, 12-15, 74, 110, 116, 122-123, 826
Subjective reading, 230, 320, 1024
Sublimation, 383, 983, 1306, 1391
Suffering, 287, 426
Suicide, 115, 316, 797, 984, 1113, 1128, 1225, 1227, 1257, 1303 1324-1325
Suicide in literature, 256
Sullivan, Harry Stack, 866
Sully, James, 993
Superego, 601, 973
Superego aggression, 355
Surrealism, 902, 969
Svevo, Italo, 1383-1385
Swallowing metaphors, 1419
Swedenborgian philosophy, 746
Swift, Jonathan, 541-545
Swinburne, Algernon Charles, 260, 867-869
Symbols, 32, 523, 865, 872, 1431
Symbolists, 872
Szasz, Thomas S., 796
Teachers, 1012
Teeth, 282

Tennyson, Alfred, 870
Thackeray, William Makepeace, 202, 871
Theater directing, 737
Theater of fact, 230
Theatrum mundi metaphor, 208
Thematic literary criticism, 33
Third force psychology, 202-204, 571, 684, 1037, 1060
Thomas, Dylan, 93, 1386-1387
Thoreau, Henry David, 153, 872-875
Tieck, Ludwig, 876-877
Time, 1039, 1048-1049, 1311
Timelessness, 1049
Tolkien, J.R.R., 236, 505, 1388
Tolstoy, Leo, 167, 256, 878-880
Tragedy, 63, 157, 220, 261, 292, 427, 1251
Tragedy, Greek, 290
Tragic hero, 793
Traherne, Thomas, 493
Transactional Analysis, 737
Transactive literary criticism, 107-108, 110-114, 117, 119-120, 123, 195, 231, 262, 386-387, 453, 645, 744, 826, 1215, 1362
Transcendence, 287
Transference-love relationship, 1057
Transformation, 325, 452
Transitional fantasies, 93
Transvestism, 299
Traven, B., 1389
Trickster Archetype, 1380
Trilling, Lionel, 1390
Tristan L'Hermite, François, 494
Trollope, Anthony, 881
Trope, 17
Turkle, Sherry, 216
Turner, Frederick Jackson, 243
Twain, Mark. See Clemens, Samuel.
Twins, 1349-1351
Unamuno, Miguel de, 1391
Uncanny, the, 782
Unconscious, the, 25, 51, 81, 233, 259, 474, 708, 882
Unconscious reactions, 392
Union of opposites, 761
Updike, John, 905, 1392-1393
Uroboros, 835
Utilitarian psychologists, 992
Utopia, 853
Valéry, Paul, 1394
Vampire superstition, 859
Van den Berg, Jan, 188, 787, 1289
Verga, Giovanni, 1196

Subject Index

Victim, 1047
Victim-introject, 659
Victimizer, 1047
Vindictiveness, 39, 140
Violence, 979, 1171, 1295, 1413
Virginity, 1343
Viscott, David S., 152
Visionary fiction, American, 550
Visionary literature, 1007
Visions, 92
Vonnegut, Mark, 910
Walker, Percy, 1289-1290
Wallant, Edward, 1218
Wangh, Martin, 228
Warren, Robert Penn, 1395
Waters, Frank, 1396
Watson, J.B., 965, 1122
Webster, John, 343, 495-497
Weiss, Peter, 220, 230
Welty, Eudora, 1397-1399
Werder, Karl, 397
West, Nathanael, 1400-1404
Wharton, Edith, 555, 1405-1406
Wheelwright, Philip, 1427
Whitman, Walt, 547-548, 556, 829, 882-891
Wilde, Oscar, 55, 892
Wilderness consciousness, 709
Williams, Charles, 1407
Williams, J.W., 1408
Williams, William Carlos, 1071, 1409-1414
Winnicott, D.W., 451, 453, 493, 1187
Wise Old Man, 893
Wish fulfillment, 722
Wolfe, Thomas, 1415
Woman imagery, 146
Women, 400, 449, 486, 509, 560, 602, 798, 863, 870, 924, 968, 1121, 1201, 1208, 1319, 1374
Women characters, 911
Women writers, 103, 551, 559, 906, 1370
Women's fiction, 169
Women's liberation, 41
Woolf, Virginia, 559, 561, 1340, 1416-1424
Wordsworth, William, 17, 70, 459, 893-898
Wright, Richard, 1425-1426
Writer, 77, 1250
Yeats, William Butler, 955, 1427-1435
Zola, Émile, 899

Author Index

The numbers following the items in this index refer to
the numbered citations in the bibliography, not to page numbers.

Aarons, Z. Alexander, 1
Abel, Elizabeth, 1319
Abood, Edward F., 296
Abram, Harry S., 1368
Abrams, Robert E., 782, 882, 1027
Adair, William, 1106
Adamowski, T.H., 1029-1031, 1182-1185
Adams, Michael I., 960
Adolf, Helen, 321
Albert, Sidney P., 1359
Albrecht, Joyce, 972
Alhadeff, Barbara, 947
Allen, James, 1427
Allen, Rupert, 1089
Allison, George, 682-683
Alston, Edwin F., 935
Altrocchi, John, 184
Anderson, Chester G., 1129
Anderson, E.W., 864
Anderson, Mary Castiglie, 919
Anderson, Roger B., 643-644
Andreasen, Nancy J.C., 348
Ansbacher, Rowena R., 519
Anshin, Roman, 1116
Arieti, S., 51
Arlow, Jacob A., 1257
Armstrong, Paul B., 747
Armstrong, Robert M., 982
Arnold, St. George Tucker, Jr., 1397
Aronson, Alexander, 349
Artinian, Robert Willard, 781

Arvanitakis, M.D., 292
Atkinson, Michael, 959
Aufhauser, Marcia C., 310
Avery, Nicholas C., 920
Axberger, Gunnar, 2
Babener, Liahna Klenman, 817
Bachelard, Gaston, 3
Bachmann, Susan, 350
Bailey, Nancy, 1102
Baird, James, 4
Baker, Robert, 811
Balakian, Anna, 966
Baldanza, Frank, 1313-1314
Baldessarini, Ross, 697, 717-718
Bales, Kent, 698
Barchilon, José, 973
Barcus, Nancy B., 1268
Bareikis, Robert, 1342
Barroll, J. Leeds, 351
Bart, Benjamin F., 677
Bartell, James, 878
Bassett, Sharon, 958
Baudry, Francis D., 678
Baum, Alwin L., 592
Beachamp, Gorman, 893
Beck, Michael, 499
Beck, Samuel J., 5
Becker, Michael, 305
Begiebing, Robert J., 614, 1230
Behrens, Roy R., 6
Beja, Morris, 546, 783, 1130
Bell, Barbara C., 484
Benert, Annette L., 1172

Author Index

Benoit, Raymond, 699
Benson, Morris, 339
Bentley, C.F., 859
Beranger, Jean, 510
Berets, Ralph, 1205
Berg, Jan Hendrick van den, 7
Berman, Jeffrey, 983-984, 1057
Berner, R.L., 1204
Bernstein, Gene, 768
Bersani, Leo, 8, 577
Bettelheim, Bruno, 9, 1329
Beyette, Kent, 894
Bickman, Martin, 548
Bierman, Joseph S., 860
Bigelow, Gordon E., 872
Binswanger, Ludwig, 733
Bjornson, Richard, 10
Black, Stephen A., 11, 883-885
Blake, Nancy, 784
Bleich, David, 12-15, 345, 748
Bleikasten, André, 1032
Blessing, Richard Allen, 1298
Bloom, Harold, 16-18
Bloomingdale, Judith, 596
Blum, H.P., 921
Bollas, Christopher, 785-786, 1303
Bolling, Douglass, 1407
Bolton, H. Philip, 1425
Boomslitter, Paul C., 19
Boulby, Mark, 527
Boyd, Wendy, 1227
Braga, Thomas J., 494
Bragg, Marvin, 521
Brand, Harry, 1154
Brantlinger, Patrick, 20
Brenkman, John, 307
Brenman-Gibson, Margaret, 21-22
Breugelmans, René, 528
Brewer, Derek, 337
Briggs, Julia, 23
Brink, A.W., 24, 1117
Brink, Andrew, 24
Brivic, Sheldon, 1131-1132
Brivic, Sheldon R., 1133
Brodtkorb, Paul, Jr., 787
Broe, Mary Lynn, 1299
Brooks, Peter, 1070
Brown, Arthur Washburn, 617
Brown, Dennis, 700
Brown, Eric, 325
Brown, Homer, 513
Brown, Jeffrey, 427
Brown, P.L., 985
Brown, P.L.R., 1428
Bryan, James E., 1333
Bufithis, Philip H., 1334

Burke, Kenneth, 25, 352, 596
Burkhart, Charles, 581
Burland, J. Alexis, 1352
Burnham, Donald L., 865-866
Burns, Wayne, 585
Burt, Forrest D., 1244
Burwell, R.M., 1265
Butery, Karen, 26, 582
Butler, David W., 818
Butler, Richard E., 986
Butturf, Doublas R., 338
Bychowski, Gustav, 1305
Byles, Joan, 353
Byles, Joan M., 354
Byles, Joan Mary, 355
Caldwell, Richard S., 283, 289
Calef, V., 356
Callan, Edward, 926
Callan, Richard J., 1010, 1086-1087, 1288, 1321
Calogeras, Roy, 27
Campbell, Harry M., 701
Carlson, Eric W., 819
Carnell, Corbin, 1216
Carothers, James B., 1217
Carr, Joan, 734
Carroll, David, 28
Carruth, Hayden, 900
Carson, Joan, 586
Carter, Thomas N., 1279
Casey, Edward S., 29-30
Cassis, A.F., 1100
Castelnuovo-Tedesco, Pietro, 549
Castillo, Ana Hernandez Del, 995
Castle, Terry J., 514
Centola, Steven, 1068
Chabot, C. Barry, 569, 788, 1033, 1080
Chaitin, Gilbert, 645, 899
Chaitin, Gilbert, D., 841, 855
Champagne, Roland A., 574
Chaplin, William H., 357
Chasseguet, Smirgel, Janine, 535
Cherry, Caroline L., 1270
Child, Irving L., 31
Chouinard, Timothy, 32, 1018
Chrzanowski, Joseph, 962
Clancier, Anne, 33
Clarke, Bruce, 1400
Clarke, Delia, 1219
Clendenning, John, 674
Cloonan, William J., 489-490
Cocks, Geoffrey, 1256
Cohan, Steven, 618
Coldwell, Joan, 957
Coles, Robert, 34

Author Index   259

Collier, Gary, 35
Cook, Harry James, 886
Cook, Reginald, 702
Cooper, David, 36
Cooper, James Glennon, 1220
Corrigan, Matthew, 1327
Corsa, Helen, 326, 1416
Corsa, Helen S., 570, 881
Coskren, Robert, 820
Costello, Jacqueline A., 789
Cowan, James C., 1034
Cowart, David, 583
Cox, Marjorie K., 358
Crews, Frederick, 37
Crews, Frederick C., 37-38
Crosby, Donald H., 776
Crow, Charles L., 729. 731
Crowley, Francis E., 749
Crowley, John W., 730-731
Culbertson, Diana, 1261
Culik, Hugh, 942
Dahlberg, Charles Clay, 1180
Dalsimer, Katherine, 1248
Dalton, Elizabeth, 646-647
Danelius, Gerhard, 306
Daniels, Marvin, 39
Dauber, Antoinette, 493
David, Michael, 40
Davidson, Cathy N., 1181, 1315
Davidson, Leah, 1237
Davies, Rosemary, 1186
Davis, D. Russell, 735
Davis, Frederick B., 967
Davis, Judith, 41
Davis, Robert Con., 42-43, 940, 1035
Davis, Robert Gorham, 1071
Deane, Paul, 1318
Deans, Thomas R., 750
Decina, Paolo, 1296
de Furia, Richard, 1125
Deleuze, Gilles, 593
Delphendahl, Renate, 529
Demetrakopoulos, Stephanie, 861
Dennis, Carl, 703
Deredita, John, 1278
Derrida, Jacques, 1072-1073
Dervin, Daniel, 44, 1134, 1187, 1360
Dervin, Daniel A., 541, 1188
Desai, Rubin W., 359
Dettmering, Peter, 45
Detweiler, Robert, 1392
Devereux, George, 290
Devlin, James E., 743
d'Heurle, Adma, 736

Diamond, Ruth, 1097
Dickes, Robert, 360
Dickstein, Morris, 500
Di Cyan, Erwin, 46
Dieckmann, Hanns, 47
Dillman, Richard H., 873
Dimeo, Steven, 579
DiStassi, Lawrence W., 1401
Dodd, William J., 1155
Doherty, Joseph F., 887
Dollard, John, 922
Donnelly, John, 446
Dooley, D.J., 1280
Doubrovsky, Serge, 1338
Downing, Christine, 48
Doyle, Charlotte Lackner, 49
Dreistadt, Roy, 1287
Dudek, Louis, 50
Duncan, Bruce, 520
Duncan, Jennifer, 686
Durand, Regis, 790
Durham, Mildred O., 361
Ebel, Henry, 362
Edel, Leon, 51-53
Edelson, Marshall, 54
Eder, Doris L., 55
Edgar, Irving, 363
Edmunds, Lowell, 56
Edinger, Edward F., 791
Edwards, Carol, 689
Edwards, Duane, 689
Efron, Arthur, 57, 587, 690, 1189
Ehrenzweig, Anton, 58
Ehrlich, Victor, 59
Eissler, Kurt Robert, 60, 364
Ekstein, Rudolf, 284
Eldredge, Patricia, 531, 619
Elldrodt, Robert, 365
Elliott, Susan M., 61
Emery, Allan Moore, 792
Empson, William, 596
Endres, Rolf C., 334
Engstrom, Alfred Garvin, 62
Erlich, Avi, 366
Evans, Martha, 846
Evans, Richard I., 1250
Evans, Timothy, 1231
Faber, M.D., 63, 311-312, 367-371, 455, 522, 639, 793, 980, 1036, 1285
Farber, Ada, 285
Farrell, Edith R., 1246
Farrell, Frederick, Jr., 1246
Feal, Gisèle, 474
Feal-Deibe, Carlos, 474, 1090

Feder, Lillian, 64, 901
Fein, Richard J., 888
Feinstein, Howard, 746
Feldman, Robert, 1272
Feldman, Robert L., 1251
Felman, Shoshana, 65, 575, 821
Fenster, Thelma, 323
Ferguson, Margaret W., 66
Fernandez, Ronald, 648
Ferris, Lesley K., 737
Fiderer, Gerald, 1281
Fineman, Joel, 372
Finholt, Richard, 550
Fish, Stanley, 67
Fisher, Marvin, 794
Fleming, Robert E., 1408
Fliess, Elenore Stratton, 373
Fliess, Robert, 373
Flower, J., 1247
Floyd, Nathaniel M., 795
Foley, John M., 324
Forrest, David V., 68, 79, 999
Forrey, Robert, 1013, 1173, 1221-1222
Fort, Keith, 69
Foster, Steven, 70
Fraiberg, Louis, 822
Frank, Lawrence, 620
Franklin, Benjamin, V, 704
Franz, Marie-Louis von, 71
Franzosa, John, 615, 705
Franzosa, John C., Jr., 72
Freedman, William, 1019
Friedman, Henry J., 1405
Friedman, Norman, 73
Friedman, Susan, 1011
Friedrich, Reindhart, 1156
Fryer, Judith, 728
Fyler, Anson C., Jr., 374
Gabbard, Lucina P., 1292
Galenbeck, Susan, 74
Gallant, Christine, 501
Gandelman, Claude, 1306
Ganim, Carole, 375
Gargano, James W., 751
Gatti-Taylor, Marisa, 732
Gedo, John E., 75
Geha, Richard, 76, 649
Geha, Richard, Jr., 1402
Geherin, D.J., 1008
George, Diana, 502-503
Gerenday, Lynn de, 376, 469
Ghiselin, Brewster, 77
Gifford, Sanford, 1353
Gilbert, Sandra M., 551
Giles, Mary E., 1095

Gilman, Sander L., 526
Gilmore, J.B., Jr., 542
Ginn, Robert M., 78
Girard, René, 1307
Girgus, Sam B., 599, 601, 823-824
Glenn, Jerry, 981
Glenn, Jules, 923, 1349-1351, 1354
Glenn, Justin, 286
Glenn, Michael L., 79
Goldiamond, Israel, 607
Goldschmidt, A.M.E., 596
Goldstein, Melvin, 80, 377
Golub, Ellen, 842
Goodman, Charlotte, 1266
Gordon, Andrew, 1232-1234
Gordon, David J., 81, 1361
Gordon, Lois G., 1330
Gordon, William A., 1135
Gorss, Gloria, 525
Gotti, Richard, 752
Gottschalk, Paul A., 378
Gounard, J.F., 1426
Graham, Neilson, 594
Grain, Frances, 738
Grant, William E., 706
Green, André, 82, 753
Green, Bernard, 892
Green, Jesse D., 1411
Greenacre, Phyllis, 596
Greenberg, Bette, 234
Greenberg, Harry, 136
Greenfield, Jerome, 83
Grenander, M.E., 84, 796
Grimaud, Michel, 85-87
Grimsley, Ronald, 88
Grimsley, Ronald R., 89
Grinstein, Alexander, 379
Griska, Joseph M., 895
Grosholz, Emily, 902
Grosman, Inge, 268
Grossvogel, David I., 90
Grotjahn, Martin, 91
Grove, T.N., 621
Grundy, Dominick, 622
Gubar, Susan, 551
Gulbertson, Diana, 1093
Gunn, Edward, 933
Gunter, G.O., 1380
Gutierrez, Donald, 1389
Gyurko, Lanin A., 797, 963, 1088
Haberstroh, Charles, 799
Haddick, Vern, 754
Hale, Frank A., 1180
Halliburton, David, 825
Halling, Steen, 1273
Hallman, Ralph J., 936

Haltresht, Michael, 92, 616, 987-988, 1115
Hamilton, James W., 93, 769, 989, 1006, 1127, 1274
Hammond, John G., 998
Handelman, Susan, 380
Hankoff, L.D., 94
Hannum, Hunter, 1238
Hans, James S., 95
Hanson, John, 1176
Hanzo, Thomas, 623
Hardin, James, 970
Harris, Phyllis, 296
Harshbarger, Karl, 313
Hartman, Geoffrey, 896
Hartman, Geoffrey H., 96
Hartocollis, P., 1171
Hartog, Curt, 515, 524
Haselswerdt, Marjorie, 1037
Haskell, Ann, 327
Haule, J., 1000
Hayes, Francis, 97
Hayman, Ronald, 98
Heller, Erich, 99-101, 903-904
Helms, Randel, 504-505
Helson, Ravena, 102-103
Henderson, Archibald, 1081
Henderson, D. James, 862
Henderson, Joseph, 381
Hendin, Josephine, 905
Hendrickson, Norejane J., 104
Henke, Suzette A., 1136-1137
Hennelly, Mark, 798
Herbert, Edward T., 382
Herbert, Wray C., 990
Herd, E.W., 105
Hernadi, Paul, 964
Herndon, Jerry A., 707
Herring, Henry, 106, 343, 1395
Herrscher, Walter, 1398
Hershey, Jane, 498
Hertz, Neil, 726
Hickey, James W., 1403
Hill, J.M., 847
Hill, James L., 552
Hines, Thomas J., 1375
Hirsch, Gordon D., 624-625, 848, 1190
Hoerner, Dennis, 1191-1192
Hoey, Thomas F., 314
Hoffman, Madelyn, 1058
Hoffman, Steven K., 1126
Hoffmeister, Charles C., 650
Hofling, Charles K., 383-384
Hogan, Patrick Colm, 385
Holland, Norman, 107-111

Holland, Norman N., 112-124, 386-387, 826, 1038, 1215, 1362
Hollis, James R., 1429
Holovinsky, Ivan Z., 854
Holsberry, John E., 708
Houghton, Donald E., 755
Hovey, Richard, 756
Hovey, Richard B., 1014
Howard, Stephen, 287
Hoy, Christopher, 1396
Hubbs, Valentine C., 671
Huber, R.J., 1335
Huber, R. John, 1336
Huffman, James, 1382
Hughes, Felicity A., 470
Hughes, Philip R., 511
Hull, Bryan D., 948
Hunt, George W., 1393
Huntley, H. Robert, 757
Hurry, D., 1409
Hurry, David, 1410
Hurt, James, 1066
Huss, Roy, 688
Hutch, Richard A., 675
Hutter, Albert D., 125, 626-628
Hutzler, Jeffrey, 651
Hyman, Stanley Edgar, 388, 1074
Ingarden, Roman, 126
Ingber, Richard, 56
Irvine, Lorna, 906
Irving, Joanne, 1337
Irwin, John, 996, 1039-1040
Iser, Wolfgang, 127-129
Jaarsma, Richard J., 389
Jackaman, Rob, 1386
Jackson, Paul R., 1255
Jacobs, Edward, 770
Jacobs, Edward C., 874
Jacobson, Irving, 1252
Jacoby, Mario, 130
Jameson, Fredric, 131, 576
Jayne, Edward, 132, 709, 1082
Jenkins, Lee, 1041
Jenkins, Lee Clinton, 1042
Jeske, Jeffrey M., 390
Jiji, Vera M., 391
Jofen, Jean, 1157
Johannsen, Pauline Renee, 1059
Johnson, Barbara, 827
Johnson, Doris V., 879
Johnson, E. Bond, 1067
Johnson, John, 1020
Johnson, Lee Ann, 758
Johnson, Paula, 595
Johnston, Kenneth G., 1107
Jones, A. David, 133

Jones, Joyce, 1021
Jones, Russell, 1015
Jordan, Mary Ellen, 691
Jordan, Robert, 480
Jørgenson, Jens Peter, 1223
Joseph, Gerhard, 849, 870
Joseph, Robert J., 844
Justman, Stewart, 799
Justman, Stuart, 652
Kahane, Claire, 134
Kahn, Coppelia, 453
Kalson, Albert E., 1381
Kann, David, 1083
Kann, David J., 744-745
Kanter, V.B., 1075
Kanzer, Mark, 392
Kaplan, Morton, 135
Kaplan, Sydney Janet, 1202, 1026
Karpowitz, Stephen, 602, 1218
Kastan, Carren Osna, 759
Katan, M., 1343
Katz, Harvey A., 136
Katz, Michael, 839
Kaufman, Pamela, 512
Kauvar, Gerald B., 553
Kavanaugh, Thomas, 516
Kavka, Jerome, 1324-1325
Keane, Susan M., 953
Keefe, Terry, 941
Keith, W.J., 1001
Kellner, R. Scott, 800
Keppler, C.F., 137
Kernan, Alvin, 138
Kerrigan, William, 340
Keyes, Margaret F., 139
Keyishian, Harry, 140
Khan, Asif Iqbal, 141
Kiell, Norman, 142, 1228
Kimball, Arthur Samuel, 336
Kimball, Jean, 1138-1139
King, Billie, 608
Kinney, Thomas, 328
Kirchner, John H., 1367
Kiremidjian, David, 653-654
Kirsch, Arthur, 393
Kist, E.M., 1028
Kleinbard, David J., 1193
Kleinschmidt, Hans, 143
Kligerman, Charles, 629
Kloss, Robert, 135, 914, 1043, 1094, 1300
Kloss, Robert J., 329, 789, 1140
Knapp, Betina, 144, 1229
Knapp, John, 1282
Knoff, William, 974
Knutson, Harold, 487

Kohut, Heinz, 145
Kolbenschlag, Madonna C., 1060
Kolodny, Annette, 146
Kovel, Joel, 679
Kramer, Maurice, 889
Kraus, Elisabeth, 1103
Kravchenko, Maria, 655
Krupnick, Mark, 1390
Kubal, David, 1076
Kudszus, Winfried G., 147
Kuenzli, Rudolf, 148
Kuhns, Richard F., 1180
Kuiken, Don, 35
Kuriyama, Constance Brown, 394
Kushen, Betty, 710, 1417-1419
La Belle, Jenijoy, 1328
Lacan, Jacques, 395, 828
Ladimer, Bethany, 968
Lale, Meta, 1177
Lameyer, Gordon, 1301
Lange, Jean, 554
Lapidus, Deborah, 244
Lauretis, Teresa de, 1383-1384
Leavy, Stanley A., 771
Lebeaux, Richard, 875
LeClair, Thomas, 1269
Leclercq, Jean, 322
Lee, C. Nicholas, 880
Lee, Ronald J., 1355
Lefcowitz, Allan, 711
Lefcowitz, Barbara F., 1207, 1236
Lefort, Guy, 197
Lehman, David, 1376
Leigh, David J., 1108
Leitch, Vincent B., 149
Lelchuk, Alan, 630
Lerner, Laurence, 150
Lesser, Simon O., 151, 301, 315, 396-399, 532, 656, 680, 712, 1158, 1293, 1430
Lester, David, 316
LeUnes, Arnold, 152
Leverenz, David, 153, 400, 473, 801
Levin, Gerald, 533-534, 867
Levine, M. Herschel, 555
Levine, Robert T., 1159
Levitt, H.N., 154
Levy, Lenore, 692
Lewis, Dorothy O., 1394
Lewis, Melvin, 1394
Lewis, Richard O., 1105
Lichtenberg, Charlotte, 401, 1275
Lichtenberg, Joseph, 401
Lichtenberg, Joseph D., 1275
Lichtenberg, Philip, 1098

Lickorish, John R., 402
Lidz, Theodore, 403
Ligocki, Llewellyn, 829
Lindauer, M.S., 404
Lindauer, Martin S., 155-156
Little, Margaret I., 739
Love, Jean O., 1420
Lower, R.B., 657
Lowry, E.D., 1109
Luke, J. Tracy, 300
Lupton, Mary, 609
Lynch, William, 157
Lyons, Charles R., 925
MacCary, W. Thomas, 309
MacPike, Loralee, 685
Magliola, Robert, 158
Magliola, Robert R., 159, 1239
Magretta, Joan, 658
Mahlendorf, Ursula, 687, 727, 777, 1096, 1344
Mahlendorf, Ursula R., 812
Mahony, Patrick, 341, 405, 1160
Maini, Darshan Singh, 160
Mairet, Philip, 406
Mais, M., 330
Mancini, Joseph, 740
Manheim, Leonard F., 161-162, 631-633, 713
Mann, Jeanette W., 1370
Mann, John S., 1224
Mannoni, Octave, 1141
Marcus, Mordecai, 1084-1085
Marcus, Steven, 506
Markert, John, 407
Markow, Alice B., 1208
Marks, W.S., III, 1162
Marotti, Arthur F., 163
Marquard, Odo, 164
Martin, Dennis M., 938
Martindale, Colin, 165-166, 830
Massey, Irving, 167
Mathews, Dorothy, 1388
May, Charles E., 603, 1371-1372, 1399
May, Keith M., 907
Mazlish, Bruce, 908
Mazzaro, Jerome, 955
Mazzeno, Laurence, 897
McAllester, E. Mary, 168
McCann, Janet, 1377
McClintock, James I., 1225
McConaghy, N., 297
McFadden, George, 1226
McGuire, Jerry, 408
McIntyre, Allan, 991
McKnight, Jeanne, 1142

McLaughlin, Ann. L., 409
McLaughlin, John J., 410, 519
McLean, Sammy, 1161
McNall, Sally, 169
McNelly, Willis E., 1114
McSweeny, Kerry, 556
Meares, Russell, 943
Meckier, Jerome, 1122
Medlicott, R.W., 294, 317
Mehlman, Jeffrey, 578
Meisel, Frederick L., 937
Meisel, Martin, 845
Meissner, W.W., 170, 659
Menaker, Esther, 171
Merivale, Patricia, 1002
Meyer, Bernard, 1332
Meyers, Jeffrey, 172, 530
Meyrowitz, J., 491
Micklus, Robert, 714
Mijuskovic, Ben Lazare, 173
Mileck, Joseph, 1118
Miller, J. Hillis, 174
Miller, R. Baxter, 1121
Miller, Ralph N., 175
Miller, Tracey R., 890
Miner-Quinn, Paula, 802
Mintz, Thomas, 293
Mishler, William, 568
Mitchell, Giles, 495, 588
Mitchell, Marilyn L., 1124
Moglen, Helene, 411
Mollinger, Robert N., 176, 831, 1260, 1378
Mollinger, Shernaz, 715
Molony, Brian, 1385
Monk, Patricia, 1003
Morel, Jean-Pierre, 969
Morey, Frederick L., 640
Morris, Christopher, 939
Morris, Humphrey, 177
Morrison, Claudia C., 178
Morrison, Ian R., 613
Morrison, Kristin, 924
Morson, Gary, 179
Mortimer, Gail L., 1178
Mosak, B., 180
Mosak, Harold H., 180
Moss, A.E., 412
Moss, A.E. St. G., 413
Moss, Judith P., 949
Mueller, Carl R., 181
Muir, Kenneth, 414
Muller, Gilbert H., 1110
Muller, John, 415
Müller-Braunschweig, Hans, 182
Murdaugh, Elaine, 1240

Author Index

Murphy, George D., 1061, 1270
Murrill, V., 1162
Muzina, Matej., 1123
Myer, John C., 557
Myerson, Paul G., 183
Nadeau, Robert L., 934
Nadel, Barbara S., 184
Nance, William, 760
Nance, William L., 185
Nash, Lee, 1059
Natoli, Joseph, 186-189, 1289
Natterson, Joseph M., 446
Neary, John, 634
Neiditz, Minerva, 416
Nelson, Benjamin, 190
Nelson, Cary, 191
Nelson, Donald F., 961
Nemiah, John C., 192
Neuhauser, Rudolf, 660
Neumann, Dwight K., 488
Neumann, Erich, 1163
Neumarkt, Paul, 335, 1164
Newman, Karen, 193
Newman, Robert D., 1143
Nnolim, C.E., 1286
Noland, Richard W., 194, 318, 417
Norris, Margot, 741, 1165
Norris, Margot C., 1144
Norris, Nancy, 1044
Norton, Rictor, 761
Ober, William B., 868
O'Brien, Darcy, 1145-1146
O'Brien, Justin, 1308
Ojo-Ade, Femi, 928
Okerlund, Arlene N., 471
Olney, James, 1431
Olshin, Toby, 517
Olson, Carol Booth, 1259
Ong, Walter J., 195
Ordway, J.A., 693
Orlando, Francesco, 492
Orr, Leonard, 196
Oughourlian, Jean-Michel, 197
Oxenhandler, Neal, 198-199, 780
Padel, J.H., 418
Palmer, Donald D., 1391
Palmer, Richard E., 200
Pankin, Shirley, 1194
Paris, Bernard J., 201-204, 419-423, 571-572, 589, 661-662, 673, 694, 871, 950
Paris, Jean, 205
Park, William, 518
Parks, A. Franklin, 539
Parloff, Gloria H., 257
Pasotti, Robert N., 206

Patterson, Rebecca, 641
Patterson, Robert G., 604
Paulissen, Mary N., 538
Paulson, A.B., 1062
Payne, Michael, 207, 424
Pearce, Howard D., 208
Pearlman, E., 331, 425, 635
Pearson, Gerald H.J., 446
Peavy, Charles D., 1045-1046
Peckham, Morse, 209
Penuel, Arnold M., 684
Perkins, M.L., 536
Perry, Nick, 929
Perry, Ruth, 298
Petrosky, Anthony R., 210
Phillips, Robert, 596
Pickering, Jean, 1209
Pinder, Donna, 426
Pinsker, Sanford, 1267
Plank, D.L., 1203
Politzer, Heinz, 1166
Pops, Martin Leonard, 803
Poresky, Louise A., 1047, 1421
Porter, Dennis, 1222
Porter, Laurence M., 211, 558, 815
Porter, Peter, 212
Porter, Thomas E., 1276
Powlick, Leonard, 1294
Pratt, Branwen, 584
Pratt, Branwen E.B., 663
Predmore, Richard, 716
Price, John, 472
Pruyser, Paul W., 300
Purdy, Strother B., 213
Quagliano, Anthony, 1290
Quinn, Bernetta, 1412
Quinn, James, 717-718
Rabaté, Jean-Michel, 1147
Rabkin, Leslie Y., 427
Rackin, Donald, 596
Radford, F.L., 1004
Ragland, Mary E., 347
Ragland-Sullivan, Ellie, 214-217, 856, 1091-1092
Ragussis, Michael, 1195
Rahv, Philip, 218, 719
Ralph, Ruth S., 1014
Rapf, Joanna, 591
Rathbauer-Vincie, Margreta, 273
Reck, Tom S., 930
Reckley, Ralph, 1119-1120
Reed, Michael, 590, 813
Reeder, Roberta, 832
Reid, Stephen, 302, 428-434, 664, 772
Reid, Stephen A., 308

Rey, Jean-Michel, 1077
Ricciardelli, Rachel M., 435
Rice, Julian C., 1331, 1356
Richmond, Hugh M., 219
Rigney, Barbara Hill, 559
Rippere, Victoria, 876
Riva, Raymond T., 944
Rizzo, Gino, 228-229
Roazen, Paul, 1283
Roberts, Patrick, 220
Robinson, James A., 1406
Robinson, Virginia P., 605
Robson, Vincent, 1063
Rodrigues, Eusebio L., 951
Rogers, Robert, 221-225, 436
Roland, Alan, 226-229, 1295
Rolfs, Daniel, 1297
Rollman-Branch, Hilda S., 230
Romig, Evelyn M., 1012
Roper, Gordon, 1005
Rose, Ellen Cronan, 1210
Rose, Gilbert J., 437, 945, 1048-1049, 1069
Rosenberg, Samuel, 670
Rosenberg, Seymour, 1015
Rosenblatt, Louise, 231
Rosenman, Stanley, 319
Rosenzweig, Paul J., 1050
Ross, Donald, 720
Rossky, William, 1051
Roth, Nathan, 725
Roth, Phyllis A., 863, 1263
Rothenberg, Alan B., 438-441
Rothenberg, Albert, 232-234, 1253, 1277
Rothman, Irving N., 543
Rovit, Earl, 560
Roy, Emil, 344, 481
Robenstein, Mark A., 850
Rubenstein, Roberta, 1211-1212
Rubin, Larry, 804
Rubin, Samuel S., 442
Rubinstein, L.H., 288
Rudat, Wolfgang E.H., 332-333, 443
Ruderman, Judith, 1196
Rusch, Frederik L., 891, 1022, 1064
Russell, Peter, 1345
Ryan, Judith, 561
Rycroft, Charles, 235
Ryder, Frank G., 778
Sachs, Erich, 975
Salamon, Lynda B., 1302
Sale, William, 299
Sanders, Kenneth, 444
Sardello, Robert, 236
Sasaki, M.S., 445

Sautter, Diana, 1387
Saveson, John E., 992-993
Schafer, Roy, 237-239
Schechter, Harold, 1007
Scheff, Thomas J., 240
Scherr, Arthur, 976
Schlack, Beverly, A., 1422
Schilder, Paul, 596
Schlesinger, Kurt O., 446
Schmidl, Fritz, 241
Schneck, Jerome M., 597, 805-806, 1065
Schneider, Daniel J., 762
Schneiderman, Stuart, 447
Schor, Naomi, 242
Schroeder, Fred E.H., 243
Schroeder, Natalie, 816
Schwaber, Paul, 833
Schwartz, Albert, 840
Schwartz, Murray M., 448-453, 840, 1197, 1303, 1413
Sears, Robert R., 244, 606
Sehmsdorf, Henning K., 580
Seidenberg, Robert, 1254
Sellery, J'nan Morse, 909
Sellner, Timothy, 877
Sellner, Timothy F., 537
Seltzer, Leon F., 1016, 1052
Semour-Smith, Martin, 454
Seward, T.C., 455
Sewell, Ernestine, 1179
Sexson, Michael, 1379
Shands, Harley C., 642
Shapiro, Barbara, 946
Shapiro, Eugene D., 1253
Shechner, Mark, 1148-1150
Sherman, Murray H., 1346
Sherwin, Paul, 851
Shinn, Thelma J., 763
Shupe, Donald R., 245, 456
Silberger, Julius, 246
Silver, Arnold, 1363
Silverman, Hugh J., 247
Silverstein, Howard, 1235
Simenauer, Erich, 1320
Simmon, Scott, 1316
Simon, Bennett, 248, 303-304
Simpson, David E., 773
Singer, June, 507
Siomopoulos, Gregory, 249
Siomopoulos, V., 250
Sizemore, Charles, 1167
Sjögren, Christine, 858
Sjögren, Christine Oertel, 1262
Skinner, John, 596
Skoller, Eleanor, 1271

Skura, Meredith, 251-252
Slaby, Andrew E., 253
Slap, Laura R., 915
Slater, Judith, 1053
Sloane, Eugene H., 610
Slochower, Harry, 254-256, 977, 1241
Slutzsky, Jacob E., 1357
Small, Michel, 721
Smith, Allan, 834
Smith, Henry Nash, 807
Smith, Joseph H., 257
Smith, M., 1284
Smith, Ralph, 1054
Snider, Clifton, 258-260, 927, 1249, 1423
Sobel, Dava, 910
Solomon, Eric, 446
Spector, Jack J., 1078
Spector, Judith, 852
Spencer, Sharon, 1264
Sperber, Michael A., 598, 665-666, 978, 994
Spilka, Mark, 636, 1424
Spivey, Ted R., 261, 916-917
Splitter, Randolph, 1309-1310
Sprague, Claire, 722
Sprich, Robert, 262
St. Armand, Barton Levi, 723, 835
Stamm, Julian L., 979, 1358
Stark, John, 1009
Steele, Richard, 1415
Steele, Robert S., 1101
Steig, Michael, 263, 476, 544, 573, 637, 695, 952
Stein, Calvert, 295
Stein, Karen F., 911
Stephenson, William, 774
Stepto, Michele, 508
Sternberg-Perrakis, Phyllis, 1213
Sterrenburg, Lee, 562
Stetner, S.C.V., 457
Stewart, Abigail J., 133
Stillman, Claudia R., 545
Stockholder, Katherine, 264, 458, 1168
Stoll, John E., 563
Stone, Albert E., 265
Stone, Carole, 1128
Stone, Donal, 1373
Storch, Margaret, 509
Storey, Robert, 1323
Stott, Jon, 266
Strauch, Carl F., 808
Street, James, 1169
Stuart, Simon, 459

Stubbs, John C., 1104
Styan, J.L., 267
Suleiman, Susan, 268
Sullivan, Ruth, 836, 1174
Sullivan, William P., 809
Sussman, Henry, 1170
Swan, Jim, 269, 478-479
Swartz, Paul, 1311-1312
Swearingen, James E., 540
Swinney, Susan V., 1101
Szalita, Alberta B., 742
Tancredi, Laurence, 253
Tarbox, Raymond, 1151, 1242, 1339
Tatar, Maria M., 764, 779
Taubenheim, Barbara Wiese, 270
Tavernier-Courbin, Jacqueline, 1111
Taylor, Gordon O., 564
Tefs, Wayne A., 1054
Tenenbaum, Elizabeth, 1198
Teplitz, Zelda, 460
Terras, Rita, 565
Thieme, John, 1369
Thompson, David, 638
Thompson, G.R., 837-838
Thornbury, Charles W., 956
Thornham, Susan, 1199
Tiberia, Vincenza, 523
Todd, Robert E., 724
Tolpin, M., 291
Tomasi, Barbara R., 1152
Townsend, Dabney W., Jr., 271
Trail, George, 1200
Trail, George Y., 696
Tremper, Ellen, 765
Tristram, Philippa, 1201
Trosman, Harry, 1023
Trouard, Dawn, 1414
Tsur, Reuven, 272
Tuch, Ronald, 1404
Turner, Dixie M., 1055
Turner, Myron, 468
Twitchell, James, 611, 775
Tytell, John, 475
Ullman, Joan C., 683
Valley, John, 1261
van den Berg, Sara, 485
Vann, Barbara, 766
Vernon, John, 810, 912, 971
Veszy-Wagner, L., 1291
Vincie, Joseph F., 273
Vineberg, Elsa, 954
Vlastos, Marion, 1214
Vranich, Stanko B., 1079
Wagatsuma, Hiroshi, 1365
Walcott, William, 1153
Waldoff, Leon, 612, 853, 898, 1024

Wall, John N., 461
Warner, Janet, 843
Warrick, Patricia, 136
Wasiolek, Edward, 274, 667-668
Wasserman, Marlie Parker, 1364
Waterman, Arthur, 918
Watt, Donald, 1112
Webster, Brenda, 1432-1433
Weinbaum, Francine, 1347
Weisberg, Richard, 462
Weisblatt, Sanford, 1304
Weisgram, Dianne H., 931-932
Weill, Allen, 275
Weiss, F., 1245
Weissman, Judith, 276
Weissman, Philip, 277
Wells, Charles E., 1258
Werman, David, 320
Wertime, Richard A., 1348
West, Fred, 463
Wheeler, Richard, 1434
Wheeler, Richard P., 464
White, John J., 965
Whitely, Deborah, 1056
Whiteside, George, 496, 1025-1026
Wigler, Stephen, 482-483
Wijsen, Louis, 278
Wijsen, Louk, 672
Wilkie, Roy, 929
Wilkinson, Charles, 497
Willbern, David P., 342, 465-466
Williams, John S., 1177
Williams, D.A., 681
Wills, Arthur, 1175
Wilson, F.A.C., 869, 1435
Wilson, Raymond J., III, 477, 669
Wilson, Roger Edward, 1017
Winter, David G., 133
Whithim, Philip, 280-281
Withim, Philip M., 279
Wolf, Ernest, 1340
Wolf, Ernest S., 467
Wolf, H.R., 1326
Wolf, Howard, 1366
Wolf, Howard R., 767
Wolfe, Gary K., 1099
Wolfe, Kary K., 1099
Wolfenstein, Martha, 346
Wolff, Cynthia G., 600
Wolfley, Lawrence C., 1317
Woodle, Gary, 1341
Woodman, Ross, 566
Woolf, Michael P., 913
Wright, Elizabeth, 567
Wright, Eugene, 495
Wyrick, Deborah, 814

Yalom, Irvin D., 1113
Yalom, Marilyn, 1113
Yalom, Marilyn K., 857
Yano, Shigeharu, 1374
Young, Gloria, 676
Zaphiropoulos, Miltiades L., 1180
Zeck, Gregory R., 997
Zimmerman, Shari, 486
Zinkin, L., 1243
Ziolkowski, Theodore, 282

About the Compilers

JOSEPH NATOLI is English and American Literature Bibliographer, Michigan State University. He is the author of *Twentieth Century Blake Criticism* and *Psychological Perspectives on Literature: Freudian Dissidents and Non-Freudians*. He is presently editing *Influences on Postmodern Literary Theory and Criticism*.

FREDERIK L. RUSCH is Associate Professor of English at the John Jay College of Criminal Justice of the City University of New York. He has contributed articles to the *Journal of Evolutionary Psychology, Walt Whitman Review, Obsidian,* and *Melus*.